Juan Rodriguez Poo

Computer-Aided Introduction to Econometrics

Springer

Juan Rodriguez Poo
Universidad de Cantabria
Depto. Economia
Avda. De los Castros s/n
39005 Santander
Spain
e-mail: rodrigjm@unican.es

Cover art: Detail of "Portrait of the Franciscan monk Luca Pacioli, humanist and mathematician (1445-1517)" by Jacopo de Barbari, Museo di Capodimonte, Naples, Italy

This book is also available as e-book on www.i-xplore.de .
Use the licence code at the end of the book to download the e-book.

Cataloging-in-Publication Data applied for

Bibliographic information published by Die Deutsche Bibliothek
Die Deutsche Bibliothek lists this publication in the Deutsche Nationalbibliografie; detailed bibliographic data is available in the Internet at <http://dnb.ddb.de>.

ISBN 3-540-44114-X Springer-Verlag Berlin Heidelberg New York

Mathematics Subject Classification (2000): 91-01, 91-08, 91B82, 91B84

Springer-Verlag Berlin Heidelberg New York
a member of BertelsmannSpringer Science+Business Media GmbH

http://www.springer.de

Printed in Germany

Cover design: *design & production GmbH*, Heidelberg
Typesetting by the author using a MD*book macro package
Printed on acid-free paper 40/3142ck-5 4 3 2 1 0

Rodriguez Poo
Computer-Aided Introduction to Econometrics

Springer
Berlin
Heidelberg
New York
Hong Kong
London
Milan
Paris
Tokyo

Preface

This book is designed for undergraduate students, applied researchers and practitioners to develop professional skills in econometrics. The contents of the book are designed to satisfy the requirements of an undergraduate econometrics course of about 90 hours. Although the book presents a clear and serious theoretical treatment, its main strength is that it incorporates an interactive computing internet based method that allows the reader to practice all the techniques he is learning theoretically along the different chapters of the book. It provides a comprehensive treatment of the theoretical issues related to linear regression analysis, univariate time series modelling and some interesting extensions such as ARCH models and dimensionality reduction techniques. Furthermore, all theoretical issues are illustrated through an internet based interactive computing method, that allows the reader to learn from theory to practice the different techniques that are developed in the book. Although the course assumes only a modest background it moves quickly between different fields of applications and in the end, the reader can expert to have theoretical and computational tools that are deep enough and rich enough to be relied on throughout future professional careers.

The computer inexperienced user of this book is softly introduced into the interactive book concept and will certainly enjoy the various practical examples. The e-book is designed as an interactive document: a stream of text and information with various hints and links to additional tools and features. Our e-book design offers also a complete PDF and HTML file with links to world wide computing servers. The reader of this book may therefore without download or purchase of software use all the presented examples and methods via a local XploRe Quantlet Server (XQS). Such QS Servers may also be installed in a department or addressed freely on the web, click to www.xplore-stat.de and www.quantlet.com.

"Computer-Aided introduction to Econometrics" consists on three main parts: Linear Regression Analysis, Univariate Time Series Modelling and Computational Methods. In the first part, Moral and Rodriguez-Poo provide the basic background for univariate linear regression models: Specification, estimation, testing and forecasting. Moreover, they provide some basic concepts on probability and inference that are required to study fruitfully further concepts in regression analysis. Aparicio and Villanua provide a deep treatment of the multivariate linear regression model: Basic assumptions, estimation methods and properties. Linear hypothesis testing and general test procedures (Likelihood ratio test, Wald test and Lagrange multiplier test) are also developed. Finally, they consider some standard extensions in regression analysis such as dummy variables and restricted regression. Čížek and Xia close this part with a chapter devoted to dimension reduction techniques and applications. Since the techniques developed in this section are rather new, this part of of higher level of difficulty than the preceding sections.

The second part starts with an introduction to Univariate Time Series Analysis by Moral and Gonzalez. Starting form the analysis of linear stationary processes, they jump to some particular cases of non-stationarity such as non-stationarity in mean and variance. They provide also some statistical tools for testing for unit roots. Furthermore, within the class of linear stationary processes they focus their attention in the sub-class of ARIMA models. Finally, as a natural extension to the previous concepts to regression analysis, cointegration and error correction models are considered. Departing from the class of ARIMA models, Chen, Schulz and Stephan propose a way to deal with seasonal time series. Olave and Alcala end this part with an introduction to Autoregressive Conditional Heteroskedastic Models, which appear to be a natural extension of ARIMA modelling to econometric models with a conditional variance that is time varying. In their work, they provide an interesting battery of tests for ARCH disturbances that appears as a nice example of the testing tools already introduced by Aparicio and Villanua in a previous chapter.

In the last part of the book, Čižkova develops several nonlinear optimization techniques that are of common use in Econometrics. The special structure of the e-book relying in a interactive computing internet based method makes it an ideal tool to comprehend optimization problems.

I gratefully acknowledge the support of Deutsche Forschungsgemeinschaft, SFB 373 Quantifikation und Simulation Ökonomischer Prozesse and Dirección General de Investigación del Ministerio de Ciencia y Tecnología under research grant BEC2001-1121. For technical production of the e-book I would like to thank Zdeněk Hlávka and Rodrigo Witzel.

Santander, October 2002, J. M. Rodriguez-Poo.

Contributors

Ignacio Moral Departamento de Economía, Universidad de Cantabria

Juan M. Rodriguez-Poo Departamento de Economía, Universidad de Cantabria

Teresa Aparicio Departamento de Análisis Económico, Universidad de Zaragoza

Inmaculada Villanua Departamento de Análisis Económico, Universidad de Zaragoza

Pavel Čížek Humboldt-Universität zu Berlin, CASE, Center of Applied Statistics and Economics

Yingcun Xia Department of Statistics and Actuarial Science, The University of Hong Kong

Paz Moral Departamento de Econometría y Estadística, Universidad del País Vasco

Pilar Gonzalez Departamento de Econometría y Estadística, Universidad del País Vasco

Rong Chen Department of Information and Decision Sciences, University of Illinois at Chicago

Rainer Schulz Humboldt-Universität zu Berlin, CASE, Center of Applied Statistics and Economics

Sabine Stephan German Institute for Economic Research

Pilar Olave Departamento de métodos estadísticos, Universidad de Zaragoza

Juan T. Alcalá Departamento de métodos estadísticos, Universidad de Zaragoza

Lenka Čížková Humboldt-Universität zu Berlin, CASE, Center of Applied Statistics and Economics

Contents

1 Univariate Linear Regression Model

Ignacio Moral and Juan M. Rodriguez-Poo

In this section we concentrate our attention in the univariate linear regression model. In economics, we can find innumerable discussions of relationships between variables in pairs: consumption and real disposable income, labor supply and real wages and many more. However, the main interest in the study of this model is not its real applicability but the fact that the mathematical and the statistical tools developed for the two variable model are foundations of other more complicated models.

An econometric study begins with a theoretical proposition about the relationship between two variables. Then, given a data set, the empirical investigation provides estimates of unknown parameters in the model, and often attempts to measure the validity of the propositions against the behavior of observable data. It is not our aim to include here a detailed discussion on econometric model building, this type of discussion can be found in Intriligator (1978), however, along the sequent subsections we will introduce, using monte carlo simulations, the main results related to estimation and inference in univariate linear regression models. The next chapters of the book develop more elaborate specifications and various problems that arise in the study and application of these techniques.

1.1 Probability and Data Generating Process

In this section we make a revision of some concepts that are necessary to understand further developments in the chapter, the purpose is to highlight some of the more important theoretical results in probability, in particular, the concept of the random variable, the probability distribution, and some related results. Note however, that we try to maintain the exposition at an introductory level. For a more formal and detailed expositions of these concepts see Härdle and Simar (1999), Mantzapoulus (1995), Newbold (1996) and Wonacot andWonacot (1990).

1.1.1 Random Variable and Probability Distribution

A random variable is a function that assigns (real) numbers to the results of an experiment. Each possible outcome of the experiment (i.e. value of the corresponding random variable) occurs with a certain probability. This outcome variable, X, is a random variable because, until the experiment is performed, it is uncertain what value X will take. Probabilities are associated with outcomes to quantify this uncertainty.

A random variable is called discrete if the set of all possible outcomes $x_1, x_2, ...$ is finite or countable. For a discrete random variable X, a probability density function is defined to be the function $f(x_i)$ such that for any real number x_i, which is a value that X can take, f gives the probability that the random variable X is equal to x_i . If x_i is not one of the values that X can take then $f(x_i) = 0$.

$$P(X = x_i) = f(x_i) \qquad i = 1, 2, \ldots$$

$$f(x_i) \geq 0, \qquad \sum_i f(x_i) = 1$$

A continuous random variable X can take any value in at least one interval on the real number line. Assume X can take values $c \leq x \leq d$. Since the possible values of X are uncountable, the probability associated with any particular point is zero. Unlike the situation for discrete random variables, the density function of a continuous random variable will not give the probability that X takes the value x_i. Instead, the density function of a continuous random variable X will be such that areas under $f(x)$ will give probabilities associated with the corresponding intervals. The probability density function is defined so that $f(x) \geq 0$ and

$$P(a < X \leq b) = \int_a^b f(x)\, dx; \; a \leq b \tag{1.1}$$

This is the area under $f(x)$ in the range from a to b. For a continuous variable

$$\int_{-\infty}^{+\infty} f(x)\,dx = 1 \tag{1.2}$$

Cumulative Distribution Function

A function closely related to the probability density function of a random variable is the corresponding *cumulative distribution function*. This function of a discrete random variable X is defined as follows:

$$F(x) = P(X \leq x) = \sum_{X \leq x} f(X) \tag{1.3}$$

That is, $F(x)$ is the probability that the random variable X takes a value less than or equal to x.

The cumulative distribution function for a continuous random variable X is given by

$$F(x) = P(X \leq x) = \int_{-\infty}^{x} f(t)dt \tag{1.4}$$

where $f(t)$ is the the probability density function. In both the continuous and the discrete case, $F(x)$ must satisfy the following properties:

- $0 \leq F(x) \leq 1$.
- If $x_2 > x_1$ then $F(x_2) \geq F(x_1)$.
- $F(+\infty) = 1$ and $F(-\infty) = 0$.

Expectations of Random Variables

The expected value of a random variable X is the value that we, on average, expect to obtain as an outcome of the experiment. It is not necessarily a value actually taken by the random variable. The expected value, denoted by $E(X)$ or μ, is a weighted average of the values taken by the random variable X, where the weights are the respective probabilities.

Let us consider the discrete random variable X with outcomes $x_1, \cdots, x_n$ and corresponding probabilities $f(x_i)$. Then, the expression

$$E(X) = \mu = \sum_{i=1}^{n} x_i f(X = x_i) \tag{1.5}$$

defines the expected value of the discrete random variable. For a continuous random variable X with density $f(x)$, we define the expected value as

$$E(X) = \mu = \int_{-\infty}^{+\infty} x f(x) \, dx \tag{1.6}$$

Joint Distribution Function

We consider an experiment that consists of two parts, and each part leads to the occurrence of specified events. We could study separately both events, however we might be interested in analyzing them jointly. The probability function defined over a pair of random variables is called the joint probability distribution. Consider two random variables X and Y, the joint probability distribution function of two random variables X and Y is defined as the probability that X is equal to x_i at the same time that Y is equal to y_j

$$P(\{X = x_i\} \cap \{Y = y_j\}) = P(X = x_i, Y = y_j) = f(x_i, y_j) \quad i, j = 1, 2, \ldots \tag{1.7}$$

If X and Y are continuous random variables, then the bivariate probability density function is:

$$P(a < X \leq b; c < Y \leq d) = \int_{c}^{d}\int_{a}^{b} f(x, y) dx dy \tag{1.8}$$

The counterparts of the requirements for a probability density function are:

$$\sum_i \sum_j f(x_i, y_j) = 1$$
$$\int_{-\infty}^{+\infty} \int_{-\infty}^{+\infty} f(x,y)dxdy = 1 \tag{1.9}$$

The *cumulative joint distribution function*, in the case that both X and Y are discrete random variables is

$$F(x,y) = P(X \leq x, Y \leq y) = \sum_{X \leq x} \sum_{Y \leq y} f(X,Y) \tag{1.10}$$

and if both X and Y are continuous random variables then

$$F(x,y) = P(X \leq x, Y \leq y) = \int_{-\infty}^{x} \int_{-\infty}^{y} f(t,v)dtdv \tag{1.11}$$

Marginal Distribution Function

Consider now that we know a bivariate random variable (X,Y) and its probability distribution, and suppose we simply want to study the probability distribution of X, say $f(x)$. How can we use the joint probability density function for (X,Y) to obtain $f(x)$?

The marginal distribution, $f(x)$, of a discrete random variable X provides the probability that the variable X is equal to x, in the joint probability $f(X,Y)$, without considering the variable Y, thus, if we want to obtain the marginal distribution of X from the joint density, it is necessary to sum out the other variable Y. The marginal distribution for the random variable Y, $f(y)$ is defined analogously.

$$P(X = x) = f(x) = \sum_Y f(x,Y) \tag{1.12}$$

$$P(Y = y) = f(y) = \sum_X f(X,y) \tag{1.13}$$

The resulting marginal distributions are one-dimensional.

Similarly, we obtain the marginal densities for a pair of continuous random variables X and Y:

$$f(x) = \int_{-\infty}^{+\infty} f(x,y)\,dy \tag{1.14}$$

$$f(y) = \int_{-\infty}^{+\infty} f(x,y)\,dx \tag{1.15}$$

Conditional Probability Distribution Function

In the setting of a joint bivariate distribution $f(X,Y)$, consider the case when we have partial information about X. More concretely, we know that the random variable X has taken some vale x. We would like to know the conditional behavior of Y given that X has taken the value x. The resultant probability distribution of Y given $X = x$ is called the conditional probability distribution function of Y given X, $F_{Y|X=x}(y)$. In the discrete case it is defined as

$$F_{Y|X=x}(y) = P(Y \leq y|X = x) = \sum_{Y\leq y} \frac{f(x,Y)}{f(x)} = \sum_{Y\leq y} f(Y|x) \tag{1.16}$$

where $f(Y|x)$ is the conditional probability density function and x must be such that $f(x) > 0$. In the continuous case $F_{Y|X=x}(y)$ is defined as

$$F_{Y|X=x}(y) = P(Y \leq y|X = x) = \int_{-\infty}^{y} f(y|x)\,dy = \int_{-\infty}^{y} \frac{f(x,y)}{f(x)}\,dy \tag{1.17}$$

$f(y|x)$ is the conditional probability density function and x must be such that $f(x) > 0$.

Conditional Expectation

The concept of mathematical expectation can be applied regardless of the kind of the probability distribution, then, for a pair of random variables (X,Y)

with conditional probability density function, namely $f(y|x)$, the conditional expectation is defined as the expected value of the conditional distribution, i.e.

$$E(Y|X=x) = \begin{cases} \sum_{j=1}^{n} y_j f(Y=y_j|X=x) & \text{if } Y \text{discrete} \\ \int_{-\infty}^{+\infty} y f(y|x)\, dy & \text{if } Y \text{ continuous} \end{cases} \tag{1.18}$$

Note that for the discrete case, $y_1, \cdots, y_n$ are values such that $f(Y = y_j|X = x) > 0$.

The Regression Function

Let us define a pair of random variables (X, Y) with a range of possible values such that the conditional expectation of Y given X is correctly defined in several values of $X = x_1, \cdots, x_n$. Then, a regression is just a function that relates different values of X, say $x_1, \cdots, x_n$, and their corresponding values in terms of the conditional expectation $E(Y|X = x_1), \cdots, E(Y|X = x_n)$.

The main objective of regression analysis is to estimate and predict the mean value (expectation) for the dependent variable Y in base of the given (fixed) values of the explanatory variable. The regression function describes dependence of a quantity Y on the quantity X, a one-directional dependence is assumed. The random variable X is referred as regressor, explanatory variable or independent variable, the random variable Y is referred as regressand or dependent variable.

1.1.2 Example

In the following Quantlet, we show a two-dimensional random variable (X, Y), we calculate the conditional expectation $E(Y|X = x)$ and generate a line by means of merging the values of the conditional expectation in each x values. The result is identical to the regression of y on x.

Let us consider 54 households as the whole population. We want to know the relationship between the *net income* and *household expenditure*, that is, we want a prediction of the expected expenditure, given the level of net income of the household. In order to do so, we separate the 54 households in 9 groups with the same income, then, we calculate the mean expenditure for every level of income.

XEGlinreg01.xpl

This program produces the output presented in Figure 1.1

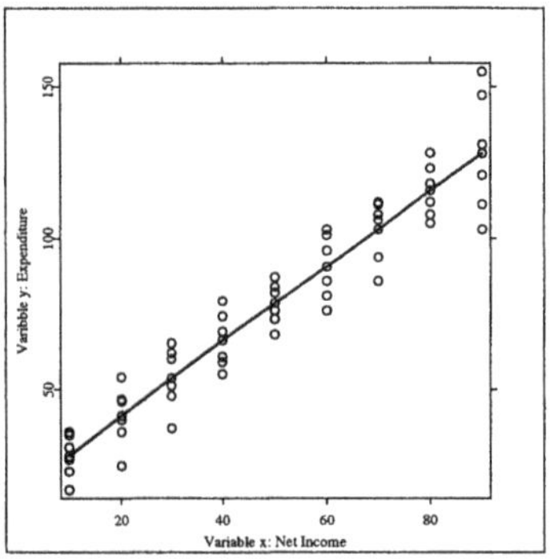

Figure 1.1. Conditional Expectation: $E(Y|X=x)$

The function $E(Y|X=x)$ is called a ***regression function.*** This function express only the fact that the (population) mean of the distribution of Y given X has a functional relationship with respect to X.

1.1.3 Data Generating Process

One of the major tasks of statistics is to obtain information about populations. A population is defined as the set of all elements that are of interest for a statistical analysis and it must be defined precisely and comprehensively so that one can immediately determine whether an element belongs to the population or not. We denote by N the population size. In fact, in most of cases, the population is unknown, and for the sake of analysis, we suppose that it is characterized by a joint probability distribution function. What is known for the researcher is a finite subset of observations drawn from this population. This is called a sample and we will denote the sample size by n. The main aim of the statistical analysis is to obtain information from the population (its joint probability distribution) through the analysis of the sample.

Unfortunately, in many situations the aim of obtaining information about the whole joint probability distribution is too complicated, and we have to orient our objective towards more modest proposals. Instead of characterizing the whole joint distribution function, one can be more interested in investigating one particular feature of this distribution such as the regression function. In this case we will denote it as *Population Regression Function* (PRF), statistical object that has been already defined in sections 1.1.1 and 1.1.2.

Since very few information is know about the population characteristics, one has to establish some assumptions about what is the behavior of this unknown quantity. Then, if we consider the observations in Figure 1.1 as the the whole population, we can state that the PRF is a linear function of the different values of X, i.e.

$$E(Y|X = x) = \alpha + \beta x \tag{1.19}$$

where α and β are fixed unknown parameters which are denoted as *regression coefficients*. Note the crucial issue that once we have determined the functional form of the regression function, estimation of the parameter values is tantamount to the estimation of the entire regression function. Therefore, once a sample is available, our task is considerably simplified since, in order to analyze the whole population, we only need to give correct estimates of the regression parameters.

One important issue related to the Population Regression Function is the so called *Error term* in the regression equation. For a pair of realizations (x_i, y_i) from the random variable (X, Y), we note that y_i will not coincide with $E(Y|X = x_i)$. We define as

$$u_i = y_i - E(Y|X = x_i) \tag{1.20}$$

the error term in the regression function that indicates the divergence between an individual value y_i and its conditional mean, $E(Y|X = x_i)$. Taking into account equations (1.19) and (1.20) we can write the following equalities

$$y_i = E(Y|X = x_i) + u_i = \alpha + \beta x_i + u_i \tag{1.21}$$

and

$$E(u|X = x_i) = 0$$

This result implies that for $X = x_i$, the divergences of all values of Y with respect to the conditional expectation $E(Y|X = x_i)$ are averaged out. There are several reasons for the existence of the error term in the regression:

- The error term is taking into account variables which are not in the model, because we do not know if this variable (regressor) has a influence in the endogenous variable
- We do not have great confidence about the correctness of the model
- Measurement errors in the variables

The PRF is a feature of the so called *Data Generating Process* DGP. This is the joint probability distribution that is supposed to characterize the entire population from which the data set has been drawn. Now, assume that from the population of N elements characterized by a bivariate random variable (X, Y), a sample of n elements, $(x_1, y_1), \cdots, (x_n, y_n)$, is selected. If we assume that the Population Regression Function (PRF) that generates the data is

$$y_i = \alpha + \beta x_i + u_i, \quad i = 1, \cdots, n \tag{1.22}$$

then, given any estimator of α and β, namely $\hat{\beta}$ and $\hat{\alpha}$, we can substitute these estimators into the regression function

$$\hat{y}_i = \hat{\alpha} + \hat{\beta} x_i, \quad i = 1, \cdots, n \tag{1.23}$$

obtaining the *sample regression function* (SRF). The relationship between the PRF and SRF is:

$$y_i = \hat{y}_i + \hat{u}_i, \quad i = 1, \cdots, n \tag{1.24}$$

where $\hat{u}_i$ is denoted the residual.

Just to illustrate the difference between Sample Regression Function and Population Regression Function, consider the data shown in Figure 1.1 (the whole population of the experiment). Let us draw a sample of 9 observations from this population.

XEGlinreg02.xpl

This is shown in Figure 1.2. If we assume that the model which generates the data is $y_i = \alpha + \beta x_i + u_i$, then using the sample we can estimate the parameters α and β.

XEGlinreg03.xpl

In Figure 1.3 we present the sample, the population regression function (thick line), and the sample regression function (thin line). For fixed values of x in the sample, the Sample Regression Function is going to depend on the sample, whereas on the contrary, the Population Regression Function will always take the same values regardless the sample values.

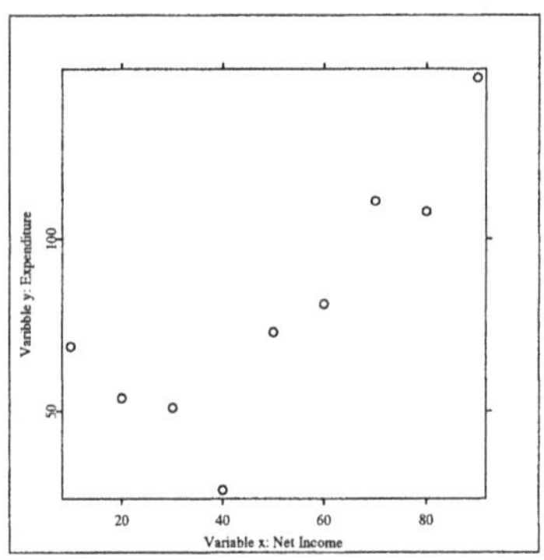

Figure 1.2. Sample $n = 9$ of (X, Y)

With a data generating process (DGP) at hand, then it is possible to create new simulated data. If α, β and the vector of exogenous variables X is known (fixed), a sample of size n is created by obtaining n values of the random variable u and then using these values, in conjunction with the rest of the model, to generate n values of Y. This yields one complete sample of size n. Note that this artificially generated set of sample data could be viewed as an example of real-world data that a researcher would be faced with when dealing with the kind of estimation problem this model represents. Note especially that the set of data obtained depends crucially on the particular set of error terms drawn. A different set of error terms would create a different data set of Y for the same problem (see for more details Kennedy (1998)).

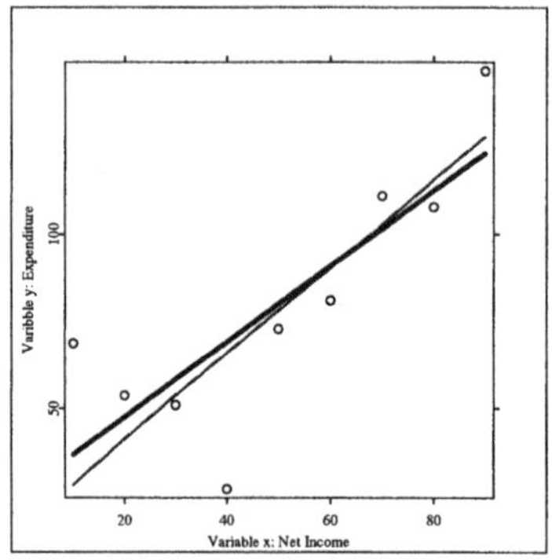

Figure 1.3. Sample and Population Regression Function

1.1.4 Example

In order to show how a DGP works, we implement the following experiment. We generate three replicates of sample $n = 10$ of the following data generating process: $y_i = 2 + 0.5x_i + u_i$. X is generated by a uniform distribution as follows $X \sim U[0,1]$.

XEGlinreg04.xpl

This code produces the values of X, which are the same for the three samples, and the corresponding values of Y, which of course differ from one sample to the other.

1.2 Estimators and Properties

If we have available a sample of n observations from the population represented by (X, Y), $(x_1, y_1), \cdots, (x_n, y_n)$, and we assume the Population Regression Function is both linear in variables and parameters

$$y_i = E(Y|X = x_i) + u_i = \alpha + \beta x_i + u_i, \quad i = 1, \cdots, n, \tag{1.25}$$

we can now face the task of estimating the unknown parameters α and β. Unfortunately, the sampling design and the linearity assumption in the PRF, are not sufficient conditions to ensure that there exists a precise statistical relationship between the estimators and its true corresponding values (see section 1.2.6 for more details). In order to do so, we need to know some additional features from the PRF. Since we do not them, we decide to establish some assumptions, making clear that in any case, the statistical properties of the estimators are going to depend crucially on the related assumptions. The basic set of assumptions that comprises the classical linear regression model is as follows:

(A.1) The explanatory variable, X, is fixed.

(A.2) For any $n > 1$,

$$\frac{1}{n}\sum_{i=1}^{n}(x_i - \bar{x})^2 > 0.$$

(A.3)

$$\lim_{n\to\infty}\frac{1}{n}\sum_{i=1}^{n}(x_i - \bar{x})^2 = m > 0.$$

(A.4) Zero mean disturbances: $E(u) = 0$.

(A.5) Homoscedasticity: $Var(u_i) = \sigma^2 < \infty$, is constant, for all i.

(A.6) Nonautocorrelation: $Cov(u_i, u_j) = 0$ if $i \neq j$.

Finally, an additional assumption that is usually employed to easier the inference is

(A.7) The error term has a gaussian distribution, $u_i \sim \mathrm{N}(0, \sigma^2)$

For a more detailed explanation and comments on the different assumption see Gujarati (1995). Assumption (A.1) is quite strong, and it is in fact very difficult to accept when dealing with economic data. However, most part of statistical results obtained under this hypothesis hold as well for weaker such as random X but independent of u (see Amemiya (1985) for the fixed design case, against Newey and McFadden (1994) for the random design).

1.2.1 Regression Parameters and their Estimation

In the univariate linear regression setting that was introduced in the previous section the following parameters need to be estimated

- α - intercept term. It gives us the value of the conditional expectation of Y given $X = x$, for $x = 0$.
- β - linear slope coefficient. It represents the sensitivity of $E(Y|X = x)$ to changes in x.
- σ^2 - Error term measure of dispersion. Large values of the variance mean that the error term u is likely to vary in a large neighborhood around the expected value. Smaller values of the standard deviation indicate that the values of u will be concentrated around the expected value.

Regression Estimation

From a given population described as

$$y = 3 + 2.5x + u \tag{1.26}$$

$X \sim U[0,1]$ and $u \sim \mathrm{N}(0,1)$, a random sample of $n = 100$ elements is generated.

`XEGlinreg05.xpl`

We show the scatter plot in Figure 1.4

Following the same reasoning as in the previous sections, the PRF is unknown for the researcher, and he has only available the data, and some information from the PRF. For example, he may know that the relationship between $E(Y|X = x)$ and x is linear, but he does not know which are the exact parameter values. In Figure 1.5 we represent the sample and several possible values of the regression functions according to different values for α and β.

`XEGlinreg06.xpl`

In order to estimate α and β, many estimation procedures are available. One of the most famous criteria is the one that chooses α and β such that they minimize the sum of the squared deviations of the regression values from their

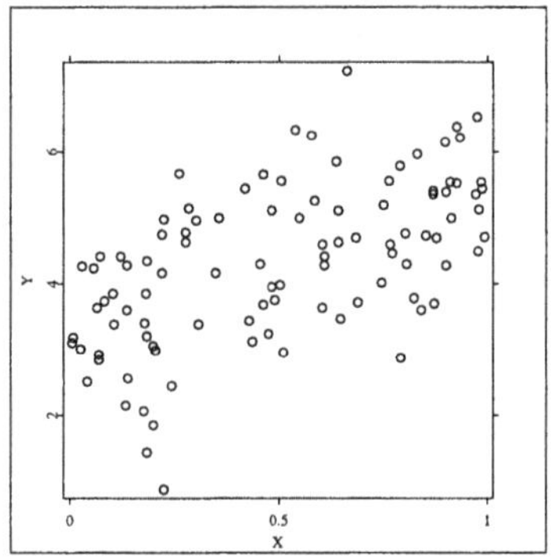

Figure 1.4. Sample $n = 100$ of (X, Y)

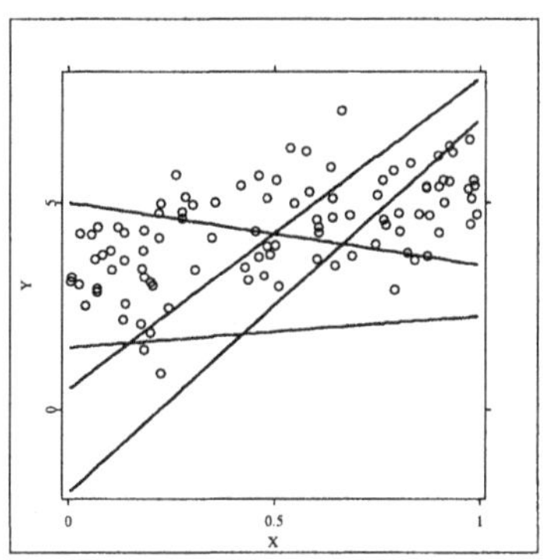

Figure 1.5. Sample of X, Y, Possible linear functions

real corresponding values. This is the so called least squares method. Applying this procedure to the previous sample,

XEGlinreg07.xpl

in Figure 1.6, we show for the sake of comparison the least squares regression curve together with the other sample regression curves.

We describe now in a more precise way how the Least Squares method is implemented, and, under a Population Regression Function that incorporates

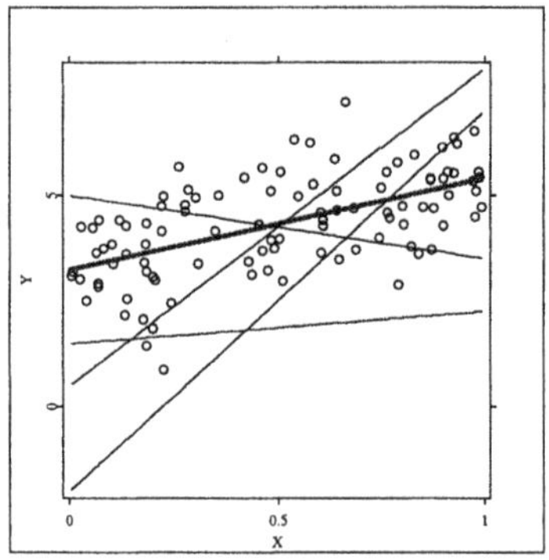

Figure 1.6. Ordinary Least Squares Estimation

assumptions (A.1) to (A.6), which are its statistical properties.

1.2.2 Least Squares Method

We begin by establishing a formal estimation criteria. Let $\hat{\hat{\alpha}}$ and $\hat{\hat{\beta}}$ be a possible estimators (some function of the sample observations) of α and β. Then, the fitted value of the endogenous variable is:

$$\hat{\hat{y}}_i = \hat{\hat{\alpha}} + \hat{\hat{\beta}} x_i \quad i = 1, ..., n \tag{1.27}$$

The residual value between the real and the fitted value is given by

$$\hat{\hat{u}}_i = y_i - \hat{\hat{y}}_i \quad i = 1, ..., n \tag{1.28}$$

The least squares method minimizes the sum of squared deviations of regression values ($\hat{\hat{y}}_i = \hat{\hat{\alpha}} + \hat{\hat{\beta}} x_i$) from the observed values (y_i), that is, the residual sum of squares–RSS.

$$\sum_{i=1}^{n} (y_i - \hat{\hat{y}}_i)^2 \rightarrow min \tag{1.29}$$

This criterion function has two variables with respect to which we are willing to minimize: $\hat{\hat{\alpha}}$ and $\hat{\hat{\beta}}$.

$$S(\hat{\hat{\alpha}}, \hat{\hat{\beta}}) = \sum_{i=1}^{n} (y_i - \hat{\hat{\alpha}} - \hat{\hat{\beta}} x_i)^2 . \tag{1.30}$$

Then, we define as Ordinary Least Squares (OLS) estimators, denoted by $\hat{\alpha}$ and $\hat{\beta}$, the values of α and β that solve the following optimization problem

$$(\hat{\alpha}, \hat{\beta}) = argmin_{\hat{\hat{\alpha}}, \hat{\hat{\beta}}} S(\hat{\hat{\alpha}}, \hat{\hat{\beta}}) \tag{1.31}$$

In order to solve it, that is, to find the minimum values, the first conditions make the first partial derivatives have to be equal to zero.

$$\begin{aligned} \frac{\partial S(\hat{\hat{\alpha}}, \hat{\hat{\beta}})}{\partial \hat{\hat{\alpha}}} &= -2 \sum_{i=1}^{n} (y_i - \hat{\hat{\alpha}} - \hat{\hat{\beta}} x_i) = 0 \\ \frac{\partial S(\hat{\hat{\alpha}}, \hat{\hat{\beta}})}{\partial \hat{\hat{\beta}}} &= -2 \sum_{i=1}^{n} (y_i - \hat{\hat{\alpha}} - \hat{\hat{\beta}} x_i) x_i = 0 \end{aligned} \tag{1.32}$$

To verify whether the solution is really a minimum, the matrix of second order derivatives of (1.32), the Hessian matrix, must be positive definite. It is easy to show that

$$H(\hat{\hat{\alpha}}, \hat{\hat{\beta}}) = 2 \begin{pmatrix} n & \sum_{i=1}^{n} x_i \\ \sum_{i=1}^{n} x_i & \sum_{i=1}^{n} x_i^2 \end{pmatrix}, \tag{1.33}$$

and this expression is positive definite if and only if, $\sum_i (x_i - \bar{x})^2 > 0$. But, this is implied by assumption (A.2). Note that this requirement is not strong at all. Without it, we might consider regression problems where no variation at all is considered in the values of X. Then, condition (A.2) rules out this degenerate case.

The first derivatives (equal to zero) lead to the so-called (least squares) normal equations from which the estimated regression parameters can be computed by solving the equations.

$$n\hat{\alpha} + \hat{\beta}\sum_{i=1}^{n} x_i = \sum_{i=1}^{n} y_i \tag{1.34}$$

$$\hat{\alpha}\sum_{i=1}^{n} x_i + \hat{\beta}\sum_{i=1}^{n} {x_i}^2 = \sum_{i=1}^{n} x_i y_i \tag{1.35}$$

Dividing the original equations by n, we get a simplified formula suitable for the computation of regression parameters

$$\begin{aligned} \hat{\alpha} + \hat{\beta}\bar{x} &= \bar{y} \\ \hat{\alpha}\bar{x} + \hat{\beta}\frac{1}{n}\sum_{i=1}^{n} {x_i}^2 &= \frac{1}{n}\sum_{i=1}^{n} x_i y_i \end{aligned}$$

For the estimated intercept $\hat{\alpha}$, we get:

$$\hat{\alpha} = \bar{y} - \hat{\beta}\bar{x} \tag{1.36}$$

For the estimated linear slope coefficient $\hat{\beta}$, we get:

$$\begin{aligned} (\bar{y} - \hat{\beta}\bar{x})\bar{x} + \hat{\beta}\frac{1}{n}\sum_{i=1}^{n} {x_i}^2 &= \frac{1}{n}\sum_{i=1}^{n} x_i y_i \\ \hat{\beta}\frac{1}{n}\sum_{i=1}^{n}({x_i}^2 - \bar{x}^2) &= \frac{1}{n}\sum_{i=1}^{n} x_i y_i - \bar{x}\bar{y} \\ \hat{\beta}{S_X}^2 &= S_{XY} \end{aligned}$$

$$\hat{\beta} = \frac{S_{XY}}{{S_X}^2} = \frac{\sum_{i=1}^{n}(x_i - \bar{x})(y_i - \bar{y})}{\sum_{i=1}^{n}(x_i - \bar{x})^2} \tag{1.37}$$

The ordinary least squares estimator of the parameter σ^2 is based on the following idea: Since σ^2 is the expected value of u_i^2 and $\hat{u}$ is an estimate of u, our initial estimator

$$\widehat{\sigma^*}^2 = \frac{1}{n}\sum_i \hat{u}_i^2 \tag{1.38}$$

would seem to be a natural estimator of σ^2, but due to the fact that $\mathrm{E}\left(\sum_i \hat{u}_i^2\right) = (n-2)\sigma^2$, this implies

$$\mathrm{E}\left(\widehat{\sigma^*}^2\right) = \frac{n-2}{n}\sigma^2 \neq \sigma^2. \tag{1.39}$$

Therefore, the unbiased estimator of σ^2 is

$$\hat{\sigma}^2 = \frac{\sum_i \hat{u}_i^2}{n-2} \tag{1.40}$$

Now, with this expression, we obtain that $E(\hat{\sigma}^2) = \sigma$.

In the next section we will introduce an example of the least squares estimation criterion.

1.2.3 Example

We can obtain a graphical representation of the least squares ordinary estimation by using the following Quantlet

```
gl = grlinreg (x)
```

The regression line computed by the least squares method using the data generated in (1.49)

XEGlinreg08.xpl

is shown in Figure 1.7 jointly with the data set.

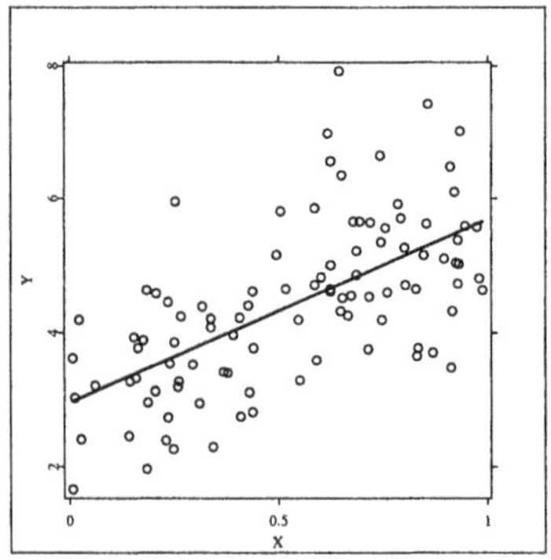

Figure 1.7. Ordinary Least Squares Estimation

1.2.4 Goodness of Fit Measures

Once the regression line is estimated, it is useful to know how well the regression line approximates the data from the sample. A measure that can describe the quality of representation is called the coefficient of determination (either R-Squared or R^2). Its computation is based on a decomposition of the variance of the values of the dependent variable Y.

The smaller is the sum of squared estimated residuals, the better is the quality of the regression line. Since the Least Squares method minimizes the variance of the estimated residuals it also maximizes the R-squared by construction.

$$\sum (y_i - \hat{y}_i)^2 = \sum \hat{u_i}^2 \rightarrow min. \tag{1.41}$$

The sample variance of the values of Y is:

$$S_Y{}^2 = \frac{\sum_{i=1}^{n} (y_i - \bar{y})^2}{n} \tag{1.42}$$

The element $\sum_{i=1}^{n} (y_i - \bar{y})^2$ is known as *Total Sum of Squares* (TSS), it is the total variation of the values of Y from $\bar{y}$. The deviation of the observed values, y_i, from the arithmetic mean, $\bar{y}$, can be decomposed into two parts: The deviation of the observed values of Y from the estimated regression values and the deviation of the estimated regression values from the sample mean. i. e.

$$y_i - \bar{y} = (y_i - \hat{y}_i + \hat{y}_i - \bar{y}) = \hat{u}_i + \hat{y}_i - \bar{y}, \quad i = 1, \cdots, n \tag{1.43}$$

where $\hat{u}_i = y_i - \hat{y}_i$ is the error term in this estimate. Note also that considering the properties of the OLS estimators it can be proved that $\bar{y} = \bar{\hat{y}}$. Taking the square of the residulas and summing over all the observations, we obtain the *Residual Sum of Squares*, $RSS = \sum_{i=1}^{n} \hat{u}_i^2$. As a goodness of fit criterion the RSS is not satisfactory because the standard errors are very sensitive to the unit in which Y is measured. In order to propose a criteria that is not sensitive to the measurement units, let us decompose the sum of the squared deviations of equation (1.43) as

$$\sum_{i=1}^{n} (y_i - \bar{y})^2 = \sum_{i=1}^{n} [(y_i - \hat{y}_i) + (\hat{y}_i - \bar{y})]^2$$

$$= \sum_{i=1}^{n} (y_i - \hat{y}_i)^2 + \sum_{i=1}^{n} (\hat{y}_i - \bar{y})^2 + 2\sum_{i=1}^{n} (y_i - \hat{y}_i)(\hat{y}_i - \bar{y}) \tag{1.44}$$

Now, noting that by the properties of the OLS estimators we have that $\sum_{i=1}^{n} (y_i - \hat{y}_i)(\hat{y}_i - \bar{y}) = 0$, expression (1.44) can be written as

$$TSS = ESS + RSS, \tag{1.45}$$

where $ESS = \sum_{i=1}^{n} (\hat{y}_i - \bar{y})^2$, is the so called *Explained Sum of Squares.* Now, dividing both sides of equation (1.45) by n, we obtain

$$\begin{aligned} \frac{\sum_i^n (y_i - \bar{y})^2}{n} &= \frac{\sum_{i=1}^{n} (y_i - \hat{y}_i)^2}{n} + \frac{\sum_{i=1}^{n} (\hat{y}_i - \bar{y})^2}{n} \\ &= \frac{\sum_{i=1}^{n} \hat{u_i}^2}{n} + \frac{\sum_{i=1}^{n} (\hat{y}_i - \bar{y})^2}{n} \end{aligned} \tag{1.46}$$

and then,

$$S_Y{}^2 = S_{\hat{u}}{}^2 + S_{\hat{Y}}{}^2 \tag{1.47}$$

The total variance of Y is equal to the sum of the sample variance of the estimated residuals (the unexplained part of the sampling variance of Y) and the part of the sampling variance of Y that is explained by the regression function (the sampling variance of the regression function).

The larger the portion of the sampling variance of the values of Y is explained by the model, the better is the fit of the regression function.

The Coefficient of Determination

The coefficient of the determination is defined as the ratio between the sampling variance of the values of Y explained by the regression function and the sampling variance of values of Y. That is, it represents the proportion of the sampling variance in the values of Y "explained" by the estimated regression function.

$$R^2 = \frac{\sum_{i=1}^{n} (\hat{y}_i - \bar{y})^2}{\sum_{i=1}^{n} (y_i - \bar{y})^2} = \frac{{S_{\hat{Y}}}^2}{{S_Y}^2} \tag{1.48}$$

This expression is unit-free because both the numerator and denominator have the same units. The higher the coefficient of determination is, the better the regression function explains the observed values. Other expressions for the coefficient are

$$R^2 = \frac{ESS}{TSS} = 1 - \frac{RSS}{TSS} = \frac{\hat{\beta} \sum_{i=1}^{n} (x_i - \bar{x})(y_i - \bar{y})}{\sum_{i=1}^{n} (y_i - \bar{y})^2} = \frac{\hat{\beta}^2 \sum_{i=1}^{n} (x_i - \bar{x})^2}{\sum_{i=1}^{n} (y_i - \bar{y})^2}$$

One special feature of this coefficient is that the R-Squared can take values in the following range: $0 \leq R^2 \leq 1$. This is always true if the model includes a constant term in the population regression function. A small value of R^2 implies that a lot of the variation in the values of Y has not been explained by the variation of the values of X.

1.2.5 Example

Ordinary Least Squares estimates of the parameters of interest are given by executing the following quantlet

```
{beta,bse,bstan,bpval}=linreg(x,y)
```

As an example, we use the original data source that was already shown in Figure 1.4

XEGlinreg09.xpl

1.2.6 Properties of the OLS Estimates of α, β and σ^2

Once the econometric model has been both specified and estimated, we are now interested in analyzing the relationship between the estimators (sample) and their respective parameter values (population). This relationship is going to be of great interest when trying to extend propositions based on econometric models that have been estimated with a unique sample to the whole population. One way to do so, is to obtain the sampling distribution of the different estimators. A sampling distribution describes the behavior of the estimators in repeated applications of the estimating formulae. A given sample yields a specific numerical estimate. Another sample from the same population will yield another numerical estimate. A sampling distribution describes the results that will be obtained for the estimators over the potentially infinite set of samples that may be drawn from the population.

Properties of $\hat{\alpha}$ and $\hat{\beta}$

We start by computing the finite sample distribution of the parameter vector $(\alpha \quad \beta)^\top$. In order to do so, note that taking the expression for $\hat{\alpha}$ in (1.36) and $\hat{\beta}$ in (1.37) we can write

$$\begin{pmatrix} \hat{\alpha} \\ \hat{\beta} \end{pmatrix} = \sum_{i=1}^{n} \begin{pmatrix} \frac{1}{n} - \bar{x}\omega_i \\ \omega_i \end{pmatrix} y_i, \tag{1.49}$$

where

$$\omega_i = \frac{x_i - \bar{x}}{\sum_{l=1}^{n} (x_l - \bar{x})^2}. \tag{1.50}$$

If we substitute now the value of y_i by the process that has generated it (equation (1.22)) we obtain

$$\begin{pmatrix}\hat{\alpha}\\ \hat{\beta}\end{pmatrix} = \begin{pmatrix}\alpha\\ \beta\end{pmatrix} + \sum_{i=1}^{n} \begin{pmatrix}\frac{1}{n} - \bar{x}\omega_i\\ \omega_i\end{pmatrix} u_i, \tag{1.51}$$

Equations (1.49) and (1.51) show the first property of the OLS estimators of α and β. They are **linear** with respect to the sampling values of the endogenous variable $y_1, \cdots, y_n$, and they also linear in the error terms $u_1, \cdots, u_n$. This property is crucial to show the finite sample distribution of the vector of parameters $(\hat{\alpha} \quad \hat{\beta})$ since then, assuming the values of X are fixed (assumption A.1), and independent gaussian errors (assumptions A.6 and A.7), linear combinations of independent gaussian variables are themselves gaussian and therefore $(\hat{\alpha} \quad \hat{\beta})$ follow a bivariate gaussian distribution.

$$\begin{pmatrix}\hat{\alpha}\\ \\ \hat{\beta}\end{pmatrix} \sim \mathrm{N}\left(\begin{pmatrix}\alpha\\ \\ \beta\end{pmatrix} \begin{pmatrix}\operatorname{Var}(\hat{\alpha}) & \operatorname{Cov}\left(\hat{\alpha},\hat{\beta}\right)\\ \\ \operatorname{Cov}\left(\hat{\alpha},\hat{\beta}\right) & \operatorname{Var}\left(\hat{\beta}\right)\end{pmatrix}\right) \tag{1.52}$$

To fully characterize the whole sampling distribution we need to determine both the mean vector, and the variance-covariance matrix of the OLS estimators. Assumptions (A.1), (A.2) and (A.3) immediately imply that

$$\mathrm{E}\left\{\begin{pmatrix}\frac{1}{n} - \bar{x}\omega_i\\ \omega_i\end{pmatrix} u_i\right\} = \begin{pmatrix}\frac{1}{n} - \bar{x}\omega_i\\ \omega_i\end{pmatrix} E(u_i) = 0, \quad \forall i \tag{1.53}$$

and therefore by equation (1.51) we obtain

$$\mathrm{E}\left\{\begin{pmatrix}\hat{\alpha}\\ \hat{\beta}\end{pmatrix}\right\} = \begin{pmatrix}\alpha\\ \beta\end{pmatrix}. \tag{1.54}$$

That is, the OLS estimators of α and β, under assumptions (A.1) to (A.7) are **unbiased**. Now we calculate the variance-covariance matrix. In order to do so, let

$$\begin{pmatrix}\operatorname{Var}(\hat{\alpha}) & \operatorname{Cov}\left(\hat{\alpha},\hat{\beta}\right)\\ \\ \operatorname{Cov}\left(\hat{\alpha},\hat{\beta}\right) & \operatorname{Var}\left(\hat{\beta}\right)\end{pmatrix} \equiv \mathrm{E}\left\{\begin{pmatrix}\hat{\alpha}-\alpha\\ \hat{\beta}-\beta\end{pmatrix} \left(\hat{\alpha}-\alpha \quad \hat{\beta}-\beta\right)\right\} \tag{1.55}$$

Then, if we substitute $\left(\hat{\alpha} - \alpha \quad \hat{\beta} - \beta\right)^{\top}$ by its definition in equation (1.51), the last expression will be equal to

$$= \sum_{i=1}^{n} \sum_{j=1}^{n} \mathrm{E} \left\{ \begin{pmatrix} (\frac{1}{n} - \bar{x}\omega_i)(\frac{1}{n} - \bar{x}\omega_j) & (\frac{1}{n} - \bar{x}\omega_i)\omega_j \\ \omega_i(\frac{1}{n} - \bar{x}\omega_j) & \omega_i\omega_j \end{pmatrix} u_i u_j \right\} \tag{1.56}$$

Now, assumptions (A.1), (A.5) and (A.6) allow us to simplify expression (1.56) and we obtain

$$= \sigma^2 \sum_{i=1}^{n} \begin{pmatrix} (\frac{1}{n} - \bar{x}\omega_i)^2 & (\frac{1}{n} - \bar{x}\omega_i)\omega_i \\ \omega_i(\frac{1}{n} - \bar{x}\omega_i) & \omega_i^2. \end{pmatrix} \tag{1.57}$$

Finally, substitute ω_i by its definition in equation (1.50) and we will obtain the following expressions for the variance covariance matrix

$$\begin{pmatrix} \mathrm{Var}(\hat{\alpha}) & \mathrm{Cov}\left(\hat{\alpha}, \hat{\beta}\right) \\ \mathrm{Cov}\left(\hat{\alpha}, \hat{\beta}\right) & \mathrm{Var}\left(\hat{\beta}\right) \end{pmatrix} = \sigma^2 \begin{pmatrix} \frac{1}{n} + \frac{\bar{x}^2}{\sum_{i=1}^{n}(x_i - \bar{x})^2} & -\frac{\bar{x}}{\sum_{i=1}^{n}(x_i - \bar{x})^2} \\ -\frac{\bar{x}}{\sum_{i=1}^{n}(x_i - \bar{x})^2} & \frac{1}{\sum_{i=1}^{n}(x_i - \bar{x})^2} \end{pmatrix} \tag{1.58}$$

We can say that the OLS method produces BLUE (Best Linear Unbiased Estimator) in the following sense: the OLS estimators are the linear, unbiased estimators which satisfy the Gauss-Markov Theorem. We now give the simplest version of the Gauss-Markov Theorem, that is proved in Johnston and Dinardo (1997), p. 36.

Gauss-Markov Theorem: Consider the regression model (1.22). Under assumptions (A.1) to (A.6) the OLS estimators of α and β are those who have minimum variance among the set of all linear and unbiased estimators of the parameters.

We remark that for the Gauss-Markov theorem to hold we do not need to include assumption (A.7) on the distribution of the error term. Furthermore, the properties of the OLS estimators mentioned above are established for finite samples. That is, the estimator divergence between the estimator and the parameter value is analyzed for a fixed sample size. Other properties of the estimators that are also of interest are the asymptotic properties. In this case, the behavior of the estimators with respect to their true parameter values are analyzed as the sample size increases. Among the asymptotic properties of the estimators we will study the so called **consistency** property.

We will say that the OLS estimators, $\hat{\alpha}$, $\hat{\beta}$, are consistent if they converge weakly in probability (see Serfling (1984) for a definition) to their respective parameter values, α and β. For weak convergence in probability, a sufficient condition is

$$\lim_{n\to\infty} E\begin{pmatrix}\hat{\alpha}\\ \hat{\beta}\end{pmatrix} = \begin{pmatrix}\alpha\\ \beta\end{pmatrix} \tag{1.59}$$

and

$$\lim_{n\to\infty}\begin{pmatrix}\operatorname{Var}(\hat{\alpha})\\ \operatorname{Var}\left(\hat{\beta}\right)\end{pmatrix} = \begin{pmatrix}0\\ 0\end{pmatrix} \tag{1.60}$$

Condition (1.59) is immediately verified since under conditions (A.1) to (A.6) we have shown that both OLS estimators are unbiased in finite sample sizes. Condition (1.60) is shown as follows:

$$\operatorname{Var}(\hat{\alpha}) = \sigma^2\left(\frac{1}{n} + \frac{\bar{x}^2}{\sum_{i=1}^n (x_i - \bar{x})^2}\right) = \frac{\sigma^2}{n}\left(1 + \frac{\bar{x}^2}{n^{-1}\sum_{i=1}^n (x_i - \bar{x})^2}\right)$$

then by the properties of the limits

$$\lim_{n\to\infty}\operatorname{Var}(\hat{\alpha}) = \lim_{n\to\infty}\frac{\sigma^2}{n} \times \lim_{n\to\infty}\left(\frac{\frac{1}{n}\sum_{i=1}^n x_i^2}{\frac{1}{n}\sum_{i=1}^n (x_i - \bar{x})^2}\right)$$

Assumption (A.3) ensures that

$$\lim_{n\to\infty}\left(\frac{\frac{1}{n}\sum_{i=1}^n x_i^2}{\frac{1}{n}\sum_{i=1}^n (x_i - \bar{x})^2}\right) < \infty$$

and since by assumption (A.5), σ^2 is constant and bounded, then $\lim_{n\to\infty}\frac{\sigma^2}{n} = 0$. This proves the first part of condition (1.60). The proof for $\hat{\beta}$ follows the same lines.

Properties of σ^2

For the statistical properties of $\hat{\sigma}^2$, we will just enumerate the different statistical results that will be proved in a more general setting in Chapter 2, Section 2.4.2. of this monograph.

Under assumptions (A.1) to (A.7), the finite sample distribution of this estimator is given by

$$\frac{(n-2)\hat{\sigma}^2}{\sigma^2} \sim \chi^2_{n-2}. \tag{1.61}$$

Then, by the properties of the χ^2 distribution it is easy to show that

$$Var\left(\frac{(n-2)\hat{\sigma}^2}{\sigma^2}\right) = 2(n-2).$$

This result allows us to calculate the variance of σ^2 as

$$Var(\hat{\sigma}^2) = \frac{2\sigma^4}{n-2}. \tag{1.62}$$

Note that to calculate this variance, the normality assumption, (A.7), plays a crucial role. In fact, by assuming that $u \sim \mathrm{N}(0, \sigma^2)$, then $E(u^3) = 0$, and the fourth order moment is already known an related to σ^2. These two properties are of great help to simplify the third and fourth order terms in equation (1.62).

Under assumptions (A.1) to (A.7) in Section 1.2 it is possible to show (see Chapter 2, Section 2.4.2 for a proof)

Unbiasedness:

$$E(\hat{\sigma}^2) = \mathrm{E}\left(\frac{\sum_{i=1}^n \hat{u}_i^2}{n-2}\right) = \frac{1}{n-2}E(\sum_{i=1}^n \hat{u}_i^2) = \frac{1}{n-2}(n-2)\sigma^2 = \sigma^2$$

Non-efficiency: The OLS estimator of σ^2 is not efficient because it does not achieve the Cramer-Rao lower bound (this bound is $\frac{2\sigma^4}{n}$).

Consistency: The OLS estimator of σ^2 converges weakly in probability to σ^2.i.e.

$$\hat{\sigma}^2 \rightarrow_p \sigma^2$$

as n tends to infinity.

Asymptotic distribution:

$$\sqrt{n}\left(\hat{\sigma}^2 - \sigma^2\right) \rightarrow_d N\left(0, 2\sigma^4\right)$$

as n tends to infinity.

From the last result, note finally that although $\hat{\sigma}^2$ is not efficient for finite sample sizes, this estimator achieves asymptotically the Cramer-Rao lower bound.

1.2.7 Examples

To illustrate the different statistical properties given in the previous section, we develop three different simulations. The first Monte Carlo experiment analyzes the finite sample distribution of both $\hat{\alpha}$, $\hat{\beta}$ and $\hat{\sigma}^2$. The second study performs a simulation to explain consistency, and finally the third study compares finite sample and asymptotic distribution of the OLS estimator of $\hat{\sigma}^2$.

Example 1

The following program illustrates the statistical properties of the OLS estimators of α and β. We implement the following Monte Carlo experiment. We have generated 500 replications of sample size n = 20 of the model $y_i = 1.5 + 2x_i + u_i \quad i = 1, \ldots, 20$. The values of X have been generated according to a uniform distribution, $X \sim U[0,1]$, and the the values for the error term have been generated following a normal distribution with zero mean and variance one, $u \sim \mathrm{N}(0,1)$. To fulfil assumption (A.1), the values of X are fixed for the 500 different replications. For each sample (replication) we have estimated the parameters α and β and their respective variances (note that σ^2 has been replaced by $\hat{\sigma}^2$). With the 500 values of the estimators of these parameters, we generate four different histograms

XEGlinreg10.xpl

The result of this procedure is presented in the Figure 1.8. With a sample size of $n = 20$, the histograms that contain the estimations of $\hat{\beta}$ and $\hat{\alpha}$ in the different replications approximate a gaussian distribution. In the other hand, the histograms for the variance estimates approximate a χ^2 distribution, as expected.

Example 2

This program analyzes by simulation the asymptotic behavior of both $\hat{\alpha}$ and $\hat{\beta}$ when the sample size increases. We generate observations using the model, $y_i = 2 + 0.5x_i + u_i$, $X \sim U[0,1]$, and $u \sim \mathrm{N}(0, 10^2)$. For 200 different sample sizes, $(n = 5, \cdots, 1000)$, we have generated 50 replications for each sample size.

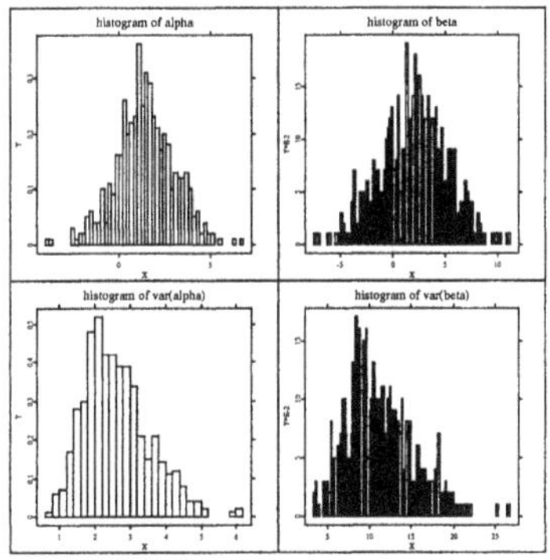

Figure 1.8. Finite sample distribution

For each sample size we estimate 50 estimators of α, β, then, we calculate $E(\hat{\beta})$ and $E(\hat{\alpha})$ conditioning on the sample size.

XEGlinreg11.xpl

The code gives the output presented in Figure 1.9. As expected, when we increase the sample size $E(\hat{\beta})$ tends to β, in this case $\beta = 0.5$, and $E(\hat{\alpha})$ tends to $\alpha = 2$.

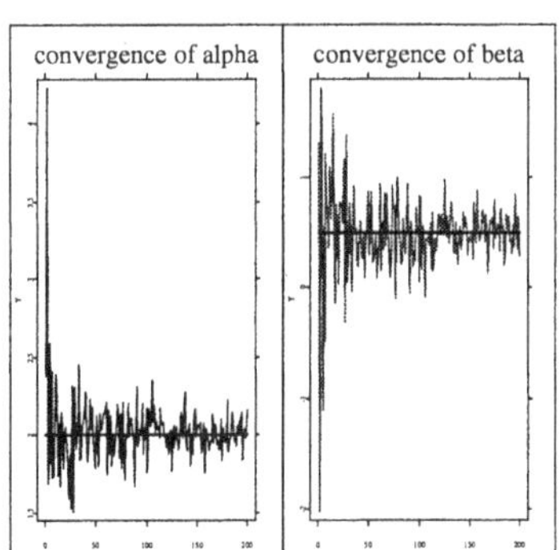

Figure 1.9. Consistency

Example 3

In the model $y_i = 1.5 + 2x_i + u_i$, $X \sim U[0,1]$, and $u \sim \mathrm{N}(0,16)$. We implement the following Monte Carlo experiment. For two different sample sizes we have generated 500 replications for each sample size. The first 500 replications have a sample size n = 10, the second n = 1000. In both sample sizes we estimate 500 estimators of σ^2. Then, we calculate two histograms for the estimates of $\frac{(n-2)\hat{\sigma}^2}{\sigma^2}$, one for $n = 10$, the other for $n = 1000$.

XEGlinreg12.xpl

The output of the code is presented in Figure 1.10. As expected, the histogram for $n = 10$ approximates a χ^2 density, whereas for $n = 1000$, the approximated density is the standard normal.

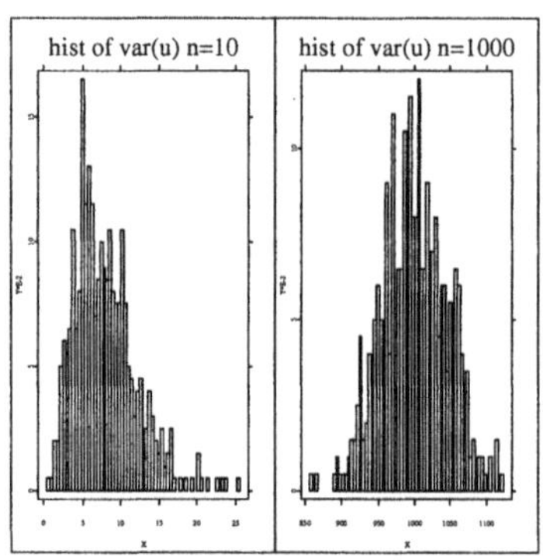

Figure 1.10. Distribution of $\hat{\sigma}^2$

1.3 Inference

In the framework of a univariate linear regression model, one can be interested in testing two different groups of hypotheses about β, α and σ^2. In the first group, the user has some prior knowledge about the value of β, for example he believes $\beta = \beta_0$, then he is interested in knowing whether this value, β_0, is compatible with the sample data. In this case the null hypothesis will be $H_0 : \beta = \beta_0$, and the alternative $H_1 : \beta \neq \beta_0$. This is what is called a **two**

sided test. In the other group, the prior knowledge about the parameter β can be more diffuse. For example we may have some knowledge about the sign of the parameter, and we want to know whether this sign agrees with our data. Then, two possible tests are available, $H_0 : \beta \leq \beta_0$ against $H_1 : \beta > \beta_0$, (for $\beta_0 = 0$ this would be a test of positive sign); and $H_0 : \beta \geq \beta_0$ against $H_1 : \beta < \beta_0$, (for $\beta_0 = 0$ this would be a test of negative sign). These are the so called **on sided tests**. Equivalent tests for α are available.

The tool we are going to use to test for the previous hypotheses is the sampling distribution for the different estimators. The key to design a testing procedure lies in being able to analyze the potential variability of the estimated value, that is, one must be able to say whether a large divergence between it and the hypothetical value is better ascribed to sampling variability alone or whether it is better ascribed to the hypothetical value being incorrect. In order to do so, we need to know the sampling distribution of the parameters.

1.3.1 Hypothesis Testing about β

In section 1.2.6, equations (1.52) to (1.58) show that the joint finite sample distribution of the OLS estimators of α and β is a normal density. Then, by standard properties of the multivariate gaussian distribution (see Greene (1993), p. 76), and under assumptions (A.1) to (A.7) from Section (1.2.6)it is possible to show that

$$\hat{\beta} \sim \mathbf{N}\left(\beta, \frac{\sigma^2}{\sum_{i=1}^{n}(x_i - \bar{x})^2}\right), \tag{1.63}$$

then, by a standard transformation

$$z = \frac{\hat{\beta} - \beta}{\sqrt{\sigma^2 / \sum_{i=1}^{n}(x_i - \bar{x})^2}} \tag{1.64}$$

is standard normal. σ^2 is unknown and therefore the previous expression is unfeasible. Replacing the unknown value of σ^2 with $\hat{\sigma}^2$ (the unbiased estimator of σ^2) the result

$$z = \frac{\hat{\beta} - \beta}{\sqrt{\hat{\sigma}^2 / \sum_{i=1}^{n}(x_i - \bar{x})^2}}, \tag{1.65}$$

is the ratio of a standard normal variable (see (1.63)) and the square root of a chi-squared variable divided by its degrees of freedom (see (1.61)). It is not difficult to show that both random variables are independent, and therefore z in (1.65) follows a student-t distribution with $n-2$ degrees of freedom (see Johnston and Dinardo (1997), p. 489 for a proof). i. e.

$$z \sim t_{(n-2)} \tag{1.66}$$

To test the hypotheses, we have the following alternative procedures:

	Null Hypothesis	Alternative Hypothesis
a) Two-sided test	$\mathrm{H}_0 : \beta = \beta_0$	$\mathrm{H}_1 : \beta \neq \beta_0$
b) one-sided test		
Right-sided test	$\mathrm{H}_0 : \beta \leq \beta_0$	$\mathrm{H}_1 : \beta > \beta_0$
Left-sided test	$\mathrm{H}_0 : \beta \geq \beta_0$	$\mathrm{H}_1 : \beta < \beta_0$

According to this set of hypotheses, next, we present the steps for a one-sided test, after this, we present the procedure for a two-sided test.

One-sided Test

The steps for a one-sided test are as follows:

Step 1: Establish the set of hypotheses

$$\mathrm{H}_0 : \beta \leq \beta_0 \quad \text{versus} \quad \mathrm{H}_1 : \beta > \beta_0.$$

Step 2: The test statistic is $\frac{\hat{\beta}-\beta_0}{\sqrt{\hat{\sigma}^2/\sum_{i=1}^n (x_i-\bar{x})^2}}$, which can be calculated from the sample. Under the null hypothesis, it has the t-distribution with $(n-2)$ degrees of freedom. If the calculated z is "large", we would suspect that β is probably not equal to β_0. This leads to the next step.

Step 3: In the t-table, look up the entry for $n-2$ degrees of freedom and the given level of significance (ϵ) and find the point $t^*_{\epsilon,n-2}$ such that $P(t > t^*) = \epsilon$

Step 4: Reject H_0 if $z > t^*_{\epsilon,n-2}$.

If the calculated t-statistic (z) falls in the critical region, then $z > t^*_{\epsilon,n-2}$. In that case the null hypothesis is rejected and we conclude that β is significantly greater than β_0

The p-value Approach to Hypothesis Testing

The t-statistic can also be carried out in an equivalent way. First, calculate the probability that the random variable t (t-distribution with $n-2$ degrees of freedom) is greater than the observed z, that is, calculate

$$p - value = P(t > z)$$

This probability is the area to the right of z in the t-distribution. A high value for this probability implies that the consequences of erroneously rejecting a true H_0 is severe. A low p-value implies that the consequences of rejecting a true H_0 erroneously are not very severe, and hence we are "safe" in rejecting H_0. The decision rule is therefore to "accept" H_0(that is, not reject it) if the p-value is too high. In other words, if the p-value is higher than the specified level of significance (say ϵ), we conclude that the regression coefficient β is not significantly greater than β_0 at the level ϵ. If the p-value is less than ϵ we reject H_0 and conclude that β is significantly greater than β_0. The modified steps for the p-value approach are as follows:

Step 3a: Calculate the probability (denoted as p-value) that t is greater than z, that is, compute the area to the right of the calculated z.

Step 4a: Reject H_0 and conclude that the coefficient is significant if the p-value is less than the given level of significance (ϵ)

If we want to establish a more constrained null hypothesis, that is, the set of possible values that β can take under the null hypothesis is only one value, we must use a two-sided test.

Two-sided Test

The procedure for a two-sided alternative is quite similar. The steps are as follows:

Step 1: Establish the set of hypotheses

$$\mathrm{H}_0 : \beta = \beta_0 \quad \text{versus} \quad \mathrm{H}_1 : \beta \neq \beta_0.$$

Step 2: The test statistic is $\frac{\hat{\beta}-\beta}{\sqrt{\hat{\sigma}^2/\sum_{i=1}^{n}(x_i-\bar{x})^2}}$, which is the same as before. Under the null hypothesis, it has the t-distribution with $(n-2)$ degrees of freedom.

Step 3: In the t-table, look up the entry for $n-2$ degrees of freedom and the given level of significance (ϵ) and find the point $t^*_{\epsilon/2,n-2}$ such that $P(t > t^*) = \epsilon/2$ (one-half of the level of significance)

Step 3a: To use the p-value approach calculate

$$p - value = P(t > z \quad \text{or} \quad t < z) = 2P(t > z)$$

because of the symmetry of the t-distribution around the origin.

Step 4: Reject H_0 if $|z| > t^*_{\epsilon/2,n-2}$ and conclude that β is significantly different form β_0 at the level ϵ

Step 4a: In case of the p-value approach, reject H_0 if p-value$< \epsilon$, the level of significance.

The different sets of hypotheses and their decision regions for testing at a significance level of ϵ can be summarized in the following table:

Test	Rejection region for H_0	Non-rejection region for H_0
Two-sided	$\left\{z \mid z < -t^*_{\epsilon/2} \text{ or } z > t^*_{\epsilon/2}\right\}$	$\left\{z \mid -t^*_{\epsilon/2} \le z \le t^*_{\epsilon/2}\right\}$
right-sided	$\{z \mid z > t^*_{\epsilon}\}$	$\{z \mid z \le t^*_{\epsilon}\}$
left-sided	$\{z \mid z < -t^*_{\epsilon}\}$	$\{z \mid z \ge -t^*_{\epsilon}\}$

1.3.2 Example

We implement the following Monte Carlo experiment. We generate one sample of size n = 20 of the model $y_i = 2 + 0.75x_i + u_i \quad i = 1, \ldots, 20$. X has a uniform distribution generated as follows $X \sim U[0,1]$, and the error term $u \sim \mathrm{N}(0,1)$. We estimate α, β, σ^2. The program gives the three possible test for β when $\beta_0 = 0$, showing the critical values and the rejection regions.

XEGlinreg13.xpl

The previous hypothesis-testing procedure is confined to the slope coefficient, β. In the next section we present the process based on the fit of the regression

1.3.3 Testing Hypothesis Based on the Regression Fit

In this section we present an alternative view to the two sided test on β that we have developed in the previous section. Recall that the null hypothesis is $H_0 \ : \beta = \beta_0$ against the alternative hypothesis that $H_0 \ : \beta \neq \beta_0$.

In order to implement the test statistic remind that the OLS estimators, $\hat{\beta}$ and $\hat{\alpha}$, are such that they minimize the residual sum of squares (RSS). Since $R^2 = 1 - RSS/TSS$, equivalently $\hat{\beta}$ and $\hat{\alpha}$ maximize the R^2, and therefore any other value of $\hat{\beta}$, leads to a relevant loss of fit. Consider, now, the value under the null, β_0 rather than $\hat{\beta}$ (the OLS estimator). We can investigate the changes in the regression fit when using β_0 instead of $\hat{\beta}$. To this end, consider the following residual sum of squares where $\hat{\beta}$ has been replaced by β_0.

$$RSS_0 = \sum_{i=1}^{n} (y_i - \alpha - \beta_0 x_i)^2. \tag{1.67}$$

Then, the value of α, α_0, that minimizes (1.67) is

$$\alpha_0 = \bar{y} - \beta_0 \bar{x}. \tag{1.68}$$

Substituting (1.68) into (1.67) we obtain

$$RSS_0 = \sum_{i=1}^{n} \left(y_i - \bar{y} - \beta_0 (x_i - \bar{x})\right)^2. \tag{1.69}$$

Doing some standard algebra we can show that this last expression is equal to

$$RSS_0 = TSS + \left(\hat{\beta} - \beta_0\right)^2 \sum_{i=1}^{n} (x_i - \bar{x})^2 - ESS, \tag{1.70}$$

and since $TSS = ESS + RSS$ and defining

$$R_0^2 = 1 - \frac{RSS_0}{TSS} \tag{1.71}$$

then (1.70) is equal to

$$R^2 - R_0^2 = \frac{(\hat{\beta} - \beta_0)^2 \sum_{i=1}^{n} (x_i - \bar{x})^2}{TSS}, \tag{1.72}$$

which is positive, because R_0^2 must be smaller than R^2, that is, the alternative regression will not fit as well as the OLS regression line. Finally,

$$F = \frac{(R^2 - R_0^2)/1}{(1 - R^2)/(n-2)} \sim F_{1,n-2} \tag{1.73}$$

where $F_{1,n-2}$ is an F-Snedecor distribution with 1 and $n-2$ degrees of freedom. The last statement is easily proved since under the assumptions established in Section 1.2.6 then

$$(\hat{\beta} - \beta_0)^2 \sum_{i=1}^{n} (x_i - \bar{x})^2 / \sigma^2 \sim \chi_1^2, \tag{1.74}$$

$$(n-2) RSS / \sigma^2 \sim \chi_{n-2}^2, \tag{1.75}$$

and

$$\frac{(R^2 - R_0^2)/1}{(1 - R^2)/(n-2)} = \frac{(\hat{\beta} - \beta_0)^2 \sum_{i=1}^{n} (x_i - \bar{x})^2 / \sigma^2}{(n-2) RSS / \sigma^2}. \tag{1.76}$$

The proof of (1.73) is closed by remarking that (1.74) and (1.75) are independent.

The procedure in the two-sided test

Step 1: Establish the set of hypotheses

$$\mathrm{H}_0 : \beta = \beta_0 \quad \text{versus} \quad \mathrm{H}_1 : \beta \neq \beta_0.$$

Step 2: The test statistic is $F = \frac{(R^2 - R_0^2)/1}{(1 - R^2)/(n-2)}$. Under the null hypothesis, it has the F-distribution with one and $(n-2)$ degrees of freedom.

Step 3: In the F-table, look up the entry for $1, n-2$ degrees of freedom and the given level of significance (ϵ) and find the point $F^*_{\epsilon/2,1,n-2}$ and $F^*_{1-\epsilon/2,1,n-2}$

Step 4: Reject H_0 if $F_0 > F^*_{\epsilon/2,1,n-2}$ or $F_0 < F^*_{1-\epsilon/2,1,n-2}$ and conclude that β is significantly different from β_0 at the level ϵ

1.3.4 Example

With the same data of the previous example, the program computes the hypothesis test for $H_0 : \beta_0 = 0$ by using the regression fit. The output is the critical value and the rejection regions.

XEGlinreg14.xpl

1.3.5 Hypothesis Testing about α

As in Section 1.3.1, by standard properties of the multivariate gaussian distribution (see Greene (1993), p. 76), and under assumptions (A.1) to (A.7) from Section (1.2.6) it is possible to show that

$$z = \frac{\hat{\alpha} - \alpha}{\hat{\sigma}\sqrt{1/n + \bar{x}^2 / \sum_{i=1}^{n}(x_i - \bar{x})^2}} \sim t_{(n-2)} \tag{1.77}$$

The construction of the test are made similar to the test of β, a two- or one-sided test will be carried out:

1)Two-sided test

$$\mathrm{H}_0 : \alpha = \alpha_0 \quad \text{versus} \quad \mathrm{H}_1 : \alpha \neq \alpha_0.$$

2) Right-sided test

$$\mathrm{H}_0 : \alpha \leq \alpha_0 \quad \text{versus} \quad \mathrm{H}_1 : \alpha > \alpha_0.$$

3) Left-sided test

$$\mathrm{H}_0 : \alpha \geq \alpha_0 \quad \text{versus} \quad \mathrm{H}_1 : \alpha < \alpha_0.$$

If we assume a two-sided test, the steps for this test are as follows

Step 1: Establish the set of hypotheses

$$\mathrm{H}_0 : \alpha = \alpha_0 \qquad \text{versus} \qquad \mathrm{H}_1 : \alpha \neq \alpha_0.$$

Step 2: The test statistic is $z = \frac{\hat{\alpha}-\alpha_0}{\hat{\sigma}_{\hat{\alpha}}}$, which is the same as before. Under the null hypothesis, it has the t-distribution with $(n-2)$ degrees of freedom.

Step 3: In the t-table, look up the entry for $n-2$ degrees of freedom and the given level of significance (ϵ) and find the point $t^*_{\epsilon/2,n-2}$ such that $P(t > t^*) = \epsilon/2$ (one-half of the level of significance)

Step 4: Reject H_0 if $|z| > t^*_{\epsilon/2,n-2}$ and conclude that α is significantly different form α_0 at the level ϵ

1.3.6 Example

With the same data of the previous example, the program gives the three possible tests for $\hat{\alpha}$ when $\alpha_0 = 2$, showing the critical values and the rejection regions.

XEGlinreg15.xpl

1.3.7 Hypotheses Testing about σ^2

Although a test for the variance of the error term σ^2 is not as common as one for the parameters of the regression line, for the sake of completeness we present it here. The test on σ^2 can be obtained from the large sample distribution of σ^2,

$$\frac{(n-2)\hat{\sigma}^2}{\sigma^2} \sim \chi^2_{n-2} \tag{1.78}$$

Using this result, one may write:

$$\mathrm{Prob}\left[\chi^2_{1-\epsilon/2} < \frac{(n-2)\hat{\sigma}^2}{\sigma^2} < \chi^2_{\epsilon/2}\right] = 1-\epsilon \tag{1.79}$$

which states that ϵ percent of the values of a χ^2 variable will lie between the values that cut off $\epsilon/2$ percent in each tail of the distribution. The critical values are taken from the χ^2 distribution with $(n-2)$ degrees of freedom. Remember that the χ^2 is an asymmetric distribution.

The $(1-\epsilon)$ percent confidence interval for σ^2 will be:

$$\left(\frac{(n-2)\hat{\sigma}^2}{\chi^2_{\epsilon/2}};\frac{(n-2)\hat{\sigma}^2}{\chi^2_{1-\epsilon/2}}\right) \tag{1.80}$$

Now, similar to test the coefficients of the regression, we can consider a test for the significance of the error variance σ^2. The steps are as follows:

Step 1: Establish the set of hypotheses

$$\mathrm{H}_0 : \sigma^2 = \sigma_0^2 \quad \text{versus} \quad \mathrm{H}_1 : \sigma^2 \neq \sigma_0^2.$$

Step 2: The test statistic is $q = (n-2)\frac{\hat{\sigma}^2}{\sigma_0^2}$. The distribution of this, under the null hypothesis, is chi-squared with $(n-2)$ degrees fo freedom. If q is "large" we would suspect that σ^2 is probably not equal to σ_0^2

Step 3: From the chi-square table, look at the value $\chi^2_{\epsilon/2,n-2}$ and $\chi^2_{1-\epsilon/2,n-2}$

Step 4: We reject H_0 if the value of the statistic $q \geq \chi^2_{\epsilon/2}$ or $q \leq \chi^2_{1-\epsilon/2}$. Otherwise, H_0 can't be rejected. This means that H_0 is accepted if σ_0^2 lay in the confidence interval of σ^2 (Chow, 1983).

1.4 Forecasting

An apparently different problem, but in actually very close to parameter estimation, is that of forecasting. We consider a situation where there is a data set available on both Y and X for elements 1 to n. We can not only estimate the relationship between Y and X. With this estimation, we can use it to forecast or predict the value of the variable Y for any given value of X. Suppose that $x^\star$ is a known value of the regressor, and we are interested in predicting $y^\star$, the value of Y associated with $x^\star$.

It is evident that, in general, if X takes the value $x^\star$, the predicted value of $y^\star$, is given by:

$$\hat{y}^\star = \hat{\alpha} + \hat{\beta}x^\star \tag{1.81}$$

The conditional mean of the predictor of Y given $X = x^\star$ is

$$E(\hat{y}|X = x^\star) = E(\hat{\alpha}) + x^\star E(\hat{\beta}) = \alpha + \beta x^\star = E(Y|X = x^\star) \tag{1.82}$$

Thus, $\hat{y}^\star$ is an unbiased conditional predictor of $y^\star$.

1.4.1 Confidence Interval for the Point Forecast

Because α and β are estimated with imprecision, $\hat{y}^\star$ is also subject to error. To take account of this, we compute the variance and confidence interval for the point predictor. The prediction error is:

$$\hat{u}^\star = y^\star - \hat{y}^\star = (\alpha - \hat{\alpha}) + (\beta - \hat{\beta})x^\star + u^\star \tag{1.83}$$

Clearly the expected prediction error is zero. The variance of $u^\star$ is

$$var(\hat{u}^\star) = \sigma^2 \left(1 + \frac{1}{n} + \frac{(x^\star - \bar{x})^2}{\sum_{i=1}^{n}(x_i - \bar{x})^2}\right) \tag{1.84}$$

We see that $\hat{u}^\star$ is a linear combination of normally distributed variables. Thus, it is also normally distributed. and so

$$\frac{\hat{u}^\star}{\sigma\sqrt{1 + \frac{1}{n} + \frac{(x^\star - \bar{x})^2}{\sum_{i=1}^{n}(x_i - \bar{x})^2}}} \sim \mathrm{N}(0,1) \tag{1.85}$$

By inserting the sample estimate $\hat{\sigma}$ for σ,

$$\frac{\hat{u}^\star}{\hat{\sigma}\sqrt{1 + \frac{1}{n} + \frac{(x^\star - \bar{x})^2}{\sum_{i=1}^{n}(x_i - \bar{x})^2}}} \sim t_{(n-2)} \tag{1.86}$$

We can construct a prediction interval for $y^\star$ in the usual way, we derive a $(1 - \epsilon)$ per cent forecast interval for $y^\star$

$$(\hat{\alpha} + \hat{\beta}x^\star) \pm t_{\epsilon/2,(n-2)}\hat{\sigma}\sqrt{1 + \frac{1}{n} + \frac{(x^\star - \bar{x})^2}{\sum_{i=1}^{n}(x_i - \bar{x})^2}} \tag{1.87}$$

where $t_{\epsilon/2,(n-2)}$ is the critical value from the t distribution with $(n-2)$ degrees of freedom.

1.4.2 Example

We implement the following experiment using the following Quantlet. We generate a sample $n = 20$ of the following data generating process: $y_i = 2 + 0.5x_i + u_i$, the vector of explanatory variables is $X = [8, ..., 27]$. First of all, we estimate α and β, then we obtain predictions for several values of X.

XEGlinreg16.xpl

In this program, the vector of X takes values from 8 to 27 for the estimation, after this we want to calculate a interval prediction for $X = [1, ..., 60]$. This procedure gives the Figure 1.11

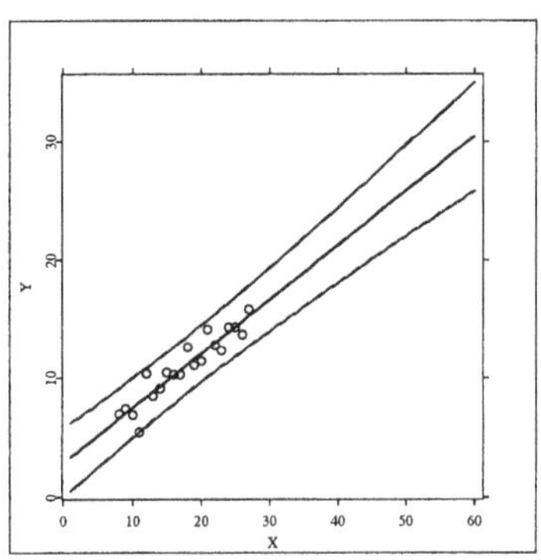

Figure 1.11. Interval prediction

1.4.3 Confidence Interval for the Mean Predictor

The sample given in the previous section is that for predicting a point. We also like the variance of the mean predictor. The variance of the prediction error for the mean $(\hat{u}_m^\star)$ is

$$var(\hat{u}_m^\star) = \sigma^2 \left(\frac{1}{n} + \frac{(x^\star - \bar{x})^2}{\sum_{i=1}^n (x_i - \bar{x})^2} \right) \tag{1.88}$$

We see that $\hat{u}_m^\star$ is a linear combination of normally distributed variables. Thus, it is also normally distributed. By inserting the sample estimate $\hat{\sigma}$ for σ

$$\frac{\hat{u}_m^\star}{\hat{\sigma}\sqrt{\frac{1}{n} + \frac{(x^\star - \bar{x})^2}{\sum_{i=1}^n (x_i - \bar{x})^2}}} \sim t_{(n-2)} \tag{1.89}$$

The $(1 - \epsilon)$ per cent confidence interval of the mean forecast is given by

$$(\hat{\alpha} + \hat{\beta}x^\star) \pm t_{\epsilon/2,(n-2)}\hat{\sigma}\sqrt{\frac{1}{n} + \frac{(x^\star - \bar{x})^2}{\sum_{i=1}^n (x_i - \bar{x})^2}} \tag{1.90}$$

where $t_{\epsilon/2,(n-2)}$ is the critical value from the t distribution with $(n-2)$ degrees of freedom.

Bibliography

Amemiya, T. (1985). *Advanced Econometrics*, Harvard University Press.

Baltagi, B.H. (1985). *Econometrics*, Springer.

Chow, G.C. (1983). *Econometrics*, McGraw-Hill.

Goldberger, A.S. (1964). *Econometric Theory*, Wiley and Sons.

Greene, W.H. (1993). *Econometric Analysis*, MacMillan Publishing Company.

Gujarati, D.M. (1995). *Basics Econometrics*, McGraw-Hill.

Härdle, W. and Simar, L. (1999). *Applied Multivariate Statistical Analysis*, Springer-Verlag.

Intriligator, M. D. (1978). *Econometric models, techniques, and applications*, McGraw-Hill. Prentice-Hall, Inc., Englewood Cliffs, N.J.

Johnston, J. and Dinardo, J. (1997). *Econometric Methods*, McGraw-Hill.

Kennedy, P. (1998). *A guide to econometrics*, Blackwell Publishers.

Mantzapoulus, V. (1995). *Statistics for the Social Sciences*, Englewood Cliffs: Prentice Hall.

Newbold, P. (1996). *Statistics for business and economics*, Prentice Hall, Englewood Cliffs.

Newey, W. K. and McFadden, D. L. (1994). Large sample estimation and hypothesis testing, *in* R. F. Engle and McFadden, D. L. (eds.) *Handbook of econometrics, Vol. IV*, North-Holland, Amsterdam.

Serfling, T. (1980). *Approximation theorems for mathematical statistics*, Wiley.

White, H. (1984). *Asymptotic Theory for Econometicians*, Academic Press.

Wonacott, T. and Wonacott, R. (1990). *Introductory statistics for business and economics*, Academic Press.

2 Multivariate Linear Regression Model

Teresa Aparicio and Inmaculada Villanua

2.1 Introduction

A **Multivariate linear regression model** (MLRM) is a generalization of the univariate linear regression model which has been dealt with in Chapter 2. In this chapter we consider an endogenous or response variable denoted by y, which depends on a set of k variables x_j $(j = 1, ..., k)$, called "regressors", "independent variables" or "explanatory variables", and an unobservable random term called "disturbance" or "error" term. The latter includes other factors (some of them non-observable, or even unknown) associated with the endogenous variable, together with possible measurement errors.

Given a sample of n observations of each variable, in such a way that the information can be referred to time periods (time-series data) or can be referred to individuals, firms, etc. (cross-section data), and assuming linearity, the model can be specified as follows:

$$y_i = \beta_1 x_{1i} + \beta_2 x_{2i} + \ldots + \beta_k x_{ki} + u_i \tag{2.1}$$

with (i=1,2,...,n), where usually $x_{1i} = 1 \ \forall \ i$, and their coefficient β_1 is called the intercept of the equation.

The right-hand side of (2.1) which includes the regressors (x_j), is called the *systematic component* of the regression function, with β_j $(j = 1, \ldots, k)$ being the coefficients or parameters of the model, which are interpreted as marginal effects, that is to say, β_j measures the change of the endogenous variable when x_j varies a unit, maintaining the rest of regressors as fixed. The error term u_i constitutes what is called the *random component* of the model.

Expression (2.1) reflects n equations, which can be written in matrix form in the following terms:

$$y = X\beta + u \tag{2.2}$$

where y is the $n \times 1$ vector of the observations of the endogenous variable, β is the $k \times 1$ vector of coefficients, and X is an $n \times k$ matrix of the form:

$$\begin{pmatrix} 1 & x_{21} & x_{31} & \dots & x_{k1} \\ 1 & x_{22} & x_{32} & \dots & x_{k2} \\ 1 & x_{23} & x_{33} & \dots & x_{k3} \\ \vdots & \vdots & \vdots & \dots & \vdots \\ 1 & x_{2n} & x_{3n} & \dots & x_{kn} \end{pmatrix} \tag{2.3}$$

in such a way that every row represents an observation. In expression (2.1) $X\beta$ represents the systematic component, while u is the random component.

Model (2.2) specifies a causality relationship among y, X and u, with X and u being considered the factors which affect y.

In general terms, model (2.2)(or(2.1)) is considered as a model of economic behavior where the variable y represents the response of the economic agents to the set of variables which are contained in X, and the error term u contains the deviation to the average behavior.

2.2 Classical Assumptions of the MLRM

In order to carry out the estimation and inference in the MLRM, the specification of this model includes a set of assumptions referring to the way of generating the data, that is to say, referring to the underlying Data Generating Process (DGP). These assumptions can be grouped into two categories:

- Hypotheses on the systematic part of the model: strict exogeneity of the explanatory variables, full rank for the X matrix, and stability of the parameter vector β.
- Hypotheses on the disturbances of the model: zero mean, constant variance, non autocorrelation, and normal distribution function.

2.2.1 The Systematic Component Assumptions

Assumption 1: Strict exogeneity of the regressors. In Economics, it is very difficult to have experimental data (obtained from a controlled experiment), so it seems reasonable to assume that the set of variables included in the model should be random variables. Following Engle, Hendry, and Richard (1983), we can say that the regressors are *strictly exogenous* if x_j is independent of u, $\forall$ j. This means that, given the DGP, for each observed sample (realization) of every variable included in X, there are infinite possible realizations of u and y; this fact leads us to deal with the distribution of $u|X$. This assumption allows us to express the joint distribution function of X and u as :

$$F(u, X) = F(u) \cdot F(X) \tag{2.4}$$

or alternatively:

$$F(u|X) = F(u) \tag{2.5}$$

Nevertheless, in this chapter we are going to adopt a more restrictive assumption, considering the variables in X as non stochastic, that is to say, the elements in X are fixed for repeated samples. Obviously, this hypothesis allows us to maintain result (2.5). Thus, we can conclude that the randomness of y is only due to the disturbance term.

Additionally, the X matrix satisfies the following condition:

$$\lim_{n \to \infty} \frac{X^\top X}{n} = Q \tag{2.6}$$

where Q is a non singular positive definite matrix with finite elements.

Assumption 2: matrix X has full rank. Analytically, this assumption is written:

$$r(X) = k \tag{2.7}$$

and it means that the columns of X are linearly independent, or in other words, no exact linear relations exist between any of the X variables. This assumption is usually denoted *non perfect multicollinearity*. A direct consequence of (2.7) is that $n \geq k$.

Assumption 3: Stability of the parameter vector β. This assumption means that the coefficients of the model do not vary across sample observations, that is to say, we assume the same model for all the sample.

2.2.2 The Random Component Assumptions

Assumption 4: Zero mean of the disturbance. Analytically, we write this as:

$$\mathrm{E}(u_i|X) = \mathrm{E}(u_i) = 0 \quad \forall i \tag{2.8}$$

or in matrix notation:

$$\mathrm{E}(u) = 0_n \tag{2.9}$$

Since u is usually considered as the sum of many individual factors whose sign is unknown, we assume that on average, these effects are null.

Assumption 5: Spherical errors. This assumption states that the disturbances have constant variance, and they are non correlated.

$$var(u_i) = \mathrm{E}(u_i^2) = \sigma^2 \quad \forall i \tag{2.10}$$

$$cov(u_i, u_{i'}) = \mathrm{E}(u_i u_{i'}) = 0 \quad \forall i \neq i' \tag{2.11}$$

The condition (2.10) is known as *homoskedasticity*, and it states that all u_i have the same dispersion around their mean, whatever the values of the regressors. The condition (2.11), related to the covariance of the disturbances, is called *non autocorrelation*, and it means that knowing the ith disturbance does not tell us anything about the i'^{th} disturbance, for $i \neq i'$. Both hypotheses can be summarized in matrix form through the variance-covariance matrix $V(u)$:

$$V(u) = \mathrm{E}[(u - \mathrm{E}u)(u - \mathrm{E}u)^\top] = \mathrm{E}(uu^\top) = \sigma^2 I_n \tag{2.12}$$

Assumption 6: The disturbance vector is normally distributed. This hypothesis, together with (2.9) and (2.12) allows us to summarize the assumptions of the disturbance term as follows:

$$u \sim N[0_n, \sigma^2 I_n] \tag{2.13}$$

From (2.13) we derive that all observations of u are independent.

We can find some text books (Baltagi (1999), Davidson (2000), Hayashi (2000), Intriligator, Bodkin, and Hsiao (1996), Judge, Carter, Griffiths, Lutkepohl and Lee (1988)) which do not initially include this last assumption in their set of classical hypotheses, but it is included later. This fact can be justified because it is possible to get the estimate of the parameters of the model by the

Least Square method, and derive some of their properties, without using the normality assumption.

From (2.13), the joint density function of the n disturbances is given by:

$$f(u) = f(u_1, u_2, \ldots, u_n) = \frac{1}{(2\pi\sigma^2)^{n/2}} exp\{-\frac{1}{2\sigma^2} u^\top u\} \tag{2.14}$$

The set of classical assumptions described above allows us to obtain the probability distribution of the endogenous variable (y) as a multivariate normal distribution, with the following moments:

$$\mathrm{E}(y) = \mathrm{E}(X\beta + u) = X\beta + \mathrm{E}(u) = X\beta \tag{2.15}$$

$$V(y) = \mathrm{E}[(y - \mathrm{E}y)(y - \mathrm{E}y)^\top] = \mathrm{E}(uu^\top) = \sigma^2 I_n \tag{2.16}$$

These results imply that, the expectation for every component of y, depends on the corresponding row of X, while all elements have the same variance, and are independent.

Obviously, we can not assure that the set of classical assumptions that we have previously described are always maintained. In practice, there are many situations for which the theoretical model which establishes the relationship among the set variables does not satisfy the classical hypotheses mentioned above. A later section of this chapter and the following chapters of this book study the consequences when some of the "ideal conditions" fails, and describe how to proceed in this case. Specifically, at the end of this chapter we deal with the non stability of the coefficient vector β.

2.3 Estimation Procedures

Having specified the MLRM given in (2.1) or (2.2), the following econometric stage to carry out is the estimation, which consists of quantifying the parameters of the model, using the observations of y and X collected in the sample of size n. The set of parameters to estimate is $k+1$: the k coefficients of the vector β, and the dispersion parameter σ^2, about which we have no a priori information.

Following the same scheme of the previous chapter, we are going to describe the two common estimation procedures: the Least Squares (LS) and the Maximum Likelihood (ML) Methods.

2.3.1 The Least Squares Estimation

The LS procedure selects those values of β that minimize the sum of squares of the distances between the actual values of y and the adjusted (or estimated) values of the endogenous variable. Let $\hat{\hat{\beta}}$ be a possible estimation (some function of the sample observations) of β. Then, the adjusted value of the endogenous variable is given by:

$$\hat{\hat{y}}_i = x_i^\top \hat{\hat{\beta}} \quad \forall i \tag{2.17}$$

where $x_i^\top = (1, x_{2i}, x_{3i}, \ldots, x_{ki})$ is the row vector of the value of the regressors for the ith observation. From (2.17), the distance defined earlier, or residual, is given by:

$$\hat{\hat{u}}_i = y_i - \hat{\hat{y}}_i = y_i - x_i^\top \hat{\hat{\beta}} \quad \forall i \tag{2.18}$$

Consequently, the function to minimize is :

$$S(\hat{\hat{\beta}}) = \sum_{i=1}^{n} \hat{\hat{u}}_i^2 = \sum_{i=1}^{n} (y_i - x_i^\top \hat{\hat{\beta}})^2 \tag{2.19}$$

and then, what we call the Ordinary Least Squares (OLS) estimator of β, denoted by $\hat{\beta}$ is the value of $\hat{\hat{\beta}}$ which satisfies:

$$\hat{\beta} = \arg\min_{\hat{\hat{\beta}}} S(\hat{\hat{\beta}}) \tag{2.20}$$

To solve this optimization problem, the first-order conditions make the first derivatives of $S(\hat{\hat{\beta}})$ with respect to $\hat{\hat{\beta}}_1$, $\hat{\hat{\beta}}_2$,…,$\hat{\hat{\beta}}_k$ equal to zero. In order to obtain such conditions in matrix form, we express (2.19) as follows:

$$S(\hat{\hat{\beta}}) = (y - X\hat{\hat{\beta}})^\top (y - X\hat{\hat{\beta}}) \tag{2.21}$$

Given that $\hat{\hat{\beta}}^\top X^\top y = (y^\top X \hat{\hat{\beta}})^\top$, and both elements are 1×1, we can group the terms, and $S(\hat{\hat{\beta}})$ is written as follows:

$$S(\hat{\hat{\beta}}) = y^\top y - 2y^\top X \hat{\hat{\beta}} + \hat{\hat{\beta}}^\top X^\top X \hat{\hat{\beta}} \tag{2.22}$$

The vector which contains the k first partial derivatives (gradient vector) is expressed as:

$$\frac{\partial S(\hat{\hat{\beta}})}{\partial \hat{\hat{\beta}}} = -2X^\top y + 2X^\top X \hat{\hat{\beta}} \tag{2.23}$$

Setting (2.23) to zero, result:

$$X^\top X\hat{\beta} = X^\top y \tag{2.24}$$

The system of k linear equations (2.24) is called the *system of normal equations.*

From assumption 2 of the last section, we know that X has full rank, and so we can state that the inverse of $X^\top X$ exists, in such a way that we can obtain $\hat{\beta}$ by premultiplying (2.24) by $(X^\top X)^{-1}$:

$$\hat{\beta} = (X^\top X)^{-1} X^\top y \tag{2.25}$$

According to (2.25), the OLS residuals vector is given by:

$$\hat{u} = y - X\hat{\beta} \tag{2.26}$$

with a typical element $\hat{u}_i = y_i - x_i^\top \hat{\beta}$. From (2.2), the residual vector can be understood as the sample counterpart of the disturbance vector u.

The second-order condition of minimization establishes that the second partial derivatives matrix (hessian matrix) has to be positive definite. In our case, such a matrix is given by:

$$\frac{\partial^2 S(\hat{\beta})}{\partial \hat{\beta} \partial \hat{\beta}^\top} = 2X^\top X \tag{2.27}$$

and given the full rank of X, it means that $X^\top X$ is positive definite.

From (2.25), and given that the regressors are fixed, it follows that $\hat{\beta}$ is a linear function of the vector y, that is to say:

$$\hat{\beta} = A^\top y \tag{2.28}$$

where $A = (X^\top X)^{-1} X^\top$ is a $k \times n$ matrix of constant elements. The set of k normal equations written in (2.24), can be expressed in the following terms:

$$\begin{pmatrix} 1 & 1 & 1 & 1 & 1 \\ x_{21} & x_{22} & x_{23} & \dots & x_{2n} \\ x_{31} & x_{32} & x_{33} & \dots & x_{3n} \\ \vdots & \vdots & \vdots & \vdots & \vdots \\ x_{k1} & x_{k2} & x_{k3} & \dots & x_{kn} \end{pmatrix} \begin{pmatrix} 1 & x_{21} & x_{31} & \dots & x_{k1} \\ 1 & x_{22} & x_{32} & \dots & x_{k2} \\ 1 & x_{23} & x_{33} & \dots & x_{k3} \\ \vdots & \vdots & \vdots & \vdots & \vdots \\ 1 & x_{2n} & x_{3n} & \dots & x_{kn} \end{pmatrix} \begin{pmatrix} \hat{\beta}_1 \\ \hat{\beta}_2 \\ \hat{\beta}_3 \\ \vdots \\ \hat{\beta}_k \end{pmatrix} =$$

$$\begin{pmatrix} 1 & 1 & 1 & 1 & 1 \\ x_{21} & x_{22} & x_{23} & \dots & x_{2n} \\ x_{31} & x_{32} & x_{33} & \dots & x_{3n} \\ \vdots & \vdots & \vdots & \vdots & \vdots \\ x_{k1} & x_{k2} & x_{k3} & \dots & x_{kn} \end{pmatrix} \begin{pmatrix} y_1 \\ y_2 \\ y_3 \\ \vdots \\ y_n \end{pmatrix}$$

resulting in:

$$\begin{pmatrix} n & \sum x_{2i} & \sum x_{3i} & \cdots & \sum x_{ki} \\ \sum x_{2i} & \sum x_{2i}^2 & \sum x_{2i}x_{3i} & \dots & \sum x_{2i}x_{ki} \\ \sum x_{3i} & \sum x_{3i}x_{2i} & \sum x_{3i}^2 & \dots & \sum x_{3i}x_{ki} \\ \vdots & \vdots & \vdots & \vdots & \vdots \\ \sum x_{ki} & \sum x_{ki}x_{2i} & \sum x_{ki}x_{3i} & \dots & \sum x_{ki}^2 \end{pmatrix} \begin{pmatrix} \hat{\beta}_1 \\ \hat{\beta}_2 \\ \hat{\beta}_3 \\ \vdots \\ \hat{\beta}_k \end{pmatrix} = \begin{pmatrix} \sum y_i \\ \sum x_{2i}y_i \\ \sum x_{3i}y_i \\ \vdots \\ \sum x_{ki}y_i \end{pmatrix} \tag{2.29}$$

where all the sums are calculated from 1 to n.

Thus, the k equations which allow us to obtain the unknown coefficients are the following:

$$\begin{aligned} \sum y_i &= n\hat{\beta}_1 + \hat{\beta}_2 \sum x_{2i} + \hat{\beta}_3 \sum x_{3i} + \ldots + \hat{\beta}_k \sum x_{ki} \\ \sum x_{2i}y_i &= \hat{\beta}_1 \sum x_{2i} + \hat{\beta}_2 \sum x_{2i}^2 + \hat{\beta}_3 \sum x_{2i}x_{3i} + \ldots + \hat{\beta}_k \sum x_{2i}x_{ki} \\ \sum x_{3i}y_i &= \hat{\beta}_1 \sum x_{3i} + \hat{\beta}_2 \sum x_{3i}x_{2i} + \hat{\beta}_3 \sum x_{3i}^2 + \ldots + \hat{\beta}_k \sum x_{3i}x_{ki} \\ &\cdots \\ \sum x_{ki}y_i &= \hat{\beta}_1 \sum x_{ki} + \hat{\beta}_2 \sum x_{ki}x_{2i} + \hat{\beta}_3 \sum x_{ki}x_{3i} + \ldots + \hat{\beta}_k \sum x_{ki}^2 \end{aligned} \tag{2.30}$$

From (2.30) we derive some algebraic properties of the OLS method:

a. The sum of the residuals is null. To show this, if we evaluate the general expression (2.17) at the OLS estimate $\hat{\beta}$ and we calculate $\sum \hat{y}_i$, we obtain:

$$\sum_{i=1}^{n} \hat{y}_i = n\hat{\beta}_1 + \hat{\beta}_2 \sum_{i=1}^{n} x_{2i} + \ldots + \hat{\beta}_k \sum_{i=1}^{n} x_{ki}$$

The right-hand side of the last expression is equal the right-hand side of the first equation of the system (2.30), so we can write:

$$\sum_{i=1}^{n} y_i = \sum_{i=1}^{n} \hat{y}_i \tag{2.31}$$

Using (2.31) and (2.18), it is proved that the residuals satisfy:

$$\sum \hat{u}_i = 0 \tag{2.32}$$

b. The regression hyperplane passes through the point of means of the data. From (2.17), the expression of this hyperplane is:

$$\hat{y}_i = \hat{\beta}_1 + \hat{\beta}_2 x_{2i} + \ldots + \hat{\beta}_k x_{ki} \quad \forall i \tag{2.33}$$

Adding up the terms of (2.33) and dividing by n, we obtain:

$$\bar{\hat{y}} = \hat{\beta}_1 + \hat{\beta}_2 \bar{x_2} + \hat{\beta}_3 \bar{x_3} + \ldots + \hat{\beta}_k \bar{x_k}$$

and given (2.31), it is obvious that $\bar{y} = \bar{\hat{y}}$, and then, we have the earlier stated property, since

$$\bar{y} = \hat{\beta}_1 + \hat{\beta}_2 \bar{x_2} + \hat{\beta}_3 \bar{x_3} + \ldots + \hat{\beta}_k \bar{x_k}$$

c. The residuals and the regressors are not correlated; this fact is mimicking the population property of independence between every x_j and u. To show this property, we calculate the sample covariance between residuals and regressors:

$$cov(x_j, \hat{u_i}) = \frac{1}{n}\sum_{i=1}^{n}[(x_{ji} - \bar{x_j})\hat{u_i}] = \frac{1}{n}\sum_{i=1}^{n} x_{ji}\hat{u_i} - \frac{1}{n}\bar{x_j}\sum_{i=1}^{n}\hat{u_i} = \frac{1}{n}\sum_{i=1}^{n} x_{ji}\hat{u_i}$$

with $j = 1, \ldots, k$. The last expression can be written in matrix form as:

$$\sum_{i=1}^{n} x_{ji}\hat{u_i} = X^\top \hat{u} = X^\top (y - X\hat{\beta}) = X^\top y - X^\top X\hat{\beta} = X^\top y - X^\top y = 0$$

where the last term uses the result (2.24).

Note that the algebraic property *c*) is always satisfied, while the properties *a*) and *b*) might not be maintained if the model has not intercept. This exception can be easily shown, because the first equation in (2.30) disappears when there is no constant term.

With respect to the OLS estimation of σ^2, we must note that it is not obtained as a result of the minimization problem, but is derived to satisfy two requirements: *i*) to use the OLS residuals ($\hat{u}$), and *ii*) to be unbiased. Generalizing the result of the previous chapter, we have:

$$\hat{\sigma}^2 = \frac{\sum_{i=1}^{n} \hat{u_i}^2}{n-k} = \frac{\hat{u}^\top \hat{u}}{n-k} \tag{2.34}$$

An alternative way of obtaining the OLS estimates of the coefficients consists of expressing the variables in deviations with respect to their means; in this case, it can be proved that the value of the estimators and the residuals are the same as that of the previous results. Suppose we have estimated the model, so that we can write it as:

$$y_i = \hat{\beta}_1 + \hat{\beta}_2 x_{2i} + \ldots + \hat{\beta}_k x_{ki} + \hat{u}_i \tag{2.35}$$

with $i = 1, \ldots, n$. Adding up both sides of (2.35) and dividing by n, we have:

$$\bar{y} = \hat{\beta}_1 + \hat{\beta}_2 \bar{x_2} + \ldots, \hat{\beta}_k \bar{x_k} \tag{2.36}$$

To obtain the last result, we have employed result (2.32). Then, we calculate (2.35) minus (2.36), leading to the following result:

$$(y_i - \bar{y}) = \hat{\beta}_2(x_{2i} - \bar{x_2}) + \hat{\beta}_3(x_{3i} - \bar{x_3}) + \ldots + \hat{\beta}_k(x_{ki} - \bar{x_k}) + \hat{u}_i \tag{2.37}$$

This model called *in deviations* differs from (2.35) in two aspects: *a*) the intercept does not explicitly appear in the equation model, and *b*) all variables are expressed in deviations from their means.

Nevertheless, researchers are usually interested in evaluating the effect of the explanatory variables on the endogenous variable, so the intercept value is not the main interest, and so, specification (2.37) contains the relevant elements. In spite of this, we can evaluate the intercept later from (2.36), in the following terms:

$$\hat{\beta}_1 = \bar{y} - \hat{\beta}_2 \bar{x_2} - \ldots - \hat{\beta}_k \bar{x_k} \tag{2.38}$$

This approach can be formalized in matrix form, writing (2.35) as:

$$y = X\hat{\beta} + \hat{u} \tag{2.39}$$

Consider $X = [\iota_n, X_2]$ a partitioned matrix, and $\hat{\beta} = [\hat{\beta}_1, \hat{\beta}_{(2)}]$ a partitioned vector, where X_2 denotes the $n \times (k-1)$ matrix whose columns are the observations of each regressor, ι_n is an $n \times 1$ vector of ones, and $\hat{\beta}_{(2)}$ is the $(k-1) \times 1$ vector of all the estimated coefficients except the intercept.

Let G be an n square matrix of the form:

$$G = I_n - \frac{1}{n}\iota_n \iota_n^\top \tag{2.40}$$

with I_n the $n \times n$ identity matrix. If we premultiply a given matrix (or vector) by G, the elements of such a matrix (or vector) are transformed in deviations with respect their means. Moreover, we have $G\iota_n = 0_n$. If we premultiply the G matrix by the model (2.39), and since $G\hat{u} = \hat{u}$ (from result (2.32)), we have:

$$Gy = GX\hat{\beta} + G\hat{u} = G\iota_n\hat{\beta}_1 + GX_2\hat{\beta}_{(2)} + G\hat{u} = GX_2\hat{\beta}_{(2)} + \hat{u} \tag{2.41}$$

This last expression is the matrix form of (2.37). Now, we premultiply (2.41) by $X_2^\top$, obtaining:

$$X_2^\top Gy = X_2^\top GX_2\hat{\beta}_{(2)} \tag{2.42}$$

Given that G is an idempotent matrix (i.e., $GG = G$), such a property allows us to write (2.42) as:

$$X_2^\top GGy = X_2^\top GGX_2\hat{\beta}_{(2)}$$

and taking advantage of the fact that G is also a symmetric matrix (i.e., $G = G^\top$), we can rewrite the last expression as follows:

$$(GX_2)^\top(Gy) = (GX_2)^\top(GX_2)\hat{\beta}_{(2)} \tag{2.43}$$

or equivalently,

$$(X_2^D)^\top y^D = ((X_2^D)^\top X_2^D)\hat{\beta}_{(2)} \tag{2.44}$$

with $X_2^D = GX_2$, that is to say, X_2^D is the $n \times (k-1)$ matrix whose columns are the observations of each regressor, evaluated in deviations. In a similar way, $y^D = Gy$, that is to say, the observed endogenous variable in deviations with respect to its mean.

The system of $k-1$ equations given by (2.44) leads to the same value of $\hat{\beta}_{(2)}$ as that obtained from (2.24). The only difference between the two systems is due to the intercept, which is estimated from (2.24), but not from (2.44). Nevertheless, as we have mentioned earlier, once we have the values of $\hat{\beta}_{(2)}$ from (2.44), we can calculate $\hat{\beta}_1$ through (2.38). Furthermore, according to (2.41), the residuals vector is the same as that obtained from (2.24), so the estimate of σ^2 is that established in (2.34).

2.3.2 The Maximum Likelihood Estimation

Assumption 6 about the normality of the disturbances allows us to apply the maximum likelihood (ML) criterion to obtain the values of the unknown parameters of the MLRM. This method consists of the maximization of the likelihood function, and the values of β and σ^2 which maximize such a function are the ML estimates. To obtain the likelihood function, we start by considering the joint density function of the sample, which establishes the probability of a sample being realized, when the parameters are known. Firstly, we consider a general framework. Let x be a random vector which is independently distributed as an n-multivariate normal , with expectations vector μ, and variance-covariance matrix Σ. The probability density function of x is given by:

$$f(x|\mu,\Sigma) = \frac{1}{(2\pi)^{n/2}|\Sigma|^{1/2}} exp\{-\frac{1}{2}(x-\mu)^\top \Sigma^{-1}(x-\mu)\} \tag{2.45}$$

Usually, we observe only one sample, so if we substitute x by an observed value x_0, the function $f(x_0|\mu,\Sigma)$ gives, for every value of (μ,Σ), the probability of obtaining such a sample value (x_0). Therefore, if the role of x and (μ,Σ) is changed, in such a way that x_0 is fixed and the parameters (μ,Σ) vary, we obtain the so called *likelihood function*, which can be written as:

$$L(\mu,\Sigma|x) = L(\mu,\Sigma) = f(x_0|\mu,\Sigma) \tag{2.46}$$

In the framework of the MLRM, the set of classical assumptions stated for the random component allowed us to conclude that the y vector is distributed as an n-multivariate normal, with $X\beta$ being the vector of means , and $\sigma^2 I_n$ the variance-covariance matrix (results (2.15) and (2.16)). From (2.45) and (2.46), the likelihood function is:

$$L(\beta,\sigma^2|y) = L(\beta,\sigma^2) = f(y|\beta,\sigma^2) = (2\pi\sigma^2)^{-n/2} exp\{-\frac{(y-X\beta)^\top(y-X\beta)}{2\sigma^2}\} \tag{2.47}$$

The ML method maximizes (2.47) in order to obtain the ML estimators of β and σ^2.

In general, the way of deriving the likelihood function (2.47) is based on the relationship between the probability distribution of y and that of u. Suppose z and w are two random vectors, where $z = h(w)$ with h being a monotonic function. If we know the probability density function of w, denoted by $g(w)$, we can obtain the probability density function of z as follows:

$$f(z) = g(h^{-1}(z))J \tag{2.48}$$

with J being the Jacobian, which is defined as the absolute value of the determinant of the matrix of partial derivatives:

$$J = abs|\frac{\partial w}{\partial z}|$$

In our case, we identify z with y, and w with u, in such a way that it is easy to show that the jacobian $J = abs|\frac{\partial u}{\partial y}|$ is the identity matrix, so expression (2.48) leads to the same result as (2.47).

Although the ML method maximizes the likelihood function, it is usually simpler to work with the log of this function. Since the logarithm is a monotonic function, the parameter values that maximize L are the same as those that maximize the log-likelihood ($\ln L$). In our case, $\ln L$ has the following form:

$$\ell = lnL(\beta, \sigma^2) = -\frac{n}{2}\ln(2\pi) - \frac{n}{2}\ln\sigma^2 - \frac{(y - X\beta)^\top (y - X\beta)}{2\sigma^2} \tag{2.49}$$

The ML estimators are the solution to the first-order conditions:

$$\frac{\partial \ell}{\partial \beta} = -\frac{1}{2\sigma^2}(-2X^\top y + 2X^\top X\beta) = 0 \tag{2.50}$$

$$\frac{\partial \ell}{\partial \sigma^2} = -\frac{n}{2\sigma^2} + \frac{(y - X\beta)^\top (y - X\beta)}{2\sigma^4} = 0 \tag{2.51}$$

Thus, the ML estimators, denoted by $\tilde{\beta}$ and $\tilde{\sigma}^2$, are:

$$\tilde{\beta} = (X^\top X)^{-1} X^\top y \tag{2.52}$$

$$\tilde{\sigma}^2 = \frac{(y - X\tilde{\beta})^\top (y - X\tilde{\beta})}{n} = \frac{\tilde{u}^\top \tilde{u}}{n} \tag{2.53}$$

As we can see, similarly to results in the univariate linear regression model of Chapter 2, under the assumption of normality of the disturbances, both ML and LS methods gives the same estimated value for the coefficients β ($\tilde{\beta} = \hat{\beta}$), and thus, the numerator of the expression of $\tilde{\sigma}^2$ is the same as that of $\hat{\sigma}^2$.

2.3.3 Example

All estimation quantlets in the `stats` quantlib have as input parameters:

x

An $n \times k$ matrix containing observations of explanatory variables ,

y

An $n \times 1$ vector containing the observed responses.

Neither the matrix `X`, nor the vector `y` should contain missing values (`NaN`) or infinite values (`Inf,-Inf`).

In the following example, we will use Spanish economic data to illustrate the MLRM estimation. The file `data.dat` contains quarterly data from 1980 to 1997 (sample size $n = 72$) for the variables consumption, exports and M1 (monetary supply). All variables are expressed in constant prices of 1995.

Descriptive statistics of the three variables which are included in the consumption function can be found in the Table 2.1.

		Min	Max	Mean	S.D.
y	**consumption**	7558200	12103000	9524600	1328800
x_2	**exports**	1439000	5590700	2778500	1017700
x_3	**M1**	9203.9	18811	13512	3140.8

Table 2.1. Descriptive statistics for consumption data.

On the basis of the information on the data file, we estimate the consumption function; the endogenous variable we want to explain is consumption, while exportations and M1 are the explanatory variables, or regressors.

The quantlet `XEGmlrm01.xpl` produces some summary statistics

`XEGmlrm01.xpl`

Computing MLRM Estimates The quantlet in the `stats` quantlib which can be employed to obtain only the OLS (or ML) estimation of the coefficients β and σ^2 is `gls`.

```
b = gls ( x, y )
```
estimates the parameters of a MLRM

In `XEGmlrl02.xpl`, we have used the quantlet `gls` to compute the OLS estimates of β (`b`), and both the OLS and ML estimates of σ^2 (`sigls` and `sigml`).

`XEGmlrl02.xpl`

2.4 Properties of the Estimators

When we want to study the properties of the obtained estimators, it is convenient to distinguish between two categories of properties: i) the small (or finite) sample properties, which are valid whatever the sample size, and ii) the asymptotic properties, which are associated with large samples, i.e., when n tends to ∞.

2.4.1 Finite Sample Properties of the OLS and ML Estimates of β

Given that, as we obtained in the previous section, the OLS and ML estimates of β lead to the same result, the following properties refer to both. In order to derive these properties, and on the basis of the classical assumptions, the vector of estimated coefficients can be written in the following alternative form:

$$\hat{\beta} = (X^\top X)^{-1}X^\top y = (X^\top X)^{-1}X^\top (X\beta + u) = \beta + (X^\top X)^{-1}X^\top u \quad (2.54)$$

- Unbiasedness. According to the concept of unbiasedness, vector $\hat{\beta}$ is an unbiased estimator vector of β since:

  $$\mathrm{E}(\hat{\beta}) = \mathrm{E}[\beta + (X^\top X)^{-1}X^\top u] = \beta + (X^\top X)^{-1}X^\top \mathrm{E}(u) = \beta \quad (2.55)$$

  The unbiasedness property of the estimators means that, if we have many samples for the random variable and we calculate the estimated value corresponding to each sample, the average of these estimated values approaches the unknown parameter. Nevertheless, we usually have only one sample (i.e, one realization of the random variable), so we can not assure anything about the distance between $\hat{\beta}$ and β. This fact leads us to employ the concept of variance, or the variance-covariance matrix if we have a vector of estimates. This concept measures the average distance between the estimated value obtained from the only sample we have and its expected value.

  From the previous argument we can deduce that, although the unbiasedness property is not sufficient in itself, it is the minimum requirement to be satisfied by an estimator.

The variance-covariance matrix of $\hat{\beta}$ has the following expression:

$$V(\hat{\beta}) = \mathrm{E}[(\hat{\beta} - \mathrm{E}\hat{\beta})(\hat{\beta} - \mathrm{E}\hat{\beta})^\top] = \mathrm{E}[(\hat{\beta} - \beta)(\hat{\beta} - \beta)^\top] =$$
$$\mathrm{E}[(X^\top X)^{-1} X^\top u u^\top X (X^\top X)^{-1}] = (X^\top X)^{-1} X^\top \mathrm{E}(u u^\top) X (X^\top X)^{-1} =$$
$$\sigma^2 (X^\top X)^{-1} \tag{2.56}$$

with the elements of this matrix meaning:

$$var(\hat{\beta}_j) = \sigma^2((X^\top X)^{-1})_{jj} \tag{2.57}$$

$$cov(\hat{\beta}_j, \hat{\beta}_h) = \sigma^2((X^\top X)^{-1})_{jh} \tag{2.58}$$

Obviously, (2.56) is a symmetric positive definite matrix.

The consideration of $V(\hat{\beta})$ allows us to define efficiency as a second finite sample property.

- Efficiency. An estimator is efficient if it is the minimum variance unbiased estimator. The Cramer Rao inequality provides verification of efficiency, since it establishes the lower bound for the variance-covariance matrix of any unbiased estimator. This lower bound is given by the corresponding element of the diagonal of the inverse of the information matrix (or sample information matrix) $I_n(\theta)$, which is defined as:

  $$I_n(\theta) = -\mathrm{E}[H(\theta)] \tag{2.59}$$

  where H denotes the hessian matrix, i.e., the matrix of the second partial derivatives of the log-likelihood function .

  In order to study the efficiency property for the OLS and ML estimates of β, we begin by defining $\theta^\top = (\beta^\top, \sigma^2)$, and the hessian matrix is expressed as a partitioned matrix of the form:

  $$\frac{\partial^2 \ell}{\partial \theta \partial \theta^\top} = \begin{pmatrix} \frac{\partial^2 \ell}{\partial \beta \partial \beta^\top} & \frac{\partial^2 \ell}{\partial \beta \partial \sigma^2} \\ \frac{\partial^2 \ell}{\partial \sigma^2 \partial \beta^\top} & \frac{\partial^2 \ell}{\partial (\sigma^2)^2} \end{pmatrix} = \begin{pmatrix} A & B \\ C & D \end{pmatrix} \tag{2.60}$$

  where A is a square k matrix, B and C are $k \times 1$ vectors, and D is a 1×1 element.

From (2.50) and (2.51), we have:

$$\frac{\partial^2 \ell}{\partial\theta\partial\theta^\top} = \begin{pmatrix} -\frac{X^\top X}{\sigma^2} & -\frac{(X^\top y - X^\top X\beta)}{\sigma^4} \\ -\frac{(y^\top X - \beta^\top X^\top X)}{\sigma^4} & \frac{n\sigma^2 - 2(y-X\beta)^\top (y-X\beta)}{2\sigma^6} \end{pmatrix}$$

$$= \begin{pmatrix} -\frac{X^\top X}{\sigma^2} & -\frac{X^\top u}{\sigma^4} \\ -\frac{u^\top X}{\sigma^4} & \frac{n\sigma^2 - 2u^\top u}{2\sigma^6} \end{pmatrix} \tag{2.61}$$

Thus, the sample information matrix is:

$$I_n(\theta) = \begin{pmatrix} \frac{X^\top X}{\sigma^2} & 0 \\ 0 & \frac{n}{2\sigma^4} \end{pmatrix} \tag{2.62}$$

and its inverse,

$$[I_n(\theta)]^{-1} = \begin{pmatrix} \sigma^2 (X^\top X)^{-1} & 0 \\ 0 & \frac{2\sigma^4}{n} \end{pmatrix} = \begin{pmatrix} I^{11} & 0 \\ 0 & I^{22} \end{pmatrix} \tag{2.63}$$

Following the Cramer-Rao inequality, I^{11} constitutes the lower bound for the variance-covariance matrix of any unbiased estimator vector of the parameter vector β, while I^{22} is the corresponding bound for the variance of an unbiased estimator of σ^2.

According to (2.56), we can conclude that $\hat{\beta}$ (or $\tilde{\beta}$), satisfies the efficiency property, given that their variance-covariance matrix coincides with I^{11}.

A property which is less strict than efficiency, is the so called best, linear unbiased estimator (BLUE) property, which also uses the variance of the estimators.

- BLUE. A vector of estimators is BLUE if it is the minimum variance linear unbiased estimator. To show this property, we use the Gauss-Markov Theorem. In the MLRM framework, this theorem provides a general expression for the variance-covariance matrix of a linear unbiased vector of estimators. Then, the comparison of this matrix with the corresponding matrix of $\hat{\beta}$ allows us to conclude that $\hat{\beta}$ (or $\tilde{\beta}$) is BLUE.

  With this aim, we define $\hat{\hat{\beta}}$ as a family of linear vectors of estimates of the parameter vector β:

$$\hat{\hat{\beta}} = C^\top y = C^\top X\beta + C^\top u \tag{2.64}$$

with C being a matrix of constant elements, where:

$$C^\top = A^\top + D^\top \tag{2.65}$$

In order to assure the unbiasedness of $\hat{\hat{\beta}}$, we suppose $C^\top X = I_k$, and then (2.64) can be written as:

$$\hat{\hat{\beta}} = \beta + C^\top u \tag{2.66}$$

From this last expression we can derive the variance-covariance matrix of $\hat{\hat{\beta}}$:

$$V(\hat{\hat{\beta}}) = \mathrm{E}[(\hat{\hat{\beta}} - \mathrm{E}\hat{\hat{\beta}})(\hat{\hat{\beta}} - \mathrm{E}\hat{\hat{\beta}})^\top]$$

$$= \mathrm{E}[(\hat{\hat{\beta}} - \beta)(\hat{\hat{\beta}} - \beta)^\top] = \mathrm{E}[C^\top u u^\top C] = \sigma^2 C^\top C \tag{2.67}$$

Taking into account (2.65) we have:

$$C^\top C = (A^\top + D^\top)(A + D) = A^\top A + A^\top D + D^\top A + D^\top D \tag{2.68}$$

and the unbiasedness condition $C^\top X = I_k$ allows us to show that $D^\top A = A^\top D = 0$:

$$C^\top X = I_k \Longrightarrow (A^\top + D^\top)X = I_k \Longrightarrow A^\top X + D^\top X = I_k \tag{2.69}$$

and given that $A^\top = (X^\top X)^{-1} X^\top$, as was established in (2.28), we derive that $A^\top X = I_k$. By substituting this result into the last term of (2.69), it must hold that $D^\top X = 0$, which implies that:

$$D^\top A = D^\top X (X^\top X)^{-1} = 0$$

and obviously, $A^\top D = 0$. We now take expression (2.67), which we can write as:

$$V(\hat{\hat{\beta}}) = \sigma^2 (A^\top A + D^\top D) \tag{2.70}$$

and given that $A^\top A = (X^\top X)^{-1}$, according to (2.56), we have:

$$V(\hat{\hat{\beta}}) = V(\hat{\beta}) + \sigma^2 D^\top D \tag{2.71}$$

or

$$V(\hat{\hat{\beta}}) - V(\hat{\beta}) = \sigma^2 D^\top D \tag{2.72}$$

A general result matrix establishes that given any matrix P, then $P^\top P$ is a positive semidefinite matrix, so we can conclude that $D^\top D$ is positive semidefinite. This property means that the elements of its diagonal are non negative, so we deduce for every β_j coefficient:

$$var(\hat{\hat{\beta}}_j) \geq var(\hat{\beta}_j) \quad j = 1, \ldots, k. \tag{2.73}$$

that is to say, we conclude that the OLS or ML estimator vector of β satisfies the Gauss-Markov theorem, and this implies that $\hat{\beta}$ (or $\tilde{\beta}$) is BLUE.

The set of results we have previously obtained, allows us to know the probability distribution for $\hat{\beta}$ (or $\tilde{\beta}$). Given that these estimator vectors are linear with respect to the y vector, and y having a normal distribution, then:

$$\hat{\beta} \sim N(\beta, \sigma^2(X^\top X)^{-1}) \tag{2.74}$$

2.4.2 Finite Sample Properties of the OLS and ML Estimates of σ^2

According to expressions (2.34) and (2.53), the OLS and ML estimators of σ^2 are different, despite both being constructed through $\hat{u}^\top \hat{u}$. In order to obtain their properties, it is convenient to express $\hat{u}^\top \hat{u}$ as a function of the disturbance of the model. From the definition of $\hat{u}$ in (2.26) we obtain:

$$\hat{u} = y - X\hat{\beta} = y - X(X^\top X)^{-1}X^\top y = [I_n - X(X^\top X)^{-1}X^\top]y = My \tag{2.75}$$

with $M = I_n - X(X^\top X)^{-1}X^\top$ a non-stochastic square n matrix, which is symmetric, idempotent and whose rank and trace are $n - k$. In addition, M fulfils $MX = 0$.

Result (2.75), which means that $\hat{u}$ is linear with respect to y, can be extended in the following way:

$$\hat{u} = My = M(X\beta + u) = Mu \tag{2.76}$$

that is to say, there is also a linear relation between $\hat{u}$ and u.

From (2.76), and under the earlier mentioned properties of M, the sum of squared residuals can be written as a quadratic form of the disturbance vector,

$$\hat{u}^\top \hat{u} = u^\top M^\top M u = u^\top M u \tag{2.77}$$

Since every element of u has a $\mathrm{N}(0,\sigma^2)$ distribution, and M is an idempotent matrix, then $\frac{u^\top Mu}{\sigma^2}$ follows a chi-squared distribution with degrees of freedom equal to the rank of M, that is to say:

$$\frac{u^\top Mu}{\sigma^2} \sim \chi^2_{n-k} \tag{2.78}$$

Note that from (2.75), it is also possible to write $\hat{u}^\top\hat{u}$ as a quadratic form of y, yielding:

$$\hat{u}^\top\hat{u} = y^\top My \tag{2.79}$$

This expression for $\hat{u}^\top\hat{u}$ allows us to obtain a very simple way to calculate the OLS or ML estimator of σ^2. For example, for $\hat{\sigma}^2$:

$$\hat{\sigma}^2 = \frac{y^\top My}{n-k} = \frac{y^\top y - y^\top X(X^\top X)^{-1}X^\top y}{n-k} = \frac{y^\top y - \hat{\beta}^\top X^\top y}{n-k} \tag{2.80}$$

Having established these relations of interest, we now define the properties of $\hat{\sigma}^2$ and $\tilde{\sigma}^2$:

- Linearity. According to (2.79) the OLS and ML estimators of σ^2 are expressed as:

  $$\hat{\sigma}^2 = \frac{\hat{u}^\top\hat{u}}{n-k} = \frac{y^\top My}{n-k}$$

  and

  $$\tilde{\sigma}^2 = \frac{\tilde{u}^\top\tilde{u}}{n} = \frac{y^\top My}{n}$$

  so both are non linear with respect to y, given that their numerators are quadratic forms of y.
- Unbiasedness. In order to show this property, we use (2.77), to obtain:

  $$\hat{\sigma}^2 = \frac{\hat{u}^\top\hat{u}}{n-k} = \frac{u^\top Mu}{n-k} \tag{2.81}$$

  $$\tilde{\sigma}^2 = \frac{\tilde{u}^\top\tilde{u}}{n} = \frac{u^\top Mu}{n} \tag{2.82}$$

  If we first consider $\hat{\sigma}^2$, we must calculate:

  $$\mathrm{E}(\hat{\sigma}^2) = \frac{1}{n-k}\mathrm{E}(u^\top Mu) \tag{2.83}$$

The calculation of $\mathrm{E}(u^\top Mu)$ requires using the distribution (2.78), in such a way that, given that a chi-square variable has expected value equal to the corresponding degree of freedom, we have:

$$\mathrm{E}(\frac{u^\top Mu}{\sigma^2}) = \frac{1}{\sigma^2}\mathrm{E}(u^\top Mu) = n - k \tag{2.84}$$

and then,

$$\mathrm{E}(u^\top Mu) = \sigma^2(n-k) \tag{2.85}$$

which allows us to obtain:

$$\mathrm{E}(\hat{\sigma}^2) = \frac{1}{n-k}\mathrm{E}(u^\top Mu) = \frac{1}{n-k}\sigma^2(n-k) = \sigma^2 \tag{2.86}$$

In a similar way, we obtain $\mathrm{E}(\tilde{\sigma}^2)$:

$$\mathrm{E}(\tilde{\sigma}^2) = \frac{1}{n}\mathrm{E}(u^\top Mu) = \frac{1}{n}\sigma^2(n-k) = \sigma^2\frac{n-k}{n} \tag{2.87}$$

so we conclude that $\hat{\sigma}^2$ is an unbiased estimator for σ^2 , while $\tilde{\sigma}^2$ is biased.

In order to analyze efficiency and BLUE properties, we must know the variance of $\hat{\sigma}^2$ and $\tilde{\sigma}^2$. From (2.78), we have $var(\frac{u^\top Mu}{\sigma^2}) = 2(n-k)$, because the variance of a chi-square variable is two times its degrees of freedom. This result leads to the following expressions for the variances:

$$var(\hat{\sigma}^2) = \frac{1}{(n-k)^2}var(u^\top Mu) = \frac{1}{(n-k)^2}2(n-k)\sigma^4 = \frac{2\sigma^4}{n-k} \tag{2.88}$$

$$var(\tilde{\sigma}^2) = \frac{1}{n^2}var(u^\top Mu) = \frac{2\sigma^4(n-k)}{n^2} \tag{2.89}$$

Nevertheless, given that $\tilde{\sigma}^2$ is biased, this estimator can not be efficient, so we focus on the study of such a property for $\hat{\sigma}^2$. With respect to the BLUE property, neither $\hat{\sigma}^2$ nor $\tilde{\sigma}^2$ are linear, so they can not be BLUE.

- Efficiency. The comparison of the variance of $\hat{\sigma}^2$ (expression (2.88)) with element I^{22} of the matrix $(I_n(\theta))^{-1}$ (expression (2.63)) allows us to deduce that this estimator does not satisfy the Cramer-Rao inequality, given that $I^{22} \neq var(\hat{\sigma}^2)$. Nevertheless, as Schmidt (1976) shows, there is no unbiased estimator of σ^2 with a smaller variance, so it can be said that $\hat{\sigma}^2$ is an efficient estimator.

The variance-covariance matrix of an estimator vector could tell us how accurate it is. However, this matrix, which was obtained in (2.56), depends on the unknown σ^2 parameter, so we can obtain an unbiased estimation of it by substituting σ^2 for its unbiased estimator $\hat{\sigma}^2$:

$$\hat{V}(\hat{\beta}) = \hat{V}(\tilde{\beta}) = \hat{\sigma}^2(X^\top X)^{-1} \tag{2.90}$$

The meaning of every element of this matrix is analogous to that presented in (2.57) and (2.58).

2.4.3 Asymptotic Properties of the OLS and ML Estimators of β

Finite sample properties try to study the behavior of an estimator under the assumption of having many samples, and consequently many estimators of the parameter of interest. Thus, the average of these estimators should approach the parameter value (unbiasedness) or the average distance to the parameter value should be the smallest possible (efficiency). However, in practice we have only one sample, and the asymptotic properties are established by keeping this fact in mind but assuming that the sample is large enough.

Specifically, the asymptotic properties study the behavior of the estimators as n increases; in this sense, an estimator which is calculated for different sample sizes can be understood as a sequence of random variables indexed by the sample sizes (for example, z_n). Two relevant aspects to analyze in this sequence are *convergence in probability* and *convergence in distribution.*

A sequence of random variables z_n is said *to converge in probability* to a constant c or to another random variable z, if

$$\lim_{n \to \infty} Pr[|z_n - c| < \epsilon] = 1 \tag{2.91}$$

or

$$\lim_{n \to \infty} Pr[|z_n - z| < \epsilon] = 1 \tag{2.92}$$

where Pr denotes probability and $\epsilon > 0$ is an arbitrary constant. Equivalently, we can express this convergence as:

$$z_n \to_p c \quad and \quad z_n \to_p z$$

or

$$plim z_n = c \quad and \quad plim z_n = z \tag{2.93}$$

Result (2.91) implies that all the probability of the distribution becomes concentrated at points close to c. Result (2.92) implies that the values that the variable may take that are not far from z become more probable as n increases, and moreover, this probability tends to one.

A second form of convergence is *convergence in distribution*. If z_n is a sequence of random variables with cumulative distribution function (*cdf*) $F_n(z)$, then the sequence *converges in distribution* to a variable z with *cdf* $F(z)$ if

$$\lim_{n \to \infty} F_n(z) = F(z) \tag{2.94}$$

which can be denoted by:

$$z_n \to_d z \tag{2.95}$$

and $F(z)$ is said to be the *limit distribution* of z.

Having established these preliminary concepts, we now consider the following desirable asymptotic properties : asymptotic unbiasedness, consistency and asymptotic efficiency.

- Asymptotic unbiasedness. There are two alternative definitions of this concept. The first states that an estimator $\hat{\hat{\theta}}$ is asymptotically unbiased if as n increases, the sequence of its first moments converges to the parameter θ. It can be expressed as:

$$\lim_{n \to \infty} \mathrm{E}(\hat{\hat{\theta}}_n) = \theta \Rightarrow \lim_{n \to \infty} \mathrm{E}(\hat{\hat{\theta}}_n) - \theta = 0 \tag{2.96}$$

  Note that the second part of (2.96) also means that the possible bias of $\hat{\hat{\theta}}$ disappears as n increases, so we can deduce that an unbiased estimator is also an asymptotic unbiased estimator.

  The second definition is based on the convergence in distribution of a sequence of random variables. According to this definition, an estimator $\hat{\hat{\theta}}$ is asymptotically unbiased if its asymptotic expectation, or expectation of its limit distribution, is the parameter θ. It is expressed as follows:

$$\mathrm{E}_{as}(\hat{\hat{\theta}}) = \theta \tag{2.97}$$

  Since this second definition requires knowing the limit distribution of the sequence of random variables, and this is not always easy to know, the first definition is very often used.

In our case, since $\hat{\beta}$ and $\tilde{\beta}$ are unbiased, it follows that they are asymptotically unbiased:

$$\lim_{n\to\infty} \mathrm{E}(\hat{\beta}_n) = \beta \Rightarrow \lim_{n\to\infty} \mathrm{E}(\hat{\beta}_n) - \beta = 0 \tag{2.98}$$

In order to simplify notation, in what follows we will use $\hat{\beta}$, instead of $\hat{\beta}_n$. Nevertheless, we must continue considering it as a sequence of random variables indexed by the sample size.

- Consistency. An estimator $\hat{\hat{\theta}}$ is said to be consistent if it converges in probability to the unknown parameter, that is to say:

$$plim \hat{\hat{\theta}}_n = \theta \tag{2.99}$$

which, in view of (2.91), means that a consistent estimator satisfies the convergence in probability to a constant, with the unknown parameter θ being such a constant.

The simplest way of showing consistency consists of proving two sufficient conditions: i) the estimator must be asymptotically unbiased, and ii) its variance must converge to zero as n increases. These conditions are derived from the convergence in quadratic mean (or convergence in second moments), given that this concept of convergence implies convergence in probability (for a detailed study of the several modes of convergence and their relations, see Amemiya (1985), Spanos (1986) and White (1984)).

In our case, since the asymptotic unbiasedness of $\hat{\beta}$ and $\tilde{\beta}$ has been shown earlier, we only have to prove the second condition. In this sense, we calculate:

$$\lim_{n\to\infty} V(\hat{\beta}) = \lim_{n\to\infty} \sigma^2 (X^\top X)^{-1} \tag{2.100}$$

Multiplying and dividing (2.100) by n, we obtain:

$$\lim_{n\to\infty} V(\hat{\beta}) = \lim_{n\to\infty} \frac{n}{n} \sigma^2 (X^\top X)^{-1} = \lim_{n\to\infty} \frac{\sigma^2}{n} (\frac{X^\top X}{n})^{-1} =$$

$$\lim_{n\to\infty} \frac{\sigma^2}{n} \lim_{n\to\infty} (\frac{X^\top X}{n})^{-1} = 0 \times Q^{-1} = 0 \tag{2.101}$$

where we have used the condition (2.6) included in assumption 1. Thus, result (2.101) proves the consistency of the OLS and ML estimators of the coefficient vector. As we mentioned before, this means that all the probability of the distribution of $\hat{\beta}$ (or β) becomes concentrated at points close to β, as n increases.

Consistency might be thought of as the minimum requirement for a useful estimator. However, given that there can be many consistent estimators of a parameter, it is convenient to consider another property such as asymptotic efficiency. This property focuses on the asymptotic variance of the estimators or asymptotic variance-covariance matrix of an estimator vector. Similar to asymptotic unbiasedness, two definitions of this concept can be found. The first of them defines it as the variance of the limit distribution of the estimator. Obviously, it is necessary to know this limit distribution. However, according to the meaning of consistency, the limit distribution of a consistent estimator is degenerated at a point, so its variance is zero. In order to obtain an approach to the limit distribution, we can use a *Central Limit Theorem* (CLT), which establishes the conditions to guaranty that the limit distribution is a normal distribution.

Suppose we have applied a CLT, and we have:

$$\sqrt{n}(\hat{\hat{\theta}} - \theta) \rightarrow_d N(0, \gamma) \tag{2.102}$$

with $\gamma = V_{as}[\sqrt{n}(\hat{\hat{\theta}} - \theta)]$, that is to say, γ is the asymptotic variance of $\sqrt{n}(\hat{\hat{\theta}} - \theta)$. This result allows us to approach the limit distribution of $\hat{\hat{\theta}}$ as:

$$\hat{\hat{\theta}} \rightarrow_{as} N(\theta, \frac{\gamma}{n}) \tag{2.103}$$

where $\rightarrow_{as}$ denotes "asymptotically distributed as", and consequently the asymptotic variance of the estimator is approached by $\frac{\gamma}{n}$.

The second definition of asymptotic variance, which does not require using any limit distribution, is obtained as:

$$V_{as}(\hat{\hat{\theta}}) = \frac{1}{n} \lim_{n \to \infty} \mathrm{E}[\sqrt{n}(\hat{\hat{\theta}} - \mathrm{E}(\hat{\hat{\theta}}))]^2 \tag{2.104}$$

In our framework, this second definition leads us to express the asymptotic variance of vector $\hat{\beta}$ as:

$$V_{as}(\hat{\beta}) = \frac{1}{n} \lim_{n \to \infty} \mathrm{E}[(\sqrt{n}(\hat{\beta} - \mathrm{E}\hat{\beta}))((\hat{\beta} - \mathrm{E}\hat{\beta})^\top \sqrt{n})] =$$

$$\frac{1}{n}\lim_{n\to\infty} n\sigma^2(X^\top X)^{-1} = \frac{1}{n}\lim_{n\to\infty}\frac{n}{n}\sigma^2(\frac{X^\top X}{n})^{-1} =$$

$$\frac{\sigma^2}{n}\lim_{n\to\infty}(\frac{X^\top X}{n})^{-1} = \frac{\sigma^2 Q^{-1}}{n} \tag{2.105}$$

If we consider the first approach of the asymptotic variance, the use of a CLT (see Judge, Carter, Griffiths, Lutkepohl and Lee (1988)) yields:

$$\sqrt{n}(\hat{\beta}-\beta) \to_d N(0,\sigma^2 Q^{-1}) \tag{2.106}$$

which leads to:

$$\hat{\beta} \to_{as} N(\beta, \frac{\sigma^2 Q^{-1}}{n}) \tag{2.107}$$

so $V_{as}(\hat{\beta})$ is approached as $\frac{\sigma^2 Q^{-1}}{n}$.

- Asymptotic efficiency A sufficient condition for a consistent asymptotically normal estimator vector to be asymptotically efficient is that its asymptotic variance-covariance matrix equals the asymptotic Cramer-Rao lower bound (see Theil (1971)), which can be expressed as:

$$\frac{1}{n}(I_\infty)^{-1} = \frac{1}{n}\left[\lim_{n\to\infty}(\frac{I_n(\theta)}{n})\right]^{-1} \tag{2.108}$$

where I_∞ denotes the so-called asymptotic information matrix, while I_n is the previously described sample information matrix (or simply, information matrix). The elements of I_∞ are:

$$I_\infty = \lim_{n\to\infty}(\frac{I_n(\theta)}{n}) = \begin{pmatrix} \frac{1}{\sigma^2}\lim_{n\to\infty}(\frac{X^\top X}{n}) & 0 \\ 0 & \frac{1}{2\sigma^4} \end{pmatrix} = \begin{pmatrix} \frac{Q}{\sigma^2} & 0 \\ 0 & \frac{1}{2\sigma^4} \end{pmatrix} \tag{2.109}$$

and so,

$$\frac{1}{n}(I_\infty)^{-1} = \begin{pmatrix} \frac{\sigma^2 Q^{-1}}{n} & 0 \\ 0 & \frac{2\sigma^4}{n} \end{pmatrix} \tag{2.110}$$

From the last expression we deduce that the variance-covariance matrix of $\hat{\beta}$ (or $\tilde{\beta}$) equals the asymptotic Cramer Rao lower bound (element (1,1) of (2.110)), so we conclude that $\hat{\beta}$ (or $\tilde{\beta}$) is an asymptotically efficient estimator vector for the parameter vector β.

Finally, we should note that the finite sample efficiency implies asymptotic efficiency, and we could have used this fact to conclude the asymptotic efficiency of $\hat{\beta}$ (or $\tilde{\beta}$), given the results of subsection about their finite sample properties.

2.4.4 Asymptotic Properties of the OLS and ML Estimators of σ^2

- Asymptotic unbiasedness. The OLS estimator of σ^2 satisfies the finite sample unbiasedness property, according to result (2.86), so we deduce that it is asymptotically unbiased.

  With respect to the ML estimator of σ^2, which does not satisfy the finite sample unbiasedness (result (2.87)), we must calculate its asymptotic expectation. On the basis of the first definition of asymptotic unbiasedness, presented in (2.96), we have:

$$\lim_{n\to\infty} \mathrm{E}(\tilde{\sigma}^2) = \lim_{n\to\infty} \frac{\sigma^2(n-k)}{n} = \lim_{n\to\infty} \sigma^2 - \lim_{n\to\infty} \frac{\sigma^2 k}{n} = \sigma^2 \tag{2.111}$$

  so we conclude that $\tilde{\sigma}^2$ is asymptotically unbiased.

- Consistency. In order to show that $\hat{\sigma}^2$ and $\tilde{\sigma}^2$ are consistent, and given that both are asymptotically unbiased, the only sufficient condition that we have to prove is that the limit of their variances is null. From (2.88) and (2.89) we have:

$$\lim_{n\to\infty} \frac{2\sigma^4}{n-k} = 0 \tag{2.112}$$

  and

$$\lim_{n\to\infty} \frac{2\sigma^4(n-k)}{n^2} = 0 \tag{2.113}$$

  so both estimators satisfy the requirements of consistency.

Finally, the study of the asymptotic efficiency property requires approaching the asymptotic variance-covariance of the estimators. Following Fomby, Carter, and Johnson (1984) we have,

$$\sqrt{n}(\hat{\sigma}^2 - \sigma^2) \to_d N(0, 2\sigma^4) \tag{2.114}$$

so the limit distribution of $\hat{\sigma}^2$ can be approached as

$$\hat{\sigma}^2 \to_{as} N(\sigma^2, \frac{2\sigma^4}{n}) \tag{2.115}$$

and then we conclude that

$$var_{as}(\hat{\sigma}^2) = \frac{2\sigma^4}{n} \tag{2.116}$$

Analogously, following Dhrymes (1974), the ML estimator $\tilde{\sigma}^2$ satisfies

$$\sqrt{n}(\tilde{\sigma}^2 - \sigma^2) \to_d N(0, 2\sigma^4) \tag{2.117}$$

so $var_{as}(\tilde{\sigma}^2)$ has the same form as that given in (2.116).

The second way to approach the asymptotic variance (see (2.104)), leads to the following expressions:

$$var_{as}(\hat{\sigma}^2) = \frac{1}{n} \lim_{n\to\infty} \mathrm{E}(\sqrt{n}(\hat{\sigma}^2 - \mathrm{E}\hat{\sigma}^2))^2 = \frac{1}{n} \lim_{n\to\infty} n\frac{2\sigma^4}{n-k} =$$

$$\frac{1}{n} \lim_{n\to\infty} \frac{2\sigma^4}{\frac{n-k}{n}} = \frac{1}{n}\left[\frac{\lim_{n\to\infty} 2\sigma^4}{\lim_{n\to\infty}(1-\frac{k}{n})}\right] = \frac{1}{n}2\sigma^4 \tag{2.118}$$

$$var_{as}(\tilde{\sigma}^2) = \frac{1}{n} \lim_{n\to\infty} n\frac{2\sigma^4(n-k)}{n^2} = \frac{1}{n}[\lim_{n\to\infty} 2\sigma^4 - \lim_{n\to\infty} \frac{2\sigma^4 k}{n}] = \frac{1}{n}2\sigma^4 \tag{2.119}$$

- Asymptotic efficiency. On the basis of the asymptotic Cramer-Rao lower bound expressed in (2.108) and calculated in (2.110), we conclude that both $\hat{\sigma}^2$ and $\tilde{\sigma}^2$ are asymptotically efficient estimators of σ^2, so their asymptotic variances equal the asymptotic Cramer-Rao lower bound.

2.4.5 Example

As we have seen in the previous section, the quantlet `gls` allows us to estimate all the parameters of the MLRM. In addition, if we want to estimate the variance-covariance matrix of $\hat{\beta}$, which is given by $\hat{\sigma}^2(X^\top X)^{-1}$, we can use the following quantlet

Q `XEGmlr103.xpl`

2.5 Interval Estimation

The LS and ML methods developed in previous sections allow us to obtain a point estimate of the parameters of the model. However, even if the estimator satisfies the desirable properties, there is some probability that it will be quite erroneous, because it tries to infer a population value from a sample. Thus, a point estimate does not provide any information on the likely range of error. The estimator should be as accurate as possible (i.e., the range of error as small as possible), and this accuracy can be quantified through the variance (or standard deviation) of the estimator. Nevertheless, if we know the sample distribution of the estimator, there is a more structured approach of presenting the accuracy measure which consists in constructing a confidence interval.

A confidence interval is defined as a range of values that is likely to include the true value of the unknown parameter. The confidence interval means that, if we have different samples, and in each case we construct the confidence intervals, then we expect that about $100(1-\epsilon)$ percent of them will contain the true parameter value. The probability amount $(1-\epsilon)$ is known as the level of confidence.

2.5.1 Interval Estimation of the Coefficients of the MLRM

As we have mentioned earlier, in order to obtain the interval estimation, we must know the sample probability distribution of the corresponding estimator. Result (2.74) allows us to obtain such a distribution for every element of the $\hat{\beta}$ vector as:

$$\hat{\beta}_j \sim N(\beta_j, \sigma^2((X^\top X)^{-1})_{jj}) \quad (j = 1, \ldots, k) \tag{2.120}$$

and thus,

$$\frac{\hat{\beta}_j - \beta_j}{\sqrt{\sigma^2((X^\top X)^{-1})_{jj}}} \sim N(0,1) \tag{2.121}$$

However, using (2.121), we can see that, in addition to β_j (whose interval estimation we want to calculate) σ^2 is also unknown. In order to solve this problem, we must remember (2.77) and (2.78), in such a way that:

$$\frac{\hat{u}^\top \hat{u}}{\sigma^2} = \frac{u^\top M u}{\sigma^2} \sim \chi^2_{n-k}$$

Given the independence between this random variable and that of (2.121) (proved in Hayashi (2000)), we can write:

$$\frac{\frac{\hat{\beta}_j - \beta_j}{\sqrt{\sigma^2((X^\top X)^{-1})_{jj}}}}{\sqrt{\frac{\frac{\hat{u}^\top \hat{u}}{\sigma^2}}{n-k}}} = \frac{\hat{\beta}_j - \beta_j}{\hat{\sigma}\sqrt{((X^\top X)^{-1})_{jj}}} = \frac{\hat{\beta}_j - \beta_j}{\hat{s}_j} \sim t_{n-k} \tag{2.122}$$

which is distributed as a t-Student with $(n-k)$ degrees of freedom, where $\hat{s}_j$ denotes the estimated standard deviation of $\hat{\beta}_j$. From (2.122), and with a fixed level of confidence $(1-\epsilon)$ (or alternatively a level of significance ϵ), we have

$$Pr[-t_{\frac{\epsilon}{2}} < \frac{\hat{\beta}_j - \beta_j}{\hat{s}_j} < t_{\frac{\epsilon}{2}}] = 1 - \epsilon \quad (j = 1, \ldots, k) \tag{2.123}$$

and then,

$$\hat{\beta}_j \pm t_{\frac{\epsilon}{2}} \hat{s}_j \quad (j = 1, \ldots, k) \tag{2.124}$$

which provides the general expression of the $100(1-\epsilon)$ percent confidence interval for β_j. Given that $\hat{s}_j$ is a component of the interval, the amplitude of the interval is a measure of the how accurate the estimator is.

2.5.2 Interval Estimation of σ^2

In order to obtain the interval estimation of σ^2 we take the distribution given in (2.78) and the expression of the OLS estimator of σ^2 given in (2.34), in such a way that,

$$\frac{\hat{u}^\top \hat{u}}{\sigma^2} = \frac{(n-k)\hat{\sigma}^2}{\sigma^2} \sim \chi^2_{n-k} \tag{2.125}$$

so that, for a fixed level of significance ϵ, or level of confidence $(1-\epsilon)$ the confidence interval is constructed as follows:

$$Pr[\chi^2_{1-\frac{\epsilon}{2}} < \frac{(n-k)\hat{\sigma}^2}{\sigma^2} < \chi^2_{\frac{\epsilon}{2}}] = 1 - \epsilon \tag{2.126}$$

and the interval estimation of σ^2 is given by:

$$\left[\frac{(n-k)\hat{\sigma}^2}{\chi^2_{\frac{\epsilon}{2}}} ; \frac{(n-k)\hat{\sigma}^2}{\chi^2_{1-\frac{\epsilon}{2}}} \right] \tag{2.127}$$

2.5.3 Example

From our consumption function example, we now want to calculate the interval confidence for the three coefficients $(\beta_1, \beta_2, \beta_3)$ and the dispersion parameter σ^2. In each case, we calculate the interval for levels of confidence of 90 and 95 percent (ϵ=0.1 and 0.05). The following quantlet allow us to obtain the previous information

`XEGmlrm04.xpl`

2.6 Goodness of Fit Measures

As was mentioned in the previous chapter, the measures of goodness of fit are aimed at quantifying how well the OLS regression we have obtained fits the data. The two measures that are usually presented are the standard error of the regression and the R^2.

In the estimation section, we proved that if the regression model contains intercept, then the sum of the residuals are null (expression 2.32), so the average magnitude of the residuals can be expressed by its sample standard deviation, that is to say, by:

$$\frac{\sum_{i=1}^{n} \hat{u}_i^2}{n-1}$$

Given the definition of residual, if the regression fits the data well, we should expect it to have a small value. Nevertheless, in the last expression we can substitute $n-1$ by $n-k$, and then, the square of this expression is an unbiased estimator of σ^2. Thus, we can use the standard error of the regression (SER), as a measure of fit:

$$SER = \sqrt{\frac{\sum_{i=1}^{n} \hat{u}_i^2}{n-k}} = \sqrt{\frac{\hat{u}^\top \hat{u}}{n-k}} = \sqrt{\hat{\sigma}^2} = \hat{\sigma} \tag{2.128}$$

In general, the smaller the SER value, the better the regression fits the data. However, in order to establish whether a value is to be considered large or small, we need a reference value. The mean of the endogenous variable $\bar{y}$ can be an adequate reference, given that both are measured in the same units, and then we can obtain the percent of $\bar{y}$ which is represented in SER. For example, a SER value of 4 percent of $\bar{y}$ would suggest that the fit seems adequate.

If we want to compare the goodness of fit between two models whose endogenous variables are different, the R^2 is a more adequate measure than the standard error of the regression, because the R^2 does not depend on the magnitude of the variables. In order to obtain this measure, we begin, similarly to the univariate linear model by writing the variance decomposition expression, which divides the sample total variation (TSS) in y, into the variation which is explained by the model, or explained sum of squares (ESS), and the variation which is not explained by the model, or residual sum of squares (RSS):

$$(y^D)^\top Y^D = (\hat{y}^D)^\top \hat{y}^D + \hat{u}^\top \hat{u} \Rightarrow TSS = ESS + RSS \tag{2.129}$$

where $\hat{y}^D$ is the estimated y vector in deviations, obtained through the matrix

G, which was defined in (2.40). On this basis, the R^2 coefficient is defined as:

$$R^2 = 1 - \frac{RSS}{TSS} = \frac{ESS}{TSS} \tag{2.130}$$

which indicates the percentage of the sample total variation in y which is explained by the regression model.

From (2.129) we can deduce that, if the regression explains all the total variation in y, then $TSS = ESS$, which implies $R^2 = 1$. However, if the regression explains nothing, then $ESS = 0$ and $R^2 = 0$. Thus, we can conclude that R^2 is bounded between 0 and 1, in such a way that values of it close to one imply a good fit of the regression.

Nevertheless, we should be careful in forming conclusions, because the magnitude of the R^2 is affected by the kind of data employed in the model. In this sense, when we use time series data and the trends of the endogenous and the explanatory variables are similar, then the R^2 is usually large, even if there is no strong relationship between these variables. However, when we work with cross-section data , the R^2 tends to be lower, because there is no trend, and also due to the substantial natural variation in individual behavior. These arguments usually lead the researcher to require a higher value of this measure if the regression is carried out with time series data.

The bounds of the R^2 we have mentioned do not hold when the estimated model does not contain an intercept. As Patterson (2000) shows, this measure can be larger than one, and even negative. In such cases, we should use an *uncentered* R^2 as a measure of fit, which is constructed in a similar way as the R^2, but where neither TSS nor ESS are calculated by using the variables in deviations, that is to say:

$$R^2_u = 1 - \frac{\hat{u}^\top \hat{u}}{y^\top y} = \frac{\hat{y}^\top \hat{y}}{y^\top y} \tag{2.131}$$

In practice, very often several regressions are estimated with the same endogenous variable, and then we want to compare them according to their goodness of fit. For this end, the R^2 is not valid, because it never decreases when we add a new explanatory variable. This is due to the mathematical properties of the optimization which underly the LS procedure. In this sense, when we increase the number of regressors, the objective function $\hat{u}^\top \hat{u}$ decreases or stays the same, but never increases. Using (2.130), we can improve the R^2 by adding variables to the regression, even if the new regressors do not explain anything about y.

In order to avoid this behavior, we compute the so-called *adjusted* R^2 ($\bar{R}^2$) as:

$$\bar{R}^2 = 1 - \frac{\frac{\hat{u}^\top \hat{u}}{n-k}}{\frac{(y^D)^\top y^D}{n-1}} = 1 - \frac{(SER)^2}{\frac{(y^D)^\top y^D}{n-1}} \tag{2.132}$$

where RSS and ESS are adjusted by their degrees of freedom.

Given that TSS does not vary when we add a new regressor, we must focus on the numerator of (2.132). When a new variable is added to the set of regressors, then k increases, and both $n-k$ and $\hat{u}^\top\hat{u}$ decrease, so we must find out how fast each of them decrease. If the decrease of $n-k$ is less than that of $\hat{u}^\top\hat{u}$, then $\bar{R}^2$ increases, while it decreases if the reduction of $\hat{u}^\top\hat{u}$ is less than that of $n-k$. The R^2 and $\bar{R}^2$ are usually presented in the softwar.

The relationship between R^2 and $\bar{R}^2$ is given by:

$$\bar{R}^2 = 1 - \frac{n-1}{n-k}(1-R^2) \tag{2.133}$$

where we can see that for $k \geq 1$, $\bar{R}^2$ is always less than R^2, and it can even be negative, so its meaning is not as clear as that of R^2.

With respect to the SER, there is an inverse relationship between it and $\bar{R}^2$: if SER increases, then $\bar{R}^2$ decreases, and vice versa.

Finally, we should note that these measures should not be used if we are comparing regressions which have a different endogenous variable, even if they are based on the same set of data (for example, y and $\ln y$). Moreover, when we want to evaluate an estimated model, other statistics, together with these measures of fit, must be calculated. These usually refer to the maintenance of the classical assumptions of the MLRM.

2.7 Linear Hypothesis Testing

The previous sections have developed, through point and interval estimation, a method to infer a population value from a sample. Hypothesis testing constitutes another method of inference which consists of formulating some assumptions about the probability distribution of the population from which the sample was extracted, and then trying to verify these assumptions for them to be considered adequate. In this sense, hypothesis testing can refer to the systematic component of the model as well as its random component. Some of these procedures will be studied in the following chapter of this book, whilst in this section we only focus on linear hypotheses about the coefficients and the parameter of dispersion of the MLRM.

In order to present how to compute hypothesis testing about the coefficients, we begin by considering the general statistic which allows us to test any linear restrictions on β. Afterwards, we will apply this method to particular cases of interest, such as the hypotheses about the value of a β_j coefficient, or about all the coefficients excepting the intercept.

2.7.1 Hypothesis Testing about the Coefficients

In order to test any linear hypothesis about the coefficient, the problem is formulated as follows:

$$\begin{aligned} H_0 &: R\beta = r \\ H_A &: R\beta \neq r \end{aligned} \tag{2.134}$$

where R is a $q \times k$ $(q \leq k)$ matrix of known elements, with q being the number of linear restrictions to test, and r is a $q \times 1$ vector of known elements. The rank of R is q, which implies that the restrictions are linearly independent.

The matrix R and the vector r can be considered as artificial instruments which allow us to express any linear restrictions in matrix form. To illustrate the role of these instruments, consider an MLRM with 4 coefficients. For example, if we want to test

$$\begin{aligned} H_0 &: 6\beta_3 - 2\beta_2 = 12 \\ H_A &: 6\beta_3 - 2\beta_2 \neq 12 \end{aligned} \tag{2.135}$$

the R matrix is a row vector of four elements:

$$R = \begin{pmatrix} 0 & -2 & 6 & 0 \end{pmatrix}$$

and $r = 12$. Then, the restriction we want to test can be expressed as $R\beta = r$, given that:

$$\begin{pmatrix} 0 & -2 & 6 & 0 \end{pmatrix} \begin{pmatrix} \beta_1 \\ \beta_2 \\ \beta_3 \\ \beta_4 \end{pmatrix} = 12 \Rightarrow 6\beta_3 - 2\beta_2 = 12$$

If the null hypothesis we test includes more than one restriction, the implementation is similar. For example, if we have the testing problem:

$$\begin{aligned} H_0 &: \quad 2\beta_1 + \beta_2 = 1 \\ & \quad\ \beta_1 + 3\beta_4 = 2 \\ H_A &: \quad noH_0 \end{aligned} \tag{2.136}$$

it follows that

$$R = \begin{pmatrix} 2 & 1 & 0 & 0 \\ 1 & 0 & 0 & 3 \end{pmatrix}$$

$$r = \begin{pmatrix} 1 \\ 2 \end{pmatrix}$$

In order to derive the statistic which allows us to test the hypothesis, we begin by obtaining the probability distribution of $R\hat{\beta}$:

$$R\hat{\beta} \sim N[R\beta, \sigma^2 R(X^\top X)^{-1}R^\top] \tag{2.137}$$

This result is obtained from (2.74), given that if the $\hat{\beta}$ vector follows a normal distribution, then a linear combination of it, such as $R\hat{\beta}$, is also normally distributed, with moments:

$$\mathrm{E}(R\hat{\beta}) = RE(\hat{\beta}) = R\beta$$

$$V(R\hat{\beta}) = \mathrm{E}[(R\hat{\beta} - R\beta)(R\hat{\beta} - R\beta)^\top] = \mathrm{E}[R(\hat{\beta} - \beta)(\hat{\beta} - \beta)^\top R^\top] =$$
$$RE[(\hat{\beta} - \beta)(\hat{\beta} - \beta)^\top]R^\top = \sigma^2 R(X^\top X)^{-1}R^\top$$

A general result establishes that, given an m dimensional ν vector, if $\nu \sim N(\mu, \Sigma)$, with Σ nonsingular, then $(\nu - \mu)^\top \Sigma^{-1}(\nu - \mu) \sim \chi^2_m$. If we substitute ν by $R\hat{\beta}$, we have

$$(R\hat{\beta} - R\beta)^\top[\sigma^2 R(X^\top X)^{-1}R^\top]^{-1}(R\hat{\beta} - R\beta) \sim \chi^2_q \tag{2.138}$$

Expression (2.138) includes the unknown parameter σ^2, so in order to obtain a value for the statistic, we have to use the independence between the quadratic form given in (2.138), and the distribution (2.125) is (see Hayashi (2000)), in such a way that:

$$\frac{\frac{(R\hat{\beta}-r)^\top[\sigma^2 R(X^\top X)^{-1}R^\top]^{-1}(R\hat{\beta}-r)}{q}}{\frac{\frac{\hat{u}^\top \hat{u}}{\sigma^2}}{n-k}}$$

$$= \frac{(R\hat{\beta} - r)^\top[R(X^\top X)^{-1}R^\top]^{-1}(R\hat{\beta} - r)}{q\hat{\sigma}^2} \sim F^q_{n-k} \tag{2.139}$$

If the null hypothesis $H_0 : R\beta = r$ is true (that is to say, $R\beta - r = 0$), then a small value of $R\hat{\beta} - r$ is expected. Consequently, small values for (2.139) are thought to be evidence in favour of H_0. This means that this is a one-sided test. As in all tests, the decision rule to carry out the test can be summarized as follows:

a. To calculate the value of the F-ratio (F^*) expressed in (2.139).

b. To search for the critical point F_ϵ of the F-Snedecor distribution for $(q, n-k)$ degrees of freedom, for a fixed level of significance ϵ.

c. If $F^* < F_\epsilon$, we conclude that there is evidence in favour of H_0. Otherwise, we have evidence against it.

The previous stages constitute the general procedure of testing, which is based on the comparison of a statistic which is obtained from the sample, with the probability distribution which such a statistic should have if H_0 is true. Nevertheless, the result obtained can be very sensitive to the fixed level of significance, which is arbitrarily chosen (usually at 1, 5 or even 10 percent). In this sense, we could find that H_0 is rejected at $\epsilon = 0.05$, while it is accepted at $\epsilon = 0.04$, which leads researchers to obtain different conclusions if they have different opinions about the adequate value of ϵ.

A way of solving this question consists of employing the so-called p-value provided by a sample in a specific test. It can be defined as the lowest significance level which allows us to reject H_0, with the available sample:

$$p - value = Pr(F \geq F^* | H_0)$$

which depends on the F^* statistic value and the sample size.

It we use the p-value, the decision rule is modified in stages *b* and *c* as follows: *b*) to calculate the p-value, and *c*) if $p - value > \epsilon$, H_0 is accepted. Otherwise, it is rejected.

Econometric softwar does not usually contain the general F-statistic, except for certain particular cases which we will discuss later. So, we must obtain it step by step, and it will not always be easy, because we have to calculate the inverses and products of matrices. Fortunately, there is a convenient alternative way involving two different residual sum of squares (RSS): that obtained from the estimation of the MLRM, now denoted RSS_u (unrestricted residual sum of squares), and that called restricted residual sum of squares, denoted RSS_R. The latter is expressed as:

$$RSS_R = \hat{u}_R^\top \hat{u}_R$$

where $\hat{u}_R$ is the residuals vector corresponding to the restricted least squares estimator (RLS) which, as we will prove in the following section, is the coefficient vector value ($\hat{\beta}_R$) that satisfies:

$$\hat{\beta}_R = \arg\min_{\hat{\hat{\beta}}} S(\hat{\hat{\beta}})$$

subject to

$$R\hat{\hat{\beta}} = r$$

From both residual sum of squares (RSS_R and RSS_u), we obtain an alternative way of expressing (2.139) as:

$$\frac{\frac{RSS_R - RSS_u}{q}}{\frac{RSS_u}{n-k}} \tag{2.140}$$

The equivalence between these two alternative ways of expressing the F-statistic will be shown in the following section.

If we use (2.140) to test a linear hypothesis about β, we only need to obtain the RSS corresponding to both the estimation of the specified MLRM, and the estimation once we have substituted the linear restriction into the model. The decision rule does not vary: if H_0 is true, RSS_R should not be much different from RSS_U, and consequently, small values of the statistic provide evidence in favour of H_0.

Having established the general F statistic, we now analyze the most useful particular cases.

2.7.2 Hypothesis Testing about a Coefficient of the MLRM

When the hypothesis to test has the form

$$\begin{aligned} H_0 &: \beta_j = \beta_j^0 \\ H_A &: \beta_j \neq \beta_j^0 \end{aligned} \tag{2.141}$$

that is to say, the null hypothesis only contains one coefficient, the general statistics given in (2.139) can be expressed as:

$$\frac{(\hat{\beta}_j - \beta_j^0)^2}{\hat{\sigma}^2((X^\top X)^{-1})_{jj}} \tag{2.142}$$

which follows an F^1_{n-k} distribution.

To obtain (2.142) we must note that, under H_0, the R matrix becomes a row vector with zero value for each element, except for the jth element which has 1 value, and $r = \beta_j^0$. Thus, the term $(R\hat{\beta} - r)$ becomes $(\hat{\beta}_j - \beta_j^0)$. Element $R(X^\top X)^{-1}R^\top$ becomes $((X^\top X)^{-1})_{jj}$.

Moreover, we know that the squared root of the F random variable expressed in (2.142) follows a t-student whose degrees of freedom are those of the denominator of the F distribution, that is to say,

$$\frac{(\hat{\beta}_j - \beta_j^0)}{\sqrt{\hat{\sigma}^2((X^\top X)^{-1})_{jj}}} \tag{2.143}$$

This t-statistic is usually computed when we want to test $H_0 : \beta_j = \beta_j^0$.

It must be noted that, given the form of H_A in (2.141), (2.143) is a two-tailed test, so once we have calculated the statistic value t^*, H_0 is rejected if $|t^*| \geq t_{\frac{\epsilon}{2}}$.

An interesting particular case of the t-statistic consists of testing $\beta_j^0 = 0$, which simplifies (2.143), yielding:

$$\frac{\hat{\beta}_j}{\hat{\sigma}\sqrt{((X^\top X)^{-1})_{jj}}} \tag{2.144}$$

which is known as the "t-ratio". This is the appropriate statistic to test whether the corresponding explanatory variable x_j has no statistically significant linear influence on the dependent variable. If we find evidence in favour of H_0, we conclude that x_j is not important to explain y. If we test the intercept, the result only allows us to decide if we have to include a constant term in the MLRM.

The statistic given in (2.143) is the same as (2.122), which was derived in order to obtain the interval estimation for a β_j coefficient. This leads us to conclude that there is an equivalence between creating a confidence interval and carrying out a two-tailed test of the hypothesis (2.141). In this sense, the confidence interval can be considered as an alternative way of testing (2.141). The decision rule will be: given a fixed level of significance ϵ and calculating a $100(1-\epsilon)$ percent confidence interval, if the β_j value in H_0 (β_j^0) belongs to the interval, we accept the null hypothesis, at a level of significance ϵ. Otherwise, H_0 should be rejected. Obviously, this equivalence holds if the significance level in the interval is the same as that of the test.

2.7.3 Testing the Overall Significance of the Model

This test tries to verify if all the coefficients, except the intercept are jointly significant, that is to say,

$$H_0 : \beta_{(2)} = 0_{k-1} \quad H_A : no \quad H_0 \tag{2.145}$$

where, as we know, $\beta_{(2)}$ is a $k-1$ vector which includes the coefficients of interest. In order to test (2.145), the matrix R and r in (2.139) are:

$$R = \begin{pmatrix} 0 & 1 & 0 & \dots & 0 \\ 0 & 0 & 1 & \dots & 0 \\ \vdots & \vdots & \vdots & \dots & \vdots \\ 0 & 0 & 0 & \dots & 1 \end{pmatrix} = \begin{pmatrix} 0_{k-1} & I_{k-1} \end{pmatrix} \tag{2.146}$$

$$r = 0_{k-1} \tag{2.147}$$

and then $(R\hat{\beta} - r)$ becomes $(\hat{\beta}_2, \hat{\beta}_3, \dots, \hat{\beta}_k)^\top = \hat{\beta}_{(2)}$. Matrix X can be partitioned as $(\imath, X_2)$ (as we have seen when we expressed the MLRM in deviations), in such a way that $R(X^\top X)^{-1}R^\top$ becomes matrix $(X^\top X)^{-1}$ adjusted by eliminating the first row and the first column. The results about the inverse of a partitioned matrix (see Greene (1993)) allow us to prove that $[R(X^\top X)^{-1}R^\top]^{-1} = ((X_2^D)^\top X_2^D)$, with X_2^D being the $n \times (k-1)$ matrix with the variables in deviations, which was defined earlier. Thus, the statistic gives:

$$\frac{\hat{\beta}_2^\top (X_2^D)^\top X_2^D \hat{\beta}_{(2)}}{(k-1)\hat{\sigma}^2} \sim F_{n-k}^{k-1} \tag{2.148}$$

If the value of (2.148) is larger than the corresponding critical point F_ϵ, we can accept that $\beta_{(2)}$ is significantly different from zero, that is to say, the set of regressors is important for explaining y. In other words, we conclude that, as a whole, the model is adequate.

Nevertheless, the F statistic (2.148) has an alternative form as a function of the explained sum of squares ESS. To prove it, we begin by considering:

$$\hat{y}^D = X_2^D \hat{\beta}_{(2)}$$

in such a way that ESS can be expressed as

$$(\hat{y}^D)^\top \hat{y}^D = \hat{\beta}_{(2)}^\top (X_2^D)^\top X_2^D \hat{\beta}_{(2)} \tag{2.149}$$

which is the numerator of expression (2.148), which can be rewritten as:

$$\frac{\frac{(\hat{y}^D)^\top \hat{y}^D}{k-1}}{\frac{\hat{u}^\top \hat{u}}{n-k}} = \frac{\frac{ESS}{k-1}}{\frac{RSS}{n-k}} \tag{2.150}$$

Furthermore, from the definition of R^2 given in (2.130) we can deduce that:

$$\frac{\frac{ESS}{k-1}}{\frac{RSS}{n-k}} = \frac{\frac{R^2}{k-1}}{\frac{1-R^2}{n-k}} \tag{2.151}$$

We must note that the equivalence between (2.148) and (2.151) is only given when the MLRM has a constant term.

2.7.4 Testing Hypothesis about σ^2

The earlier mentioned relationship between the confidence interval and hypothesis testing, allows us to derive the test of the following hypothesis easily:

$$\begin{array}{l} H_0 : \sigma^2 = \sigma_0^2 \\ H_A : \sigma^2 \neq \sigma_0^2 \end{array} \tag{2.152}$$

with $\sigma_0^2 \geq 0$. Under H_0, the statistic to test (2.152) is that given in (2.125):

$$\frac{(n-k)\hat{\sigma}^2}{\sigma^2} \sim \chi^2_{n-k}$$

The decision rule consists of rejecting H_0 if the value of the statistic $(\chi^2)^* \leq \chi^2_{\frac{\epsilon}{2}}$ or $(\chi^2)^* \geq \chi^2_{1-\frac{\epsilon}{2}}$. Otherwise, H_0 will be accepted. In other words, fixing a level of significance, H_0 is accepted if σ_0^2 belongs to the confidence interval for σ^2.

2.7.5 Example

Now, we present the quantlet `linreg` in the `stats` quantlib which allows us to obtain the main measures of fit and testing hypothesis that we have just described in both this section and the previous section.

```
{beta,bse,bstan,bpval}= linreg ( x, y )
```
estimates the parameters of a MLRM and obtains the main statistics.

For the example of the consumption function which we presented in previous sections, the quantlet *XEGmlrm05.xpl* obtains the statistical information

Q XEGmlrm05.xpl

The column SS represents the squared sum of the regression (ESS), the squared sum of the residuals (RSS) and the total squared sum (TSS). The MSS column represents the means of SS calculated by dividing SS by the corresponding degrees of freedom(df). The F-test is the statistic to test $H_0 : \beta_2 = \beta_3 = 0$, which is followed by the corresponding p-value. Afterwards, we have the measures of fit we presented in the previous section, that is to say, R^2, adjusted-$R^2(\bar{R}^2)$, and Standard Error (SER). Moreover, multiple R represents the squared root of R^2.

Finally, the output presents the columns of the values of the estimated coefficients (beta) and their corresponding standard deviations (SE). It also presents the t-ratios (t-test) together with their corresponding p-values. By observing the p-values, we see that all the p-values are very low, so we reject $H_0 : \beta_j = 0$, whatever the significance level (usually 1, 5 or 10 percent), which means that all the coefficients are statistically significant. Moreover, the p-value of the F-tests also allows us to conclude that we reject $H_0 : \beta_2 = \beta_3 = 0$, or in other words, the overall regression explains the y variable. Finally, with this quntlet it is also possible to illustrate the computation of the F statistic to test the hypothesis $H_0 : \beta_2 = 1$.

2.8 Restricted and Unrestricted Regression

In previous sections we made use of the LS and ML principles to derive estimators of the unknown parameters of the MLRM. In using these principles, we assumed that our information level was only the sample information, so it was considered there was no a priori information on the parameters of the model. However, in some situations it is possible to have some non-sample information (a priori information on the parameters), which can be of several kinds. Now we focus only on exact a priori information about β coefficients (useful references for this topic are Fomby, Carter, and Johnson (1984) and Judge, Griffiths, Carter, Lutkepohl and Lee (1985)).

In general, this previous information on the coefficients can be expressed as follows:

$$R\beta = r \tag{2.153}$$

where R and r are the matrix and the vector which was defined to establish the test given in (2.134). Now (2.153) can be thought of as the way of expressing the a priori information about the elements of the β vector.

In this section, our objective consists of estimating the parameters of the MLRM by considering the a priori information. Basically, there are two equivalent ways of carrying out such an estimation. One of them consists of incorporating the a priori information into the specified model, in such a way that a transformed model is obtained whose unknown parameters are estimated by OLS or ML. The other way of operating consists of applying either what we call the restricted least squares (RLS) method, or what we call the restricted maximum likelihood (RML) method.

2.8.1 Restricted Least Squares and Restricted Maximum Likelihood Estimators

Given the MLRM

$$y = X\beta + u$$

and the a priori information about β expressed as $R\beta = r$, we try to find the vector $\hat{\hat{\beta}}_R$ which minimizes the squared sum of residuals (if we use the LS method) or maximizes the likelihood function (in the case of the ML method), subject to $R\hat{\hat{\beta}}_R = r$. Then, the estimator which we obtain by combining all the information is called *Restricted Least Squares* or *Restricted Maximum Likelihood*, respectively.

The conditioned optimization problem can be solved through the classical Lagrangian procedures. If we first consider the LS method, the corresponding Lagrange function is:

$$\Im = (y - X\hat{\hat{\beta}}_R)^\top (y - X\hat{\hat{\beta}}_R) - 2\lambda^\top (R\hat{\hat{\beta}}_R - r) =$$

$$y^\top y - 2\hat{\hat{\beta}}_R^\top X^\top y + \hat{\hat{\beta}}_R^\top X^\top X\hat{\hat{\beta}}_R - 2\lambda^\top (R\hat{\hat{\beta}}_R - r) \tag{2.154}$$

where λ is the $q \times 1$ vector of Lagrange multipliers. The 2 in the last term appears to make the derivation easier and does not affect the outcome.

To determine the optimum values, we set the partial derivatives of $\Im$ with respect to β and λ equal to zero:

$$\frac{\partial \Im}{\partial \hat{\hat{\beta}}_R} = -2X^\top y + 2X^\top X\hat{\hat{\beta}}_R - 2R^\top \lambda = 0 \tag{2.155}$$

$$\frac{\partial \Im}{\partial \lambda} = -2(R\hat{\hat{\beta}}_R - r) = 0 \tag{2.156}$$

We substitute $\hat{\hat{\beta}}_R$ by $\hat{\beta}_R$ in order to obtain the value of $\hat{\hat{\beta}}_R$ which satisfies the first-order conditions. Then, from (2.155) we have:

$$X^\top X\hat{\beta}_R = X^\top y + R^\top \hat{\lambda} \tag{2.157}$$

In premultiplying the last expression by $(X^\top X)^{-1}$ we get:

$$(X^\top X)^{-1}X^\top X\hat{\beta}_R = (X^\top X)^{-1}(X^\top y + R^\top \hat{\lambda})$$

$$\Rightarrow \hat{\beta}_R = \hat{\beta} + (X^\top X)^{-1}R^\top \hat{\lambda} \tag{2.158}$$

where $\hat{\beta}$ is the unrestricted least squares estimator which was obtained in (2.25).

Expression (2.158) is premultiplied by R and we get:

$$R\hat{\beta}_R = R\hat{\beta} + R(X^\top X)^{-1}R^\top \hat{\lambda} \tag{2.159}$$

Since $(X^\top X)^{-1}$ is a positive definite matrix, $R(X^\top X)^{-1}R^\top$ is also positive definite, and moreover, its rank is $q \leq k$ and it is nonsingular. Then, from (2.159) we may obtain:

$$\hat{\lambda} = [R(X^\top X)^{-1}R^\top]^{-1}(R\hat{\beta}_R - R\hat{\beta})$$

or

$$\hat{\lambda} = [R(X^\top X)^{-1}R^\top]^{-1}(r - R\hat{\beta}) \tag{2.160}$$

because from (2.156), the restricted minimization problem must satisfy the side condition $R\hat{\beta}_R = r$. Using the value (2.160) for the vector λ, we get from (2.158) the estimator:

$$\hat{\beta}_R = \hat{\beta} + (X^\top X)^{-1}R^\top[R(X^\top X)^{-1}R^\top]^{-1}(r - R\hat{\beta}) \tag{2.161}$$

which is denoted as the restricted least squares (RLS) estimator.

Given that $(X^\top X)^{-1}R^\top[R(X^\top X)^{-1}R^\top]^{-1}$ is a matrix of constant elements, from (2.161) we can see that the difference between $\hat{\beta}_R$ and $\hat{\beta}$ is a linear function of the $(r - R\hat{\beta})$ vector. Moreover, we deduce that this difference increases the further $\hat{\beta}$ (unrestricted LS) is from satisfying the restriction.

According to the RLS estimator, the residuals vector can be defined as:

$$\hat{u}_R = y - X\hat{\beta}_R \tag{2.162}$$

and, analogously to the procedure followed to obtain $\hat{\sigma}^2$, the RLS estimator of σ^2 is given by:

$$\hat{\sigma}_R^2 = \frac{\hat{u}_R^\top \hat{u}_R}{n - k + q} \tag{2.163}$$

which is an unbiased estimator of σ^2, given that $\mathrm{E}(\hat{u}_R^\top \hat{u}_R) = \sigma^2(n - (k - q))$.

Having obtained the expressions of the RLS estimators of the parameters in the MLRM, we now have the required information in order to prove the equivalence between (2.139) and (2.140), established in the previous section. In order to show such equivalence, we begin by adding and subtracting $X\hat{\beta}$ to and from (2.162):

$$\hat{u}_R = y - X\hat{\beta}_R + X\hat{\beta} - X\hat{\beta} = (y - X\hat{\beta}) - X(\hat{\beta}_R - \hat{\beta}) = \hat{u} - X(\hat{\beta}_R - \hat{\beta}) \tag{2.164}$$

and then, given that $X^\top \hat{u} = \hat{u}^\top X = 0$ (an algebraic property of the LS method, described in the estimation section), we have:

$$\hat{u}_R^\top \hat{u}_R = [\hat{u} - X(\hat{\beta}_R - \hat{\beta})]^\top [\hat{u} - X(\hat{\beta}_R - \hat{\beta})] = \hat{u}^\top \hat{u} + (\hat{\beta}_R - \hat{\beta})^\top X^\top X(\hat{\beta}_R - \hat{\beta}) \tag{2.165}$$

From (2.165), we can write:

$$\hat{u}_R^\top \hat{u}_R - \hat{u}^\top \hat{u} = (\hat{\beta}_R - \hat{\beta})^\top X^\top X(\hat{\beta}_R - \hat{\beta}) \tag{2.166}$$

and if we substitute $(\hat{\beta}_R - \hat{\beta})$ according to (2.161), we have

$$\hat{u}_R^\top \hat{u}_R - \hat{u}^\top \hat{u} = (r - R\hat{\beta})^\top [R(X^\top X)^{-1}R^\top]^{-1}(r - R\hat{\beta}) \tag{2.167}$$

This last expression allows us to conclude that (2.139) and (2.140) are equivalent. Additionally, from (2.167) it is satisfied that $\hat{u}_R^\top \hat{u}_R > \hat{u}^\top \hat{u}$, given that $[R(X^\top X)^{-1}R^\top]^{-1}$ is a positive definite matrix.

In order to derive now the RML estimators, the Lagrange function according to the ML principle is written as:

$$\Im = -\frac{n}{2}\ln 2\pi - \frac{n}{2}\ln \sigma_R^2 - \frac{(y - X\beta_R)^\top (y - X\beta_R)}{2\sigma_R^2} + 2\lambda^\top (R\beta_R - r) \tag{2.168}$$

and the first-order conditions are:

$$\frac{\partial \Im}{\partial \beta_R} = -\frac{1}{2\sigma_R^2}(-2X^\top y + 2X^\top X\beta_R) + 2R^\top \lambda = 0 \tag{2.169}$$

$$\frac{\partial \Im}{\partial \sigma_R^2} = -\frac{n}{2\sigma_R^2} + \frac{(y - X\beta_R)^\top (y - X\beta_R)}{2\sigma_R^4} = 0 \tag{2.170}$$

$$\frac{\partial \Im}{\partial \lambda} = -2(R\beta_R - r) = 0 \tag{2.171}$$

From (2.169)-(2.171), and putting $\sim$ to the parameters, in a similar way to the RLS procedure, we deduce:

$$\tilde{\beta}_R = \tilde{\beta} + (X^\top X)^{-1}R^\top [R(X^\top X)^{-1}R^\top]^{-1}(r - R\tilde{\beta}) \tag{2.172}$$

$$\tilde{\sigma}_R^2 = \frac{(y - X\tilde{\beta}_R)^\top (y - X\tilde{\beta}_R)}{n} = \frac{\hat{u}_R^\top \hat{u}_R}{n} \tag{2.173}$$

$$\tilde{\lambda} = \frac{[R(X^\top X)^{-1}R^\top]^{-1}(r - R\tilde{\beta})}{\tilde{\sigma}_R^2} \tag{2.174}$$

so we conclude that, in a MLRM which satisfies the classical assumptions, the RLS estimators of the coefficients are the same as the RML estimators. This allows us to write the equality given in (2.173).

2.8.2 Finite Sample Properties of the Restricted Estimator Vector

Given the equality between $\hat{\beta}_R$ and $\tilde{\beta}_R$, the following proofs are valid for both procedures.

Before deriving some properties, it is convenient to obtain the expectation vector and the variance-covariance matrix of the restricted estimator vector. Using (2.161), the expected value of $\hat{\beta}_R$ is :

$$\mathrm{E}(\hat{\beta}_R) = \mathrm{E}(\hat{\beta}) + (X^\top X)^{-1}R^\top [R(X^\top X)^{-1}R^\top]^{-1}(r - R\mathrm{E}(\hat{\beta})) =$$

$$\beta + (X^\top X)^{-1}R^\top [R(X^\top X)^{-1}R^\top]^{-1}(r - R\beta) \tag{2.175}$$

and the variance-covariance matrix:

$$V(\tilde{\beta}_R) = \mathrm{E}[(\hat{\beta}_R - \mathrm{E}\hat{\beta}_R)(\hat{\beta}_R - \mathrm{E}\hat{\beta}_R)^\top]$$

If we consider expression (2.54) and it is substituted into (2.161), we can write:

$$\begin{aligned}\hat{\beta}_R - \mathrm{E}\hat{\beta}_R &= (X^\top X)^{-1}X^\top u - (X^\top X)^{-1}R^\top[R(X^\top X)^{-1}R^\top]^{-1}R(X^\top X)^{-1}X^\top u \\ &= [I_k - (X^\top X)^{-1}R^\top[R(X^\top X)^{-1}R^\top]^{-1}R](X^\top X)^{-1}X^\top u \\ &= \Phi(X^\top X)^{-1}X^\top u \qquad (2.176)\end{aligned}$$

The Φ matrix (which premultiplies to $(X^\top X)^{-1}X^\top u$ in (2.176), is a $k \times k$ idempotent matrix of constant elements. From this last expression we obtain:

$$\begin{aligned}V(\hat{\beta}_R) &= \mathrm{E}[\Phi(X^\top X)^{-1}X^\top uu^\top X(X^\top X)^{-1}\Phi^\top] \\ &= \sigma^2\Phi(X^\top X)^{-1}\Phi^\top = \sigma^2\Phi(X^\top X)^{-1} \qquad (2.177)\end{aligned}$$

The last equality of (2.177) is written according to the proof presented in Judge, Carter, Griffiths, Lutkepohl and Lee (1988)

From (2.177), it is possible to deduce the relationship between $V(\hat{\beta}_R)$ and $V(\hat{\beta})$, by replacing Φ by its expression, and thus:

$$V(\hat{\beta}_R) = \sigma^2(X^\top X)^{-1} - \sigma^2(X^\top X)^{-1}R^\top[R(X^\top X)^{-1}R^\top]^{-1}R(X^\top X)^{-1} \Rightarrow$$

$$V(\hat{\beta}_R) - V(\hat{\beta}) = \sigma^2(X^\top X)^{-1}R^\top[R(X^\top X)^{-1}R^\top]^{-1}R(X^\top X)^{-1} = \sigma^2 C$$

with C being a positive semidefinite matrix, as Fomby, Carter, and Johnson (1984) show. Consequently, the diagonal elements of $V(\hat{\beta}_R)$ (variances of each $\hat{\beta}_{Rj}$) are equal to or less than the corresponding elements of $V(\hat{\beta})$ (variances of each $\hat{\beta}_j$). This means that, if the a priori information is correct (as we will show later , in this case $\mathrm{E}(\hat{\beta}_R) = \beta$), the estimator vector $\hat{\beta}_R$ is more efficient than the OLS estimator.

On the basis of these previous results, we can establish the finite properties of the RLS estimator.

- Linearity. If we substitute expression (2.54) of $\hat{\beta}$ into (2.161), and then we group terms, we obtain:

$$\hat{\beta}_R = (X^\top X)^{-1}R^\top[R(X^\top X)^{-1}R^\top]^{-1}r+ \qquad (2.178)$$

$$[(X^\top X)^{-1}X^\top - (X^\top X)^{-1}R^\top[R(X^\top X)^{-1}R^\top]^{-1}R(X^\top X)^{-1}X^\top]\, y$$

Given that the first term of the right-hand side of (2.178) is a vector of constant elements, and the second term is the product of a matrix of constant elements multiplied by the vector y, it follows that $\hat{\beta}_R$ satisfies the linearity property.

- Unbiasedness. According to (2.175), $\hat{\beta}_R$ is unbiased only if $r - R\beta = 0$, that is to say, if the a priori information is true.

- BLUE. With correct a priori information, the estimator vector $\hat{\beta}_R$ is the best linear unbiased vector within the class of unbiased estimators that are linear functions of the endogenous variable and that also satisfy the a priori information (2.153). This property, which we will not prove here, is based on the Gauss-Markov Theorem.

- Efficiency. As Rothemberg (1973) shows, when the a priori information is correct, the estimator vector $\hat{\beta}_R$ satisfies the Cramer-Rao inequality, and consequently, it is efficient.

From (2.177) it can be deduced that the expression of $V(\hat{\beta}_R)$ does not change if the a priori information is correct or non correct, which means that $V(\hat{\beta}_R) \leq V(\hat{\beta})$ is maintained whatever the situation.

Finally, given the linearity of $\hat{\beta}_R$ with respect to y, and this vector being normally distributed, if the a priori information is correct, we have:

$$\hat{\beta}_R \sim N(\beta, \sigma^2 \Phi(X^\top X)^{-1}) \tag{2.179}$$

2.8.3 Example

We now consider that we have the following a priori information on the coefficients: $\beta_2 = 1$, in such a way that we calculate the restricted estimators of the coefficients. Jointly with these estimators the quantlet `XEGmlrm06.xpl` computes the F statistic as a function of the restricted and unrestricted squared sum of the residuals which allows us to test $H_0 : \beta_2 = 1$.

`XEGmlrm06.xpl`

Note that the RML estimator satisfies the formulated restriction, and the value of the F statistic is the same as the one obtained in Section 2.7.4

2.9 Three General Test Procedures

Under the classical assumptions of the MLRM, in the section on the testing hypotheses we have derived appropriate finite sample test statistics in order to verify linear restrictions on the coefficients. Nevertheless, these exact tests are not always available, so in these cases it is very useful to consider the following three approaches, which allow us to derive large sample tests, which are asymptotically equivalent. Several situations which require making use of these tests will be presented in following chapters of this book. In this chapter we now focus on their general derivation, and on their illustration in the context of an MLRM under classical assumptions.

All three test procedures are developed within the framework of ML estimation and they use the information included in the log-likelihood in different but asymptotically equivalent ways.

The general framework to implement these principles is defined as follows:

$$\begin{aligned} H_0 &: h(\theta) = 0 \\ H_A &: h(\theta) \neq 0 \end{aligned} \tag{2.180}$$

where $h(\theta)$ includes q restrictions ($q \leq k$) on the elements of the parameter vector θ which has k dimension. Furthermore, suppose we have estimated by both unrestricted and restricted ML, so that we have the vectors θ and $\tilde{\theta}_R$.

Formal derivation of these tests can be found, for example, in Davidson and MacKinnon (1993).

2.9.1 Likelihood Ratio Test (LR)

This test is based on the distance between the log-likelihood function evaluated at the ML and the RML estimators. Thus, it is defined as:

$$LR = 2[\ell(\tilde{\theta}) - \ell(\tilde{\theta}_R)] \tag{2.181}$$

which, under the null hypothesis (2.180) is asymptotically distributed as a χ^2_q. This result is obtained through a Taylor expansion of second order of the restricted log-likelihood around the ML estimator vector.

Taking (2.181) it can be thought that if the restriction $h(\theta) = 0$ is true when it is included, the log-likelihood should not reduce its value by a significant amount and thus, both $\ell(\tilde{\theta})$ and $\ell(\tilde{\theta}_R)$ should be similar. Given that the inequality

$\ell(\tilde{\theta}) \geq \ell(\tilde{\theta}_R)$ always holds (because a maximum subject to restrictions is never larger than an unrestricted maximum), significant discrepancies between both estimated log-likelihoods can be thought of as evidence against H_0, since the RML estimator moves far away from the unrestricted ML.

Another way of understanding what underlies this test focuses on the asymptotic properties of the ML estimators under correct specification. Given several regularity conditions, the ML estimators are consistent, asymptotically efficient and their asymptotic distribution is normal. Moreover, it is shown that the RML estimators are consistent when the restrictions are true (correct a priori information). According to these results, we can say that, if H_0 is true, then both ML and RML estimators are consistent, so it is expected that $\ell(\tilde{\theta}) \cong \ell(\tilde{\theta}_R)$. Thus, small values of (2.181) provide evidence in favour of the null hypothesis.

As it was earlier described, the decision rule consists of, for a fixed significance level ϵ, comparing the value of the LR statistic for a given sample (LR^*) with the corresponding critical point χ^2_ϵ (with q degrees of freedom), and concluding the rejection of H_0 if $LR^* > \chi^2_\epsilon$. Equivalently, we reject H_0 if the p-value is less than ϵ.

2.9.2 The Wald Test (W)

This test is based on the distance between $\tilde{\theta}_R$ and $\tilde{\theta}$, so it tries to find out if the unrestricted estimators nearly satisfy the restrictions implied by the null hypothesis. The statistic is defined as :

$$W = nh(\tilde{\theta})^\top [H_{\tilde{\theta}}^\top (I_\infty(\tilde{\theta}))^{-1} H_{\tilde{\theta}}]^{-1} h(\tilde{\theta}) \tag{2.182}$$

where H_θ is the $k \times q$ matrix of the derivatives $\frac{\partial h(\theta)}{\partial \theta}$, in such a way that $H_{\tilde{\theta}}$ means that it is evaluated at the unrestricted ML estimators.

According to the result:

$$\sqrt{n} h(\theta) \rightarrow_{as} N[0, H_\theta^\top (I_\infty(\theta))^{-1} H_\theta] \tag{2.183}$$

The construction of a quadratic form from (2.183), under H_0 and evaluated at the ML estimators, leads to the conclusion that (2.182) follows a χ^2_q.

Given that $\tilde{\theta}$ is consistent, if H_0 is true, we expect that $h(\tilde{\theta})$ takes a value close to zero and consequently the value of W for a given sample (W^*) adopts a small value. However, H_0 is rejected if $W^* > \chi^2_\epsilon$. This amounts to saying that H_0 is rejected if $h(\tilde{\theta})$ is "very distant" from zero.

Finally, we must note that the asymptotic information matrix, which appears in (2.182), is usually non observable. In order to be able to implement the test, $I_\infty(\theta)$ is substituted by $\frac{I_n(\theta)}{n}$. Thus, the W statistic for a given sample of size n is written as:

$$W_n = nh(\tilde{\theta})^\top \left[H_{\tilde{\theta}}^\top \left(\frac{I_n(\tilde{\theta})}{n} \right)^{-1} H_{\tilde{\theta}} \right]^{-1} h(\tilde{\theta}) = h(\tilde{\theta})^\top [H_{\tilde{\theta}}^\top (I_n(\tilde{\theta}))^{-1} H_{\tilde{\theta}}]^{-1} h(\tilde{\theta}) \tag{2.184}$$

which converges to the statistic W of (2.182) as n increases.

2.9.3 Lagrange Multiplier Test (LM)

This test is also known as the Rao efficient score test. It is defined as:

$$LM = \frac{1}{n} \tilde{\lambda}^\top H_{\tilde{\theta}_R}^\top [I_\infty(\tilde{\theta}_R)]^{-1} H_{\tilde{\theta}_R} \tilde{\lambda} \tag{2.185}$$

which under the null hypothesis has an asymptotic distribution χ^2_q. Remember that $\tilde{\lambda}$ is the estimated Lagrange multiplier vector which emerges if one maximizes the likelihood function subject to constraints by means of a Lagrange function.

This asymptotic distribution is obtained from the result:

$$\frac{\tilde{\lambda}}{\sqrt{n}} \rightarrow_{as} N[0, (H_\theta^\top [I(\theta)]^{-1} H_\theta)^{-1}] \tag{2.186}$$

This result allows us to construct a quadratic form that, evaluated at $\tilde{\theta}_R$ and under H_0 leads to the χ^2_q distribution of (2.185).

The idea which underlies this test can be thought of as follows. If the restrictions of H_0 are true, the penalization for including them in the model is minimum. Thus, $\tilde{\lambda}$ is close to zero, and LM also tends to zero. Consequently, large values of the statistic provide evidence against the null hypothesis.

Again, we must note that expression (2.185) contains the asymptotic information matrix, which is a problem for implementing the test. In a similar way to that described in the Wald test, we have:

$$LM_n = \frac{1}{n} \tilde{\lambda}^\top H_{\tilde{\theta}_R}^\top [\frac{I_n(\tilde{\theta}_R)}{n}]^{-1} H_{\tilde{\theta}_R} \tilde{\lambda} = \tilde{\lambda}^\top H_{\tilde{\theta}_R}^\top [I_n(\tilde{\theta}_R)]^{-1} H_{\tilde{\theta}_R} \tilde{\lambda} \tag{2.187}$$

which converges to (2.185) as n tends to ∞.

If we remember the restricted maximization problem, which in our case is solved by means of the Lagrange function:

$$\Im = \ell(\theta) - \lambda^\top h(\theta)$$

the set of first order conditions can be expressed as:

$$\frac{\partial \Im}{\partial \theta} = g(\theta) - H\lambda = 0$$

$$\frac{\partial \Im}{\partial \lambda} = h(\theta) = 0 \tag{2.188}$$

with $g(\theta)$ being the gradient or score vector, that is to say, the first derivatives of the log-likelihood with respect to the parameters.

From the first set of first-order conditions in (2.188) one can deduce that $g(\theta) = H\lambda$. Thus, $H\tilde{\lambda}$ can be substituted by $g(\tilde{\theta}_R)$, leading to the known score form of the LM test (or simply the score test):

$$LM = \frac{1}{n} g(\tilde{\theta}_R)^\top [I_\infty(\tilde{\theta}_R)]^{-1} g(\tilde{\theta}_R) \tag{2.189}$$

So, when the null hypothesis is true, the restricted ML estimator is close to the unrestricted ML estimator, so we expect that $g(\tilde{\theta}_R) \cong 0$, since we know that in the unrestricted optimization it is maintained that $g(\tilde{\theta}) = 0$. It is evident that this test is based on the distance between $g(\tilde{\theta}_R)$ and $g(\tilde{\theta})$. Small values of the statistic provide evidence in favour of the null hypothesis.

Again $I_\infty(\cdot)$ is substituted by $\frac{I_n(\cdot)}{n}$, and the expression of the statistic for a sample of size n is given by:

$$LM_n = g(\tilde{\theta}_R)^\top [I_n(\tilde{\theta}_R)]^{-1} g(\tilde{\theta}_R) \tag{2.190}$$

Very often, the LM test statistic is asymptotically equal to n times the non centered R^2 of an artificial linear regression (for a more detailed description of this approach, see Davidson and Mackinnon (1984).

2.9.4 Relationships and Properties of the Three General Testing Procedures

The main property of these three statistics is that, under H_0, all of them tend to the same random variable, as $n \to \infty$. This random variable is distributed as a χ^2_q. In other words, in the asymptotic context we are dealing with the same statistic, although they have very different definitions. Thus, in large samples, it does not really matter which of the three tests we use. The choice of which of the three test statistics to use depends on the convenience in their computation. LR requires obtaining two estimators (under H_0 and H_A). If $\tilde{\theta}$ is easy to compute but $\tilde{\theta}_R$ is not, as may be the case of non linear restrictions in a linear model, then the Wald statistic becomes attractive. On the other hand, if $\tilde{\theta}_R$ is easier to compute than $\tilde{\theta}$, as is often the case of tests for autocorrelation and heteroskedasticity, then the LM test is more convenient. When the sample size is not large, choosing from the three statistics is complicated because of the fact that they may have very different finite-sample properties.

These tests satisfy the "consistency of size ε" property, and moreover, they are "locally uniformly more powerful". The first property means that, when H_0 is true, the probability of deciding erroneously (rejecting H_0) is equal or less than the fixed significance level. The second property implies that these tests have maximum power (the probability of rejecting H_0 when it is false) against alternative hypotheses such as:

$$h(\theta) = \frac{b}{\sqrt{n}}$$

with $b \neq 0$.

We shall now examine some questions related to the use of these tests. In a finite sample context, the asymptotic distribution used for the three tests is different from the exact distribution, which is unknown (except in some situations, as an MLRM under the classical assumptions), and furthermore, may not be equal in the three tests.

Moreover, once a significance level ϵ is adopted, the same critical point χ^2_ϵ is used in the three cases because they have the same asymptotic distribution. But the values the three tests take, given the same sample data, are different, so this can lead to opposite conclusions. Specifically, it has been shown that for most models the following holds:

$$W \geq LR \geq LM$$

that is to say, one test may indicate rejecting the null hypothesis whereas the other may indicate its acceptance.

2.9.5 The Three General Testing Procedures in the MLRM Context

In this subsection we try to present the implementation of the LR, W and LM tests in the framework of an MLRM under the classical assumptions, when we want to test a set of linear restrictions on β, as was established earlier :

$$\begin{aligned} H_0 &: R\beta = r \\ H_A &: R\beta \neq r \end{aligned} \tag{2.191}$$

Our aim is mainly didactic, because in the framework of the MLRM there are finite sample tests which can be applied, and the asymptotic tests here derived will be unnecessary. Nevertheless, the following derivations allows us to illustrate all the concepts we have to know in order to construct these tests, and moreover, allows us to show some relationships between them.

In order to obtain the form which the LR, W and LM adopt, when the q linear restrictions (2.191) are tested, it is convenient to remember some results that were obtained in the previous sections referring to the ML and the RML estimation. First, the set of parameters of the MLRM are denoted:

$$\theta^\top = (\beta^\top, \sigma^2)$$

The log-likelihood function and the ML estimators ($\tilde{\theta}$) are rewritten as follows:

$$\ell(\theta) = -\frac{n}{2}\ln 2\pi - \frac{n}{2}\ln\sigma^2 - \frac{(y - X\beta)^\top (y - X\beta)}{2\sigma^2} \tag{2.192}$$

$$\tilde{\beta} = (X^\top X)^{-1} X^\top y \tag{2.193}$$

$$\tilde{\sigma}^2 = \frac{\tilde{u}^\top \tilde{u}}{n} \tag{2.194}$$

Analogously, the gradient vector and the information matrix are given by:

$$g(\theta) = \begin{pmatrix} \frac{\partial \ell(\theta)}{\partial \beta} \\ \frac{\partial \ell(\theta)}{\partial \sigma^2} \end{pmatrix} = \begin{pmatrix} \frac{1}{\sigma^2}(X^\top y - X^\top X\beta) \\ -\frac{n}{2\sigma^2} + \frac{u^\top u}{2\sigma^4} \end{pmatrix} \tag{2.195}$$

$$I_n(\theta) = \begin{pmatrix} \frac{X^\top X}{\sigma^2} & 0 \\ 0 & \frac{n}{2\sigma^4} \end{pmatrix} \tag{2.196}$$

$$[I_n(\theta)]^{-1} = \begin{pmatrix} \sigma^2 (X^\top X)^{-1} & 0 \\ 0 & \frac{2\sigma^4}{n} \end{pmatrix} \tag{2.197}$$

In order to obtain the restricted maximum likelihood estimators (RML), the Lagrange function is expressed as:

$$\Im = \ell(\theta) + 2\lambda^\top(R\beta - r) \tag{2.198}$$

The first-order condition of optimization

$$\frac{\partial \Im}{\partial \beta} = 0; \quad \frac{\partial \Im}{\partial \sigma^2} = 0; \quad \frac{\partial \Im}{\partial \lambda} = 0$$

leads to the obtainment of the RML estimators included in $\tilde{\theta}_R$:

$$\tilde{\beta}_R = \tilde{\beta} + (X^\top X)^{-1}R^\top[R(X^\top X)^{-1}R^\top]^{-1}(r - R\tilde{\beta}) \tag{2.199}$$

$$\tilde{\sigma}_R^2 = \frac{\tilde{u}_R^\top \tilde{u}_R}{n} \tag{2.200}$$

together with the estimated Lagrange multiplier vector:

$$\tilde{\lambda} = \frac{[R(X^\top X)^{-1}R^\top]^{-1}(r - R\tilde{\beta})}{\tilde{\sigma}_R^2} \tag{2.201}$$

To obtain the form of the LR test in the MLRM, given its general expression

$$LR = 2(\ell(\tilde{\theta}) - \ell(\tilde{\theta}_R))$$

we substitute the parameters of expression (2.192) for the ML and RML estimators, obtaining $\ell(\tilde{\theta})$ and $\ell(\tilde{\theta}_R)$, respectively:

$$\ell(\tilde{\theta}) = -\frac{n}{2}\ln 2\pi - \frac{n}{2}\ln\tilde{\sigma}^2 - \frac{(y - X\tilde{\beta})^\top(y - X\tilde{\beta})}{2\tilde{\sigma}^2} =$$

$$-\frac{n}{2}\ln 2\pi - \frac{n}{2}\ln\tilde{\sigma}^2 - \frac{\tilde{u}^\top\tilde{u}}{2\tilde{\sigma}^2} = -\frac{n}{2}\ln 2\pi - \frac{n}{2}\ln\tilde{\sigma}^2 - \frac{n}{2} \tag{2.202}$$

$$\ell(\tilde{\theta}_R) = -\frac{n}{2}\ln 2\pi - \frac{n}{2}\ln\tilde{\sigma}_R^2 - \frac{(y - X\tilde{\beta}_R)^\top(y - X\tilde{\beta}_R)}{2\tilde{\sigma}_R^2} =$$

$$-\frac{n}{2}\ln 2\pi - \frac{n}{2}\ln\tilde{\sigma}_R^2 - \frac{\tilde{u}_R^\top\tilde{u}_R}{2\tilde{\sigma}_R^2} = -\frac{n}{2}\ln 2\pi - \frac{n}{2}\ln\tilde{\sigma}_R^2 - \frac{n}{2} \tag{2.203}$$

Note that, in order to obtain the last terms of (2.202) and (2.203), the sums of squared residuals $\tilde{u}^\top\tilde{u}$ and $\tilde{u}_R^\top\tilde{u}_R$ are written as a function of $\tilde{\sigma}^2$ and $\tilde{\sigma}_R^2$ respectively, by taking their corresponding expressions (2.194) and (2.200).

We now substitute the two last expressions in the general form of the LR test, to obtain:

$$LR = 2\left[-\frac{n}{2}\ln\tilde{\sigma}^2 + \frac{n}{2}\ln\tilde{\sigma}_R^2\right] = n\ln\frac{\tilde{\sigma}_R^2}{\tilde{\sigma}^2} \tag{2.204}$$

Thus, (2.204) is the expression of the LR statistic which is used to test linear hypothesis in an MLRM under classical assumptions.

In order to derive the form of the Wald test in this context, we remember the general expression of this test which is presented in (2.184):

$$W_n = (h(\tilde{\theta}))^\top [H_{\tilde{\theta}}^\top (I_n(\tilde{\theta}))^{-1} H_{\tilde{\theta}}]^{-1} h(\tilde{\theta})$$

The elements of the last expression in the context of the MLRM are:

$$h(\theta) = R\beta - r \tag{2.205}$$

$$H_\theta = \begin{pmatrix} \frac{\partial h(\theta)}{\partial \beta} \\ \frac{\partial h(\theta)}{\partial \sigma^2} \end{pmatrix} = \begin{pmatrix} R \\ 0 \end{pmatrix} \tag{2.206}$$

with H_θ being a $(k+1) \times q$ matrix.

Then, from (2.197) and (2.206) we get:

$$H_\theta^\top [I_n(\theta)]^{-1} H_\theta = \sigma^2 R(X^\top X)^{-1} R^\top$$

Making the inverse of this matrix, and evaluating it at the ML estimators, we have:

$$[H_{\tilde{\theta}}^\top [I_n(\tilde{\theta})]^{-1} H_{\tilde{\theta}}]^{-1} = \frac{1}{\tilde{\sigma}^2}[R(X^\top X)^{-1} R^\top]^{-1}$$

Thus, in the context we have considered, the Wald statistic can be expressed as:

$$W_n = \frac{1}{\tilde{\sigma}^2}(R\tilde{\beta} - r)^\top [R(X^\top X)^{-1} R^\top]^{-1} (R\tilde{\beta} - r) \tag{2.207}$$

or equivalently, in agreement with the equality given in (2.167), it can be written:

$$W_n = \frac{\tilde{u}_R^\top \tilde{u}_R - \tilde{u}^\top \tilde{u}}{\frac{\tilde{u}^\top \tilde{u}}{n}} = n\frac{\tilde{u}_R^\top \tilde{u}_R - \tilde{u}^\top \tilde{u}}{\tilde{u}^\top \tilde{u}} = n\frac{\tilde{\sigma}_R^2 - \tilde{\sigma}^2}{\tilde{\sigma}^2} \tag{2.208}$$

(Note that the vector $(r - R\tilde{\beta})$ in (2.167) and $(R\tilde{\beta} - r)$ in (2.207) leads to the same quadratic form).

With respect to the LM test, it must be remembered that it had two alternative forms, and both will be considered in this illustration.

If we focus on the first one, which was written as:

$$LM_n = \tilde{\lambda}^\top H_{\tilde{\theta}_R}^\top [I_n(\tilde{\theta}_R)]^{-1} H_{\tilde{\theta}_R} \tilde{\lambda}$$

their elements were previously defined, so we can write:

$$H_{\tilde{\theta}_R}^\top [I_n(\tilde{\theta}_R)]^{-1} H_{\tilde{\theta}_R} = \tilde{\sigma}_R^2 R(X^\top X)^{-1} R^\top \tag{2.209}$$

Thus, the LM statistic in an MLRM under classical assumptions gives:

$$LM_n = \tilde{\lambda}^\top H_{\tilde{\theta}_R}^\top [I_n(\tilde{\theta}_R)]^{-1} H_{\tilde{\theta}_R} \tilde{\lambda} =$$

$$\frac{(r - R\tilde{\beta})^\top [R(X^\top X)^{-1} R^\top]^{-1}}{\tilde{\sigma}_R^2} \tilde{\sigma}_R^2 R(X^\top X)^{-1} R^\top \frac{[R(X^\top X)^{-1} R^\top]^{-1}(r - R\tilde{\beta})}{\tilde{\sigma}_R^2} =$$

$$\frac{1}{\tilde{\sigma}_R^2}(r - R\tilde{\beta})^\top [R(X^\top X)^{-1} R^\top]^{-1}(r - R\tilde{\beta}) \tag{2.210}$$

Again, we consider the equality (2.167), so we obtain:

$$LM_n = \frac{\tilde{u}_R^\top \tilde{u}_R - \tilde{u}^\top \tilde{u}}{\frac{\tilde{u}_R^\top \tilde{u}_R}{n}} = n\frac{\tilde{u}_R^\top \tilde{u}_R - \tilde{u}^\top \tilde{u}}{\tilde{u}_R^\top \tilde{u}_R} = n\frac{\tilde{\sigma}_R^2 - \tilde{\sigma}^2}{\tilde{\sigma}_R^2} \tag{2.211}$$

Now, we shall consider the second form of the LM test, which is given by:

$$LM = g(\tilde{\theta}_R)^\top [I_n(\tilde{\theta}_R)]^{-1} g(\tilde{\theta}_R)$$

According to the expressions (2.195) and (2.197), evaluated at the RML estimator vector, we have:

$$g(\tilde{\theta}_R) = \begin{pmatrix} \frac{1}{\tilde{\sigma}_R^2}(X^\top y - X^\top X\tilde{\beta}_R) \\ -\frac{n}{2\tilde{\sigma}_R^2} + \frac{\tilde{u}_R^\top \tilde{u}_R}{2\tilde{\sigma}_R^4} \end{pmatrix} = \begin{pmatrix} \frac{1}{\tilde{\sigma}_R^2} X^\top \tilde{u}_R \\ 0 \end{pmatrix}$$

and consequently,

$$LM_n = \begin{pmatrix} \frac{1}{\tilde{\sigma}_R^2}\tilde{u}_R^\top X & 0 \end{pmatrix} \begin{pmatrix} \tilde{\sigma}_R^2 (X^\top X)^{-1} & 0 \\ 0 & \frac{2\tilde{\sigma}_R^4}{n} \end{pmatrix} \begin{pmatrix} \frac{1}{\tilde{\sigma}_R^2} X^\top \tilde{u}_R \\ 0 \end{pmatrix}$$

$$= \frac{1}{\tilde{\sigma}_R^2} \tilde{u}_R^\top X(X^\top X)^{-1} X^\top \tilde{u}_R \tag{2.212}$$

It the restricted residual vector given in (2.162) is substituted in (2.212), one leads to the same expression (2.211) after some calculations.

Having presented the corresponding expressions of the three statistics for testing linear restrictions, it is convenient to derive a last result which consists in obtaining the each statistic as a function of the general F test given in (2.139) or (2.140). If we take this last expression, we have that:

$$F = \frac{\frac{\tilde{u}_R^\top \tilde{u}_R - \tilde{u}^\top \tilde{u}}{q}}{\frac{\tilde{u}^\top \tilde{u}}{n-k}} = \frac{n}{q\hat{\sigma}^2}(\tilde{\sigma}_R^2 - \tilde{\sigma}^2) \tag{2.213}$$

According to the relationship between $\tilde{\sigma}^2$ and $\hat{\sigma}^2$, given by:

$$\hat{\sigma}^2 = \frac{n\tilde{\sigma}^2}{n-k}$$

it is straightforward that

$$F = \frac{n-k}{q} \frac{(\tilde{\sigma}_R^2 - \tilde{\sigma}^2)}{\tilde{\sigma}^2} \tag{2.214}$$

From this last result, we have:

$$\frac{(\tilde{\sigma}_R^2 - \tilde{\sigma}^2)}{\tilde{\sigma}^2} = \frac{Fq}{n-k} \Rightarrow \frac{\tilde{\sigma}_R^2}{\tilde{\sigma}^2} = 1 + \frac{Fq}{n-k} \tag{2.215}$$

Expression (2.215) is substituted in (2.204), (2.208) and (2.211), in order to obtain LR, W and LM tests as functions of F. The corresponding expressions are:

$$LR = n \ln(1 + \frac{Fq}{n-k}) \tag{2.216}$$

$$W = \frac{nqF}{n-k} \tag{2.217}$$

$$LM = \frac{nq}{(n-k)F^{-1} + q} \tag{2.218}$$

The set of results (2.216) to (2.218) allows us to understand some arguments mentioned in the previous subsection. Specifically, in the context of an MLRM under the classical assumptions, it is possible to obtain the exact distribution of each statistic, by means of their relationship with the F statistic. Moreover, we can see that such exact distributions are not the same as their corresponding asymptotic distributions, and furthermore the three statistics are different in the finite sample framework. This fact can lead to obtain opposite conclusions from their decision rules, because, as Berndt, and Savin (1977) show, it is satisfied $W \geq LR \geq LM$.

2.9.6 Example

With the aim of testing the same restriction as in previous sections, in the quantlet `XEGmlrm07.xpl` we calculate the three asymptotic tests LR, W and LM. Note that the RML and ML estimation of β and σ^2, were obtained in the previous quantlet, `XEGmlrm06`.

`XEGmlrm07.xpl`

The p-values associated with the LR, W and LM statistics show that the null hypothesis is rejected in all the cases.

2.10 Dummy Variables

Up to now, we have carried out the study of the MLRM on the basis of a set of variables (regressors and the endogenous variable) that are quantitative, i.e. which adopt real continuous values. However, the MLRM can be applied in a wider framework which allows us to include as regressors non-quantitative factors such as time effects, space effects, qualitative variables or quantitative grouped variables. In order to include these factors in an MLRM, the so-called dummy variables are defined. These variables will be included in the X matrix of regressors, and they can be thought of as artificial variables which have the aim of representing the non quantitative factors. To understand what dummy variables mean, we will consider some common situations which require including this class of factors in such a way that it will be necessary to use dummy variables.

- Sometimes the researcher can suspect that a given behaviour relation varies from one period to another. For example, it can be expected that the consumption function in war time has a lower value than that in peace time. Analogously, if we have dealt with quarterly or monthly data we may expect some variations between the seasons. To analyse how war time, or a given season, affect the corresponding endogenous variable, they are considered as time effects which can not be included in the model by means of quantitative variables but require using dummy variables.

- In several cases, researchers can expect some changes in an economic function between different geographic areas, due to the different economic structures of these places. So, these non-quantitative space effects are represented by means of dummy variables.
- Some qualitative variables such as sex, marital status, race, etc. can be considered as important factors to explain economic behaviour, so these should be included in the systematic component of the MLRM. These qualitative variables are represented by means of dummy variables.
- In some frameworks we try to study certain behaviour relations on the basis of microeconomic data. In some of these cases constructing intervals by grouping data could be interesting. For this, we also make use of dummy variables.

To sum up, we can define dummy variables as those which are constructed by researchers in order to include non-quantitative factors in a regression model. These factors can distinguish two o more categories, in such a way that each dummy variables takes one value for the category we consider, and zero value for the rest of categories. In other words, what we mean is that a sample can be divided into two or more partitions in which some or all of the coefficients may differ.

2.10.1 Models with Changes in the Intercept

Suppose the factors reflected by means of dummy variables affect only the intercept of the relation. In this case, these dummy variables are included in "additive" form, that is to say, as another regressor together with its corresponding coefficient. Some examples of this situation include the following:

Example 1. Time change in the intercept. We want to explain the consumption behaviour in a country during a time period, which includes some war time. It is thought of that the autonomous consumption in war periods is lower that that in peace periods. Additionally, we assume that the propensity to consume is the same. In other words, what we want to reflect is a possible non stability of the intercept during the sample period.

Example 2. Qualitative variables as explanatory factors of the model. Suppose we want to analyze the behaviour of the wages of a set of workers, and it is suspected that, independently of other quantitative factors, the variable sex can be considered as another explanatory factor.

In the above examples it is possible to specify and estimate a different model for every category. That is to say, in example 1 we could specify one model for a war period, and another for a peace period. Analogously, in example 2 we could specify one model for men and another for women. Alternatively, it is possible to specify one only model, by including dummy variables, in such a way that the behaviour of the endogenous variable for each category is differentiated. In this case we use all the sample information, so that the estimation of the parameters is more efficient.

When a regression model is specified, the inclusion of the non quantitative factor is carried out by defining dummy variables. If we suppose that the non quantitative factor has only two categories, we can represent them by means of one only dummy variable:

$$d_i = \begin{matrix} 1 & \forall i \in category1 \\ 0 & \forall i \in category2 \end{matrix}$$

with $(i = 1, 2, \ldots, n)$, where the assignation of zero or one to each category is usually arbitrary.

In general, if we consider a model with $k-1$ quantitative explanatory variables and a non-quantitative factor which distinguishes two categories, the corresponding specification could be:

$$y_i = \beta_1 + \beta_2 x_{2i} + \ldots + \beta_k x_{ki} + \beta_{k+1} d_i + u_i \quad (i = 1, 2, \ldots, n) \tag{2.219}$$

The inclusion of the term $\beta_{k+1} d_i$ allows us to differentiate the intercept term in the two categories or to consider a qualitative factor as a relevant variable. To see this, note that if all the usual regression assumptions hold for (2.219) then:

$$\begin{aligned} \mathrm{E}(y_i|d_i = 1) &= (\beta_1 + \beta_{k+1}) + +\beta_2 x_{2i} + \ldots + \beta_k x_{ki} \\ \mathrm{E}(y_i|d_i = 0) &= \beta_1 + \beta_2 x_{2i} + \ldots + \beta_k x_{ki} \end{aligned} \tag{2.220}$$

Thus, for the first category the intercept is $(\beta_1 + \beta_{k+1})$ rather than β_1, and the parameter β_{k+1} represents the difference between the intercept values in the two categories. In the framework of Example 2, result (2.220) allows us to see that the coefficient of the dummy variable represents the impact on the expected value of y of an observation which is being in the included group (first category) rather than the excluded group (second category), maintaining all the other regressors constant.

Once we have estimated the parameter vector of the model by OLS or ML, we can test several hypotheses about the significance of such parameters. Specifically, the most interesting tests are the following:

- Testing the statistical significance of the intercept corresponding to the first category:
$$H_0 : \beta_1 + \beta_{k+1} = 0$$
$$H_A : \beta_1 + \beta_{k+1} \neq 0$$
To solve this test, we can use the general F-statistic.

- Testing the statistical significance of the intercept corresponding to the second category:
$$H_0 : \beta_1 = 0$$
$$H_A : \beta_1 \neq 0$$

- Testing whether there is a statistically significant difference between the intercept of the two categories. This can be also thought of as testing the stability of the intercept. Alternatively, this test can be thought of as testing the statistical significance of the qualitative variable under consideration.
$$H_0 : \beta_{k+1} = 0$$
$$H_A : \beta_{k+1} \neq 0$$
We must note that accepting this null hypothesis in Example 1 implies concluding the stability of the intercept.

The last two tests can be solved by using a t-ratio statistic.

Alternatively, in the previous examples we could specify the model by defining two dummy variables as follows:

$$d_{1i} = \begin{matrix} 1 & \forall i \in category1 \\ 0 & \forall i \in category2 \end{matrix}$$

$$d_{2i} = \begin{array}{ll} 1 & \forall i \in category2 \\ 0 & \forall i \in category1 \end{array}$$

In this case, the specified model should be:

$$y_i = \beta_1 + \beta_2 x_{2i} + \ldots + \beta_k x_{ki} + \beta_{k+1} d_{1i} + \beta_{k+2} d_{2i} + u_i \quad (i = 1, 2, \ldots, n) \tag{2.221}$$

and analogously to (2.220) we have:

$$\begin{array}{r} \mathrm{E}(y_i|d_{1i} = 1, d_{2i} = 0) = (\beta_1 + \beta_{k+1}) + +\beta_2 x_{2i} + \ldots + \beta_k x_{ki} \\ \mathrm{E}(y_i|d_{1i} = 0, d_{2i} = 1) = (\beta_1 + \beta_{k+2}) + \beta_2 x_{2i} + \ldots + \beta_k x_{ki} \end{array} \tag{2.222}$$

which allows us to differentiate the effect of the intercept in the two categories, so we could think that (2.221) is also a correct specification.

However, model (2.221) leads us to the so-called "dummy variable trap". This term means that, if the model to estimate is (2.221), then matrix X will be:

$$X = \begin{pmatrix} 1 & x_{21} & \ldots & x_{k1} & 0 & 1 \\ 1 & x_{22} & \ldots & x_{k2} & 0 & 1 \\ 1 & x_{23} & \ldots & x_{k3} & 1 & 0 \\ 1 & x_{24} & \ldots & x_{k4} & 1 & 0 \\ 1 & x_{25} & \ldots & x_{k5} & 1 & 0 \\ \vdots & \vdots & \vdots & \vdots & \vdots & \vdots \\ 1 & x_{2n} & \ldots & x_{kn} & 0 & 1 \end{pmatrix} = \begin{pmatrix} x_1 & x_2 & \ldots & x_k & x_{k+1} & x_{k+2} \end{pmatrix} \tag{2.223}$$

where the last two columns reflect the sample observations of the dummy variables. Given this X matrix, it follows that:

$$x_{1i} = x_{(k+1)i} + x_{(k+2)i} \quad \forall i = 1, 2, \ldots, n$$

That is to say, the observations of the first column in X are an exact linear combination of those of the two last columns. This means that model (2.221) does not satisfy the full rank property, or in other words, there is perfect multicollinearity. Given that the rank of X is less than $k+2$, matrix $X^{\top}X$ is nonsingular, so its inverse does not exist and so $\hat{\beta}$ can not be obtained. This fact allows us to conclude that, for the examples previously defined, the correct specification is (2.219), which includes only one dummy variable.

Nevertheless, if the model is specified without intercept, there should not be any problem to estimate it(given the corresponding matrix X, without the column of ones).

Including intercept is usually advised in order to assure that certain properties are satisfied and the meaning of some measures is maintained. Thus, if we specify a model with intercept and a non-quantitative factor which has m categories, including $m-1$ dummy variables is enough. Although it is the general rule, we can consider the possibility of not including intercept (remember that some results will be not satisfied) and then including m categories.

Having solved the question about the number of dummy variables to include, we now generalize the way of proceeding for the two following situations:

a) To represent a factor which has more that two categories. This is the case of the so-called seasonality models.

b) To represent several non-quantitative factors which have different number of categories.

The first case allows us, among other situations, to use dummy variables to deal with seasonality, that is to say, to allow the regression to have some heterogeneity between seasons (quarters or months). In this case, given that the non quantitative factor distinguishes four categories for quarters (12 for months), and considering that the model has an intercept, we define three dummy variables (11 for months) as follows:

$$d_{ji} = \begin{matrix} 1 & \forall i \in quarter(month)j \\ 0 & otherwise \end{matrix}$$

With respect to the second generalization (b)), suppose a model in which we want to consider the sex variable (two categories) and the race variable (three categories). Analogously to the previous case, we have to define a dummy variable for sex, and two dummies for race.

2.10.2 Models with Changes in some Slope Parameters

We now consider the situation where the non-quantitative factors affect one or more coefficients of the explanatory variables (slopes). In this situation, the dummy variables are included in "multiplicative" or "interactive" mode, that is to say, multiplied by the corresponding regressor. Some examples of this situation are the following:

Example 3. Time varying of a slope. Taking the situation of Example 1, now it is supposed that the phenomenon war/peace affects only the propensity to consume. In this sense, we try to analyze whether the coefficient of a given explanatory variable is homogeneous during the sample period.

Example 4. Taking the case of Example 2, we now try to analyze the behaviour of the wages of a set of workers. This wage depends, together with other quantitative factors, on the years of experience, and these are considered as not independent of sex, that is to say, there is an "interaction effect" between both variables.

Again, these situations could be specified through two models: one model for the war period and another for the peace period in Example 3, and analogously, a model for men and another for women in Example 4. Alternatively, we can specify one unique model which includes dummy variables, allowing it a more efficient estimation of the parameters.

The general regression model which allows an interaction effect between a non quantitative factor (represented by means of a dummy variable d_i) and a given quantitative variable (suppose x_2), is written as:

$$y_i = \beta_1 + \beta_2 x_{2i} + \ldots + \beta_k x_{ki} + \beta_{k+1}(d_i x_{2i}) + u_i \quad \forall i = 1, 2, \ldots, n. \tag{2.224}$$

where it is supposed that the non-quantitative factor has only two categories. In order to prove that model (2.224) adequately reflects the situations of the previous examples, we calculate:

$$\begin{aligned} \mathrm{E}(y_i|d_i = 1) &= \beta_1 + (\beta_2 + \beta_{k+1})x_{2i} + \ldots + \beta_k x_{ki} \\ \mathrm{E}(y_i|d_i = 0) &= \beta_1 + \beta_2 x_{2i} + \ldots + \beta_k x_{ki} \end{aligned} \tag{2.225}$$

We suppose that in Example 3 the income variable is x_2, so the propensity to consume is given by its corresponding coefficient. For the first category this slope or propensity is $(\beta_2 + \beta_{k+1})$ rather than β_2, and the parameter β_{k+1} reflects the difference between the slope values in the two categories (war/peace). For Example 4, if we consider that x_2 is the variable years of experience, it is obvious that specification (2.224) adequately reflects the interaction effect mentioned earlier .

Again, once the model has been estimated, the most interesting testing hypotheses we can carry out are the following:

- Testing the statistical significance of the coefficient of x_2 in the first category.

$$H_0 : \beta_2 + \beta_{k+1} = 0$$
$$H_A : \beta_2 + \beta_{k+1} \neq 0$$

We use a F-statistic to test this hypothesis.

- Testing the statistical significance of the coefficient of x_2 in the second category.

$$H_0 : \beta_2 = 0$$
$$H_A : \beta_2 \neq 0$$

- Testing whether there are non-significant differences between the coefficients of x_2 for the two categories. In other words, testing the statistical significance of the interaction effect defined earlier.

$$H_0 : \beta_{k+1} = 0$$
$$H_A : \beta_{k+1} \neq 0$$

Similarly to the previous subsection, these last two hypotheses can be tested by using a t-ratio statistic.

2.10.3 Models with Changes in all the Coefficients

In this case, we try to analyze jointly each of the situations which have been considered separately in previous subsections. Thus, we assume that the non quantitative factor represented by dummy variables affects both the intercept and all the coefficients of the regressors. Obviously, this is the more general situation, which contains particularly the influence of a non-quantitative factor on a subset of coefficients.

In order to reflect the effect of the non-quantitative factor on the intercept, the dummy variables should be included in additive form, while they should be included in multiplicative form to reflect the effect on the slopes.

Thus, the general specification, under the assumption of having a non quantitative factor which distinguishes only two categories, is given by:

$$y_i = \beta_1 + \beta_2 x_{2i} + \ldots + \beta_k x_{ki} + \beta_{k+1} d_i + \beta_{k+2}(d_i x_{2i}) + \ldots + \beta_{k+k}(d_i x_{ki}) + u_i \tag{2.226}$$

From (2.226) we obtain the expected value of the endogenous variable conditioned to each of the categories considered, with the aim of verifying that the specification adequately reflects our objective:

$$
\begin{aligned}
\mathrm{E}(y_i|d_i = 1) &= (\beta_1 + \beta_{k+1}) + (\beta_2 + \beta_{k+2})x_{2i} + \ldots + (\beta_k + \beta_{k+k})x_{ki} \\
\mathrm{E}(y_i|d_i = 0) &= \beta_1 + \beta_2 x_{2i} + \ldots + \beta_k x_{ki}
\end{aligned}
\tag{2.227}
$$

According to (2.227), $(\beta_1 + \beta_{k+1})$ and β_1 denote, respectively, the constant terms for the first and second categories, while $(\beta_j + \beta_{k+j})$ and β_j $(j = 2, 3, \ldots, k)$ denote the slopes of x_j $(j = 2, 3, \ldots, k)$ for the first and second categories. By contrast to previous cases, when the non-quantitative factor affects all the coefficients of the model, there is no gain of efficiency of specifying (2.226) compared to considering one model for each category. This is due, as Goldberger (1964) argues to the fact that the normal equations of the estimation of (2.226) are constituted by two blocks of independent equations: that corresponding to the observations of the first category, and those of the second category. However, the t and F-statistics and R^2 of the two ways of dealing with the information are not equivalent.

Having estimated (2.226), the most interesting hypotheses testing we can carry out are the following:

- Testing the significance of the slope of x_j (j=2,3,...,k) corresponding to the first category:

  $$
  \begin{aligned}
  H_0 &: \beta_j + \beta_{k+j} = 0 \\
  H_A &: \beta_j + \beta_{k+j} \neq 0
  \end{aligned}
  $$

  We use the general F-statistic to solve this test.

- Testing the significance of the slope of x_j (j=2,3,...,k) corresponding to the second category:

  $$
  \begin{aligned}
  H_0 &: \beta_j = 0 \\
  H_A &: \beta_j \neq 0
  \end{aligned}
  $$

- Testing whether there is a non-significant difference between the coefficient of x_j of the two categories:

  $$
  \begin{aligned}
  H_0 &: \beta_{k+j} = 0 \\
  H_A &: \beta_{k+j} \neq 0
  \end{aligned}
  $$

- Testing whether there is a non-significant difference between the intercept of both categories:

  $$
  \begin{aligned}
  H_0 &: \beta_{k+1} = 0 \\
  H_A &: \beta_{k+1} \neq 0
  \end{aligned}
  $$

To solve these tests, we will use the t-ratio statistic.

- Testing the joint hypothesis that the endogenous variable has no different behaviour between the two categories:

$$H_0 : \beta_{k+1} = \beta_{k+2} = \ldots = \beta_{k+k} = 0$$
$$H_A : noH_0$$

  This test is solved by using a general F statistic. It can also be denoted as a test of stability, given that accepting H_0 leads us to conclude that all the coefficients of the model are invariant during the sample period.

Thus, dummy variables provide a method of verifying one of the classical assumptions of the MLRM: that referring to the stability of the coefficients. Nevertheless, note that this method requires knowing (or supposing) the point (observation) of possible change in the behaviour of the model.

2.10.4 Example

Considering the same example than in previous sections, we now want to illustrate the way of testing structural change, that is to say, testing the stability of the coefficients. For this end, we suppose that a possible change in the consumption behavior can be produced in 1986, so it is thought of that the incorporation of Spain to the European Union can affect the coefficients. We are interested in testing the following cases: a) the change affects the autonomous consumption; b) the change affects the slope of the export variable, and c) the change affects all the model. To carry out this test, we begin by defining the dummy variable which allows us to differentiate the periods before and after 1986, that is to say:

$$d_i = \begin{cases} 1 & \text{i=1986,...,1997} \\ 0 & \text{otherwise.} \end{cases}$$

Thus, we have to estimate the following three regression models:

a. $y_i = \beta_1 + \beta_2 x_{2i} + \beta_3 x_{3i} + \beta_4 d_i + u_i$

b. $y_i = \beta_1 + \beta_2 x_{2i} + \beta_3 x_{3i} + \beta_4 (x_{2i} d_i) + u_i$

c. $y_i = \beta_1 + \beta_2 x_{2i} + \beta_3 x_{3i} + \beta_4 d_i + \beta_5 (x_{2i} d_i) + \beta_6 (x_{3i} d_i) + u_i$

In regression a) we test structural change in the intercept, that is to say, $H_0 : \beta_4 = 0$. The second regression allows us to test structural change which affects the coefficient of the export variable by means of the same hypothesis as that of the first regression. Both hypotheses are tested using the t-ratio statistic. The third regression allows us to test structural change which affects all the model, that is to say, $H_0 : \beta_4 = \beta_5 = \beta_6 = 0$, by means of the general F statistic.

The quantlet `XEGmlrm08.xpl` allows to estimate these regression models and test the corresponding hypotheses. Furthermore, the corresponding output includes the results of the four regressions

`XEGmlrm08.xpl`

The first regression is used for calculating the restricted residual sum of squares, given that including the restriction $\beta_4 = \beta_5 = \beta_6 = 0$ in regression c), we have the first regression of the output, that is to say $y_i = \beta_1 + \beta_2 x_{2i} + \beta_3 x_{3i} + u_i$. Observing the value of the F statistic (5.0059) and its corresponding p-value, we conclude rejection the null hypotheses. This conclusion means that there is structural change which affects all the model. Note that the t-ratio of β_4 in regressions a) and b) leads to reject the null hypothesis $H_0 : \beta_4 = 0$, that is to say, each parameter is not stable.

2.11 Forecasting

A possible use of an MLRM consists of obtaining predictions for the endogenous variable when the set of regressors adopt a given value. That is to say, an MLRM can only provide predictions conditioned to the value of the regressors.

Prediction must be thought of as the final step of econometric methodology. Thus, in order to minimize the possible errors in the predictions, we must have evidence in favour of the stability of the model during the sample period, and also of the accuracy of the estimated coefficients.

The first of these two aspects refers to the maintenance of the classical assumption of coefficient stability, which can be verified (among other approaches) by means of dummy variables, as we saw in the previous sections. Thus, if we have evidence in favour of the stability of the model during the sample period, we will maintain this evidence for the out-sample (prediction) period. Nevertheless, we are not sure that this stability holds in this out-sample period.

The second aspect refers to the maintenance of the classical assumptions in every specific application. We have proved in previous sections of this chapter that, under the classical assumptions, the OLS and ML estimators of the coefficients satisfy desirable properties in both finite samples and in the asymptotic framework. Thus, the violation of one or more "ideal conditions" in an empirical application can affect the properties of the estimators, and then, it can be the cause of some errors in the prediction.

Similarly to the estimation stage, we can obtain two class of predictions: point prediction and interval prediction.

2.11.1 Point Prediction

We assume the data set is divided into subsets of size n (the sample size we have used to estimate) and n_p (the out-sample period), where $n_p \geq 1$, but is small relative to n. The idea consists of using the fitted model to generate predictions of y_p from X_p. The general expression of an MLRM is given by:

$$y_i = x_i^\top \beta + u_i \quad (i = 1, \dots, n) \tag{2.228}$$

where $x_i^\top$ represents the row vector of the ith observation of every regressor, including the intercept. We also consider that classical assumptions are satisfied.

If we assume that model (2.228) is stable, the relation for the out-sample period is given by:

$$y_p = x_p^\top \beta + u_p \quad (p = n+1, \dots, n_p) \tag{2.229}$$

where $\mathrm{E}(u_p) = 0$, $var(u_p) = \sigma^2$ and $cov(u_p u_i) = 0$ $(\forall i = 1, \dots, n)$ are satisfied.

In the following, we consider $p = n + 1$, i.e. we are interested in the prediction one period ahead; nevertheless, this can be easily generalized.

First, we focus on the prediction of the mean value of y_p which, from (2.229) and under classical assumptions, is:

$$\mathrm{E}(y_p) = x_p^\top \beta$$

Using the Gauss-Markov theorem, it follows that

$$\hat{y}_p = x_p^\top \hat{\beta} \tag{2.230}$$

is the best linear unbiased predictor of $\mathrm{E}(y_p)$. We can intuitively understand this result, given that $\mathrm{E}(y_p)$ is an unknown parameter $(x_p^\top \beta)$. Thus, if we substitute β for $\hat{\beta}$, which is BLUE, we obtain the best predictor of $\mathrm{E}(y_p)$. In other words, among the class of linear and unbiased predictors, the OLS predictor has minimum variance. This variance is obtained as:

$$var(\hat{y}_p) = \mathrm{E}[(\hat{y}_p - \mathrm{E}(\hat{y}_p))^2] = \mathrm{E}[(\hat{y}_p - \mathrm{E}(\hat{y}_p))(\hat{y}_p - \mathrm{E}(\hat{y}_p))^\top] =$$

$$\mathrm{E}[(x_p^\top \hat{\beta} - x_p^\top \beta)(x_p^\top \hat{\beta} - x_p^\top \beta)^\top] = \mathrm{E}[x_p^\top (\hat{\beta} - \beta)(\hat{\beta} - \beta)^\top x_p] =$$

$$x_p^\top \mathrm{E}[(\hat{\beta} - \beta)(\hat{\beta} - \beta)^\top] x_p = \sigma^2 x_p^\top (X^\top X)^{-1} x_p \qquad (2.231)$$

where we have used result (2.56) about the variance-covariance matrix of $\hat{\beta}$.

If we are interested in the prediction for y_p itself, the best linear unbiased predictor is still $\hat{y}_p$. This result can be easily explained because the only difference between y_p and $\mathrm{E}(y_p)$ is the error term u_p. So, taking into account that the best prediction of u_p is zero (given that the best prediction of a random variable is its expectation when we have no sample information), we derive that the OLS predictor $\hat{y}_p$ is still optimum for predicting y_p.

The prediction error (e_p) is defined as the difference between the variable we want to predict and the prediction. Thus, we have:

$$e_p = y_p - \hat{y}_p = x_p^\top \beta + u_p - x_p^\top \hat{\beta} = u_p - x_p^\top (\hat{\beta} - \beta) \qquad (2.232)$$

in such a way that its expected value is zero, and its variance is:

$$var(e_p) = \mathrm{E}(e_p - \mathrm{E}(e_p))^2 = \mathrm{E}(e_p)^2 = \mathrm{E}[u_p - x_p^\top (\hat{\beta} - \beta)]^2 =$$

$$\mathrm{E}[u_p^2 + x_p^\top (\hat{\beta} - \beta)(\hat{\beta} - \beta)^\top x_p - 2x_p^\top (\hat{\beta} - \beta) u_p] =$$

$$\mathrm{E}[u_p^2 + x_p^\top (\hat{\beta} - \beta)(\hat{\beta} - \beta)^\top x_p - 2x_p^\top (X^\top X)^{-1} X^\top u u_p]$$

The previous result has been obtained from (2.54) which establishes $\hat{\beta} - \beta = (X^\top X)^{-1} X^\top u$. We have also taken into account that the new disturbance u_p is not correlated with the disturbances in the sample, so the last term is null, and:

$$var(e_p) = \sigma^2 [1 + x_p^\top (X^\top X)^{-1} x_p] \qquad (2.233)$$

We can see that the variance of the prediction error adds $var(u_p)$ to the variance of the predictor given in (2.231).

2.11.2 Interval Prediction

To provide an interval prediction of $\mathrm{E}(y_p)$ or y_p, we begin by establishing the sample distributions of $\hat{y}_p$ and e_p. From (2.230) and (2.232) we can see that both $\hat{y}_p$ and e_p are linear combinations of normal random variables, so they also follow a normal distribution. Specifically:

$$\hat{y}_p \sim N[x_p^\top \beta, \sigma^2 x_p^\top (X^\top X)^{-1} x_p] \tag{2.234}$$

$$e_p \sim N[0, \sigma^2(1 + x_p^\top (X^\top X)^{-1} x_p)] \tag{2.235}$$

Similarly to the interval estimation and given that $\mathrm{E}(y_p) = x_p^\top \beta$ is an unknown parameter, we obtain:

$$\frac{\hat{y}_p - \mathrm{E}(y_p)}{\sigma \sqrt{x_p^\top (X^\top X)^{-1} x_p}} \sim N(0,1) \tag{2.236}$$

Again, we must eliminate the unknown σ^2 parameter, so from (2.125) and using the independence between the variables (2.236) and (2.125), we have:

$$\frac{\hat{y}_p - \mathrm{E}(y_p)}{\hat{\sigma} \sqrt{x_p^\top (X^\top X)^{-1} x_p}} = \frac{\hat{y}_p - \mathrm{E}(y_p)}{\hat{\sigma}_{\hat{y}_p}} \sim t_{n-k} \tag{2.237}$$

where $\hat{\sigma}_{\hat{y}_p}$ denotes the estimated standard deviation of the predictor.

Therefore, the $100(1-\epsilon)$ percent confidence interval for $\mathrm{E}(y_p)$ is given by:

$$\hat{y}_p \pm t_{\frac{\epsilon}{2}} \hat{\sigma}_{\hat{y}_p} \tag{2.238}$$

with $t_{\frac{\epsilon}{2}}$ being the critical point of the t-distribution.

Note that the statistic (2.237) or the interval prediction (2.238) allow us to carry out testing hypotheses on the value of $\mathrm{E}(y_p)$.

With respect to the interval prediction for y_p, we use (2.235) to derive:

$$\frac{e_p}{\sigma \sqrt{1 + x_p^\top (X^\top X)^{-1} x_p}} = \frac{y_p - \hat{y}_p}{\sigma \sqrt{1 + x_p^\top (X^\top X)^{-1} x_p}} \sim N(0,1) \tag{2.239}$$

and then, in order to eliminate σ^2,(2.239) is transformed to obtain:

$$\frac{y_p - \hat{y}_p}{\hat{\sigma} \sqrt{1 + x_p^\top (X^\top X)^{-1} x_p}} = \frac{y_p - \hat{y}_p}{\hat{\sigma}_{e_p}} \sim t_{n-k} \tag{2.240}$$

with $\hat{\sigma}_{e_p}$ being the standard deviation of the prediction error associated with y_p. Again, result (2.240) is based on the independence between the distributions given in (2.239) and (2.125).

Therefore, the $100(1-\epsilon)$ percent confidence interval for y_p is given by:

$$\hat{y}_p \pm t_{\frac{\epsilon}{2}} \hat{\sigma}_{e_p} \tag{2.241}$$

The statistic (2.240) or the confidence interval (2.241) lead to a test of the hypothesis that a new data point (y_p, x_p^{*t}) is generated by the same structure as that of the sample data. This test is called test for stability. We denote y_p as the real value of the endogenous variable in the period p, and x_p^{*t} as the row vector with the pth real observation of the k explanatory variables. This vector x_p^{*t} could not be the same as the vector $x_p^\top$, because the latter has been used to carry out a conditioned prediction. In other words, we want to test the model stability hypothesis at the prediction period. In this context, the t-value for this new data point is given by:

$$t = \frac{y_p - x_p^{*t}\hat{\beta}}{\hat{\sigma}\sqrt{1 + x_p^{*t}(X^\top X)^{-1}x_p^*}} \tag{2.242}$$

If there is no structural change in the out-sample period, the difference between y_p (real value) and $\hat{y}_p$ (predicted value) should not be large and so, (2.242) should tend to adopt a small value. Thus, fixing a significance level ϵ, when $|t| > t_{\frac{\epsilon}{2}}$, we can conclude that the new observation may be generated by a different structure. That is to say, the null hypothesis of structural stability can be rejected for the out-sample period.

We can generalize this test for the case of several out-sample periods. In this situation, the statistic test becomes:

$$\frac{\frac{RSS_R - RSS_u}{n_2}}{\frac{RSS_u}{n_1 - k}} \tag{2.243}$$

which follows a F-Snedecor with n_1 (the sample size) and $n_2 - k$ degrees of freedom, where n_2 is the out-sample size. In 2.243, RSS_R is the residual sum of squares from the regression based on $(n_1 + n_2)$ observations, and RSS_U is the residual sum of squares from the regression based on n_1 observations.

2.11.3 Measures of the Accuracy of Forecast

Once the prediction periods has passed, the researcher knows the true values of the dependent variable, and then, he can evaluate the goodness of the obtained predictions. With this aim, various measures have been proposed. Most of them are based on the residuals from the forecast.

- Root mean-squared error (RMSE)

$$RMSE = \sqrt{\frac{1}{n_p} \sum_{p=n+1}^{n_p} (y_p - \hat{y}_p)^2}$$

- Root mean-squared error, expressed in percentages (RMSEP)

$$RMSEP = \sqrt{\frac{1}{n_p} \sum_{p=n+1}^{n_p} (\frac{y_p - \hat{y}_p}{y_p})^2}$$

- Mean absolute error (MAE)

$$MAE = \frac{1}{n_p} \sum_{p=n+1}^{n_p} |y_p - \hat{y}_p|$$

- Theil U statistic

$$U = \sqrt{\frac{\frac{1}{n_p} \sum_{p=n+1}^{n_p} (y_p - \hat{y}_p)^2}{\frac{1}{n_p} \sum_{p=n+1}^{n_p} y_p^2}}$$

  Large values of the U statistic indicate a poor forecasting performance. Sometimes this measure is calculated in terms of the changes in y_p:

$$U_{\triangle} = \sqrt{\frac{\frac{1}{n_p} \sum_{p=n+1}^{n_p} (\triangle y_p - \triangle \hat{y}_p)^2}{\frac{1}{n_p} \sum_{p=n+1}^{n_p} (\triangle y_p)^2}}$$

  where $\triangle y_p = y_p - y_{p-1}$ and $\triangle \hat{y}_p = \hat{y}_p - y_{p-1}$ or, in percentage changes, $\triangle y_p = \frac{y_p - y_{p-1}}{y_{p-1}}$ and $\triangle \hat{y}_p = \frac{\hat{y}_p - y_{p-1}}{y_{p-1}}$.

The latter measure reflects the ability of model to track the turning points in the data.

2.11.4 Example

To carry out the forecasting of the value of the consumption for the out-sample period 1998, we need information about the value of the explanatory variables in this period. In this sense, we suppose that the values of x_2 (exports) and x_3 (M1) are those of Table 2.2.

	X2	X3
quarter 1	5403791	19290.1904
quarter 2	5924731	19827.894
quarter 3	5626585	20356.7381
quarter 4	5749398	20973.5399

Table 2.2. Assumed values for x_2 and x_3

On the basis of this information, we obtain the point and interval prediction of y and $\mathrm{E}(y)$. When the period 1998 passes, we know that the true value of y for the first, second, third and fourth quarters are 11432012, 12113995, 11813440 and 12585278. The explanatory variables adopt the values we previously supposed. This new information allows us to test the hypothesis of stability model in the out-sample period. Additionally we calculate some measures of accuracy. The following quantlet provides the corresponding results:

`XEGmlrm09.xpl`

Note that the p-value is high, and so we accept the null hypothesis of stability in the out-sample periods, for the usual significance levels. Additionally the values of RMSEP and the statistic U of Theil are low, which means a good forecasting performance.

Bibliography

Amemiya, T. (1985). *Advanced Econometrics*, Harvard University Press.

Baltagi, B.H. (1999). *Econometrics*, Springer.

Berndt, E., Hendry, D. and Savin, N.E. (1977). Conflict Among Criteria for Testing Hypotheses in the Multivariate Linear Regression Model, *Econometrica*, Vol. 45, pp. 1263–1277.

Davidson, J. (2000). *Econometric Theory*, Blackwell Publishers.

Davidson, R. and Mackinnon, G. J. (1984). Model Specification Test Based on Artificial Linear Regressions, *International Economic Review*, Vol. 25 ,pp. 485-502.

Davidson, R. and Mackinnon, G. J. (1993). *Estimation and Inference in Econometrics*, Oxford University Press.

Drhymes, P. J. (1974). *Econometrics*, Springer-Verlag.

Engle, R., Hendry, D. and Richard, J.F. (1983). Exogeneity, *Econometrica*, Vol. 51, pp. 277–304.

Fomby, T. B., Carter Hill, R. and Johnson, S. R. (1984). *Advanced Econometric Methods*, Springer-Verlag.

Goldberger, A. S. (1964). *Econometric Theory*, Wiley and Sons.

Greene, W. H. (1993). *Econometric Analysis*, Macmillan Publishing Company.

Hayashi, F. (2000). *Econometrics*, Princenton University Press.

Intriligator, M. D., Bodkin, R.G. and Hsiao, C. (1996). *Econometric Models.Techniques and Applications*, 2 edn, Prentice Hall.

Judge, G.G., Griffiths, W.E.,Carter Hill, R., Lutkepohl, H. and Lee, T. (1985). *The Theory and Practice of Econometrics*, 2 edn, Wiley and Sons.

Judge, G.G., Carter Hill, R., Griffiths, W.E., Lutkepohl, H. and Lee, T. (1988). *Introduction to the Theory and Practice of Econometrics*, 2 edn, Wiley and Sons.

Patterson, K. (2000). *An Introduction to Applied Econometrics. A Time Series Approach*, Palgrave.

Rothemberg, T. J. (1973). Efficent Estimation with A Priori Information, *Cowles Commission Monograph 23* Yale University Press.

Schmidt, P. (1976). *Econometrics*, Marcel Dekker.

Spanos, A. (1986). *Statistical Foundations of Econometric Modelling*, Cambridge University Press.

Theil, H. (1971). *Principles of Econometrics*, North Holland.

White, H. (1984). *Asymptotic Theory for Econometricians*, Academic Press.

3 Dimension Reduction and Its Applications

Pavel Čížek and Yingcun Xia

3.1 Introduction

3.1.1 Real Data Sets

This chapter is motivated by our attempt to answer pertinent questions concerning a number of real data sets, some of which are listed below.

Example 3.1.1. Consider the relationship between the levels of pollutants and weather with the total number (y_t) of daily hospital admissions for circulatory and respiratory problems. The covariates are the average levels of sulphur dioxide (x_{1t}, unit $\mu g m^{-3}$), nitrogen dioxide (x_{2t}, unit $\mu g m^{-3}$), respirable suspended particulates (x_{3t}, unit $\mu g m^{-3}$), ozone (x_{4t}, unit $\mu g m^{-3}$), temperature (x_{5t}, unit ^oC) and humidity (x_{6t}, unit %). The data set was collected daily in Hong Kong from January 1, 1994 to December 31, 1995 (Courtesy of Professor T.S. Lau). The basic question is this: Are the prevailing levels of the pollutants a cause for concern?

The relationship between y_t and $x_{1t}, x_{2t}, x_{3t}, x_{4t}, x_{5t}, x_{6t}$ is quite complicated. A naive approach may be to start with a simple linear regression model such as

$$
\begin{aligned}
y_t \quad = \quad & \underset{(20.64)}{255.45} - \underset{(0.18)}{0.55 x_{t1}} + \underset{(0.17)}{0.58 x_{2t}} + \underset{(0.13)}{0.18 x_{3t}} - \\
& - \underset{(0.11)}{0.33 x_{4t}} - \underset{(0.46)}{0.12 x_{5t}} - \underset{(0.23)}{0.16 x_{6t}}.
\end{aligned}
\tag{3.1}
$$

XEGeq1.xpl

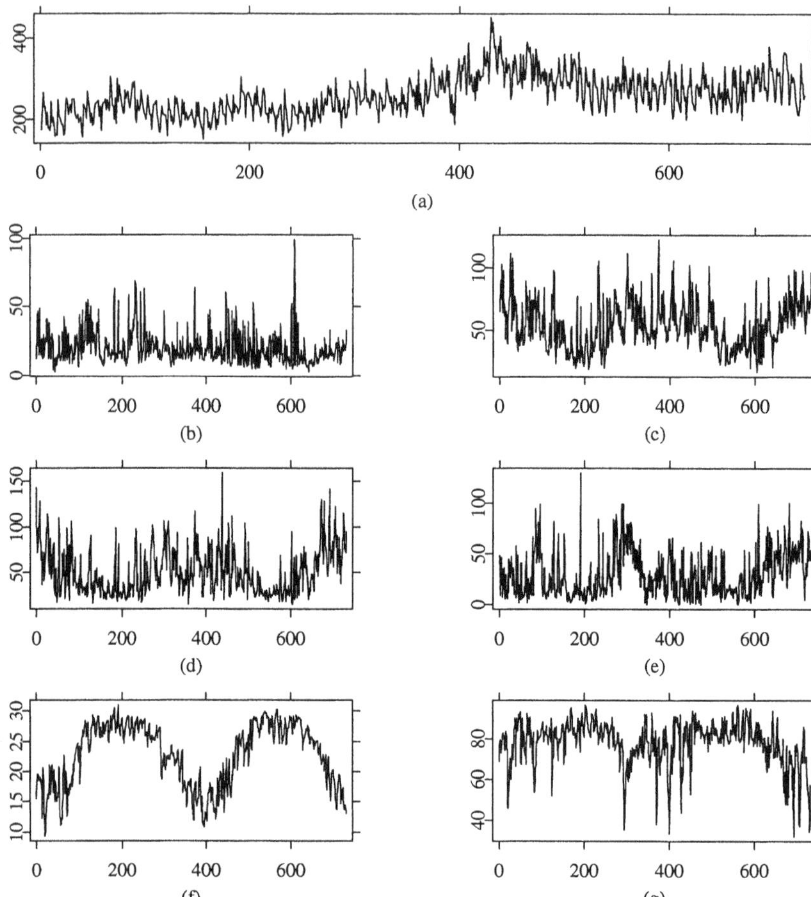

Figure 3.1. (a) Total number of daily hospital admissions for circulatory and respiratory problems. (b) the average levels of sulphur dioxide. (c) nitrogen dioxide. (d) respirable suspended particulates. (e) ozone. (f) temperature. (g) humidity.

XEGfig1.xpl

Note that the coefficients of x_{3t}, x_{5t} and x_{6t} are not significantly different from 0 (at the 5% level of significance) and the negative coefficients of x_{t1} and x_{t4} are difficult to interpret. Refinements of the above model are, of course, possible within the linear framework but it is unlikely that they will throw much light in respect of the opening question because, as we shall see, the situation is quite complex.

Example 3.1.2. We revisit the Mackenzie River Lynx data for 1821-1934. Following common practice in ecology and statistics, let y_t denote log(number recorded as trapped in year 1820+t) ($t = 1, 2, \cdots, 114$). The series is shown in Figure 1.2. It is interesting to see that the relation between y_t and y_{t-1} seems quite linear as shown in Figure 1.2(b). However, the relation between y_t and y_{t-2} shows some nonlinearity. A number of time series models have been proposed in the literature. Do they have points of contact with one another?

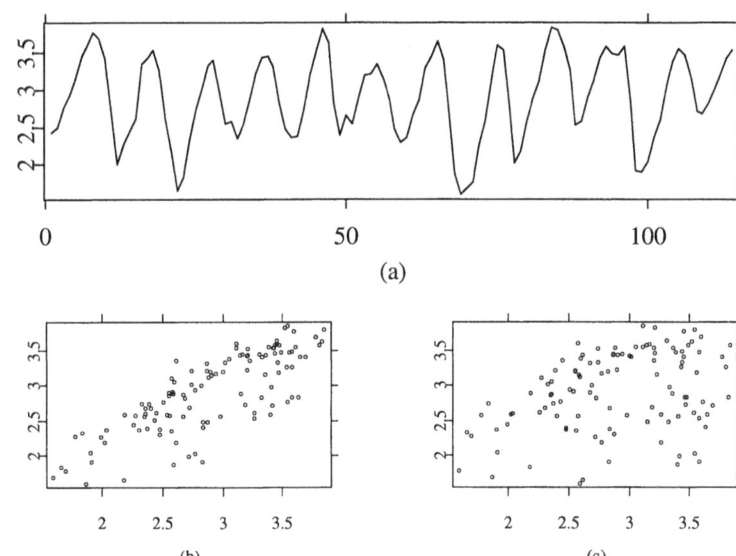

Figure 3.2. The Mackenzie River Lynx data for 1821-1934. (a) The series y_t = log(number recorded as trapped in year 1820+t). (b) Directed scatter diagrams of y_t against y_{t-1}. (c) Directed scatter diagrams of y_t against y_{t-2}.

XEGfig2.xpl

3.1.2 Theoretical Consideration

Let (X, Z, y) be respectively $\mathbb{R}^p$-valued, $\mathbb{R}^q$-valued, and $\mathbb{R}$-valued random variables. In the absence of any prior knowledge about the relation between y and (X, Z), a nonparametric regression model is usually adopted, i.e. $y = g(X, Z) + \varepsilon$, where $\mathrm{E}(\varepsilon|X, Z) = 0$ almost surely. More recently, there is a tendency to use instead some semiparametric models to fit the relations between y and (X, Z). There are three reasons for this. The first is to reduce the impact of the curse of dimensionality in nonparametric estimation. The second is that a parametric form allows us some explicit expression, perhaps based on intuition or prior information, about part of the relation between variables. The third is that for one reason or another (e.g. availability of some background information) some restrictions have to be imposed on the relations. The latter two reasons also mean that we have some information about some of the explanatory variables but not the others. A general semiparametric model can be written as

$$y = G(g_1(B^\top X), \cdots, g_\gamma(B^\top X), Z, \theta) + \varepsilon, \tag{3.2}$$

where G is a *known* function up to a parameter vector $\theta \in \mathbb{R}^l$, $g_1(\cdot), \cdots, g_\gamma(\cdot)$ are *unknown* functions and $\mathrm{E}(\varepsilon|X, Z) = 0$ almost surely. Covariates X and Z may have some common components. Matrix B is a $p \times D$ orthogonal matrix with $D < p$. Note that model (3.2) still contains unknown multivariate functions $g_1, \cdots, g_\gamma$. For model (3.2), parameter θ, matrix B and functions $g_1(\cdot), \cdots, g_\gamma(\cdot)$ are typically chosen to minimize

$$E\Big[y - G(g_1(B^\top X), \cdots, g_\gamma(B^\top X), Z, \theta)\Big]^2. \tag{3.3}$$

Note that the space spanned by the column vectors of B is uniquely defined under some mild conditions and is our focus of interest. For convenience, we shall refer to these column vectors the efficient dimension reduction (e.d.r.) directions, which are unique up to orthogonal transformations. The above idea underlines many useful semiparametric models, of which the following are some examples.

(1) The following model has been quite often considered.

$$y = g(B_0^\top X) + \varepsilon, \tag{3.4}$$

where $B_0^\top B_0 = I_{D\times D}$ $(D \le p)$ and $\mathrm{E}(\varepsilon|X) = 0$ almost surely. Here, both g and B_0 are unknown. Li (1991) gave an interesting approach to the estimation of

B_0. Li (1991) used model (3.4) to investigate the e.d.r. directions of $\mathrm{E}(y|X = x)$. Specifically, for any k, the *k-indexing directions* $\beta_1, \cdots, \beta_k$ are defined such that $B_k = (\beta_1, \cdots, \beta_k)$ minimizes

$$E[y - \mathrm{E}(y|B_k^\top X)]^2. \tag{3.5}$$

(2) A slightly more complicated model is the multi-index model proposed by Ichimura and Lee (1991), namely

$$y = \theta_0^\top X + g(B_0^\top X) + \varepsilon. \tag{3.6}$$

The linear restriction of the first component is of some interest. See Xia, Tong, and Li (1999). Carroll et al. (1997) proposed a slightly simpler form. To fit model (3.6), we also need to estimate the e.d.r. directions or equivalently B_0, a $p \times D$ matrix. An important special case of (3.6) is the single-index model, in which $\theta_0 = 0$ and $D = 1$.

(3) The varying-coefficient model proposed by Hastie and Tibshirani (1993),

$$y = c_0(X) + c_1(X)z_1 + \cdots + c_q(X)z_q + \varepsilon, \tag{3.7}$$

is a generalized linear regression with unknown varying-coefficients $c_0, \cdots, c_q$, which are functions of X. Here, $Z = (z_1, \cdots, z_q)^\top$. A similar model was proposed by Chen and Tsay (1993) in the time series context. The question is how to find the e.d.r. directions for the X within the c_k's. More precisely, we seek the model

$$y = g_0(B_0^\top X) + g_1(B_0^\top X)z_1 + \cdots + g_q(B_0^\top X)z_q + \varepsilon, \tag{3.8}$$

where $g_1, \cdots, g_q$ are unknown functions and the columns in $B_0 : p \times D$ are unknown directions. The case $D = 1$ has an important application in nonlinear time series analysis: it can be used to select the (sometimes hidden) threshold variable (previously called the indicator variable) of a threshold autoregressive model (Tong, 1990). See also Xia and Li (1999).

The above discussion and examples highlight the importance of dimension reduction for semiparametric models. For some special cases of model (3.2), some dimension reduction methods have been introduced. Next, we give a brief review of these methods.

The projection pursuit regression (PPR) was proposed by Friedman and Stuetzle (1981). Huber (1985) gave a comprehensive discussion. The commonly used PPR aims to find univariate functions $g_1, g_2, \cdots, g_D$ and directions $\beta_1, \beta_2, \cdots, \beta_D$ which satisfy the following sequence of minimizations,

$$\min_{\beta_1} E[y - g_1(\beta_1^\top X)]^2, \ \cdots, \ \min_{\beta_D} E\{y - \sum_{j=1}^{D-1} g_j(\beta_j^\top X) - g_D(\beta_D^\top X)\}^2. \quad (3.9)$$

Actually, $g_1(\beta^\top X) = \mathrm{E}(y|\beta^\top X)$ and $g_k(\beta^\top X) = E\Big[\{y - \sum_{i=1}^{k-1} g_i(\beta_i^\top X)\}|\beta^\top X\Big]$, $k = 1, \cdots, D$. Because both β_k and g_k are unknown, the implementation of the above minimizations is non-trivial. Compared with (3.4), the PPR assumes that $g(x) = \mathrm{E}(y|X = x)$ depends *additively* on its e.d.r. directions. The primary focus of the PPR is more on the approximation of $g(x)$ by a sum of ridge functions $g_k(\cdot)$, namely $g(X) \approx \sum_{k=1}^{D} g_k(\beta_k^\top X)$, than on looking for the e.d.r. directions. To illustrate, let $y = (x_1 + x_2)^2(1 + x_3) + \varepsilon$, where $x_1, x_2, x_3, \varepsilon$ are i.i.d. random variables with the common distribution $N(0, 1)$. The e.d.r. directions are $(1/\sqrt{2}, 1/\sqrt{2}, 0)^\top$ and $(0, 0, 1)^\top$. However, the PPR cannot find the directions correctly because the components are not additive.

Another simple approach related to the estimation of the e.d.r. direction is the average derivative estimation (ADE) proposed by Härdle and Stoker (1989). Suppose that $g(x) = g_1(\beta_1^\top x)$. Then $\bigtriangledown g(x) = g_1'(\beta_1^\top x)\beta_1$, where $\bigtriangledown g(\cdot)$ is the gradient of the unknown regression function $g(\cdot)$ with respect to its arguments. It follows that $E \bigtriangledown g(X) = \{Eg_1'(\beta_1^\top X)\}\beta_1$. Therefore, the difference between β_1 and the expectation of the gradient is a scalar constant. We can estimate $\bigtriangledown g(x)$ nonparametrically, and then obtain an estimate of β_1 by the direction of the estimate of $E \bigtriangledown g(X)$. An interesting result is that the estimator of β_1 can achieve root-n consistency even when we use high-dimensional kernel smoothing method to estimate $E\bigtriangledown g(X)$. However, there are several limitations with the ADE: (i) To obtain the estimate of β_1, the condition $Eg_1'(\beta_1^\top X) \neq 0$ is needed. This condition is violated when $g_1(\cdot)$ is an even function and X is symmetrically distributed. (ii) As far as we known, there is no successful extension to the case of more than one e.d.r. direction.

The sliced inverse regression (SIR) method proposed by Li (1991) is perhaps up to now the most powerful method for searching for the e.d.r. directions. However, to ensure that such an inverse regression can be taken, the SIR method imposes some strong probabilistic structure on X. Specifically, the method requires that for any constant vector $b = (b_1, \cdots, b_p)$, there are constants c_0 and $c = (c_1, \cdots, c_D)$ such that for any B,

$$\mathrm{E}(bX|B^\top X) = c_0 + cB^\top X. \quad (3.10)$$

In times series analysis, we typically set $X = (y_{t-1}, \cdots, y_{t-p})^\top$, where $\{y_t\}$ is a time series. Then the above restriction of probability structure is tantamount to assuming that $\{y_t\}$ is time-reversible. However, it is well known that time-reversibility is the exception rather than the rule for time series. Another important problem for dimension reduction is the determination of the number of the e.d.r. directions. Based on the SIR method, Li (1991) proposed a testing method. For reasons similar to the above, the method is typically not relevant in time series analysis.

For the general model (3.2), the methods listed above may fail in one way or another. For instance, the SIR method fails with most nonlinear times series models and the ADE fails with model (3.8) when X and Z have common variables. In this chapter, we shall propose a new method to estimate the e.d.r. directions for the general model (3.2). Our approach is inspired by the SIR method, the ADE method and the idea of local linear smoothers (see, for example, Fan and Gibbers (1996)). It is easy to implement and needs no strong assumptions on the probabilistic structure of X. In particular, it can handle time series data. Our simulations show that the proposed method has better performance than the existing ones. Based on the properties of our direction estimation methods, we shall propose a method to estimate the number of the e.d.r. directions, which again does not require special assumptions on the design X and is applicable to many complicated models.

To explain the basic ideas of our approach, we shall refer mostly to models (3.4) and (3.8). Extension to other models is not difficult. The rest of this chapter is organized as follows. Section 3.2 gives some properties of the e.d.r. directions and extends the ADE method to the average outer product of gradients estimation method. These properties are important for the implementation of our estimation procedure. Section 3.3 describes the the minimum average (conditional) variance estimation procedure and gives some results. Some comparisons with the existing methods are also discussed. An algorithm is proposed in Section 3.5. To check the feasibility of our approach, we have conducted a substantial volume of simulations, typical ones of which are reported in Section 3.6. Section 3.7 gives some real applications of our method to both independently observed data sets and time series data sets.

3.2 Average Outer Product of Gradients and its Estimation

In this section, we give some properties of the e.d.r. directions. The e.d.r. directions coincide with the eigenvectors of the so-called Hessian matrix of the regression function. Slightly different from the usual one, the outer product of gradients simplifies the calculation and extends the ADE of Härdle and Stoker (1989) to the case of more than one direction. For ease of exposition, we always assume the eigenvectors of a semi-positive matrix be arranged according to their corresponding eigenvalues in descending order.

3.2.1 The Simple Case

Consider the relation between y and X in model (3.4). The k-indexing e.d.r. directions are as defined in (3.5). Let $\tilde{g}(X) = \mathrm{E}(y|X)$ and $\triangledown\tilde{g}$ denote the gradients of the function $\tilde{g}$ with respect to the arguments of $\tilde{g}$. Under model (3.4), i.e. $\tilde{g}(X) = g(B_0^\top X)$, we have $\triangledown\tilde{g}(X) = B_0 \triangledown g(B_0^\top X)$. Therefore

$$E[\triangledown\tilde{g}(X) \triangledown^\top \tilde{g}(X)] = B_0 H B_0^\top,$$

where $H = E[\triangledown g(B_0^\top X) \triangledown^\top g(B_0^\top X)]$, the average outer product of gradients of $g(\cdot)$. It is easy to see that the following lemma holds.

LEMMA 3.1 *Suppose that $\tilde{g}(\cdot)$ is differentiable. If model (3.4) is true, then B_0 is in the space spanned by the first D eigenvectors of $E[\triangledown\tilde{g}(X) \triangledown^\top \tilde{g}(X)]$.*

Lemma 3.1 provides a simple method to estimate B_0 through the eigenvectors of $E[\triangledown\tilde{g}(X) \triangledown^\top \tilde{g}(X)]$. Härdle and Stoker (1989) noted this fact in passing but seemed to have stopped short of exploiting it. Instead, they proposed the so-called ADE method, which suffers from the disadvantages as stated in Section 3.1. Li (1992) proposed the principal Hessian directions (pHd) method by estimating the Hessian matrix of $g(\cdot)$. For a normally distributed design X, the Hessian matrix can be properly estimated simply by the Stein's Lemma. (Cook (1998) claimed that the result can be extended to symmetric design X). However, in time series analysis, the assumption of symmetric design X is frequently violated. As an example, see (3.28) and Figure 3.5 in the next section. Now, we propose a direct estimation method as follows. Suppose that $\{(y_i, X_i), i = 1, 2, \cdots, n\}$ is a random sample. First, estimate the gradients

$\bigtriangledown g(X_j)$ by local polynomial smoothing. Thus, we consider the local r-th order polynomial fitting in the form of the following minimization problem

$$\min_{a_j,b_j,c_j} \sum_{i=1}^n \Big[y_i - a_j - b_j^\top (X_i - X_j) - \sum_{1<k\le r} \sum_{i_1+\cdots+i_p=k} \Big(c_{i_1,i_2,\cdots,i_p} \tag{3.11}$$

$$\times \{X_i - X_j\}_1^{i_1}\{X_i - X_j\}_2^{i_2}\cdots\{X_i - X_j\}_p^{i_p}\Big)\Big]^2 K_h(X_i - X_j),$$

where $\{X_i - x\}_k$ denotes the kth element of matrix $X_i - x$. Here, $K(x)$ is a kernel function, h is a bandwidth and $K_h(\cdot) = K(\cdot/h)/h^p$. A special case is the local linear fitting with $r = 1$. The minimizer $\hat{b}_j = (\hat{b}_{j1}, \cdots, \hat{b}_{jp})^\top$ is the estimator of $\bigtriangledown\tilde{g}(X_j)$. We therefore obtain the estimator of $E\{\bigtriangledown\tilde{g}(X)\bigtriangledown^\top\tilde{g}(X)\}$ as

$$\hat{\Sigma} = \frac{1}{n}\sum_{j=1}^n \hat{b}_j\hat{b}_j^\top.$$

Finally, we estimate the k-indexing e.d.r. directions by the first k eigenvectors of $\hat{\Sigma}$. We call this method the method of outer product of gradients estimation (OPG). The difference between the OPG method and the ADE method is that the former uses the second moment of the derivative but the latter uses only the first moment. Unlike the ADE, the OPG method still works even if $E\bigtriangledown\tilde{g}(X) = 0$. Moreover, the OPG method can handle multiple e.d.r. directions simultaneously whereas the ADE can only handle the first e.d.r. direction (i.e. single-index model).

THEOREM 3.1 *Let $\hat{\beta}_1, \cdots, \hat{\beta}_p$ be the eigenvectors of $\hat{\Sigma}$. Suppose that (C1)-(C6) (in Appendix 3.9) hold and model (3.4) is true. If $nh^p/\log n \to \infty$ and $h \to 0$, then for any $k \le D$,*

$$\|(I - B_0B_0^\top)\hat{\beta}_k\| = O_P(h^r + \delta_n^2 h^{-1}),$$

where $\delta_n = \{\log n/(nh^p)\}^{1/2}$ and $\|M\|$ denotes the Euclidean norm of M. If further, $r > p - 2$ and $h = O(n^{-\tau})$ with $\{2(p-2)\}^{-1} > \tau > (2r)^{-1}$, then

$$\|(I - B_0B_0^\top)\hat{\beta}_k\| = O_P(n^{-1/2}).$$

Similar results were obtained by Härdle and Stoker (1989) for the ADE method. Note that the optimal bandwidth for the estimation of the regression function (or the derivatives) in the sense of the mean integrated squared errors (MISE) is $h_{opt} \sim n^{-1/\{2(r+1)+p\}}$. The fastest convergence rate for the estimator of the directions can never be achieved at the bandwidth of this value, but is actually achieved at $h \sim n^{-1/(r+1+p)}$, which is smaller than h_{opt}. This point has been noticed by many authors in other contexts. See for example Hall (1984), Weisberg and Welsh (1994), and Carroll et al. (1997).

3.2.2 The Varying-coefficient Model

Let $Z = (1, z_1, \cdots, z_q)^\top$ and $C(X) = (c_0(X), c_1(X), \cdots, c_q(X))^\top$. Then model (3.7) can be written as $y = Z^\top C(X)$. It is easy to see that

$$C(x) = \{\mathrm{E}(ZZ^\top|X = x)\}^{-1}\mathrm{E}(Zy|X = x).$$

LEMMA 3.2 *Suppose that $c_0(x), \cdots, c_q(x)$ are differentiable. If model (3.8) is true, then B_0 is in the space spanned by the first D eigenvectors of $E\{\triangledown C(X) \triangledown^\top C(X)]$, where $\triangledown C(X) = (\triangledown c_0(X), \cdots, \triangledown c_q(X))$.*

Similarly, we can estimate the gradient $\triangledown C(x)$ using a nonparametric method. For example, if we use the local linear smoothing method, we can estimate the gradients by solving the following minimization problem

$$\min_{c_k, b_k : k=0,1,\cdots,q} \sum_{i=1}^{n} \left\{ y_i - \sum_{k=0}^{q} [c_k(x) + b_k^\top(x)(X_i - x)] z_k \right\}^2 K_h(X_i - x).$$

Let $\{\hat{c}_k(x), \hat{b}_k(x) : k = 0, \cdots, q\}$ be the solutions. Then, we get the estimate $\widehat{\triangledown C}(X_j) = (\hat{b}_0(X_j), \hat{b}_1(X_j), \cdots, \hat{b}_q(X_j))$. Finally, B_0 can be estimated by the first D eigenvectors of $n^{-1}\sum_{j=1}^{n} \widehat{\triangledown C}(X_j)\widehat{\triangledown C}^\top(X_j)$.

3.3 A Unified Estimation Method

As we have discussed above, the e.d.r. directions can be obtained from the relevant outer product of gradients. Further, the proposed OPG method can achieve root-n consistency. Unlike the SIR method, the OPG method does not need strong assumptions on the design X and can be used for more complicated models. However, its estimators still suffer from poor performance when a high-dimensional kernel is used in (3.12). Now, we discuss how to improve the OPG method.

Note that all the existing methods adopt two separate steps to estimate the directions. First estimate the regression function and then estimate the directions based on the estimated regression function. See for example Hall (1984), Härdle and Stoker (1989), Carroll et al. (1997) and the OPG method above. It is therefore not surprising that the performance of the direction estimator suffers from the bias problem in nonparametric estimation. Härdle, Hall, and Ichimura (1993) noticed this point and estimated the bandwidth and the directions simultaneously in a single-index model by minimizing the sum of squares of the residuals. They further showed that the optimal bandwidth for the estimation of the regression function in the sense of MISE enables the estimator of the direction to achieve root-n consistency. Inspired by this, we propose to estimate the direction by minimizing the mean of the conditional variance simultaneously with respect to the regression function and the directions. As we shall see, similar results as Härdle, Hall, and Ichimura (1993) can be obtained and the improvement over the OPG method achieved.

3.3.1 The Simple Case

In this subsection, we investigate the relation between y and X. The idea was proposed by Xia et al. (2002). Consider model (3.4). For any orthogonal matrix $B = (\beta_1, \cdots, \beta_d)$, the conditional variance given $B^\top X$ is

$$\sigma_B^2(B^\top X) = E[\{y - \mathrm{E}(y|B^\top X)\}^2 | B^\top X]. \tag{3.12}$$

It follows that

$$E\left[y - \mathrm{E}(y|B^\top X)\right]^2 = E\sigma_B^2(B^\top X).$$

Therefore, minimizing (3.5) is equivalent to minimizing, with respect to B,

$$E\sigma_B^2(B^\top X) \quad \text{subject to} \quad B^\top B = I. \tag{3.13}$$

We shall call this the the minimum average (conditional) variance (MAVE) estimation. Suppose $\{(X_i, y_i)\ i = 1, 2, \cdots, n\}$ is a random sample from (X, y). Let $g_B(v_1, \cdots, v_d) = \mathrm{E}(y|\beta_1^\top X = v_1, \cdots, \beta_d^\top X = v_d)$. For any given X_0, a local linear expansion of $\mathrm{E}(y_i|B^\top X_i)$ at X_0 is

$$\mathrm{E}(y_i|B^\top X_i) \approx a + bB^\top (X_i - X_0),$$

where $a = g_B(B^\top X_0)$ and $b = (b_1, \cdots, b_D)$ with

$$b_k = \left.\frac{\partial g_B(v_1, \cdots, v_d)}{\partial v_k}\right|_{v_1 = \beta_1^\top X_0, \cdots, v_d = \beta_d^\top X_0}, \qquad k = 1, \cdots, d.$$

The residuals are then

$$y_i - g_B(B^\top X_i) \approx y_i - \left[a + bB^\top (X_i - X_0)\right].$$

Following the idea of Nadaraya-Watson estimation, we can estimate $\sigma_B^2(B^\top X_0)$ by exploiting the approximation

$$\sum_{i=1}^{n} \left[y_i - \mathrm{E}(y_i|B^\top X_i)\right]^2 w_{i0} \approx \sum_{i=1}^{n} \left[y_i - \{a + bB^\top (X_i - X_0)\}\right]^2 w_{i0}, \quad (3.14)$$

where $w_{i0} \geq 0$ are some weights with $\sum_{i=1}^n w_{i0} = 1$ and typically centered around $B^\top X_0$. The choice of the weights w_{i0} plays a key role in the different approaches to searching for the e.d.r. directions in this chapter. We shall discuss this issue in detail later. Usually, $w_{i0} = K_h(B^\top(X_i - X_0))/\sum_{l=1}^n K_h(B^\top(X_l - X_0))$. For ease of exposition, we use $K(\cdot)$ to denote different kernel functions at different places. let $K_h(\cdot) = h^d K(\cdot/h)$, d being the dimension of $K(\cdot)$. Note that the estimators of a and b are just the minimum point of (3.14). Therefore, the estimator of σ_B^2 at $B^\top X_0$ is just the minimum value of (3.14), namely

$$\hat{\sigma}_B^2(B^\top X_0) = \min_{a, b_1, b_2, \cdots, b_d} \sum_{i=1}^{n} \Big[y_i - \{a + bB^\top (X_i - X_0)\}\Big]^2 w_{i0}. \quad (3.15)$$

Note that the estimator $\hat{\sigma}_B^2(B^\top x)$ is different from existing ones. See, for example, Fan and Yao (1998). For this estimator, the following holds.

LEMMA 3.3 *Under assumptions (C1)-(C6) (in Appendix 3.9) and* $w_{i0} = K_h(B^\top(X_i - X_0))/\sum_{i=1}^n K_h(B^\top(X_i - X_0))$, *we have*

$$\hat{\sigma}_B^2(B^\top X_0) - \sigma_B^2(B^\top X_0) = o_P(1)$$

Based on (3.5), (3.13), and (3.15), we can estimate the e.d.r. directions by solving the following minimization problem.

$$\begin{aligned} \min_{B:\ B^\top B = I} \sum_{j=1}^{n} \hat{\sigma}_B^2(B^\top X_j) &= \\ = \min_{\substack{B:\ B^\top B=I \\ a_j, b_j, j=1,\cdots,n}} \sum_{j=1}^{n}\sum_{i=1}^{n} &\Big[y_i - \{a_j + b_j B^\top (X_i - X_j)\}\Big]^2 w_{ij}, \quad (3.16) \end{aligned}$$

where $b_j = (b_{j1}, \cdots, b_{jd})$. The MAVE method or the minimization in (3.16) can be seen as a combination of nonparametric function estimation and direction estimation, which minimizes (3.16) simultaneously with respect to the directions and the nonparametric regression function. As we shall see, we benefit from this simultaneous minimization.

Note that the weights depend on B. Therefore, to implement the minimization in (3.16) is non-trivial. The weight w_{i0} in (3.14) should be chosen such that *the value of* w_{i0} *is proportional to the difference between* X_i *and* X_0. Next, we give two choices of w_{i0}.

(1) Multi-dimensional kernel. To simplify (3.16), a natural choice is $w_{i0} = K_h(X_i - X_0)/\sum_{l=1}^n K_h(X_l - X_0)$. If our primary interest is on dimension reduction, this multidimensional kernel will not slow down the convergence rate in the estimation of the e.d.r. directions. This was first observed by Härdle and Stoker (1989). See also Theorem 3.1. For such weights, the right hand side of (3.16) does not tend to $\sigma_B^2(B^\top X_0)$. However, we have

LEMMA 3.4 *Suppose* $y = \tilde{g}(X) + \varepsilon$ *with* $E(\varepsilon|X) = 0$ *a.s. Under assumptions (C1)-(C6) (in Appendix 3.9) and* $w_{i0} = K_h(X_i - X_0)/\sum_{l=1}^n K_h(X_l - X_0)$, *we have*

$$\min_{a,b_1,b_1,\cdots,b_d} \sum_{i=1}^n \Big[y_i - \{a + bB^\top(X_i - X_0)\}\Big]^2 w_{i0}$$
$$= \hat{\sigma}^2(X_0) + h^2 \bigtriangledown^\top \tilde{g}(X_0)(I_{p\times p} - BB^\top) \bigtriangledown \tilde{g}(X_0) + o_P(h^2),$$

where $\hat{\sigma}^2(X_0) = n^{-1}\sum_{i=1}^n \varepsilon_i^2 w_{i0}$ *does not depend on* B.

Note that $BB^\top$ is a projection matrix. The bias term on the right hand side above is asymptotically non-negative. Therefore, by the law of large numbers and Lemma 3.4, the minimization problem (3.16) depends mainly on

$$\begin{aligned} & E\{\bigtriangledown^\top \tilde{g}(X)(I_{p\times p} - BB^\top) \bigtriangledown \tilde{g}(X)\} \\ &= tr\left[(I_{p\times p} - BB^\top)E\{\bigtriangledown\tilde{g}(X) \bigtriangledown^\top \tilde{g}(X)\}\right] \\ &= tr\Big[E\{\bigtriangledown\tilde{g}(X) \bigtriangledown^\top \tilde{g}(X)\}\Big] - tr\Big[B^\top E\{\bigtriangledown\tilde{g}(X) \bigtriangledown^\top \tilde{g}(X)\}B\Big]. \end{aligned} \quad (3.17)$$

Therefore, the B which minimizes the above equation is close to the first d eigenvectors of $E\{\bigtriangledown\tilde{g}(X) \bigtriangledown^\top \tilde{g}(X)\}$. By Lemma 3.4, we can still use (3.16) to find an estimator for B if we use the weight $w_{ij} = K_h(X_i - X_j)/\sum_{l=1}^n K_h(X_l - X_j)$. To improve the convergence rate, we can further use the r-th ($r \geq 1$) order local polynomial fittings as follows.

$$\min_{\substack{B:\ B^\top B=I \\ a_j,b_j,j=1,\cdots,n}} \sum_{j=1}^{n}\sum_{i=1}^{n}\Big[y_i - a_j - b_j B^\top (X_i - X_j) - \tag{3.18}$$
$$- \sum_{1<k\le r}\ \sum_{i_1+\cdots+i_p=k} \Big(c_{i_1,i_2,\cdots,i_p} \times$$
$$\times \{X_i - X_j\}_1^{i_1}\{X_i - X_j\}_2^{i_2}\cdots\{X_i - X_j\}_p^{i_p}\Big)\Big]^2 w_{ij},$$

where $b_j = (b_{j1}, \cdots, b_{jd})$ and we assume the summation over an empty set to be 0 in order to include the case of $r = 1$. Note that the minimization in (3.18) can be effected by alternating between (a_j, b_j) and B. See the next section for details.

The root-n consistency for the MAVE estimator of e.d.r. directions with sufficiently large order r can also be proved. Besides the difference between the MAVE method and the other methods as stated at the beginning of this section, we need to address another difference between the multi-dimensional kernel MAVE method and the OPG method or the other existing estimation methods. The MAVE method uses the common e.d.r directions as the prior information. Therefore, it can be expected that the MAVE method outperforms the OPG method as well as other existing methods. In order not to be distracted by the complexity of the expressions using high-order local polynomial methods, we now focus on the case $r = 1$.

THEOREM 3.2 *Suppose that (C1)-(C6) (in Appendix 3.9) hold and model (3.4) is true. Take $r = 1$. If $nh^p/\log n \to \infty$, $h \to 0$ and $d \ge D$, then*

$$||(I - \hat{B}\hat{B}^\top)B_0|| = O_P(h^3 + h\delta_n + h^{-1}\delta_n^2).$$

Note that the convergence rate is of $O_P(h^3(\log n)^{1/2})$ if we use the optimal bandwidth h_{opt} of the regression function estimation in the sense of MISE, in which case $\delta_n = O_P(h^2(\log n)^{1/2})$. This is faster than the rate for the other methods, which is of $O_P(h^2)$. Note that the convergence rate for the local linear estimator of the function is also $O_P(h^2)$. As far as we know, if we use the optimal bandwidth h_{opt} for the nonparametric function estimation in the sense of MISE, then for all the non-MAVE methods, the convergence rate for the estimators of directions is the same as that for the estimators of the nonparametric functions. As a typical illustration, consider the ADE method and the single-index model $y = g_0(\beta_0^\top X)+\varepsilon$. The direction β_0 can be estimated as

$$\hat{\beta}_0 = \sum_{j=1}^n \hat{b}_j / || \sum_{j=1}^n \hat{b}_j ||,$$

where $\hat{b}_j$ is obtained by the minimization in (3.12). If we take $r = 1$ in (3.12), then we have

$$\begin{aligned}\hat{\beta}_0 &= \pm\beta_0 + \frac{1}{2}h^2\{Eg_0'(\beta_0^\top X)\}^{-1}(I - \beta_0\beta_0^\top)E\{g_0''(\beta_0^\top X)f^{-1}(X) \bigtriangledown f(X)\} \\ &\quad + o_P(h^2), \qquad (3.19)\end{aligned}$$

from which we can see that the convergence rate for $\hat{\beta}_0$ is also $O_P(h^2)$. In order to improve the convergence rate, a popular device is to undersmooth the regression function g_0 by taking $h = o(h_{opt})$. Although the undersmooth method is proved asymptotically useful, there are two disadvantages in practice. (1) There is no general guidance on the selection of such a smaller bandwidth. (2) All our simulations show that the estimation errors of the estimators for the directions become large very quickly as the bandwidth gets small, in contrast to the case when the bandwidth gets large. See Figures 3.3, 3.4 and 3.5. Thus a small bandwidth can be quite dangerous.

To illustrate this, consider the model

$$y = (\theta_1 x_1 + \theta_2 x_2 + \theta_3 x_3)^2 + 0.5\varepsilon, \qquad (3.20)$$

where x_1, x_2, x_3 and ε are i.i.d. $\sim N(0,1)$ and $(\theta_1, \theta_2, \theta_3) = (4,1,0)/\sqrt{17}$. With sample size $n = 100$, 500 samples are drawn independently. With different choices of the bandwidth, the average absolute errors $\sum_{i=1}^3 |\hat{\theta}_i - \theta_i|$ are computed using both the OPG method and the MAVE method. As a more complicated example, we also investigate the nonlinear autoregressive model

$$y_t = \sin(\pi(\theta^\top X_t)) + 0.2\varepsilon_t, \qquad (3.21)$$

with $X_t = (y_{t-1}, \cdots, y_{t-5})^\top$, $\varepsilon_t \sim N(0,1)$ and $\theta = (1,0,1,0,1)/\sqrt{3}$. With sample size $n = 200$, we perform a similar comparison as for model (3.20). In Figure 3.3, the solid lines are the errors of the MAVE method and the dashed lines are those of the OPG method. The MAVE method always outperforms the OPG method across all bandwidths. The MAVE method also outperforms the PPR method, which are shown by the dotted line in Figure 3.3 (a). [For model (3.21), the PPR error is 0.9211, which is much worse than our simulation results]. The asterisks refer to the errors when using the bandwidth chosen by the cross-validation method. It seems that this bandwidth is close to the optimal bandwidth as measured by the errors of the estimated directions. This observation suggests the feasibility of using the cross-validation bandwidth for the MAVE method. It also supports our theoretical result that the optimal bandwidth for the estimation of nonparametric function is also suitable for the MAVE estimation of the directions.

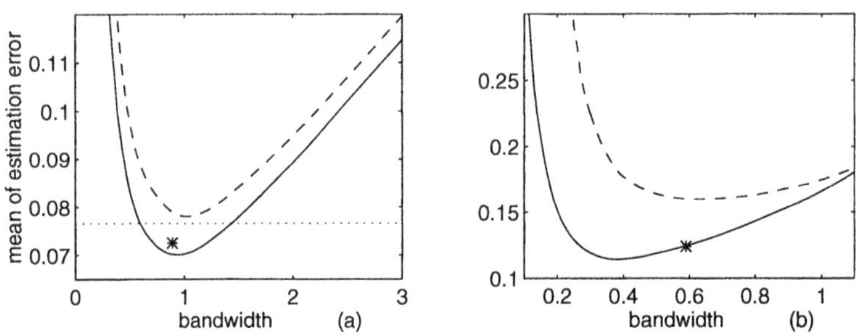

Figure 3.3. (a) and (b) are the simulation results for model (3.20) and model (3.21) respectively. The dash lines are the estimation errors by the OPG method and the solid lines are the errors by the MAVE method. The asterisks refer to the errors when using the bandwidth chosen by the cross-validation method

(2) Inverse regression weight. If $\{y_i\}$ and $\{X_i\}$ have an approximate 1-1 correspondence, then we can use y instead of X to produce the weights. As an example, suppose $\mathrm{E}(y|X) = g_0(\beta_0^\top X)$ and $g_0(\cdot)$ is invertible. Then we may choose

$$w_{ij} = K_h(y_i - y_j) / \sum_{\ell=1}^{n} K_h(y_\ell - y_j). \tag{3.22}$$

For this weight function, the minimization in (3.15) becomes the minimization of

$$\sum_{i=1}^{n} \Big[y_i - \{a + b\beta_0^\top (X_i - X_0)\} \Big]^2 w_{i0}.$$

Following the idea of the MAVE method above, we should minimize

$$n^{-1} \sum_{i=1}^{n} \sum_{j=1}^{n} \Big[y_i - \{a_j + b_j \beta^\top (X_i - X_j)\} \Big]^2 w_{ij}. \tag{3.23}$$

We may also consider a 'dual' of (3.23) and minimize

$$n^{-1}\sum_{j=1}^{n}\sum_{i=1}^{n}\Big[\beta^{\top}X_i - c_j - d_j(y_j - y_i)\Big]^2 w_{ij}. \tag{3.24}$$

This may be considered an alternative derivation of the SIR method. Extension of (3.24) to more than one direction can be stated as follows. Suppose that the first k directions have been calculated and are denoted by $\hat{\beta}_1, \cdots, \hat{\beta}_k$ respectively. To obtain the $(k+1)$th direction, we need to perform

$$\min_{\alpha_1,\cdots,\alpha_k,c_j,d_j,\beta}\sum_{j=1}^{n}\sum_{i=1}^{n}\Big\{\beta^{\top}X_i + \cdots + \alpha_k\hat{\beta}_k^{\top}X_i - c_j - d_j(y_i - y_j)\Big\}^2 w_{ij}$$

$$\text{subject to:} \qquad \beta^{\top}(\hat{\beta}_1, \cdots, \hat{\beta}_k) = 0 \text{ and } \|\beta\| = 1. \tag{3.25}$$

We call the estimation method by minimizing (3.23) with w_{ij} as defined in (3.22) the inverse MAVE (iMAVE) method. Under similar conditions as for the SIR method, the root-n consistency for the estimators can be proved.

THEOREM 3.3 *Suppose that (3.10) and assumptions (C1), (C2′), (C3′), (C4), (C5′) and (C6) (in Appendix 3.9) hold. Then for any $h \to 0$ and $nh^2/\log n \to \infty$*

$$\|(I - B_0B_0^{\top})\hat{B}\| = O_P(h^2 + n^{-1/2}).$$

If further $nh^4 \to 0$, then

$$\|(I - B_0B_0^{\top})\hat{B}\| = O_P(n^{-1/2}).$$

The result is similar to that of Zhu and Fang (1996). However, in our simulations the method based on the minimization in (3.25) always outperforms the SIR method. To illustrate, we adopt the examples used in Li (1991),

$$y = x_1(x_1 + x_2 + 1) + 0.5\varepsilon, \tag{3.26}$$

$$y = x_1/(0.5 + (x_2 + 1.5)^2) + 0.5\varepsilon, \tag{3.27}$$

where $\varepsilon, x_1, x_2, \cdots, x_{10}$ are independent and standard normally distributed. The sample size is set to $n = 200$ and 400. Let $\beta_1 = (1, 0, \cdots, 0)^{\top}$ and $\beta_2 = (0, 1, \cdots, 0)^{\top}$ and $P = 1 - (\beta_1, \beta_2)(\beta_1, \beta_2)^{\top}$. Then the estimation errors can be measured by $\hat{\beta}_1^{\top}P\hat{\beta}_1$ and $\hat{\beta}_2^{\top}P\hat{\beta}_2$. Figure 3.4 shows the means of the estimation errors defined above; they are labeled by "1" and "2" for β_1 and β_2 respectively. The iMAVE method has outperformed the SIR method in our simulations. Furthermore, we find that the MAVE method outperforms the iMAVE method in our simulation. Zhu and Fang (1996) proposed a kernel smooth version of the SIR method. However, their method does not show significant improvement over the original SIR method.

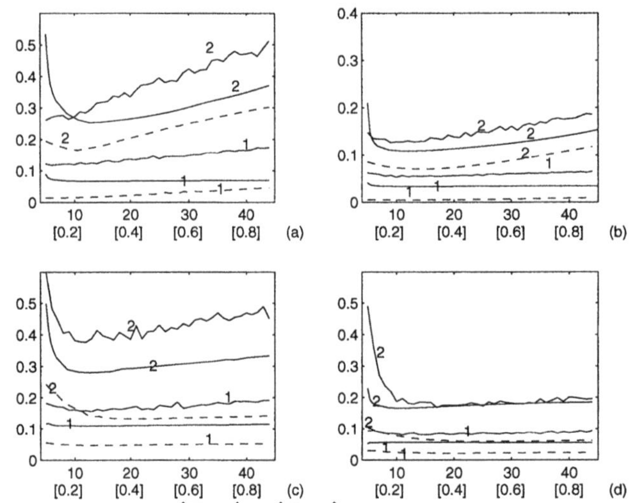

Figure 3.4. means of $\hat{\beta}_1^\top P \hat{\beta}_1$ $[\hat{\beta}_2^\top P \hat{\beta}_2]$ are labelled "1" ["2"]. Figures (a) and (b) [(c) and (d)] are for model (3.26) [(3.27)]. Figures (a) and (c) [(b) and (d)] are based on a sample size of 200 [400]. Dashed [smooth] lines are based on the MAVE [iMAVE] method. The wavy lines are based on the SIR method. The horizontal axes give the number of slices/bandwidth (in square brackets) for the SIR method/iMAVE method. For the MAVE method, the range of bandwidth extends from 2 to 7 for (a) and (c), 1.5 to 4 for (b) and (d).

As noticed previously, the assumption of symmetry on the design X can be a handicap as far as applications of the SIR method are concerned. Interestingly, simulations show that the SIR method sometimes works in the case of independent data even when the assumption of symmetry is violated. However, for time series data, we find that the SIR often fails. As a typical illustration, consider the nonparametric times series model

$$y_t = \{\sqrt{5}(\theta_1 y_{t-1} + \theta_2 y_{t-2})/2\}^{1/3} + \varepsilon_t, \tag{3.28}$$

where ε_t are i.i.d. standard normal and $(\theta_1, \theta_2) = (2, 1)/\sqrt{5}$. A typical data set is generated with size $n = 1000$ and is plotted in Figure 3.5 (a). Clearly, the assumption (3.10) is violated and the SIR method is inappropriate here.

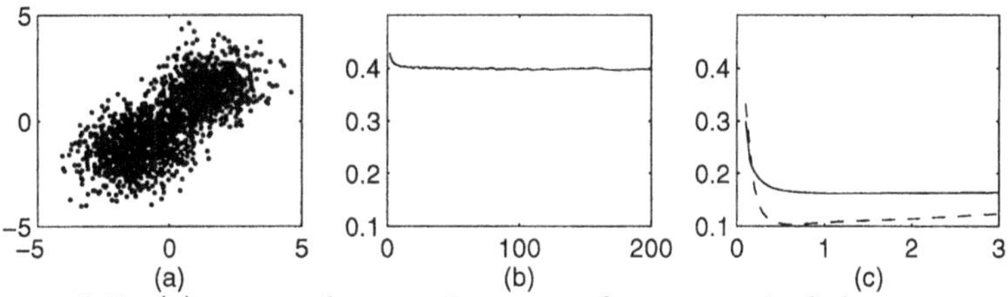

Figure 3.5. (a): y_{t-1} plots against y_{t-2} from a typical data sets with $n = 1000$. (b): the mean of absolute estimated error using SIR plotted against the number of slices. (c) the means of estimated errors using the iMAVE method (solid line) and the MAVE method (dashed line) against bandwidth respectively.

For sample size $n = 500$, we draw 200 samples from model (3.28). Using the SIR method with different number of slices, the mean of the estimated errors $|\hat{\theta}_1 - \theta_1| + |\hat{\theta}_2 - \theta_2|$ is plotted in Figure 3.5 (b). The estimation is quite poor. However, the iMAVE estimation gives much better results, and the MAVE $(r = 1)$ method is even better.

Now, we make a comparison between the MAVE method and the iMAVE method (or the SIR method). Besides the fact that the MAVE method is applicable to an asymmetric design X, the MAVE method (with $r = 1$) has better performance than the iMAVE (or SIR) method for the above models and for all the other simulations we have done. We even tried the same models with higher dimensionality p. All our simulation results show that the iMAVE method performs better than the SIR method and the MAVE method performs better than both of them. Intuitively, we may think that the iMAVE method and the SIR method should benefit from the use of one-dimensional kernels, unlike the MAVE method, which uses a multi-dimensional kernel. However, if the regression function g is symmetric about 0, then the SIR method and the iMAVE method usually fails to find the directions. Furthermore, any fluctuation in the regression function may reduce the efficiency of the estimation. (To overcome the effect of symmetry in the regression function, Li (1992) used a third moment method to estimate the Hessian matrix. This method has, however, a larger variance in practice). Another reason in addition to Theorem 3.2 why the iCMV method and the SIR method perform poorly may be the following. Note that for the MAVE method

$$B_0 - \hat{B}(\hat{B}^\top B_0) = (I - B_0 B_0^\top) \sum_{i=1}^{n} \nabla g(B_0^\top X_j) \nabla f(X_i)\varepsilon_i \times \Big(E\{\nabla g(B_0^\top X) \nabla^\top g(B_0^\top X)\Big)^{-1} + O_P(h^3 + h\delta_n) \quad (3.29)$$

Now consider the iMAVE method. Let $S(y) = E\Big(\{X - \mathrm{E}(X|y)\}\{X - \mathrm{E}(X|y)\}^\top\Big)$ The estimator $\hat{B}$ consists of the eigenvectors of $ES(y) + n^{-1}H_n + O_P(h^2)$, where

$$H_n = n^{-1}\sum_{j=1}^{n}\Big[\{S(y_i) - ES(y_i)\} + \{nf(y_j)\}^{-1}\sum_{i=1}^{n}\Big(K_{h,i}(y_j)\{X_i - A(y_j)\} \times\{X_i - A(y_j)\}^\top - EK_{h,i}(y_j)\{X_i - A(y_j)\}\{X_i - A(y_j)\}^\top\Big)\Big].$$

Note that H_n is a $p \times p$ matrix. The variance of the eigenvectors of $ES(y) + n^{-1}H_n + O_P(h^2)$ is a summation of p^2 terms. See Zhu and Fang (1996). The variance is quite large for large p. A theoretical comparison between the MAVE method and the iMAVE (or SIR) method is unavailable but we conjecture that the gain in using the univariate kernel will not be sufficient to compensate for the loss in other aspects such as the variance and the effect of fluctuations in the regression function.

3.3.2 The Varying-coefficient Model

Consider model (3.8). Note that B_0 is the solution of the following minimization problem

$$\min_{B:\ B^\top B = I} E\Big[y - \sum_{\ell=0}^{q} z_\ell g_\ell(B^\top X)\Big]^2. \quad (3.30)$$

Here and later, we take $z_0 = 1$ for ease of exposition. Consider the conditional variance of y given $B^\top X$

$$\sigma_B^2(B^\top X) = E\Big[\{y - \sum_{\ell=0}^{q} z_\ell g_\ell(B^\top X)\}^2 | B^\top X\Big]. \quad (3.31)$$

It follows that

$$E\left[E[\{y - \sum_{\ell=1}^{d} z_\ell g_\ell(B^\top X)\}^2 | B^\top X]\right] = E\sigma_B^2(B^\top X).$$

Therefore, the minimization of (3.3) is equivalent to

$$\min_{B:\ B^\top B = I} E\sigma_B^2(B^\top X). \tag{3.32}$$

Suppose $\{(X_i, Z_i, y_i)\ i = 1, 2, \cdots, n\}$ is a random sample from (X, Z, y). For any given X_0, a local linear expansion of $g_\ell(B^\top X_i)$ at X_0 is

$$g_\ell(B^\top X_i) \approx a_\ell + b_\ell B^\top (X_i - X_0), \tag{3.33}$$

where $a_\ell = g_\ell(B^\top X_0)$ and $b_\ell = (b_{\ell 1}, \cdots, b_{\ell d})$ with

$$b_{\ell k} = \frac{\partial g_\ell(v_1, \cdots, v_d)}{\partial v_k}\bigg|_{(v_1,\cdots,v_d)^\top = B^\top X_0}, \quad k = 1, \cdots, d; \;\; \ell = 1, \cdots, q.$$

The residuals are then

$$y_i - \sum_{\ell=0}^{\ell} z_\ell g_\ell(B^\top X) \approx y_i - \sum_{\ell=0}^{q} \{a_\ell z_\ell + b_\ell B^\top (X_i - X_0) z_\ell\}.$$

Following the idea of Nadaraya-Watson estimation, we can estimate σ_B^2 at $B^\top X_0$ by

$$\sum_{i=1}^{n} \Big[y_i - \mathrm{E}(y_i | B^\top X_i = B^\top X_0)\Big]^2 w_{0i}$$
$$\approx \sum_{i=1}^{n} \Big[y_i - \sum_{\ell=0}^{q} \{a_\ell z_\ell + b_\ell B^\top (X_i - X_0) z_\ell\}\Big]^2 w_{i0}. \tag{3.34}$$

As in the nonparametric case, the choice of w_{i0} is important. However, the model is now more complicated. Even if the g_ℓ's are monotonic functions, we can not guarantee a 1-1 correspondence between y and X. Therefore a possible choice is the multi-dimensional kernel, i.e. $w_{i0} = K_h(X_i - X_0)/\sum_{\ell=1}^{n} K_h(X_\ell - X_0)$. To improve the accuracy, we can also use a higher order local polynomial smoothing since

$$\sum_{i=1}^{n} \Big[y_i - \mathrm{E}(y_i | B^\top X_0)\Big]^2 w_{0i} \approx \sum_{i=1}^{n} \Big[y_i - \sum_{\ell=0}^{q} \{a_\ell z_\ell + b_\ell B^\top (X_i - X_0) z_\ell\}$$
$$- \sum_{\ell=0}^{q} z_\ell \sum_{1 < k \le r} \sum_{i_1 + \cdots + i_p = k} c_{\ell, i_1, i_2, \cdots, i_p} \{X_i - X_j\}_1^{i_1} \{X_i - X_j\}_2^{i_2} \cdots \{X_i - X_j\}_p^{i_p}\Big]^2 w_{i0}.$$

Finally, we can estimate the directions by minimizing

$$\sum_{j=1}^{n}\sum_{i=1}^{n}\Big[y_i - \sum_{\ell=0}^{q}\{a_\ell z_\ell + b_\ell B^\top (X_i - X_j) z_\ell\} - \sum_{\ell=0}^{q} z_\ell$$

$$\sum_{1<k\leq r}\sum_{i_1+\cdots+i_p=k} \times c_{\ell,i_1,i_2,\cdots,i_p}\{X_i - X_j\}_1^{i_1}\{X_i - X_j\}_2^{i_2}\cdots\{X_i - X_j\}_p^{i_p}\Big]^2 w_{ij}$$

Now, returning to the general model (3.2), suppose $G(v_1,\cdots,v_\gamma,Z,\theta)$ is differentiable. Let $G'_k(v_1,\cdots,v_\gamma,Z,\theta) = \partial G(v_1,\cdots,v_\gamma,Z,\theta)/\partial v_k$, $k = 1,\cdots,\gamma$. By (3.33), for $B^\top X_i$ close to $B^\top X_0$ we have

$$G(g_1(B^\top X_i),\cdots,g_\gamma(B^\top X_i),Z_i,\theta) \approx G(g_1(B^\top X_0),\cdots,g_\gamma(B^\top X_0),Z_i,\theta)$$
$$+\sum_{k=1}^{\gamma} G'_k(g_1(B^\top X_0),\cdots,g_\gamma(B^\top X_0),Z_i,\theta)\bigtriangledown^\top g_k(B^\top X_0)B^\top(X_i - X_0).$$

To estimate B, we minimize

$$\sum_{j=1}^{n}\sum_{i=1}^{n}\Big\{y_i - G(a_{1j},\cdots,a_{\gamma j},Z_i,\theta) +$$
$$+\sum_{k=1}^{\gamma} G'_k(a_{1j},\cdots,a_{\gamma j},Z_i,\theta)b_{kj}^\top B^\top(X_i - X_j)\Big\}^2 w_{i,j}$$

with respect to $a_{1j},\cdots,a_{\gamma j}$, $b_{1j},\cdots,b_{\gamma j}$, $j = 1,\cdots,n$, θ and B.

3.4 Number of E.D.R. Directions

Methods have been proposed for the determination of the number of the e.d.r. directions. See, for example, Li (1992), Schott (1994), and Cook (1998). Their approaches are based on the assumption of symmetry of the distribution of the explanatory variable X. We now extend the cross-validation method (Cheng and Tong (1992); Yao and Tong (1994)) to solve the above problem, having selected the explanatory variables using the referenced cross-validation method. A similar extension may be effected by using the approach of Auestad and Tjøstheim (1990), which is asymptotically equivalent to the cross-validation method

Suppose that $\beta_1, \cdots, \beta_D$ are the e.d.r. directions, i.e. $y = g(\beta_1^\top X, \cdots, \beta_D^\top X) + \varepsilon$ with $\mathrm{E}(\varepsilon|X) = 0$ *a.s.*. If $D < p$, we can nominally extend the number of directions to p, say $\{\beta_1, \cdots, \beta_D, \cdots, \beta_p\}$, such that they are perpendicular to one another.

Now, the problem becomes the selection of the explanatory variables among $\{\beta_1^\top X, \cdots, \beta_p^\top X\}$. However, because $\beta_1, \cdots, \beta_p$ are unknown, we have to replace β_k's by their estimator $\hat{\beta}_k$'s. As we have proved that the convergence rate of $\hat{\beta}_k$'s is faster than that of the nonparametric function estimators, the replacement is justified.

Let $\hat{a}_{d0,j}, \hat{a}_{d1,j}, \cdots \hat{a}_{dd,j}$ be the minimizers of

$$\sum_{i=1,\ i\neq j}^{n} \{y_i - a_{d0,j} - a_{d1,j}\hat{\beta}_1^\top (X_i - X_j) - \cdots - a_{dd,j}\hat{\beta}_d^\top (X_i - X_j)\}^2 K_{d,h}^{(i,j)} \tag{3.35}$$

where $K_{d,h}^{(i,j)} = K_h(\hat{\beta}_1^\top (X_i - X_j), \cdots, \hat{\beta}_d^\top (X_i - X_j))$. Let

$$CV(d) = n^{-1} \sum_{j=1}^{n} \{y_j - \hat{a}_{d0,j}\}^2, \quad d = 1, \cdots, p.$$

We estimate the number of e.d.r. as

$$\hat{d} = \arg \min_{1 \le d \le p} CV(d).$$

THEOREM 3.4 *Suppose that the assumptions of (C1)-(C6) (in Appendix 3.9) hold. Under model (3.4), we have*

$$\lim_{n\to\infty} P(\hat{d} = D) = 1.$$

In theory, we ought to select the explanatory variables among all possible combinations of $\{\beta_1^\top X, \cdots, \beta_p^\top X\}$. However, in practice because $\{\hat{\beta}_1, \cdots, \hat{\beta}_d\}$ have been ordered according to their contributions (see the algorithm in the next section), we need only calculate $CV(d), d = 1, \cdots, p$, and compare their values.

After determining the number of directions, which is usually less than p, we can then search for the e.d.r. directions on a lower dimensional space, thereby reducing the effect of high dimensionality and improving the accuracy of the estimation. Denote the corresponding estimate of B_0 by $\hat{B} : p \times \hat{d}$. Let

$$\tilde{w}_{ij} = K_h(\hat{B}^\top (X_i - X_j)) / \sum_{\ell=1}^{n} K_h(\hat{B}^\top (X_\ell - X_j)) \tag{3.36}$$

Re-estimate B_0 by the minimization in (3.18) with weights $\tilde{w}_{ij}$ replacing w_{ij}. By an abuse of notation, we denote the new estimator of B_0 by $\hat{B}$ too. Replace $\hat{B}$ in (3.36) by the latest $\hat{B}$ and estimate B_0. Repeat this procedure until $\hat{B}$ converges. Let $\tilde{B}$ be the final estimator. We call it the refined MAVE (rMAVE) estimator.

THEOREM 3.5 *Suppose that (C1)-(C6) (in Appendix 3.9) hold. Assume that model (3.4) is true and $g(\cdot)$ has derivatives of all order. Let $r = 1$. If $nh^D/\log n \to \infty$, $h \to 0$, then*

$$\|(I - \tilde{B}\tilde{B}^\top)B_0\| = O_P(h^3 + h\delta_n + h^{-1}\delta_n^2 + n^{-1/2}).$$

To illustrate, we apply the procedure to models (3.20) and (3.21) to see the improvement of the rMAVE method. The mean of the estimation absolute errors against the bandwidth is shown in Figure 3.6. The improvement is significant.

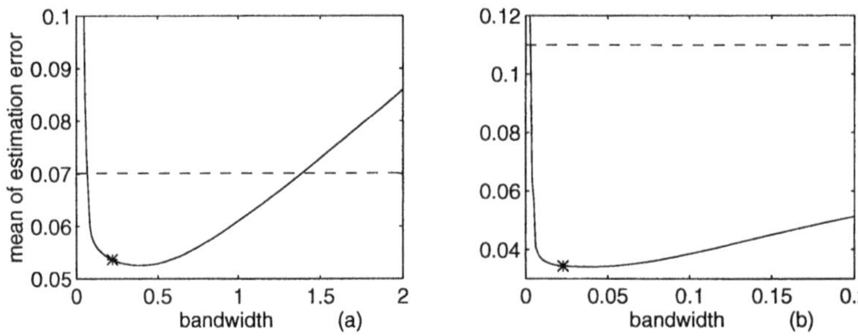

Figure 3.6. (a) and (b) are the simulation results for model (3.20) and model (3.21) respectively. The curves are the means of the estimation errors using the rMAVE method. The dash lines are the smallest means of estimation errors using MAVE among all possible choice of bandwidths. The asterisks refer to the errors when using the bandwidth chosen by the cross-validation method

As a special case, we can estimate the direction in a single-index model by the rMAVE method (with $r = 1$). The root-n consistency can be achieved even if we use the bandwidth $h \sim n^{-1/5}$. A similar result was obtained by Härdle, Hall, and Ichimura (1993) by minimizing the sum of squares of the residuals simultaneously with respect to the direction and the bandwidth.

3.5 The Algorithm

In this section, we first give some guidance on the selection of the bandwidth, the estimation of e.d.r. directions and the determination of the number of e.d.r. directions. Then we give an algorithm for the calculation of the e.d.r. directions.

We first standardize the original data. Write $X_i = (x_{i1}, \cdots, x_{ip})^\top$, $i = 1, 2, \cdots, n$. Let $\bar{X} = (\bar{x}_1, \cdots, \bar{x}_p)^\top = n^{-1}\sum_{i=1}^n X_i$ and $x_{i,k} := (x_{i,k} - \bar{x}_k)$ / $(\sum_{l=1}^n (x_{l,k} - \bar{x}_k)^2/n)^{1/2}$, $k = 1, 2, \cdots, p$ and $i = 1, 2, \cdots, n$. We use the cross-validation method to select the bandwidth h. For each j, let $\hat{a}_{h,j}$ and $\hat{b}_{h,j}$ be the arguments of

$$\min_{a_{h,j}, b_{h,j}} n^{-1} \sum_{i=1}^n \{y_i - a_{h,j} - b_{h,j}^\top (X_i - X_j)\}^2 K_{h,i}(X_j)$$

The bandwidth is then chosen as

$$h_{cv} = \arg\min_h \sum_{j=1}^n \{y_j - \hat{a}_{h,j}\}^2.$$

With the bandwidth h_{cv}, we now proceed to the calculation of the e.d.r. directions below by reference to the minimization (3.16). By (3.17) and Theorem 3.2, we can estimate the e.d.r. directions using the backfitting method. To save space, we give here the details for model (3.4) to illustrate the general idea. For any d, let $\mathcal{B} = (\beta_1, \cdots, \beta_d)$ with $\beta_1 = \beta_2 = \cdots = \beta_d = 0$ as the initial value and $\mathcal{B}_{l,k} = (\beta_1, \cdots, \beta_{k-1})$ and $\mathcal{B}_{r,k} = (\beta_{k+1}, \cdots, \beta_d)$, $k = 1, 2, \cdots, d$. Minimize

$$S_{n,k} = \sum_{j=1}^n \sum_{i=1}^n \left[y_i - a_j - (X_i - X_j)^\top (\mathcal{B}_{l,k}, b, \mathcal{B}_{r,k}) \begin{pmatrix} c_j \\ d_j \\ e_j \end{pmatrix} \right]^2 w_{ij}$$

$$\text{subject to :} \quad \mathcal{B}_{l,k}^\top b = 0 \text{ and } \mathcal{B}_{r,k}^\top b = 0,$$

where c_j is a $(k-1) \times 1$ vector, d_j a scalar and e_j a $(d-k) \times 1$ vector. This is a typical constrained quadratic programming problem. See, for example, Rao (1973, p. 232). Let

$$C_j = \sum_{i=1}^n w_{ij}(X_i - X_j), \quad D_j = \sum_{i=1}^n w_{ij}(X_i - X_j)(X_i - X_j)^\top,$$

$$E_j = \sum_{i=1}^n w_{ij} y_i, \quad F_j = \sum_{i=1}^n w_{ij}(X_i - X_j) y_i.$$

With b given, (a_j, c_j, d_j, e_j) which minimizes $S_{n,k+1}$ is given by

$$\begin{pmatrix} a_j \\ c_j \\ d_j \\ e_j \end{pmatrix} = \begin{pmatrix} 1 & C_j^\top(\mathcal{B}_{l,k}, b, \mathcal{B}_{r,k}) \\ (\mathcal{B}_{l,k}, b, \mathcal{B}_{r,k})^\top C_j & (\mathcal{B}_{l,k}, b, \mathcal{B}_{r,k})^\top D_j (\mathcal{B}_{l,k}, b, \mathcal{B}_{r,k}) \end{pmatrix}^{-1} \times \begin{pmatrix} E_j \\ (\mathcal{B}_{l,k}, b, \mathcal{B}_{r,k})^\top F_j \end{pmatrix}, \tag{3.37}$$

$j = 1, \cdots, n$. If a_j, c_j, d_j and e_j are given, then the b which minimizes $S_{n,k+1}$ is given by

$$\begin{pmatrix} b \\ \lambda \end{pmatrix} = \begin{pmatrix} \sum_{j=1}^n d_j^2 D_j & \tilde{\mathcal{B}}_k \\ \tilde{\mathcal{B}}_k^\top & 0 \end{pmatrix}^+ \begin{pmatrix} \sum_{j=1}^n d_j \{F_j - a_j - D_j \tilde{\mathcal{B}}_k \begin{pmatrix} c_j \\ e_j \end{pmatrix}\} \\ 0 \end{pmatrix} \tag{3.38}$$

where $\tilde{\mathcal{B}}_k = (\mathcal{B}_{l,k}, \mathcal{B}_{r,k})$ and A^+ denotes the Moore-Penrose inverse of a matrix A. Therefore, we can then minimize $S_{n,k+1}$ iteratively as follows.

0. initial $\mathcal{B} = 0$ and $k = 1$;

1. initialize b such that $\mathcal{B}_{l,k}^\top b = 0$, $\mathcal{B}_{r,k}^\top b = 0$ and $||b|| = 1$ and repeat the following steps

   a. Calculate (a_j, c_j, d_j, e_j) as in (3.37);

   b. Calculate b as in (3.38) and let $b := b/||b||$;

2. replace $\mathcal{B}$ by $(\mathcal{B}_{l,k}, b, \mathcal{B}_{r,k})$, let $k := k + 1$ if $k + 1 \le d$, 1 otherwise, return to step 1.

Repeat steps 1 and 2 until convergence is obtained.

The above algorithm is quite efficient. Note that to search for the minimum point we do not have to use the derivative of the unknown functions as required by the Newton-Raphson method, which is hard to estimate. See for example Weisberg and Welsh (1994). Indeed, the subsequent numerical examples suggest the above algorithm has a wider domain of convergence than the Newton-Raphson based algorithm.

3.6 Simulation Results

In this section, we carry out simulations to check the performance of the proposed OPG method and MAVE method. Some comparisons of the methods are made. Let $\mathcal{S}(B)$ be the space spanned by the column vectors in B. To describe the error of estimation, we define the distance from b to $\mathcal{S}(B)$ as $d(b, B) = b^\top(I - BB^\top)b$, where the columns of B form an orthogonal standard basis of the space. It is easy to see that $0 \le d(b, B) \le 1$. If $d(b, B) = 0$ then $b \in \mathcal{S}(B)$; if $d(b, B) = 1$ then $b \perp \mathcal{S}(B)$.

Example 3.6.1. Consider the following model

$$y = X^\top\beta_1(X^\top\beta_2)^2 + (X^\top\beta_3)(X^\top\beta_4) + 0.5\varepsilon, \tag{3.39}$$

where $X \sim N(0, I_{10})$ and $\varepsilon \sim N(0, 1)$ and they are independent. In model (3.39), the coefficients $\beta_1 = (1, 2, 3, 4, 0, 0, 0, 0, 0, 0)^\top/\sqrt{30}$, $\beta_2 = (-2, 1, -4, 3, 1, 2, 0, 0, 0, 0)^\top/\sqrt{35}$, $\beta_3 = (0, 0, 0, 0, 2, -1, 2, 1, 2, 1)^\top/\sqrt{15}$, $\beta_4 = (0, 0, 0, 0, 0, 0, -1, -1, 1, 1)^\top/2$ and there are four e.d.r. directions. Let $B_0 = (\beta_1, \beta_2, \beta_3, \beta_4)$. In our simulations, the SIR method and the ADE method perform quite poorly for this model. Next, we use this model to check the OPG method and the MAVE method.

n	Methods	$d(\hat\beta_k, B_0)$				Freq. of Est. No. of e.d.r directions		
		$k=1$	$k=2$	$k=3$	$k=4$			
100	pHd	.2769	.2992	.4544	.5818	f_1=0	f_2=10	f_3=23
	OPG	.1524	.2438	.3444	.4886	f_4=78	f_5=44	f_6=32
	MAVE	.1364	.1870	.2165	.3395	f_7=11	f_8=1	f_9=1
	rMAVE	.1137	.1397	.1848	.3356	f_{10}=0		
200	pHd	.1684	.1892	.3917	.6006	f_1=0	f_2=0	f_3=5
	OPG	.0713	.1013	.1349	.2604	f_4=121	f_5=50	f_6=16
	MAVE	.0710	.0810	.0752	.1093	f_7=8	f_8=0	f_9=0
	rMAVE	.0469	.0464	.0437	.0609	f_{10}=0		
400	pHd	.0961	.1151	.3559	.6020	f_1=0	f_2=0	f_3=0
	OPG	.0286	.0388	.0448	.0565	f_4=188	f_5=16	f_6=6
	MAVE	.0300	.0344	.0292	.0303	f_7=0	f_8=0	f_9=0
	rMAVE	.0170	.0119	.0116	.0115	f_{10}=0		

Table 3.1. Average distance $d(\hat\beta_k, B_0)$ for model (3.39) using different methods

With sample sizes n = 100, 200 and 400, 200 independent samples are drawn. The average distance from the estimated e.d.r. directions to $\mathcal{S}(B_0)$ is calculated for the pHd method (Li, 1992), the OPG method, the MAVE method and the rMAVE method. The results are listed in Table 3.1. The proposed OPG and

MAVE methods work quite well. The results also show that the MAVE method is better than the OPG method, while the rMAVE method shows significant improvement over the MAVE method. Our method for the estimation of the number of e.d.r. directions also works quite well.

Example 3.6.2. We next consider the nonlinear time series model

$$y_t = -1 + 0.4\beta_1^\top X_{t-1} - \cos(\frac{\pi}{2}\beta_2^\top X_{t-1}) + \exp\{-(\beta_3^\top X_{t-1})^2\} + 0.2\varepsilon_t, \quad (3.40)$$

where $X_{t-1} = (y_{t-1}, \cdots, y_{t-6})^\top$, ε are i.i.d. $N(0,1)$, $\beta_1 = (1,0,0,2,0,0)^\top/\sqrt{5}$, $\beta_2 = (0,0,2,0,0,1)^\top/\sqrt{5}$ and $\beta_3 = (-2,2,-2,1,-1,1)^\top/\sqrt{15}$. A typical data set sample with size 1000 was drawn from this model. The points (y_t, y_{t-k}), $t = 1, \ldots, 1000$, and $k = 1, \cdots, 6$ are plotted in Figures 3.7 (a)–(f). As there is no discernible symmetry, the SIR method will not be appropriate.

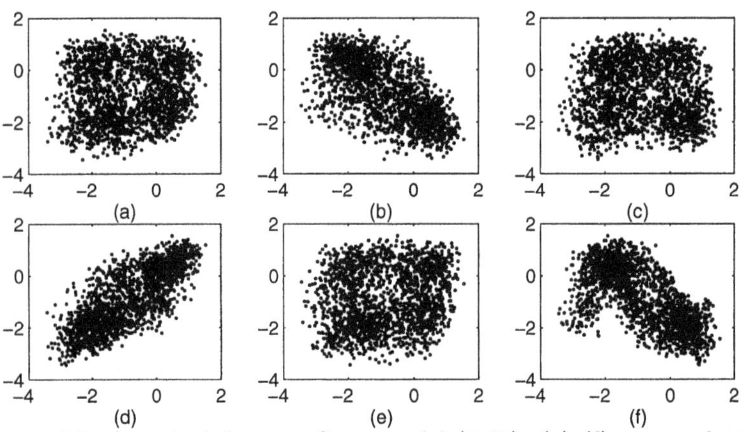

Figure 3.7. A typical data set from model (3.40). (a)-(f) are y_t plotted against y_{t-k}, $k = 1, \cdots, 6$, respectively.

Now, we use the OPG method and the MAVE method. The simulation results are listed in Table 3.2. Both methods have quite small estimation errors. As expected, the rMAVE method works better than the MAVE method, and the MAVE method outperforms the OPG method. The number of the e.d.r. directions is also estimated correctly most of the time for suitable sample size.

Example 3.6.3. The multi-index model (3.6). For simplicity, we discuss only the generalized partially linear single-index models. This model was proposed by Xia, Tong, and Li (1999), which has been found adequate for quite a lot of

n	Method	$d(\hat{\beta}_k, B_0)$ for k =			Freq. of Est. No. of e.d.r. directions	
		1	2	3		
100	pHd	.1582	.2742	.3817	f_1=3	f_2=73
	OPG	.0427	.1202	.2803	f_3=94	f_4=25
	MAVE	.0295	.1201	.2924	f_5=4	f_6=1
	rMAVE	.0096	.0712	.2003		
200	pHd	.1565	.2656	.3690	f_1=0	f_2=34
	OPG	.0117	.0613	.1170	f_3=160	f_4=5
	MAVE	.0059	.0399	.1209	f_5=1	f_6=0
	rMAVE	.0030	.0224	.0632		
300	pHd	.1619	.2681	.3710	f_1=0	f_2=11
	OPG	.0076	.0364	.0809	f_3=185	f_4=4
	MAVE	.0040	.0274	.0666	f_5=0	f_6=0
	rMAVE	.0017	.0106	.0262		

Table 3.2. Mean of the distance $d(\hat{\beta}_k, B_0)$ for model (3.40) using different methods

real data sets. The model can be written as

$$y = \theta_0^\top X + g(\beta_0^\top X) + \varepsilon, \tag{3.41}$$

where $\theta_0 \perp \beta_0$ and $||\beta_0|| = 1$. Following the idea of the MAVE method, we may estimate θ_0 and β_0 by minimizing

$$\sum_{j=1}^{n}\sum_{i=1}^{n} \Big[y_i - \theta^\top X_i - a_j - b_j\beta^\top(X_i - X_j)\Big]^2 w_{ij},$$
$$\text{subject to } \ \theta \perp \beta. \tag{3.42}$$

Suppose that $\tilde{\theta}$ and $\tilde{\beta}$ constitute the minimum point. Then we have the estimates

$$\hat{\theta} = \tilde{\theta} - (\tilde{\theta}^\top \tilde{\beta})\tilde{\beta} \quad \text{and} \quad \hat{\beta} = \tilde{\beta}.$$

To illustrate the performance of the above algorithm, we further consider the following model

$$y = 3x_2 + 2x_3 + (x_1 - 2x_2 + 3x_3)^2 + \varepsilon, \tag{3.43}$$

where x_1, x_2, x_3 and ε are i.i.d. $\sim N(0,\ 1)$. In this model, $\theta_0 = (0,3,2)^\top$ and $\beta_0 = (1,-2,3)^\top/\sqrt{14} = (0.2673, -0.5345, 0.8018)^\top$. Let $\theta_1 = \theta_0/||\theta_0|| =$

$(0, 0.8321, 0.5547)^\top$ and $B_0 = (\beta_0, \theta_1)$. We can estimate the model using the MAVE method without assuming its specific form. The simulation results listed in Table 3.3 suggest that the estimation is quite successful. If we further assume that it is a generalized partially linear single-index model and estimate θ_1 and β_0 by minimizing (3.42), the estimation is much better as shown in Table 3.3.

n		no model specification		model specified	
50	β_0	(0.2703 -0.5147 0.8136)	[.000329]	(0.2678 -0.5346 0.8014)	[.000052]
	θ_1	(0.0264 0.8487 0.5281)	[.013229]	(0.0108 0.8319 0.5513)	[.003946]
100	β_0	(0.2679 -0.5307 0.8041)	[.000052]	(0.2665 -0.5346 0.8020)	[.000019]
	θ_1	(0.0035 0.8341 0.5516)	[.002244]	(0.0014 0.8318 0.5540)	[.001142]

Table 3.3. Mean of the estimated directions and average distance $d(\hat\beta_0, B_0)$ or $d(\hat\theta_1, B_0)$ in square brackets for model (3.43)

Example 3.6.4. The varying-coefficient model (3.7). For simplicity, here we only discuss the single-index coefficient linear model proposed by Xia and Li (1999). The model can be written as

$$y_t = c_0(\beta_0^\top X_{t-1}) + c_1(\beta_0^\top X_{t-1})y_{t-1} + \cdots + c_p(\beta_0^\top X_{t-1})y_{t-p} + \varepsilon_t, \quad (3.44)$$

where $X_{t-1} = (y_{t-1}, \cdots, y_{t-p})^\top$.

To see the performance of the MAVE method discussed in Section 3.3.2, we further consider the following model

$$y_t = 0.4\sin(x_t) + 0.5\Phi(x_t + 0.6)y_{t-4} + 0.6\exp(-x_t^2/4)y_{t-5} + 0.2\varepsilon_t, \quad (3.45)$$

where $x_t = 2(0.5y_{t-1} + y_{t-2} + 1.5y_{t-3})$, $t = 0, \pm1, \pm2, \cdots$, and ε_t are i.i.d. $\sim N(0,\ 1)$. In this model, $\beta_0 = (1,2,3)^\top/\sqrt{13} = (0.2774\ 0.5547\ 0.8321)^\top$. Model (3.45) is a combination of the TAR model and the EXPAR model (cf. Tong (1990)). Table 3.4 shows the simulation results, which also suggest that the estimation is satisfactory.

n	Estimated direction	s.d.
$n = 100$	(0.2794 0.5306 0.7895)	[0.07896 0.0817 0.0646]
$n = 200$	(0.2637 0.5243 0.8052)	[0.06310 0.0468 0.0303]

Table 3.4. Mean of the estimated directions and the standard deviation for model (3.45)

3.7 Applications

In this section, we return to the opening questions of this chapter concerning some real data sets. In our calculation, we use the Gaussian kernel throughout.

Example 3.7.1. We return to the data set in Example 3.1.1. Previous analyses, such as Fan and Zhang (1999), have ignored the weather effect. The omission of the weather effect seems reasonable from the point of view linear regression, such as model (3.2). However, as we shall see, the weather has an important role to play.

The daily admissions shown in Figure 3.8 (a) suggest non-stationarity, which is, however, not discernible in the explanatory variables. This kind of trend was also observed by Smith, Davis, and Speckman (1999) in their study of the effect of particulates on human health. They conjecture that the trend is due to the epidemic effect. We therefore estimate the time dependence by a simple kernel method and the result is show in Figure 3.8 (a). Another factor is the day-of-the-week effect, presumably due to the booking system. The effect of the day-of-the-week effect can be estimated by a simple regression method using dummy variables. To better assess the effect of pollutants, we remove these two factors first. By an abuse of notation, we shall continue to use the y_t to denote the 'filtered' data, now shown in Figure 3.8 (b).

As the different pollutant-based and weather-based covariates may affect the circulatory and respiratory system after different time delay, we first use the method of Yao and Tong (1994) to select a suitable lag for each covariate within the model framework

$$y_t = g(x_{k,t-\ell}) + \varepsilon_{k,t}, \qquad k = 1, 2, \cdots, 6, \quad \ell = 1, 2, \cdots, 8.$$

The selected lag variables are $x_{1,t-6}, x_{2,t-1}, x_{3,t-1}, x_{4,t-7}, x_{5,t-6}, x_{6,t-4}$ respectively. Since it is expected that the rapid changes in the temperature may also affect the health, we also incorporate the local temperature variation $v_{5,t}$. See, Fan and Yao (1998). Finally, we consider the model

$$y_t = g(X_t) + \varepsilon_t, \text{ with } X_t = (x_{1,t-6}, x_{2,t-1}, x_{3,t-1}, x_{4,t-7}, v_{5,t-6}, x_{5,t-6}, x_{6,t-4})^\top,$$

where all the variables are standardized.

Now, using the MAVE method and with the bandwidth $h = 0.8$, we have $CV(1) = 0.3802, CV(2) = 0.3632, CV(3) = 0.3614, CV(4) = 0.3563, CV(5) = 0.3613, CV(6) = 0.3800, CV(7) = 0.4241$. Therefore, the number of e.d.r. directions is 4. The corresponding directions are

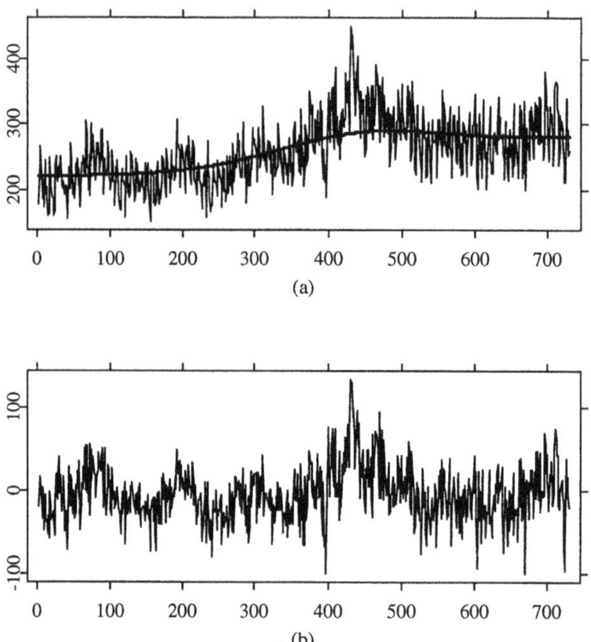

Figure 3.8. For Example 3.7.1. (a) the original data set and the time trend, (b) after removing the time trend and the day-of-the-weak effect.

XEGfig9.xpl

$$
\begin{array}{lcl}
\hat{\beta}_1 & = & (\text{-}0.0606 \quad 0.5394 \quad \text{-}0.2396 \quad \text{-}0.1286 \quad \text{-}0.4652 \quad \text{-}0.6435 \quad 0.0305)^\top, \\
\hat{\beta}_2 & = & (\text{-}0.0930 \quad \text{-}0.0453 \quad \text{-}0.0048 \quad 0.6045 \quad 0.0587 \quad \text{-}0.2264 \quad \text{-}0.7544)^\top, \\
\hat{\beta}_3 & = & (0.2193 \quad 0.7568 \quad \text{-}0.0707 \quad 0.2136 \quad 0.5232 \quad 0.2226 \quad 0.0730)^\top, \\
\hat{\beta}_4 & = & (\text{-}0.1018 \quad 0.0271 \quad 0.8051 \quad \text{-}0.0255 \quad 0.3033 \quad \text{-}0.4745 \quad 0.1514)^\top.
\end{array}
$$

XEGex71.xpl

Figures 3.9 (a)–(d) show y_t plotted against the e.d.r. directions. Figures 3.9 (a$'$)-(d$'$) are the estimated regression function of y_t on the e.d.r. directions and pointwise 95% confidence bands. See for example Fan and Gibbers (1996). It suggests that along these directions, there are discernible changes in the function value.

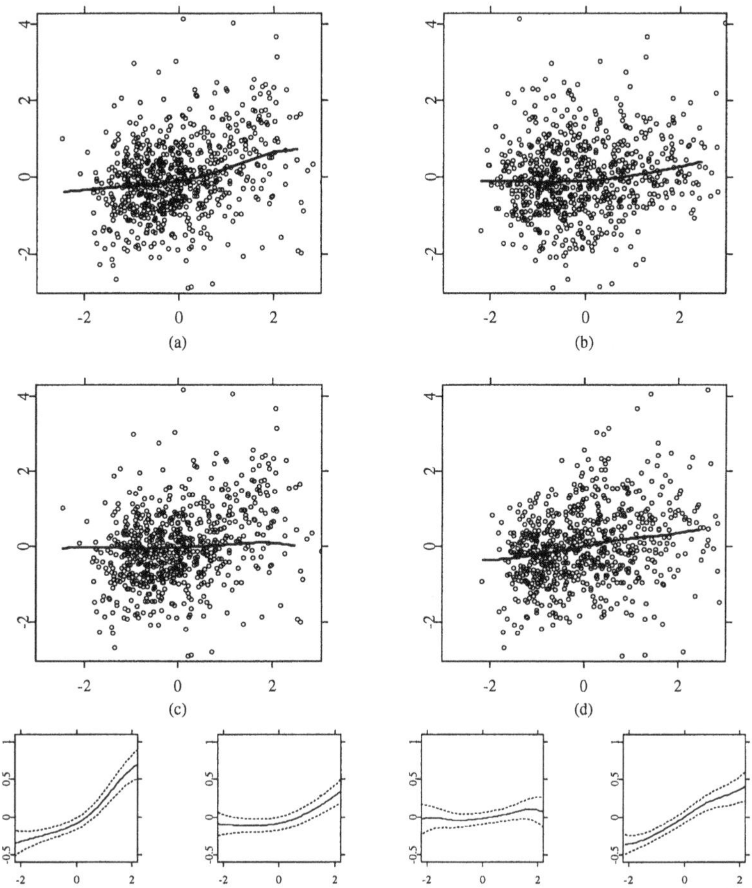

Figure 3.9. Example 3.7.1. (a)–(d) are the y_t plotted against $\hat{\beta}_1^\top X$, $\hat{\beta}_2^\top X$, $\hat{\beta}_3^\top X$ and $\hat{\beta}_4^\top X$ respectively. (a′)–(d′) are the estimates of regression functions of y_t on $\hat{\beta}_i^\top X$, $i = 1, 2, 3, 4$, and the pointwise 95% confidence bands.

XEGfig10.xpl

We may draw some preliminary conclusions about which weather-pollutant conditions are more likely to produce adverse effects on the human circulatory and respiratory system. We have identified four conditions, which we list in descending order of importance as follows. (i) The main covariates in $\hat{\beta}_1^\top X$ are nitrogen dioxide (x_2), variation of temperature (v_5) and temperature x_5, with coefficients 0.5394, -0.4652 and -0.6435 respectively. From Figures 3.9 (a) and (a$'$), the first e.d.r. direction suggests that continuous cool days with high nitrogen dioxide level constitute the most important condition. This kind of weather is very common in the winter in Hong Kong. (ii) The main covariates in $\hat{\beta}_2^\top X$ are ozone (x_4) and humidity (x_6), with coefficients 0.6045 and -0.7544 respectively. Figures 3.10 (b) and (b1) suggest that dry days with high ozone level constitute the second most important condition. Dry days are very common in the autumn time in Hong Kong. (iii) The main covariates in $\hat{\beta}_3^\top X$ are nitrogen dioxide (x_2) and the variation of the temperature (v_5), with coefficients 0.7568 and 0.5232 respectively. Figures 3.9 (c) and (c$'$) suggest that rapid temperature variation with high level of nitrogen dioxide constitutes the third important condition. Rapid temperature variations can take place at almost any time in Hong Kong. (iv) The main covariates in $\hat{\beta}_4^\top X$ are the respirable suspended particulates x_3, the variation of temperature v_5 and the level of temperature x_5, with coefficients 0.8051, 0.3033 and -0.4745 respectively. Figures 3.9 (d) and (d') suggest that high particulate level with rapid temperature variation in the winter constitutes the fourth important condition.

Although individually the levels of major pollutants may be considered to be below the acceptable threshold values according to the National Ambient Quality Standard (NAQS) of U.S.A. as shown in Figure 3.10, there is evidence to suggest that give certain weather conditions which exist in Hong Kong, current levels of nitrogen dioxide, ozone and particulates in the territory already pose a considerable health risk to its citizens. Our results have points of contact with the analysis of Smith, Davis, and Speckman (1999), which focused on the effect of particulates on human health.

Q XEGfig11.xpl

Example 3.7.2. We continue with Example 3.1.2. The first model was fitted by Maran (1953):

$$y_t = 1.05 + 1.41 y_{t-1} - 0.77 y_{t-2} + \varepsilon_t, \tag{3.46}$$

where $\varepsilon_t \overset{i.i.d.}{\sim} N(0, 0.0459)$. The fit of this linear model is known to be inadequate (see e.g. Tong (1990)). Let us consider a nonlinear (nonparametric)

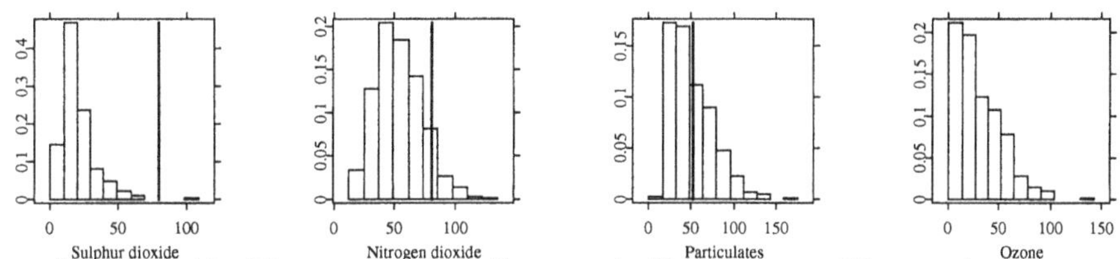

Figure 3.10. Histograms of pollutants in Hong Kong. The vertical lines are the threshold NAQS values, which pollutants are considered to have significant effect on the circulatory and respiratory system. (We do not have the corresponding value for ozone).

Model	SS of residuals	cv*	bandwidth by cv
$y_t = g_0(\hat{\beta}_1^\top X_t, \hat{\beta}_2^\top X_t) + \varepsilon_t$	0.0417	0.0475	0.5316
$y_t = g_1(\hat{\beta}_1^\top X_t) + \varepsilon_t$	0.0475	0.0504	0.2236
$y_t - \hat{g}_1(\hat{\beta}_1^\top X_t) = g_2(\hat{\beta}_1^\top X_t) + \varepsilon_t$	0.0420	0.0449	0.5136
$y_t = \theta^\top X_t + g(\beta^\top X_t) + \varepsilon_t$	0.0401	0.0450	0.2240

* The data have not been standardised because we want to compare the results with Maran's (1953)

Table 3.5. Estimations of models for the Lynx data in Example 3.7.2.

autoregressive model say

$$y_t = g(X_t) + \varepsilon_t, \tag{3.47}$$

where $X_t = (y_{t-1}, y_{t-2})^\top$.

Now, using the dimension reduction method, we obtain the e.d.r. directions as $\hat{\beta}_1 = (.87, -.49)^\top$ and $\hat{\beta}_2 = (.49, .87)^\top$. No dimensional reduction is needed and the number of e.d.r. is 2. It is interesting to see that the first e.d.r. direction practically coincides with that of model (3.46). (Note that $1.41/(-0.77) \approx 0.87/(-0.49)$). Without the benefit of the second direction, the inadequacy of model (3.46) is not surprising. Next, the sum of squared (SS) of the residuals listed in Table 3.5 suggests that an additive model can achieve almost the same SS of the residuals. Therefore, we may entertain an additive model of the form

$$y_t = g_1(\beta_1^\top X_t) + g_2(\beta_2^\top X_t) + \varepsilon_t. \tag{3.48}$$

The estimated g_1 and g_2 are shown in Figures 3.11 (a) and (b) respectively. Note that g_1 is nearly a linear function.

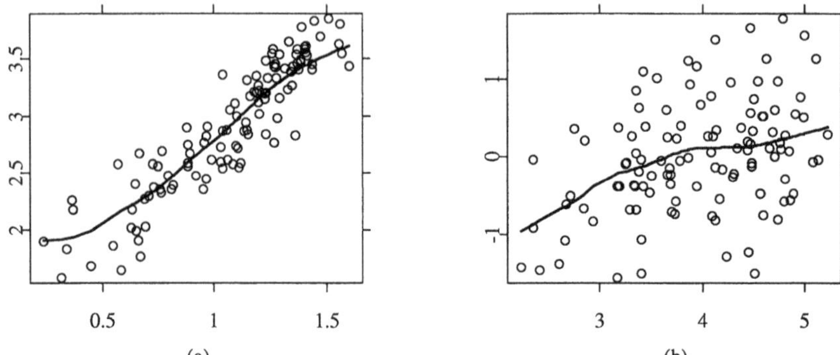

Figure 3.11. For Example 3.7.2. (a) and (b) are the estimated g_1 and g_2 respectively.
XEGfig12.xpl

Based on the above observation, it further seems reasonable to fit a generalized partially linear single-index model of the form (3.41). Using the method described in Example 3.6.3, we have fitted the model

$$y_t = 1.1339 y_{t-1} + 0.2420 y_{t-2} + g(-0.2088 y_{t-1} + 0.9780 y_{t-2}) + \varepsilon_t.$$

By comparing the sum of square of the residuals in Table 3.5, the partially linear single-index model fits the lynx data quite well. Removing the linear part, g may be written in the form

$$\begin{aligned} g(-0.2088 y_{t-1} + 0.9780 y_{t-2}) &= 1.0986 - 0.9794(-0.2088 y_{t-1} + 0.9780 y_{t-2}) \\ &\quad + g_o(-0.2088 y_{t-1} + 0.9780 y_{t-2}), \end{aligned}$$

where $Corr(g_o(-0.2088 y_{t-1} + 0.9780 y_{t-2}), X_t) = 0$. Then, the fitted partially linear single-index model can be written as

$$y_t = 1.099 + 1.3384 y_{t-1} - 0.716 y_{t-2} + g_o(-0.209 y_{t-1} + 0.978 y_{t-2}) + \varepsilon_t, \quad (3.49)$$

which looks quite similar to model (3.46) except for g_o. Note that the coefficient of y_{t-1} in g_o is small compared with that of y_{t-2}. Therefore, model (3.49) can be further approximated to

$$y_t \approx 1.3384 y_{t-1} + f_o(y_{t-2}) + \varepsilon_t.$$

This is close to the model suggested by Lin and Pourahmadi (1998) and has clearly points of contact with the threshold models, where the "thresholding" is at lag 2. (Tong, 1990).

3.8 Conclusions and Further Discussion

In this chapter, we first extend the ADE method of Härdle and Stoker (1989) to the case of more than one e.d.r direction, i.e. the OPG method. This method has wide applicability in respect of designs for X and regression functions. To improve the accuracy of the estimation, we then propose our basic method, i.e. the MAVE method. Both theoretical analysis and simulations show that the MAVE method has many attractive properties. Different from all existing methods for the estimation of the directions, the MAVE estimators of the directions have a faster convergence rate than the corresponding estimators of the regression function. Based on the faster convergence rate, a method for the determination of the number of e.d.r directions is proposed. The MAVE method can also be extended easily to more complicated models. It does not require strong assumptions on the design of X and the regression functions.

Following the basic idea, we proposed the iMAVE method, which is closely related to the SIR method. In our simulations, the iMAVE method has better performance than the SIR method. The refined kernel based on the determination of the number of the directions can further improve the estimation accuracy of the directions. Our simulations show that substantial improvements can be achieved.

Unlike the SIR method, the MAVE method is well adapted to time series. Furthermore, all of our simulations show that the MAVE method has much better performance than the SIR method (even with $r = 1$ in the MAVE). This is rather intriguing because the SIR uses the one-dimensional kernel (for the kernel version) while the MAVE method uses a multi-dimensional kernel. However, because the SIR method uses y to produce the kernel weight, its efficiency will suffer from fluctuations in the regression function. The gain by using the y-based one-dimensional kernel does not seem to be sufficient to compensate for the loss in efficiency caused by the fluctuation in the regression function. Further research is needed here.

3.9 Appendix. Assumptions and Remarks

Note that the observations of X should be centralized before analyzed. Therefore, we assume X is centralized for ease of exposition. In our proofs, we need the following conditions. (In all our theorems, weaker conditions can be adopted at the expense of much lengthier proofs.)

(C1) $\{(X_i, y_i)\}$ is a stationary (with the same distribution as (X, y)) and absolutely regular sequence, i.e.

$$\beta(k) = \sup_{i \geq 1} E\Big\{ \sup_{\mathcal{F}_{i+k}^{\infty}} |P(A|\mathcal{F}_1^i) - P(A)| \Big\} \to 0 \quad \text{as} \quad k \to \infty,$$

where $\mathcal{F}_i^k$ denotes the σ-field generated by $\{(X_\ell, y_\ell) : i \leq \ell \leq k\}$. Further, $\beta(k)$ decreases at a geometric rate.

(C2) $\mathrm{E}|y|^k < \infty$ for all $k > 0$.

(C2′) $\mathrm{E}|X||^k < \infty$ for all $k > 0$.

(C3) The density function f of X has bounded fourth derivative and is bounded away from 0 in a neighbor $\mathcal{D}$ around 0.

(C3′) The density function f_y of y has bounded derivative and is bounded away from 0 on a compact support.

(C4) The conditional densities $f_{X|y}(x|y)$ of X given y and $f_{(X_0,X_l)|(y_0,y_l)}$ of (X_0, X_l) given (y_0, y_l) are bounded for all $l \geq 1$.

(C5) g has bounded, continuous (r+2)th derivatives.

(C5′) $\mathrm{E}(X|y)$ and $\mathrm{E}(XX^\top|y)$ have bounded, continuous third derivatives.

(C6) $K(\cdot)$ is a spherical symmetric density function with a bounded derivative. All the moments of $K(\cdot)$ exist.

(C1) is made only for the purpose of simplicity of proof. It can be weakened to $\beta(k) = O(k^{-\iota})$ for some $\iota > 0$. Many time series models, including the autoregression single-index model (Xia and Li, 1999), satisfy assumption (C1). Assumption (C2) is also made for simplicity of proof. See, for example, Härdle, Hall, and Ichimura (1993). The existence of finite moments is sufficient. (C3) is needed for the uniform consistency of the kernel smoothing methods. Assumption (C4) is needed for kernel estimation of dependent data. Assumption (C5) is made to meet the continuous requirement for kernel smoothing. The kernel assumption (C6) is satisfied by most of the commonly used kernel functions. For ease of exposition, we further assume $\int UU^\top K(U)dU = I$.

Bibliography

Auestad, B. and Tjøstheim, D. (1990). Identification of nonlinear time series: first order characterisation and order determination. *Biometrika*, **77**: 669–688.

Carroll, R.J., Fan. J., Gijbels, I. and Wand, M.P. (1997). Generalized partially linear single-index models. *J. Am. Statist. Ass.*, **92**: 477–489.

Chen, R. and Tsay, S. (1993). Functional-coefficient autoregressive models. *J. Am. Statist. Ass.*, 88, 298–308.

Cheng, B. and Tong, H. (1992). On consistent nonparametric order determination and chaos (with discussion), *J. R. Statist. Soc. B.* **54**: 427–449.

Cook, R.D. (1998). Principle Hessian directions revisited (with discussions). *J. Am. Statist. Ass.*, **93**: 85–100.

Fan, J. and Gibbers, I. (1996). *Local Polynomial Modeling and Its Applications.* Chapman & Hall, London.

Fan, J. and Yao, Q. (1998). . Efficient estimation of conditional variance functions in Stochastic regression. *Biometrika*, **85**: 645–660.

Friedman, J.H. and Stuetzle, W. (1981). Projection pursuit regression, *J. Am. Statist. Ass.*, **76**: 817–823.

Fuller, W.A. (1976). *Introduction to Statistical Time Series.* New York: John Wiley & Sons.

Hall, P. (1984). Central limit theorem for integrated square error of multivariate nonparametric density estimators. *J. Mult. Anal.* **14**: 1-16.

Hannan, E. J. (1969). The estimation of mixed moving average autoregressive system. *Biometrika* **56**: 579–593.

Härdle, W., Hall, P. and Ichimura, H. (1993). Optimal smoothing in single-index models. *Ann. Statist.*, **21**, 157–178.

Härdle, W. and Stoker, T. M. (1989). Investigating smooth multiple regression by method of average derivatives. *J. Amer. Stat. Ass.* **84**: 986–995.

Hastie, T. and Tibshirani, R. (1993). Varying-coefficient models (with discussion) *J. R. Statist. Soc. B.* **55**: 757–796.

Huber, P.J. (1985). . Projection pursuit (with discussion). *Ann. Statist.*, **13**, 435–525.

Ichimura, H. and Lee, L. (1991). Semiparametric least squares estimation of multiple index models: Single equation estimation. *Nonparametric and Semiparametric Methods in Econometrics and Statistics*, edited by Barnett, W., Powell, J. and Tauchen, G.. Cambridge University Press.

Li, K. C. (1991). Sliced inverse regression for dimension reduction (with discussion). *Amer. Statist. Ass.* **86**: 316–342

Li, K. C. (1992). On principle Hessian directions for data visualization and dimension reduction: another application of Stein's Lemma. *Ann. Statist.* **87**: 1025–1039.

Li, W. K. (1992). On the asymptotic standard errors of residual autocorrelations in nonlinear time series modelling. *Biometrika* **79**: 435–437.

Lin, T. C. and Pourahmadi, M. (1998). Nonparametric and non-linear models and data mining in time series: A case-study on the Canadian lynx data. *Appl. Statist.* **47**: 187–201.

Masry, E.(1996). . Multivariate local polynomial regression for time series: uniform strong consistency and rates. *Journal of Time Series Analysis* **17**: 571–599.

Rao, C. R. (1973). *Linear Statistical Inference and Its Applications.* John Wiely & Sons.

Schott, J. R. (1994). Determining the dimensionality in sliced inverse regression. *J. Amer. Statist. Ass.* **89**: 141–148.

Smith, R. L., Davis, J. M. and Speckman, P. (1999). Assessing the human health risk of atmospheric particles. *Environmental Statistics: Analysing Data For Environmental Policy.* Novartis Foundation Symposium 220. John Wiley & Sons.

Sugihara, G. and May, R. M. (1990). Nonlinear forecasting as a way of distinguishing chaos from measurement errors. *Nature*, **344**: 734–741.

Tong, H. (1990). *Nonlinear Time Series Analysis: a Dynamic Approach.* Oxford University Press, London.

Weisberg, S. and Welsh, A. H. (1994). Estimating the missing link functions, *Ann. of Statist.* **22**, 1674–1700.

Xia, Y. and Li, W. K. (1999). On single-index coefficient regression models. *J. Amer. Statist. Ass.* **94**: 1275–1285.

Xia, Y., Tong, H., and W. K. Li (1999). On extended partially linear single-index models. *Biometrika*, 86, 831–842.

Xia, Y., Tong, H., W. K. Li, and Zhu, L-X. (2002). An adaptive method of dimension reduction. *J. R. Statist. Soc. B.* (to appear)

Yao, Q. and Tong, H. (1994). On subset selection in nonparametric stochastic regression. *Statistica Sinica, 4*, 51–70.

Yoshihara, K. I. (1976). Limiting behavior of U-statistics for stationary, absolutely regular process. *Z, Wahrsch. verw. Gebiete* **35**: 237–252.

Zhu, L. X. and Fang K.-T. (1996). Asymptotics for kernel estimate of sliced inverse regression. *Ann. Statist.* **24**: 1053–1068.

4 Univariate Time Series Modelling

Paz Moral and Pilar González

Data in economics are frequently collected in form of time series. A time series is a set of observations ordered in time and dependent of each other. We may find time series data in a wide variety of fields: macroeconomics, finance, demographics, etc. The intrinsic nature of a time series is that its observations are ordered in time and the modelling strategies of time series must take into account this property. This does not occur with cross-section data where the sequence of data points does not matter. Due to this order in time, it is likely that the value of a variable y at moment t reflects the past history of the series, that is, the observations of a time series are likely to be correlated. Since the observations are measurements of the same variable, it is usually said that y is correlated with itself, that is, it is autocorrelated.

Time Series Analysis is the set of statistical methodologies that analyze this kind of data. The main tool in Time Series Analysis is a model that should reproduce the past behavior of the series, exploiting its autocorrelation structure. The objectives of Time Series Analysis are basically two: to describe the regularity patterns present in the data and to forecast future observations. Since a pure time series model does not include explanatory variables, these forecasts of future observations are simply extrapolations of the observed series at the end of the sample. If we consider a single variable in our study, we shall construct what is called a *univariate time series model.* But if two of more variables are available, the possibility of dynamic interactions among them may be important. We can think, for instance, in economic variables such as consumption, investment and income that influence each other. In this case, *multivariate time series models* can be constructed to take into account these relations among variables (Lütkepohl, 1991).

This chapter will focus on which is called Univariate Time Series Analysis, that is, building a model and forecasting one variable in terms of its past observations. It is centered in time series models based on the theory of linear stochastic processes. A good survey on nonlinear formulations of time series models may be found in Granger and Teräsvirta (1993) among others. The chapter starts with a brief introduction of some basic ideas about the main characteristics of a time series that have to be considered when building a time series model (section 4.1). Section 4.2 presents the general class of nonseasonal linear models, denoted by $ARMA$ models that can be shown to be able to approximate most stationary processes. Since few time series in economics and business are stationary, section 4.3 presents models capable of reproducing nonstationary behavior. Focus is set on $ARIMA$ models, obtained by assuming that a series can be represented by an $ARMA$ stationary model after differencing. In section 4.4, the theory to obtain Minimum Mean Squared Error forecasts is presented. Model building and selection strategy for $ARIMA$ models is explained in section 4.5 along with an economic application analyzing the European Union G.D.P. series. Finally, in section 4.6 the issue of regression models with time series data is brought up briefly.

4.1 Introduction

A univariate time series consists of a set of observations on a single variable, y. If there are T observations, they may be denoted by $y_t, t = 1, 2, \ldots, T$. A univariate time series model for y_t is formulated in terms of past values of y_t and/or its position in relation to time.

Time series of economic data display many different characteristics and one easy way of starting the analysis of a series is to display the data by means of a timeplot in which the series of interest is graphed against time. A visual inspection of a time series plot allows us to see the relevant feature of dependence among observations and other important characteristics such as trends (long-run movements of the series), seasonalities, cycles of period longer than a year, structural breaks, conditional heteroskedasticity, etc.

Figure 4.1 shows graphics of four economic time series that exhibit some of these characteristics. The $Minks$ series plotted in graphic (a) evolves around a constant mean with cycles of period approximately 10 years, while the GDP series presents an upward trending pattern (graphic (b)) and the $Tourists$ series is dominated by a cyclical behavior that repeats itself more or less every year and which is called seasonality (graphic (c)). On the other hand, finance time series usually present variances that change over time as can be observed in graphic (d). This behavior can be captured by conditional heteroskedasticity

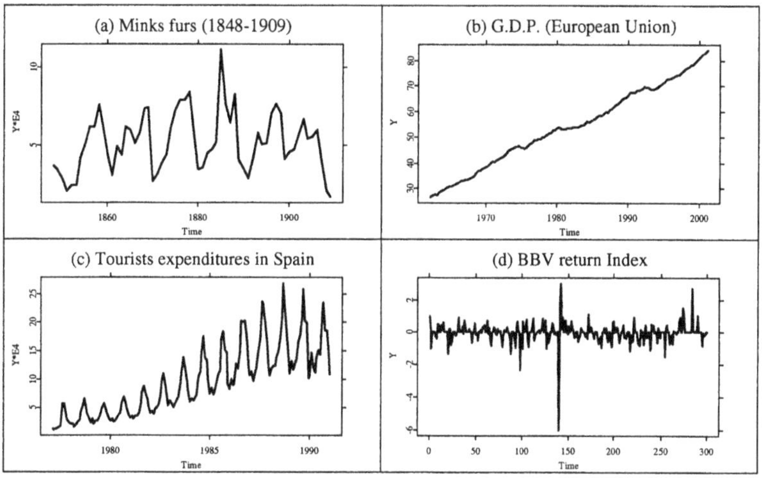

Figure 4.1. Time series plots

XEGutsm01.xpl

models that will be treated in detail in Chapter 6.

A time series model should reproduce these characteristics but there is no unique model to perform this analysis. With regard to trends and seasonalities, a simple way to deal with them is working within the framework of linear regression models (Diebold, 1997). In these models, the trend is specified as a deterministic function of time about which the series is constrained to move forever. For instance, a simple linear regression model able to represent the trending behaviour of the *GDP* series can be formulated as follows:

$$y_t = \alpha + \beta t + u_t$$

where u_t is the error term that may be correlated. The variable t is constructed artificially as a 'dummy variable' that takes the value 1 in the first period of the sample, 2 in the second period and so on.

As far as seasonality is concerned, it can be easily modelled as a deterministic function of time by including in the regression model a set of s seasonal dummies:

$$D_{jt} = \begin{cases} 1 & t \in \text{season}\, j \\ 0 & \text{otherwise} \end{cases} \quad j = 1, 2, \ldots, s$$

where s is the number of seasons in a year, thus, $s = 4$ if we have quarterly data, $s = 12$ if we have monthly data, and so forth. A linear regression model for a time series with a linear trend and seasonal behaviour can be formulated as follows:

$$y_t = \alpha + \beta t + \sum_{j=1}^{s} \gamma_j D_{jt} + u_t$$

where γ_j are the seasonal coefficients constrained to sum zero.

This kind of models are very simple and may be easily estimated by least squares. Trends and seasonalities estimated by these models are *global* since they are represented by a deterministic function of time which holds at all points throughtout the sample. Forecasting is straightforward as well: it consists of extrapolating these *global* components into the future.

A classical alternative to these models are the Exponential Smoothing Procedures (see Gardner (1985) for a survey). These models are *local* in the sense that they fit trends and seasonalities placing more weight on the more recent observations. In this way, these methods allow the components to change slowly within the sample and the most recent estimations of these components are extrapolated into the future in forecasting. These models are easy to implement and can be quite effective. However, they are *ad hoc* models because they are implemented without a properly defined statistical model. A class of unobserved components models that allow trends and seasonalities to evolve in time stochastically may be found in Harvey (1989). Last, modelling time series with trend and/or seasonal behaviour within the ARIMA framework will be presented in section 4.3 and in Chapter 5 respectively.

4.2 Linear Stationary Models for Time Series

A *stochastic process* $\{y_t\}_{t=-\infty}^{\infty}$ is a model that describes the probability structure of a sequence of observations over time. A time series y_t is a sample realization of a stochastic process that is observed only for a finite number of periods, indexed by $t = 1, \ldots, T$.

Any stochastic process can be partially characterized by the first and second moments of the joint probability distribution: the set of means, $\mu_t = \mathrm{E} y_t$, and the set of variances and covariances $cov(y_t, y_s) = \mathrm{E}(y_t - \mu_t)(y_s - \mu_s)$, $\forall t,\ s$. In order to get consistent forecast methods, we need that the underlying probabilistic structure would be stable over time. So a stochastic process is called *weak stationary* or *covariance stationary* when the mean, the variance and the covariance structure of the process is stable over time, that is:

$$\begin{aligned} \mathrm{E}\, y_t &= \mu < \infty && (4.1)\\ E(y_t - \mu)^2 &= \gamma_0 < \infty && (4.2)\\ E(y_t - \mu)(y_s - \mu) &= \gamma_{|t-s|} \qquad \forall t, s \quad t \neq s && (4.3) \end{aligned}$$

Given condition (4.3), the covariance between y_t and y_s depends only on the displacement $|t - s| = j$ and it is called *autocovariance* at lag j, γ_j. The set of autocovariances γ_j, $j = 0, \pm 1, \pm 2, \ldots$, is called the autocovariance function of a stationary process.

The general **Autoregressive Moving Average** model $ARMA(p, q)$ is a linear stochastic model where the variable y_t is modelled in terms of its own past values and a disturbance. It is defined as follows:

$$\begin{aligned} y_t &= \delta + \phi_1 y_{t-1} + \phi_2 y_{t-2} + \cdots + \phi_p y_{t-p} + u_t \qquad (4.4)\\ u_t &= \varepsilon_t + \theta_1 \varepsilon_{t-1} + \theta_2 \varepsilon_{t-2} + \cdots + \theta_q \varepsilon_{t-q}\\ \varepsilon_t &\sim i.i.d.(0, \sigma_\varepsilon^2) \end{aligned}$$

where the random variable ε_t is called the *innovation* because it represents the part of the observed variable y_t that is unpredictable given the past values $y_{t-1}, y_{t-2}, \ldots$.

The general $ARMA$ model (4.4) assumes that y_t is the output of a linear filter that transforms the past innovations $\varepsilon_{t-i}, i = 0, 1, \ldots, \infty$, that is, y_t is a linear process. This linearity assumption is based on the Wold's decomposition theorem (Wold, 1938) that says that any discrete stationary covariance process y_t can be expressed as the sum of two uncorrelated processes,

$$y_t = d_t + u_t \qquad (4.5)$$

where d_t is purely deterministic and u_t is a purely indeterministic process that can be written as a linear sum of the innovation process ε_t:

$$u_t = \sum_{i=0}^{\infty} \psi_i \varepsilon_{t-i} \quad \text{with} \quad \psi_0 = 1, \qquad \sum_{i=0}^{\infty} \psi_i^2 < \infty \qquad (4.6)$$

where ε_t is a sequence of serially uncorrelated random variables with zero mean and common variance σ_ε^2. Condition $\sum_i \psi_i^2 < \infty$ is necessary for stationarity.

The $ARMA(p,q)$ formulation (4.4) is a finite reparametrization of the infinite representation (4.5)-(4.6) with d_t constant. It is usually written in terms of the lag operator L defined by $L^j y_t = y_{t-j}$, that gives a shorter expression:

$$\begin{aligned}(1-\phi_1 L - \cdots - \phi_p L^p) y_t &= \delta + (1+\theta_1 L + \cdots + \theta_q L^q)\varepsilon_t \\ \Phi(L) y_t &= \delta + \Theta(L)\varepsilon_t \qquad (4.7)\end{aligned}$$

where the lag operator polynomials $\Theta(L)$ and $\Phi(L)$ are called the MA polynomial and the AR polynomial, respectively. In order to avoid parameter redundancy, we assume that there are not common factors between the AR and the MA components.

Next, we will study the plot of some time series generated by stationary $ARMA$ models with the aim of determining the main patterns of their temporal evolution. Figure 4.2 includes two series generated from the following stationary processes computed by means of the `genarma` quantlet:

Series 1: $y1_t = 1.4\, y1_{t-1} - 0.8\, y1_{t-2} + \varepsilon_t, \qquad \varepsilon_t \sim N.I.D.(0,1)$

Series 2: $y2_t = 0.9 + 0.7\, y2_{t-1} + 0.5\varepsilon_{t-1} + \varepsilon_t, \quad \varepsilon_t \sim N.I.D.(0,1)$

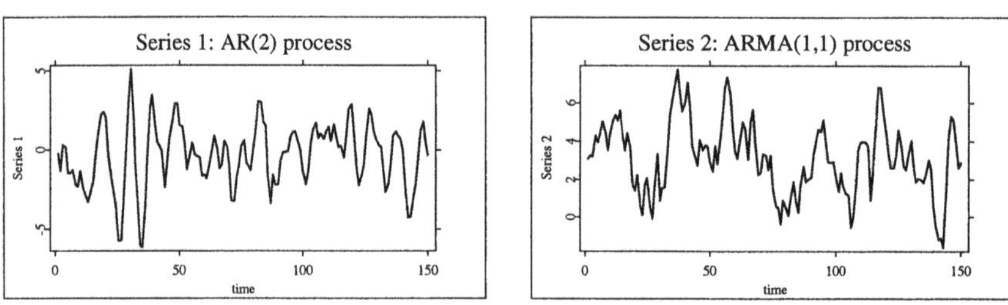

Figure 4.2. Time series generated by $ARMA$ models

`XEGutsm02.xpl`

As expected, both time series move around a constant level without changes in variance due to the stationary property. Moreover, this level is close to the theoretical mean of the process, μ, and the distance of each point to this value is very rarely outside the bounds $\pm 2\sigma$. Furthermore, the evolution of the series shows local departures from the mean of the process, which is known as the mean reversion behavior that characterizes the stationary time series.

Let us study with some detail the properties of the different $ARMA$ processes, in particular, the autocovariance function which captures the dynamic properties of a stochastic stationary process. This function depends on the units of measure, so the usual measure of the degree of linearity between variables is the correlation coefficient. In the case of stationary processes, the *autocorrelation coefficient* at lag j, denoted by ρ_j, is defined as the correlation between y_t and y_{t-j}:

$$\rho_j = \frac{cov(y_t, y_{t-j})}{\sqrt{V(y_t)}\sqrt{V(y_{t-j})}} = \frac{\gamma_j}{\gamma_0}, \qquad j = 0, \pm 1, \pm 2, \ldots$$

Thus, the autocorrelation function (ACF) is the autocovariance function standarized by the variance γ_0. The properties of the ACF are:

$$\rho_0 = 1 \tag{4.8}$$

$$|\rho_j| \leq 1 \tag{4.9}$$

$$\rho_j = \rho_{-j} \tag{4.10}$$

Given the symmetry property (4.10), the ACF is usually represented by means of a bar graph at the nonnegative lags that is called the simple correlogram.

Another useful tool to describe the dynamics of a stationary process is the partial autocorrelation function (PACF). The *partial autocorrelation coefficient* at lag j measures the linear association between y_t and y_{t-j} adjusted for the effects of the intermediate values $y_{t-1}, \ldots, y_{t-j+1}$. Therefore, it is just the coefficient ϕ_{jj} in the linear regression model:

$$y_t = \alpha + \phi_{j1} y_{t-1} + \phi_{j2} y_{t-2} + \cdots + \phi_{jj} y_{t-j} + e_t \tag{4.11}$$

The properties of the PACF are equivalent to those of the ACF (4.8)-(4.10) and it is easy to prove that $\phi_{11} = \rho_1$ (Box and Jenkins, 1976). Like the ACF, the partial autocorrelation function does not depend on the units of measure and it is represented by means of a bar graph at the nonnegative lags that is called partial correlogram.

The dynamic properties of each stationary model determine a particular shape of the correlograms. Moreover, it can be shown that, for any stationary process, both functions, ACF and PACF, approach to zero as the lag j tends to infinity.

The $ARMA$ models are not always stationary processes, so it is necessary first to determine the conditions for stationarity. There are subclasses of $ARMA$ models which have special properties so we shall study them separately. Thus, when $p = q = 0$ and $\delta = 0$, it is a *white noise process*, when $p = 0$, it is a pure *moving average process of order* q, $MA(q)$, and when $q = 0$ it is a pure *autoregressive process of order* p, $AR(p)$.

4.2.1 White Noise Process

The simplest $ARMA$ model is a white noise process, where y_t is a sequence of uncorrelated zero mean variables with constant variance σ^2. It is denoted by $y_t \sim WN(0, \sigma^2)$. This process is stationary if its variance is finite, $\sigma^2 < \infty$, since given that:

$$\begin{aligned} Ey_t &= 0 && \forall t \\ V(y_t) &= \sigma^2 && \forall t \\ Cov(y_t, y_s) &= 0 && \forall t \neq s \end{aligned}$$

y_t verifies conditions (4.1)-(4.3). Moreover, y_t is uncorrelated over time, so its autocovariance function is:

$$\gamma_j = \begin{cases} \sigma^2 & j = 0 \\ 0 & j \neq 1 \end{cases}$$

And its ACF and PACF are as follows:

$$\rho_j = \begin{cases} 1 & j = 0 \\ 0 & j \neq 1 \end{cases} \qquad \phi_{jj} = \begin{cases} 1 & j = 0 \\ 0 & j \neq 1 \end{cases}$$

To understand the behavior of a white noise, we will generate a time series of size 150 from a gaussian white noise process $y_t \sim N.I.D.(0, 1)$. Figure 4.3 shows the simulated series that moves around a constant level randomly, without any kind of pattern, as corresponds to the uncorrelation over time. The economic time series will follow white noise patterns very rarely, but this process is the key for the formulation of more complex models. In fact, it is the starting point of the derivation of the properties of $ARMA$ processes given that we are assuming that the innovation of the model is a white noise.

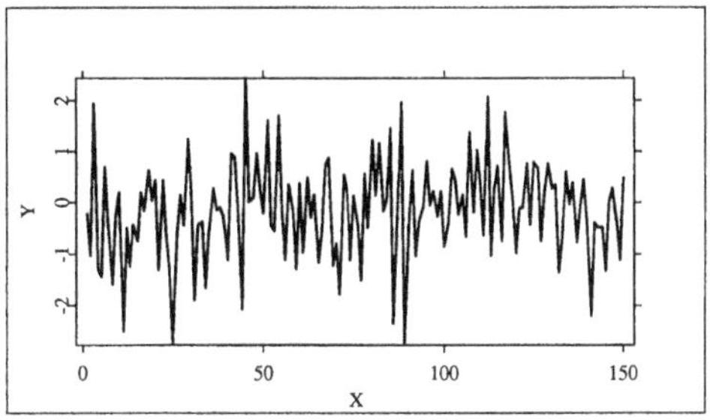

Figure 4.3. Realization from a white noise process

XEGutsm03.xpl

4.2.2 Moving Average Model

The general (finite-order) moving average model of order q, $MA(q)$ is:

$$\begin{aligned} y_t &= \delta + \varepsilon_t + \theta_1\varepsilon_{t-1} + \cdots + \theta_q\varepsilon_{t-q} && (4.12)\\ y_t &= \delta + \Theta(L)\varepsilon_t, && \varepsilon_t \sim \mathrm{WN}(0, \sigma_\varepsilon^2) \end{aligned}$$

It can be easily shown that MA processes are always stationary, given that the parameters of any finite MA processes always verify condition (4.6). Moreover, we are interested in *invertible* MA processes. When a process is invertible, it is possible to invert the process, that is, to express the current value of the variable y_t in terms of a current shock ε_t and its observable past values $y_{t-1}, y_{t-2}, \ldots$. Then, we say that the model has an autoregressive representation. This requirement provides a sensible way of associating present events with past happenings. A $MA(q)$ model is invertible if the q roots of the characteristic equation $\Theta(L) = 0$ lie outside the unit circle. When the root R_j is real, this condition means that the absolute value must be greater than unity, $|R_j| > 1$. If there are a pair of complex roots, they may be written as $R_j = a \pm bi$, where a, b are real numbers and $i = \sqrt{-1}$, and then the invertibility condition means that its *moduli* must be greater than unity, $\sqrt{a^2 + b^2} > 1$.

Let us consider the moving average process of first order, $MA(1)$:

$$\begin{aligned} y_t &= \delta + \varepsilon_t + \theta\varepsilon_{t-1}, \qquad \varepsilon_t \sim WN(0, \sigma_\varepsilon^2)\\ y_t &= \delta + (1 + \theta L)\varepsilon_t \end{aligned}$$

It is invertible when the root of $1+\theta L=0$ lies outside the unit circle, that is, $|R|=|-1/\theta|>1$. This condition implies the invertibility restriction on the parameter, $-1<\theta<1$.

Let us study this simple MA process in detail. Figure 4.4 plots simulated series of length 150 from two $MA(1)$ processes where the parameters (δ,θ) take the values (0, 0.8) in the first model and (4, -0.5) in the second one. It can be noted that the series show the general patterns associated with stationary and mean reversion processes. More specifically, given that only a past innovation ε_{t-1} affects the current value of the series y_t (positively for $\theta>0$ and negatively for $\theta<0$), the $MA(1)$ process is known as a very short memory process and so, there is not a 'strong' dynamic pattern in the series. Nevertheless, it can be observed that the time evolution is smoother for the positive value of θ.

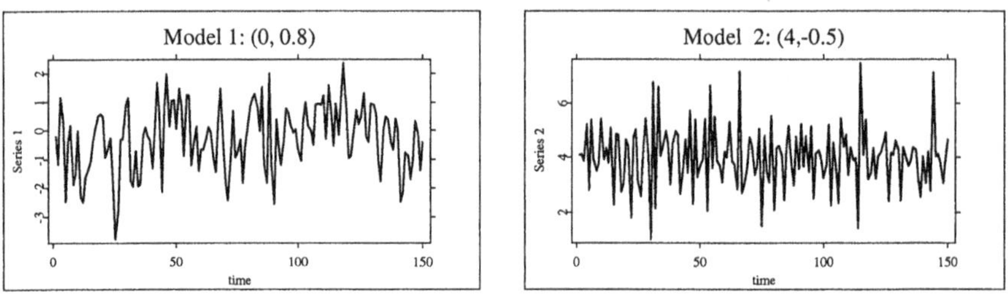

Figure 4.4. Realizations of $MA(1)$ models with $\varepsilon_t \sim N.I.D.(0,1)$

XEGutsm04.xpl

The ACF for $MA(1)$ models is derived from the following moments:

$$\begin{aligned}
Ey_t &= \mathrm{E}(\delta+\varepsilon_t+\theta\varepsilon_{t-1}) &&= \delta \\
V(y_t) &= \mathrm{E}(\varepsilon_t+\theta\varepsilon_{t-1})^2 &&= \sigma_\varepsilon^2(1+\theta^2) \\
Cov(y_t,y_{t-1}) &= \mathrm{E}(\varepsilon_t+\theta\varepsilon_{t-1})(\varepsilon_{t-1}+\theta\varepsilon_{t-2}) &&= \sigma_\varepsilon^2\theta \\
Cov(y_t,y_{t-j}) &= \mathrm{E}(\varepsilon_t+\theta\varepsilon_{t-1})(a_{t-j}+\theta\varepsilon_{t-j-1}) &&= 0 \qquad \forall j>1
\end{aligned}$$

given that, for all $j>1$ and for all t, the innovations $\varepsilon_t,\varepsilon_{t-1}$ are uncorrelated with $\varepsilon_{t-j},\varepsilon_{t-j-1}$. Then, the autocorrelation function is:

$$\rho_j = \begin{cases} \dfrac{\theta}{1+\theta^2} & j=1 \\ 0 & j>1 \end{cases}$$

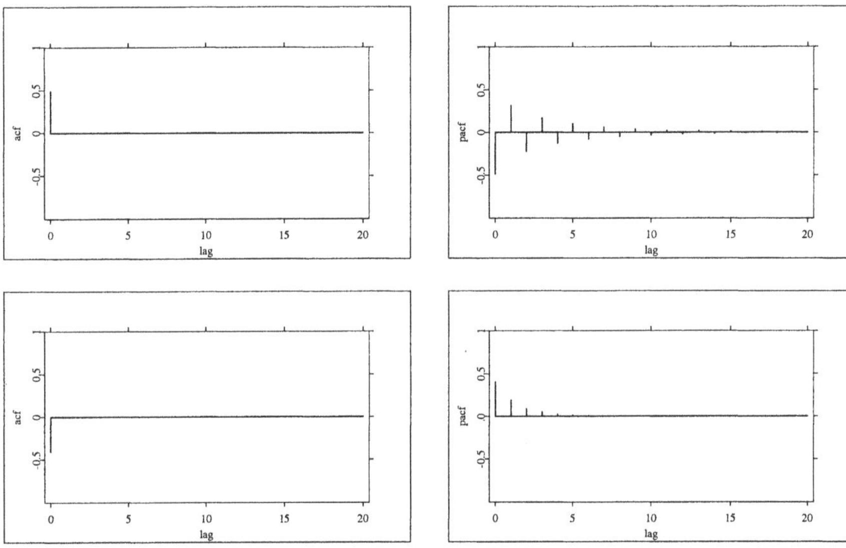

Figure 4.5. Population ACF and PACF for $MA(1)$

That is, there is a cutoff in the ACF at the first lag. Finally, the partial autocorrelation function shows an exponential decay. Figure 4.5 shows typical profiles of this ACF jointly with the PACF.

It can be shown that the general stationary and invertible $MA(q)$ process has the following properties (Box and Jenkins, 1976):

- The mean is equal to δ and the variance is given by $\sigma_\varepsilon^2(1 + \sum_{i=1}^q \theta_i^2)$.
- The ACF shows a cutoff at the q lag, that is, $\rho_j = 0, \ \ \forall j > q$.
- The PACF decays to zero, exponentially when $\Theta(L) = 0$ has real roots or with sine-cosine wave fluctuations when the roots are complex.

Figure 4.6 shows the simple and partial correlograms for two different $MA(2)$ processes. Both ACF exhibit a cutoff at lag two. The roots of the MA polynomial of the first series are real, so the PACF decays exponentially while for the second series with complex roots the PACF decays as a damping sine-cosine wave.

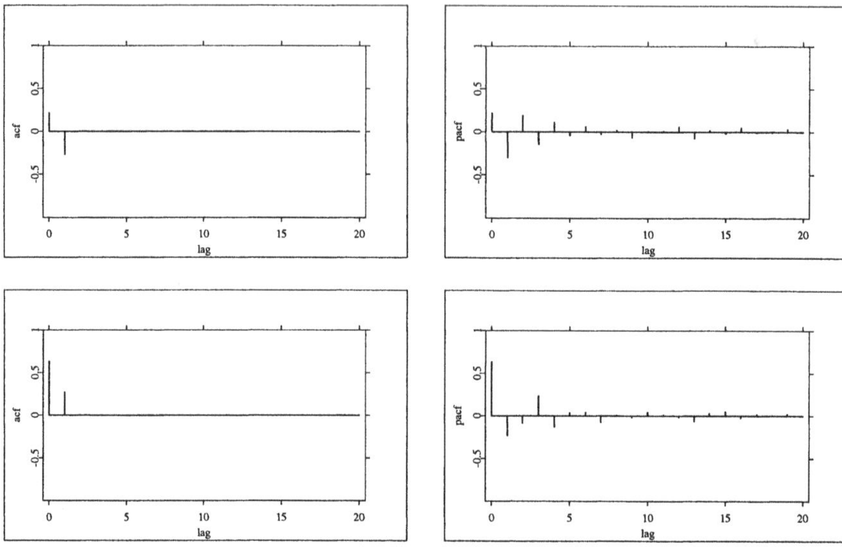

Figure 4.6. Population ACF and PACF for $MA(2)$ processes

4.2.3 Autoregressive Model

The general (finite-order) autoregressive model of order p, $AR(p)$, is:

$$\begin{aligned} y_t &= \delta + \phi_1 y_{t-1} + \cdots + \phi_p y_{t-p} + \varepsilon_t \\ \Phi(L) y_t &= \delta + \varepsilon_t, \qquad \varepsilon_t \sim \mathrm{WN}(0, \sigma_\varepsilon^2) \end{aligned} \tag{4.13}$$

Let us begin with the simplest AR process, the autoregressive process of first order, $AR(1)$, that is defined as:

$$\begin{aligned} y_t &= \delta + \phi\, y_{t-1} + \varepsilon_t \\ (1 - \phi L)\, y_t &= \delta + \varepsilon_t, \qquad \varepsilon_t \sim WN(0, \sigma_\varepsilon^2) \end{aligned} \tag{4.14}$$

Figure 4.7 shows two simulated time series generated from $AR(1)$ processes with zero mean and parameters $\phi = 0.7$ and -0.7, respectively. The autoregressive parameter measures the persistence of past events into the current values. For example, if $\phi > 0$, a positive (or negative) shock ε_t affects positively (or

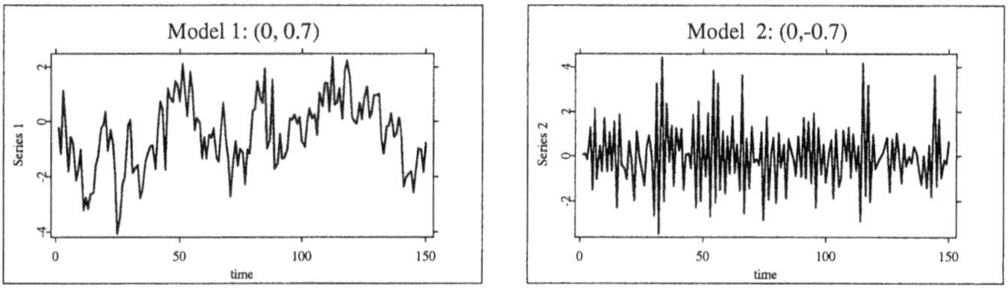

Figure 4.7. Realizations of $AR(1)$ models with $\varepsilon_t \sim N.I.D.(0,1)$

XEGutsm05.xpl

negatively) for a period of time which is longer the larger the value of ϕ. When $\phi < 0$, the series moves more roughly around the mean due to the alternation in the direction of the effect of ε_t, that is, a shock that affects positively in moment t, has negative effects on $t+1$, positive in $t+2$, ...

The $AR(1)$ process is always invertible and it is stationary when the parameter of the model is constrained to lie in the region $-1 < \phi < 1$. To prove the stationary condition, first we write the y_t in the moving average form by recursive substitution of y_{t-i} in (4.14):

$$y_t = \delta \sum_{i=0}^{\infty} \phi^i + \sum_{i=0}^{\infty} \phi^i \varepsilon_{t-i} \tag{4.15}$$

That is, y_t is a weighted sum of past innovations. The weights depend on the value of the parameter ϕ: when $|\phi| > 1$, (or $|\phi| < 1$), the influence of a given innovation ε_t increases (or decreases) through time. Taking expectations to (4.15) in order to compute the mean of the process, we get:

$$\mathrm{E}\, y_t = \delta \sum_{i=0}^{\infty} \phi^i + \sum_{i=0}^{\infty} \phi^i \mathrm{E}\, \varepsilon_{t-i}$$

Given that $E\varepsilon_{t-i} = 0$, the result is a sum of infinite terms that converges for all value of δ only if $|\phi| < 1$, in which case $Ey_t = \delta(1-\phi)^{-1}$. A similar problem appears when we compute the second moment. The proof can be simplified assuming that $\delta = 0$, that is, $Ey_t = 0$. Then, variance is:

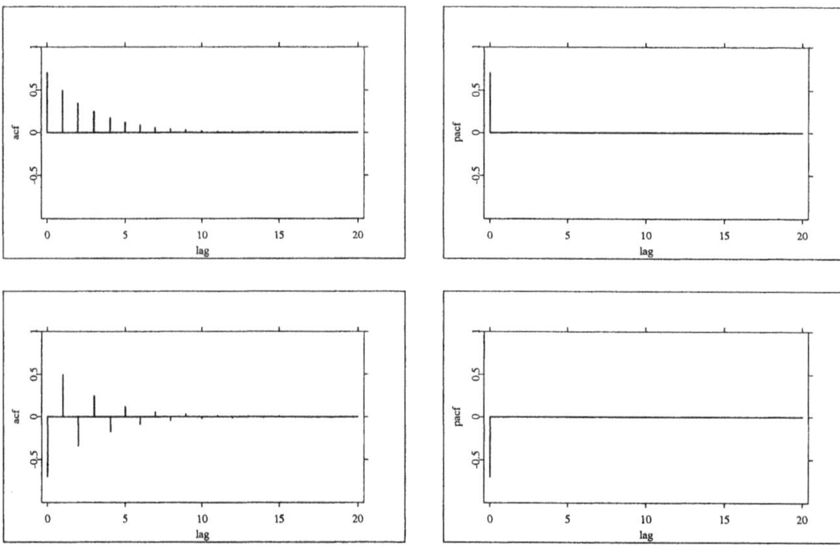

Figure 4.8. Population correlograms for $AR(1)$ processes

$$
\begin{aligned}
V(y_t) &= \mathrm{E}\left(\sum_{i=0}^{\infty} \phi^i \varepsilon_{t-i}\right)^2 \\
&= \sum_{i=0}^{\infty} \phi^{2i} V(\varepsilon_{t-i}) = \sigma_\varepsilon^2 \sum_{i=1}^{\infty} \phi^{2i}
\end{aligned}
$$

Again, the variance goes to infinity except for $-1 < \phi < 1$, in which case $V(y_t) = \sigma_\varepsilon^2(1-\phi^2)^{-1}$. It is easy to verify that both the mean and the variance explode when that condition doesn't hold.

The autocovariance function of a stationary $AR(1)$ process is

$$\gamma_j = \mathrm{E}\{(\phi y_{t-1} + \varepsilon_t) y_{t-j}\} = \phi\gamma_{j-1} = \sigma_\varepsilon^2(1-\phi^2)^{-1}\,\phi^j \qquad \forall j > 0$$

Therefore, the autocorrelation function for the stationary $AR(1)$ model is:

$$\rho_j = \frac{\phi\gamma_{j-1}}{\gamma_0} = \phi\rho_{j-1} = \phi^j \qquad \forall j$$

That is, the correlogram shows an exponential decay with positive values always if ϕ is positive and with negative-positive oscillations if ϕ is negative (see figure 4.8). Furthermore, the rate of decay decreases as ϕ increases, so the greater the value of ϕ the stronger the dynamic correlation in the process. Finally, there is a cutoff in the partial autocorrelation function at the first lag.

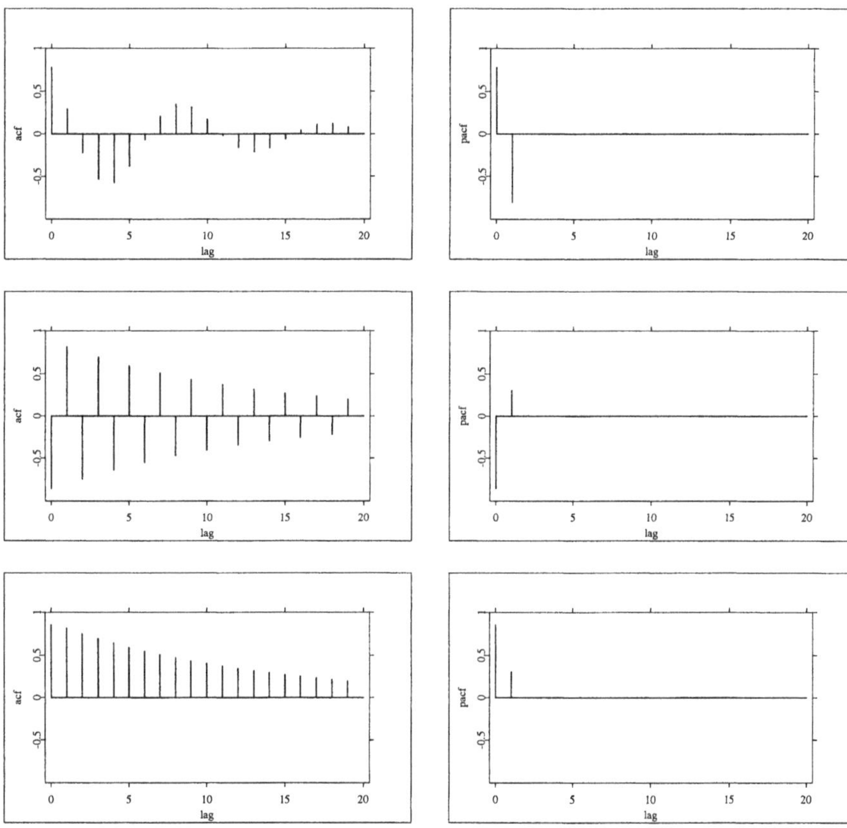

Figure 4.9. Population correlograms for $AR(2)$ processes

It can be shown that the general $AR(p)$ process (Box and Jenkins, 1976):

- Is stationary only if the p roots of the characteristic equation of the AR polynomial $\Phi(L) = 0$ lie outside the unit circle. The mean of a stationary

$AR(p)$ model is $\mu = \delta\left(1 - \sum_{i=1}^{p} \phi_i\right)^{-1}$.

- Is always invertible for any values of the parameters δ, Φ.
- Its ACF goes to zero exponentially when the roots of $\Phi(L) = 0$ are real or with sine-cosine wave fluctuations when they are complex.
- Its PACF has a cutoff at the p lag, that is, $\phi_{jj} = 0, \quad \forall j > p$.

Some examples of correlograms for more complex AR models, such as the $AR(2)$, can be seen in figure 4.9. They are very similar to the $AR(1)$ patterns when the processes have real roots, but take a very different shape when the roots are complex (see the first pair of graphics of figure 4.9).

4.2.4 Autoregressive Moving Average Model

The general (finite-order) autoregressive moving average model of orders (p, q), $ARMA(p, q)$, is:

$$\begin{aligned} y_t &= \delta + \phi_1 y_{t-1} + \cdots + \phi_p y_{t-p} + \varepsilon_t + \theta_1 \varepsilon_{t-1} + \cdots + \theta_q \varepsilon_{t-q} \\ \Phi(L) y_t &= \delta + \Theta(L)\varepsilon_t, \qquad \varepsilon_t \sim \text{WN}(0, \sigma_\varepsilon^2) \end{aligned}$$

It can be shown that the general $ARMA(p, q)$ process (Box and Jenkins, 1976):

- Is stationary if the AR component is stationary, that is, the roots of the characteristic equation $\Phi(L) = 0$ lie outside the unit circle. The mean of a stationary $ARMA(p, q)$ model is

  $$\mu = \frac{\delta}{1 - \sum_{i=1}^{p} \phi_i}$$

  A necessary condition to hold stationarity is the following that ensures a finite mean process:

  $$\sum_{i=1}^{p} \phi_i < 1 \tag{4.16}$$

- Is invertible if the MA component is invertible, that is, the roots of the characteristic equation $\Theta(L) = 0$ lie outside the unit circle.

- Its ACF approaches to zero as lag j tends to infinity, exponentially when $\Phi(L) = 0$ has real roots or with sine-cosine wave fluctuations when these roots are complex.
- Its PACF decays to zero, exponentially when $\Theta(L) = 0$ has real roots or with sine-cosine wave fluctuations when these roots are complex.

For example, the $ARMA(1,1)$ process is defined as:

$$\begin{aligned} y_t &= \delta + \phi y_{t-1} + \theta \varepsilon_{t-1} + \varepsilon_t \\ (1 - \phi L)\, y_t &= \delta + (1 + \theta L)\varepsilon_t, \qquad \varepsilon_t \sim WN(0, \sigma_\varepsilon^2) \end{aligned}$$

This model is stationary if $|\phi| < 1$ and is invertible if $|\theta| < 1$. The mean of the $ARMA(1,1)$ stationary process can be derived as follows:

$$Ey_t = \delta + \phi \mathrm{E}y_{t-1} + \theta \mathrm{E}\varepsilon_{t-1} + \mathrm{E}\varepsilon_t$$

by stationarity $Ey_t = \mathrm{E}y_{t-1} = \mu$, and so $\mu = \dfrac{\delta}{1 - \phi}$.

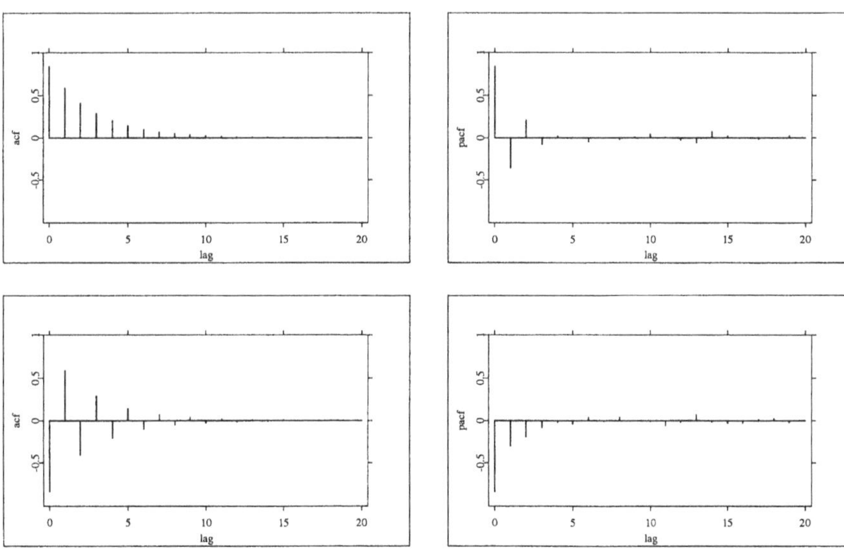

Figure 4.10. Population correlograms for $ARMA(1,1)$ processes

The autovariance function for an $ARMA(1,1)$ stationary process (assuming $\delta \doteq 0$) is as follows:

$$\begin{aligned}
\gamma_0 &= \mathrm{E}(\phi y_{t-1} + \theta\varepsilon_{t-1} + \varepsilon_t)^2 &&= \phi^2\gamma_0 + \sigma_\varepsilon^2(\theta^2 + 1 + 2\phi\theta) \\
&= \sigma_\varepsilon^2(1 + \theta^2 + 2\phi\theta)(1 - \phi^2)^{-1} \\
\gamma_1 &= \mathrm{E}\{(\phi y_{t-1} + \theta\varepsilon_{t-1} + \varepsilon_t)y_{t-1}\} &&= \phi\gamma_0 + \theta\sigma_\varepsilon^2 \\
\gamma_j &= \mathrm{E}\{(\phi y_{t-1} + \theta\varepsilon_{t-1} + \varepsilon_t)y_{t-j}\} &&= \phi\gamma_{j-1} \qquad \forall j > 1
\end{aligned}$$

The autocorrelation function for the stationary $ARMA(1,1)$ model is:

$$\rho_j = \begin{cases} \phi + \dfrac{\theta(1-\phi^2)}{1+\theta^2+2\theta\phi} & j = 1 \\ \phi\rho_{j-1} & j > 1 \end{cases}$$

Figure 4.10 shows typical profiles of the ACF and PACF for $ARMA(1,1)$ stationary e invertible processes.

4.3 Nonstationary Models for Time Series

The models presented so far are based on the stationarity assumption, that is, the mean and the variance of the underlying process are constant and the autocovariances depend only on the time lag. But many economic and business time series are nonstationary. Nonstationary time series can occur in many different ways. In particular, economic time series usually show time-changing levels, μ_t, (see graph (b) in figure 4.1) and/or variances (see graph (c) in figure 4.1).

4.3.1 Nonstationary in the Variance

When a time series is not stationary in variance we need a proper variance stabilizing transformation. It is very common for the variance of a nonstationary process to change as its level changes. Thus, let us assume that the variance of the process is:

$$V(y_t) = kf(\mu_t)$$

for some positive constant k and some known function f. The objective is to find a function h such that the transformed series $h(y_t)$ has a constant variance. Expanding $h(y_t)$ in a first-order Taylor series around μ_t:

$$h(y_t) \simeq h(\mu_t) + (y_t - \mu_t)h'(\mu_t)$$

where $h'(\mu_t)$ is the first derivative of $h(y_t)$ evaluated at μ_t. The variance of $h(y_t)$ can be approximated as:

$$\begin{aligned} V[h(y_t)] &\simeq V[h(\mu_t) + (y_t - \mu_t)h'(\mu_t)] \\ &= [h'(\mu_t)]^2 V(y_t) = [h'(\mu_t)]^2\, k\, f(\mu_t) \end{aligned}$$

Thus, the transformation $h(y_t)$ must be chosen so that:

$$h'(\mu_t) = \frac{1}{\sqrt{f(\mu_t)}}$$

For example, if the standard deviation of a series y_t is proportional to its level, then $f(\mu_t) = \mu_t^2$ and the transformation $h(\mu_t)$ has to satisfy $h'(\mu_t) = \mu_t^{-1}$. This implies that $h(\mu_t) = \ln(\mu_t)$. Hence, a logarithmic transformation of the series will give a constant variance. If the variance of a series is proportional to its level, so that $f(\mu_t) = \mu_t$, then a square root transformation of the series, $\sqrt{y_t}$, will give a constant variance.

More generally, to stabilize the variance, we can use the power transformation introduced by Box and Cox (1964):

$$y_t^{(\lambda)} = \begin{cases} \frac{y_t^\lambda - 1}{\lambda} & \lambda \neq 0 \\ \ln(y_t) & \lambda = 0 \end{cases} \tag{4.17}$$

where λ is called the transformation parameter. It should be noted that, frequently, the Box-Cox transformation not only stabilizes the variance but also improves the approximation to normality of process y_t.

4.3.2 Nonstationarity in the Mean

One of the dominant features of many economic and business time series is the trend. Trend is slow, long-run evolution in the variables that we want to model. In business, economics, and finance time series, trend is usually produced by slowly evolving preferences, technologies and demographics. This trend behavior can be upward or downward, steep or not, and exponential or approximately linear. With such a trending pattern, a time series is nonstationary, it does not show a tendency of mean reversion.

Nonstationarity in the mean, that is a non constant level, can be modelled in different ways. The most common alternatives are deterministic trends and stochastic trends.

Deterministic Trends

Let us consider the extension of Wold's decomposition theorem for nonstationary series given by Cramer (1961):

$$y_t = \mu_t + u_t$$

where u_t is a zero mean stationary process. The changing mean of a nonstationary process or trend, μ_t can be represented by a deterministic function of time. These models for the trend imply that the series trend evolves in a perfectly predictable way, therefore they are called deterministic trend models.

For example, if the mean function μ_t follows a linear trend, one can use the deterministic linear trend model:

$$y_t = \alpha + \beta\, t + u_t \tag{4.18}$$

The parameter α is the intercept; it is the value of the trend at time $t = 0$ and β is the slope; it is positive if the trend is increasing and negative if the trend is decreasing. The larger the absolute value of β the steeper the trend's slope.

Sometimes trend appears nonlinear, or curved, as for example when a variable increases at an increasing or decreasing rate. In fact, it is not required that trends be linear only that they be smooth. Quadratic trend models can potentially capture nonlinearities such as those observed in some series. Such trends are quadratic as opposed to linear functions of time,

$$y_t = \alpha + \beta_1\, t + \beta_2\, t^2 + u_t$$

Higher order polynomial trends are sometimes considered, but it is important to use low-order polynomials to maintain smoothness. Other types of nonlinear trends that are sometimes appropriate are the exponential trends. If trend is characterized by constant growth at rate β, then we can write:

$$y_t = \alpha\, e^{\beta t}\, U_t$$

Trend has been modelled as a nonlinear (exponential) function of time in levels, but in logarithms we have

$$\ln(y_t) = \ln(\alpha) + \beta t + u_t$$

Thus, trend is a linear function of time. This situation, in which a trend appears nonlinear in levels but linear in logarithms is called exponential trend or log-linear trend and is very common in economics because economic variables often displays roughly constant growth rates.

Stochastic Trends

Nonstationarity in the mean can be dealt within the class of the $ARMA(p,q)$ models (4.7). An $ARMA$ model is nonstationary if its AR polynomial does not satisfy the stationarity condition, that is, if some of its roots do not lie outside the unit circle. If the AR polynomial contains at least one root inside the unit circle, the behavior of a realization of the process will be explosive. However, this is not the sort of evolution that can be observed in economic and business time series. Although many of them are nonstationary, these series behave very much alike except for their difference in the local mean levels. If we want to model the evolution of the series independent of its level within the framework of $ARMA$ models, the AR polynomial must satisfy:

$$\Phi(L)(y_t - \mu) = \Theta(L)\varepsilon_t$$

that is:

$$\Phi(L)\mu = 0 \quad \Rightarrow \quad \Phi(1) = 0$$

so that the $\Phi(L)$ polynomial can be factorised as:

$$\Phi(L) = \Phi^*(L)(1 - L)$$

Applying this decomposition to the general $ARMA$ model:

$$\Phi^*(L)(1 - L)y_t = \Theta(L)\varepsilon_t$$

or

$$\Phi^*(L)\Delta y_t = \Theta(L)\varepsilon_t$$

where $\Phi^*(L)$ is a polynomial of order $(p-1)$ and $\Delta = (1 - L)$. If $\Phi^*(L)$ is a stationary AR polynomial, we say that y_t has a unit autoregressive root. When the nonstationary AR polynomial presents more than one unit root, for instance d, it can be decomposed as:

$$\Phi(L) = \Phi^*(L)(1 - L)^d$$

Applying again this decomposition to the general $ARMA$ model we get:

$$\Phi^*(L)\Delta^d y_t = \Theta(L)\varepsilon_t$$

for some $d > 0$ where $\Phi^*(L)$ is a stationary AR polynomial of order $(p-d)$.

In short, if we use $ARMA$ processes for modelling nonstationary time series, the nonstationarity leads to the presence of unit roots in the autoregressive polynomial. In other words, the series y_t is nonstationary but its dth differenced series, $(1-L)^d y_t$, for some integer $d \geq 1$, follows a stationary and invertible $ARMA(p-d,q)$ model. A process y_t with these characteristics is called an **integrated process** of order **d** and it is denoted by $y_t \sim I(d)$. It can be noted that the order of integration of a process is the number of differences needed to achieve stationarity, *i.e.*, the number of unit roots present in the process. In practice $I(0)$ and $I(1)$ processes are by far the most important cases for economic and business time series, arising $I(2)$ series much less frequently. Box and Jenkins (1976) refer to this kind of nonstationary behavior as homogeneous nonstationarity, indicating that the local behavior of this sort of series is independent of its level (for $I(1)$ processes) and of its level and slope (for $I(2)$ processes).

In general, if the series y_t is integrated of order d, it can be represented by the following model:

$$\Phi_p(L)(1-L)^d y_t = \delta + \Theta_q(L)\varepsilon_t \tag{4.19}$$

where the stationary AR operator $\Phi_p(L)$ and the invertible MA operator $\Theta_q(L)$ share no common factors.

The resulting homogeneous nonstationary model (4.19) has been referred to as the **Autoregressive Integrated Moving Average** model of order (p,d,q) and is denoted as the $ARIMA(p,d,q)$ model. When $p=0$, the $ARIMA(0,d,q)$ is also called the Integrated Moving Average model of order (d,q) and it is denoted as the $IMA(d,q)$ model. When $q=0$, the resulting model is called the Autoregressive Integrated model $ARI(p,d)$.

In order to get more insight into the kind of nonstationary behavior implied by integrated processes, let us study with some detail two of the most simple $ARIMA$ models: random walk and random walk with drift models.

Random Walk Model. The random walk model is simply an $AR(1)$ with coefficient $\phi = 1$:

$$\begin{aligned} \Delta y_t &= \varepsilon_t, \qquad \varepsilon_t \sim WN(0,\sigma_\varepsilon^2) \\ y_t &= y_{t-1} + \varepsilon_t \end{aligned} \tag{4.20}$$

That is, in the random walk model the value of y at time t is equal to its value at time $t-1$ plus a random shock. The random walk model is not covariance stationary because the $AR(1)$ coefficient is not less than one. But since the first difference of the series follows a white noise process, y_t is an integrated process

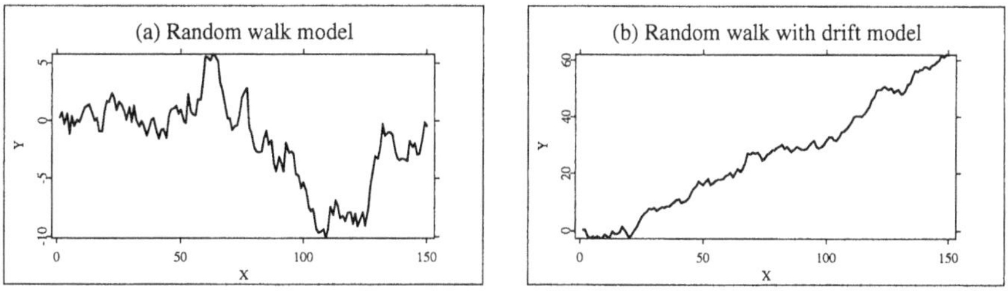

Figure 4.11. Realizations from nonstationary processes

XEGutsm06.xpl

of order 1, $I(1)$. This model has been widely used to describe the behavior of finance time series such as stock prices, exchange rates, etc.

Graph (a) of figure 4.11 shows a simulated realization of size 150 of a random walk process, with $\sigma_\varepsilon^2 = 1$. It can be observed that the series does not display what is known as a mean reversion behavior: it wanders up and down randomly with no tendency to return to any particular point. If a shock increases the value of a random walk, there is no tendency for it to necessarily lower again, it is expected to stay permanently higher.

Taking expectations in (4.20) given the past information $y_{t-1}, y_{t-2}, \ldots$, we get:

$$E[y_t | y_{t-1}, y_{t-2}, \ldots] = \mu_{t|t-1} = y_{t-1}$$

This implies that the level at time t of a series generated by a random walk model is subject to the stochastic disturbance at time $(t-1)$. That is, the mean level of the process y_t changes through time stochastically, and the process is characterized as having a stochastic trend. This is different from the deterministic trend model (4.18) of the previous section, where the parameter β remains constant through time and the mean level of the process is a pure deterministic function of time.

Assuming that the random walk started at some time t_0 with value y_0, we get:

$$y_t = y_0 + \sum_{i=t_0+1}^{t} \varepsilon_i$$

Therefore,

$$\mathrm{E}(y_t) = y_0 \qquad V(y_t) = (t - t_0)\sigma_\varepsilon^2$$

so that the variance grows continuously rather than converging to some finite unconditional variance. The correlation between y_t and y_{t-k} is:

$$\rho_{k,t} = \frac{t - t_0 - k}{\sqrt{(t-t_0)(t-t_0-k)}} = \sqrt{\frac{t-t_0-k}{t-t_0}}$$

If $(t - t_0)$ is large compared to k, the correlation coefficients will be close to one. Therefore, the random walk model process can be characterized by coefficients in the sample ACF of the original series y_t that decay very slowly.

Random Walk with Drift Model. The random walk with drift model results of adding a nonzero constant term to the random walk model:

$$\Delta y_t = \delta + \varepsilon_t$$

or

$$y_t = y_{t-1} + \delta + \varepsilon_t \tag{4.21}$$

So the process y_t is integrated of order 1, $I(1)$. Assuming that the process started at some time t_0, by successive substitution, we have:

$$y_t = y_0 + (t - t_0)\,\delta + \sum_{i=t_0+1}^{t} \varepsilon_i$$

It can be observed that y_t contains a deterministic trend with slope or drift δ, as well as a stochastic trend. Given the past information $y_{t-1}, y_{t-2}, \ldots$, the level of the series at time t is given by:

$$E[y_t | y_{t-1}, y_{t-2}, \ldots] = \mu_{t|t-1} = y_{t-1} + \delta$$

which is influenced by the stochastic disturbance at time $(t-1)$ through the term y_{t-1} as well as by the deterministic component through the parameter δ.

The random walk with drift is a model that on average grows each period by the drift, δ. This drift parameter δ plays the same role as the slope parameter in the linear deterministic trend model (4.18). Just as the random walk has no particular level to which it returns, so the random walk with drift model has no particular trend to which it returns. If a shock moves the value of the process below the currently projected trend, there is no tendency for it to return; a new trend simply begins from the new position of the series (see graph (b) in figure 4.11).

In general, if a process is integrated, that is, $y_t \sim ARIMA(p, d, q)$ for some $d > 0$, shocks have completely permanent effects; a unit shock moves the expected future path of the series by one unit forever. Moreover, the parameter δ plays very different roles for $d = 0$ and $d > 0$. When $d = 0$, the process is stationary and the parameter δ is related to the mean of the process, μ:

$$\delta = \mu(1 - \phi_1 - \ldots - \phi_p) \tag{4.22}$$

However, when $d > 0$, the presence of the constant term δ introduces a deterministic linear trend in the process (see graph (b) in figure 4.11). More generally, for models involving the dth differenced series $(1 - L)^d y_t$, the nonzero parameter δ can be shown to correspond to the coefficient β_d of t^d in the deterministic trend, $\beta_0 + \beta_1 t + \ldots + \beta_d t^d$. That is why, when $d > 0$, the parameter δ is referred to as the deterministic trend term. In this case, the models may be interpreted as including a deterministic trend buried in a nonstationary noise.

4.3.3 Testing for Unit Roots and Stationarity

As we have seen the properties of a time series depend on its order of integration, d, that is on the presence of unit roots. It is important to have techniques available to determine the actual form of nonstationarity and to distinguish between stochastic and deterministic trends if possible. There are two kinds of statistical tests: one group is based on the unit root hypothesis while the other is on the stationary null hypothesis.

Unit Root Tests

There is a large literature on testing for unit roots theory. A good survey may be found in Dickey and Bell and Miller (1986), among others. Let us consider the simple $AR(1)$ model:

$$y_t = \phi y_{t-1} + \varepsilon_t, \tag{4.23}$$

where $y_0 = 0$ and the innovations ε_t are a white noise sequence with constant variance. We can regress y_t on y_{t-1} and then use the standard t-statistic for testing the null hypothesis H_0: $\phi = \phi_0$. The problem arises because we do not know *a priori* whether the model is stationary. If $|\phi| < 1$, the $AR(1)$ model is stationary and the least-squares (LS) estimator of ϕ, $\hat{\phi}_{LS}$, equals the Maximum Likelihood estimator under normality and follows a normal asymptotic distribution. Furthermore, the statistic given by:

$$t_\phi = \frac{\hat{\phi}_{LS} - \phi_0}{s_{\hat{\phi}}}$$

where $s_{\hat{\phi}}$ is the estimated standard deviation of $\hat{\phi}_{LS}$, follows an asymptotic distribution $N(0,1)$. For small samples, this statistic is distributed approximately as a Student's t with $(T-1)$ degrees of freedom. Nevertheless, when $\phi = 1$, this result does not hold. It can be shown that the LS estimator of ϕ is biased downwards and that the t-statistic under the unit-root null hypothesis, does not have a Student's t distribution even in the limit as the sample size becomes infinite.

The $AR(1)$ model (4.23) can be written as follows by substracting y_{t-1} to both sides of the equation:

$$\begin{aligned} y_t - y_{t-1} &= (\phi - 1)\, y_{t-1} + \varepsilon_t \\ \Delta y_t &= \rho\, y_{t-1} + \varepsilon_t \end{aligned} \tag{4.24}$$

where $\rho = \phi - 1$. The relevant unit-root null hypothesis is $\rho = 0$ and the alternative is one sided H_a: $\rho < 0$, since $\rho > 0$ corresponds to explosive time series models. Dickey (1976) tabulated the percentiles of this statistic under the unit root null hypothesis. The H_0 of a unit root is rejected when the value of the statistic is lower than the critical value. This statistic, denoted by τ, is called the **Dickey-Fuller statistic** and their critical values are published in Fuller (1976).

Up to now it has been shown how to test the null hypothesis of a random walk (one unit root) against the alternative of a zero mean, stationary $AR(1)$. For economic time series, it could be of interest to consider alternative hypothesis including stationarity around a constant and/or a linear trend. This could be achieved by introducing these terms in model (4.24):

$$\Delta y_t = \alpha + \rho\, y_{t-1} + \varepsilon_t \tag{4.25}$$

$$\Delta y_t = \alpha + \beta t + \rho\, y_{t-1} + \varepsilon_t \tag{4.26}$$

The unit-root null hypothesis is simply H_0: $\rho = 0$ in both models (4.25)-(4.26). Dickey-Fuller tabulated the critical values for the corresponding statistics, denoted by τ_μ and τ_τ respectively. It should be noted that model (4.26) under the null hypothesis becomes a random walk plus drift model, which is a hypothesis that frequently arises in economic applications.

The tests presented so far have the disadvantage that they assume that the three models considered (4.24), (4.25) and (4.26) cover all the possibilities under the null hypothesis. However, many $I(1)$ series do not behave in that way. In particular, their Data Generating Process may include nuisance parameters, like an autocorrelated process for the error term, for example. One method to allow a more flexible dynamic behavior in the series of interest is to consider that the series y_t follows an $AR(p)$ model:

$$y_t = \phi_1 y_{t-1} + \phi_2 y_{t-2} + \ldots + \phi_p y_{t-p} + \varepsilon_t$$

This assumption is not particularly restrictive since every $ARMA$ model always have an AR representation if its moving average polynomial is invertible. The $AR(p)$ model can be rewritten as the following regression model:

$$\Delta y_t = \rho y_{t-1} + \sum_{i=1}^{p-1} \gamma_i \Delta y_{t-i} + \varepsilon_t \tag{4.27}$$

where $\rho = \sum_{i=1}^{p} \phi_i - 1$ and $\gamma_i = -\sum_{j=1}^{i} \phi_{p-i+j}$. Since the autoregressive polynomial will have a unit root if $\sum_{i=1}^{p} \phi_i = 1$, the presence of such a root is formally equivalent to the null hypothesis $\rho = 0$. In this case, the unit root test, denoted as the **Augmented Dickey-Fuller** (Dickey and Fuller, 1979), is based on the LS estimation of the ρ coefficient and the corresponding t-statistic. The distribution of this statistic is the same that the distribution of τ, so we may use the same critical values. This model may include a constant and/or a linear trend:

$$\Delta y_t = \alpha + \rho y_{t-1} + \sum_{i=1}^{p-1} \gamma_i \Delta y_{t-i} + \varepsilon_t \tag{4.28}$$

$$\Delta y_t = \alpha + \beta t + \rho y_{t-1} + \sum_{i=1}^{p-1} \gamma_i \Delta y_{t-i} + \varepsilon_t \tag{4.29}$$

and the t-statistics for the unit root null hypothesis follow the same distribution as τ_μ and τ_τ respectively.

The most common values for d are zero and 1 in economic and business time series. That is why we have concentrated so far in testing the null hypothesis of one unit root against the alternative of stationarity (possibly in deviations from a mean or a linear trend). But it is possible that the series present more than one unit root. If we want to test, in general, the hypothesis that a series is $I(d)$

against the alternative that it is $I(d-1)$, Dickey and Pantula (1987) suggest to follow a sequential procedure. First, we should test the null hypothesis of d unit roots against the alternative of $(d-1)$ unit roots. If we reject this H_0, then the null hypothesis of $(d-1)$ unit roots should be tested against the alternative of $(d-2)$ unit roots. Last, the null of one unit root is tested against the alternative of stationarity.

Example. The `XEGutsm07.xpl` code computes the ADF statistic to test the unit root hypothesis for a simulated random walk series of size 1000. The value of the τ_μ is -0.93178, which rejects the null hypothesis at the 5% significance level. This output provides as well with the critical values 1%, 5%, 10%, 90%, 95% and 99%. It can be observed that the differences between the distributions of the conventional t-statistic and τ_μ are important. For example, using a 0.05 significance level the critical τ_μ value is -2.86 while that of the normal approximation to Student's t is -1.96 for large samples.

`XEGutsm07.xpl`

Testing for Stationarity

If we want to check the stationarity of a time series or a linear combination of time series, it would be interesting to test the null hypothesis of stationarity directly. Bearing in mind that the classical hypothesis testing methodology ensures that the null hypothesis is accepted unless there is strong evidence against it, it is not surprising that a good number of empirical work show that standard unit-root tests fail to reject the null hypothesis for many economic time series. Therefore, in trying to decide wether economic data are stationary or integrated, it would be useful to perform tests of the null hypothesis of stationarity as well as tests of the unit-root null hypothesis.

Kwiatkowski, Phillips, Schmidt and Shin (1992) (KPSS) have developed a test for the null hypothesis of stationarity against the alternative of unit root. Let us consider the following Data Generating Process:

$$y_t = \beta t + \alpha_t + u_t \tag{4.30}$$

The term α_t is a random walk:

$$\alpha_t - \alpha_{t-1} = \zeta_t$$

where the initial value α_0 is treated as fixed and plays the role of intercept, the error term $\zeta_t \sim i.i.d.(0, \sigma_\zeta^2)$ and u_t is assumed to be a stationary process independent of ζ_t. If α_t is not a random walk the series y_t would be trend stationary. Therefore, the stationarity hypothesis is simply H_0: $\sigma_\zeta^2 = 0$.

Let $\hat{u}_t$, $t = 1, 2, \ldots, T$, be the LS residuals of the auxiliary regression:

$$y_t = \alpha + \beta t + u_t$$

and let us define the partial sum of the residuals as:

$$S_t = \sum_{i=1}^{t} \hat{u}_i$$

The test statistic developed by KPSS is based on the idea that for a trend stationary process, the variance of the sum series S_t should be relative small, while it should be important in the presence of one unit root. Then, the test statistic for the null hypothesis of trend stationarity versus a stochastic trend representation is:

$$\eta = \frac{\sum_{t=1}^{T} S_t^2}{T^2 \hat{\sigma}^2} \tag{4.31}$$

where $\hat{\sigma}^2$ stands for a consistent estimation of the 'long-term' variance of the error term u_t. KPSS derived the asymptotic distribution of this test statistic under the stronger assumptions that ζ_t is normal and $u_t \sim N.I.D.(0, \sigma_u^2)$, and tabulated the corresponding critical values. Since η only takes positive values, this test procedure is an upper tail test. The null hypothesis of trend stationarity is rejected when η exceeds the critical value.

The distribution of this test statistic has been tabulated as well for the special case in which the slope parameter of model (4.30) is $\beta = 0$. In such a case, the process y_t is stationary around a level (α_0) rather than around a trend under the null hypothesis. Therefore, the residual $\hat{u}_t$, is obtained from the auxiliary regression of y_t on an intercept only, that is $\hat{u}_t = y_t - \bar{y}$.

Example. The `XEGutsm08.xpl` code tests the stationarity hypothesis for a simulated $AR(1)$ series with $\phi = 0.4$ and $T = 1000$. The results do not reject the null hypothesis of stationarity.

```
[1,]   Order   Test    Statistic          Crit. Value
[2,]                                  0.1    0.05   0.01
[3,] -----------------------------------------------------
[4,]       2  const        0.105    0.347  0.463  0.739
[5,]       2  trend        0.103    0.119  0.146  0.216
```

XEGutsm08.xpl

4.4 Forecasting with ARIMA Models

4.4.1 The Optimal Forecast

Let us assume that the series $y_1, y_2, \ldots, y_T$ follows the general $ARIMA(p,d,q)$ model that can be rewritten in terms of the present and past values of ε_t:

$$y_t = \frac{\Theta(L)}{\Phi(L)\Delta^d}\,\varepsilon_t = \psi_\infty(L)\,\varepsilon_t = (1 + \psi_1 L + \psi_2 L^2 + \ldots)\,\varepsilon_t \tag{4.32}$$

Our objective is to forecast a future value $y_{T+\ell}$ given our information set that consists of the past values $Y_T = (y_T, y_{T-1}, \ldots)$. The future value $y_{T+\ell}$ is generated by model (4.32), thus

$$y_{T+\ell} = \varepsilon_{T+\ell} + \psi_1 \varepsilon_{T+\ell-1} + \psi_2 \varepsilon_{T+\ell-2} + \ldots$$

Let us denote by $y_T(\ell)$ the ℓ-step ahead forecast of $y_{T+\ell}$ made at origin T. It can be shown that, under reasonable weak conditions, the optimal forecast of $y_{T+\ell}$ is the conditional expectation of $y_{T+\ell}$ given the information set, denoted by $E[y_{T+\ell}|Y_T]$. The term optimal is used in the sense that minimizes the Mean Squared Error (MSE). Although the conditional expectation does not have to be a linear function of the present and past values of y_t, we shall consider linear forecasts because they are fairly easy to work with. Furthermore, if the process is normal, the Minimum MSE forecast (MMSE) is linear. Therefore, the optimal forecast ℓ-step ahead is:

$$\begin{aligned} y_T(\ell) &= E[y_{T+\ell}|Y_T] = E[\varepsilon_{T+\ell} + \psi_1 \varepsilon_{T+\ell-1} + \psi_2 \varepsilon_{T+\ell-2} + \ldots |Y_T] \\ &= \psi_\ell \varepsilon_T + \psi_{\ell+1} \varepsilon_{T-1} + \psi_{\ell+2} \varepsilon_{T-2} + \ldots \end{aligned}$$

since past values of ε_{T+j}, for $j \leq 0$, are known and future values of ε_{T+j}, for $j > 0$, have zero expectation.

The ℓ-step ahead forecast error is a linear combination of the future shocks entering the system after time T:

$$e_T(\ell) = y_{T+\ell} - y_T(\ell) = \varepsilon_{T+\ell} + \psi_1 \varepsilon_{T+\ell-1} + \ldots + \psi_{\ell-1}\varepsilon_{T+1}$$

Since $E[e_T(\ell)|Y_T] = 0$, the forecast $y_T(\ell)$ is unbiased with MSE:

$$MSE[y_T(\ell)] = V(e_T(\ell)) = \sigma_\varepsilon^2 (1 + \psi_1^2 + \ldots + \psi_\ell^2) \tag{4.33}$$

Given these results, if the process is normal, the $(1-\alpha)$ forecast interval is:

$$\left[\, y_T(\ell) \pm N_{\alpha/2}\sqrt{V(e_T(\ell))}\,\right] \tag{4.34}$$

For $\ell = 1$, the one-step ahead forecast error is $e_T(1) = y_{T+1} - y_T(1) = \varepsilon_{T+1}$, therefore σ_ε^2 can be interpreted as the one-step ahead prediction error variance.

4.4.2 Computation of Forecasts

Let us consider again the general $ARIMA(p,d,q)$ model that can be written as well as:

$$\Pi_{p+d}(L) y_t = (1 - \pi_1 L - \pi_2 L^2 - \ldots - \pi_{p+d} L^{p+d}) y_t = \Theta(L)\varepsilon_t \tag{4.35}$$

where $\Pi_{p+d}(L) = \Phi_p(L)(1-L)^d$. Thus, the future value of $y_{T+\ell}$ generated by (4.35) is:

$$y_{T+\ell} = \pi_1 y_{T+\ell-1} + \ldots + \pi_{p+d} y_{T+\ell-p-d} + \varepsilon_{T+\ell} + \theta_1 \varepsilon_{T+\ell-1} + \ldots + \theta_q \varepsilon_{T+\ell-q}$$

and the MMSE forecast is given by the expectation conditional to the information set:

$$\begin{aligned} y_T(\ell) &= \mathrm{E}[\, y_{T+\ell}|Y_T] = \pi_1 E[y_{T+\ell-1}|Y_T] + \ldots + \pi_{p+d} E[y_{T+\ell-p-d}|Y_T] \\ &+ E[\varepsilon_{T+\ell}|Y_T] + \theta_1 E[\varepsilon_{T+\ell-1}|Y_T] + \ldots + \theta_q E[\varepsilon_{T+\ell-q}|Y_T] \end{aligned}$$

The forecast $y_T(\ell)$ is computed substituting past expectations for known values and future expectations by forecast values, that is:

$$E[y_{T+j}|Y_T] = \begin{cases} y_{T+j} & j \leq 0 \\ y_T(j) & j > 0 \end{cases}$$

$$E[\varepsilon_{T+j}|Y_T] = \begin{cases} \varepsilon_{T+j} & j \leq 0 \\ 0 & j > 0 \end{cases}$$

In practice, the parameters of the $ARIMA(p, d, q)$ model should be estimated, but for convenience, we assume that they are given.

4.4.3 Eventual Forecast Functions

Following the results of section 4.4.2, if the series y_t follows an $ARIMA(p, d, q)$ model, the ℓ-step ahead forecast at origin T is given by:

$$y_T(\ell) = \pi_1 y_T(\ell-1) + \ldots + \pi_{p+d}\, y_T(\ell-p-d) + \theta_1 \varepsilon_T(\ell-1) + \ldots + \theta_q \varepsilon_T(\ell-q)$$

Therefore, when the forecast horizon $\ell > q$:

$$y_T(\ell) = \pi_1\, y_T(\ell-1) + \pi_2\, y_T(\ell-2) + \ldots + \pi_{p+d}\, y_T(\ell-p-d)$$

That is, the ℓ-step ahead forecast for $\ell > q$ satisfies the homogeneous difference equation of order $(p+d)$:

$$y_T(\ell) - \pi_1\, y_T(\ell-1) - \pi_2\, y_T(\ell-2) - \ldots - \pi_{p+d}\, y_T(\ell-p-d) = 0 \qquad (4.36)$$

Let us factorize the polynomial $\Pi(L)$ in terms of its roots as follows:

$$\Pi(L) = (1 - \pi_1 L - \pi_2 L^2 - \ldots - \pi_{p+d} L^{p+d}) = \prod_{i=1}^{N} (1 - R_i^{-1} L)^{n_i}$$

where $\sum_1^N n_i = p+d$. Then, the general solution of the homogeneous difference equation (4.36) is:

$$y_T(\ell) = \sum_{i=1}^{N} \left[\sum_{j=0}^{n_i-1} k_{ij}^T\, \ell^j \right] (R_i^{-1})^{\ell} \qquad \ell > q-p-d \qquad (4.37)$$

where k_{ij}^T are constants that depend on time origin T, that is, these constants change when the forecast origin is changed.

The expression (4.37) is called the eventual forecast function, because it holds only for $\ell > q-p-d$. If $q < p+d$, then the eventual forecast function holds for all $\ell > 0$. This eventual forecast function passes through the $(p+d)$ values given by $y_T(q), y_T(q-1), \ldots, y_T(q-p-d+1)$.

Example 1: Stationary processes. Let us consider the $ARIMA(1,0,1)$ process in deviations to the mean μ:

$$(1-\phi L)(y_t-\mu) = (1+\theta L)\varepsilon_t \qquad |\phi| < 1$$

For $\ell > q = 1$, the forecast function $y_T(\ell)$ satisfies the difference equation:

$$(1-\phi L)(y_t-\mu) = 0$$

Therefore, the eventual forecast function is given by:

$$\begin{aligned} y_T(\ell)-\mu &= k^T\phi^\ell \\ y_T(\ell) &= \mu + k^T\phi^\ell \qquad \ell > q-p-d = 0 \end{aligned}$$

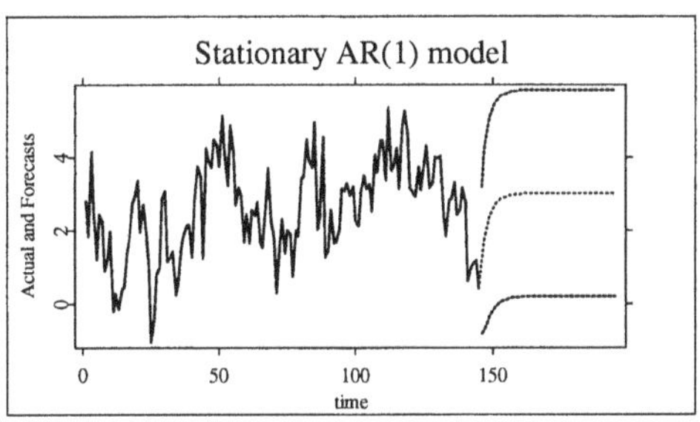

Figure 4.12. Forecast of $AR(1)$ model

XEGutsm09.xpl

Let us take as an example the forecast of an $AR(1)$ process with $\delta = 0.9$ and $\phi = 0.7$. Figure 4.12 shows the eventual forecast function of the model considered (dotted line). It can be observed that this function increases at the beginning until it reaches the mean value, 3. This result, that is,

$$\lim_{\ell\to\infty} y_T(\ell) = \mu$$

holds for every stationary process. The dashed lines give the interval forecasts, whose limits approach to horizontal parallel lines. This is due to the fact that for every stationary process the $\lim_{\ell\to\infty} V(e_T(\ell))$ exists and it is equal to $V(y_t)$.

Example 2: Integrated processes of order 1. Let us consider the following $ARIMA(0,1,1)$ model:

$$(1-L)y_t = (1+\theta L)\varepsilon_t$$

The eventual forecast function is the solution to the difference equation:

$$(1-L)y_t = 0 \qquad \ell > q = 1$$

that is given by:

$$y_T(\ell) = k^T 1^\ell = k^T \qquad \ell > q-p-d = 0$$

This eventual forecast function passes through the one-step ahead forecast $y_T(1)$ and remains there as ℓ increases.

If $\theta = 0$, we get the **random walk** model (4.20) and the eventual forecast function takes the form:

$$y_T(\ell) = y_T \qquad \ell > 0$$

That is, the optimal forecast is simply the current value, regardless of the forecast horizon. If a shock occurs at time T, its effect does not disappear as the forecast horizon increases, because there is no mean to which the process may revert (see graph (a) in figure 4.13).

The eventual forecast function for the **random walk plus drift** model (4.21) is the solution to the following difference equation:

$$(1-L)y_t = \delta$$

Thus:

$$y_T(\ell) = k^T 1^\ell + \delta\ell = k^T + \delta\ell \tag{4.38}$$

Therefore the eventual forecast function is a straight line in which only the intercept depends on the time origin, T, through the constant k^T (see graph (b) in figure 4.13).

It can be observed in figure 4.13 that the interval forecast limits increase continuously as the forecast horizon ℓ becomes larger. It should be taken into account that when the process is nonstationary the limit $\lim_{\ell\to\infty} V(e_T(\ell))$ does not exist.

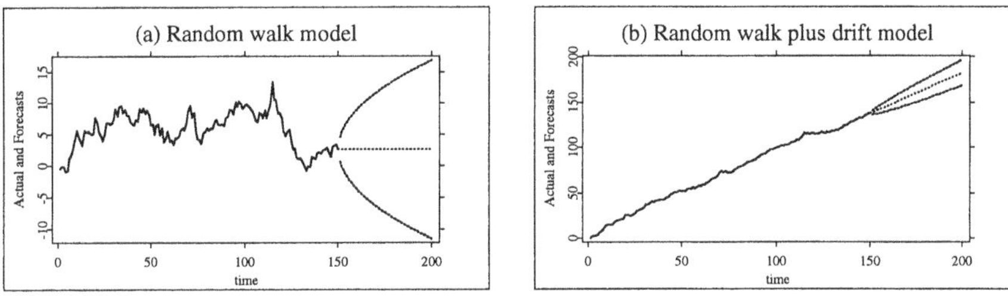

Figure 4.13. Forecast of $I(1)$ models

XEGutsm10.xpl

Example 3: Integrated processes of order 2. Let us consider the $ARIMA(0,2,2)$ model:

$$(1-L)^2 y_t = (1+\theta_1 L + \theta_2 L^2)\varepsilon_t$$

Solving the homogeneous difference equation: $(1-L)^2 y_t = 0 \quad \ell > 2$ we get the eventual forecast function as:

$$y_T(\ell) = k_1^T 1^\ell + k_2^T 1^\ell \ell = k_1^T + k_2^T \ell$$

Thus, the eventual forecast function is a straight line passing through the forecasts $y_T(1)$ and $y_T(2)$. Although this forecast function shows the same structure as equation (4.38), it should be noted that both the intercept and the slope of the eventual forecast function depend on the time origin T.

4.5 ARIMA Model Building

We have determined the population properties of the wide class of $ARIMA$ models but, in practice, we have a time series and we want to infer which $ARIMA$ model can have generated this time series. The selection of the appropriate $ARIMA$ model for the data is achieved by a iterative procedure based on three steps (Box, Jenkins and Reinsel, 1994):

- *Identification*: use of the data and of any available information to suggest a subclass of parsimonious models to describe how the data have been generated.

- *Estimation*: efficient use of the data to make inference about the parameters. It is conditioned on the adequacy of the selected model.
- *Diagnostic checking*: checks the adequacy of fitted model to the data in order to reveal model inadequacies and to achieve model improvement.

In this section we will explain this procedure in detail illustrating each step with an example.

4.5.1 Inference for the Moments of Stationary Processes

Since a stationary $ARMA$ process is characterized in terms of the moments of the distribution, meanly its mean, ACF and PACF, it is necessary to estimate them using the available data in order to make inference about the underlying process.

Mean. A consistent estimator of the mean of the process, μ, is the sample mean of the time series $\overline{y}$:

$$\overline{y} = \frac{1}{T}\sum_{t=1}^{T} y_t \tag{4.39}$$

whose asymptotic variance can be approximated by $\frac{1}{T}$ times the sample variance S_y^2.

Sometimes it is useful to check whether the mean of a process is zero or not, that is, to test $H_0\colon \mu = 0$ against $H_a\colon \mu \neq 0$. Under H_0 the test statistic $\sqrt{T}\frac{\overline{y}}{S_y}$ follows approximately a normal distribution.

Autocorrelation Function. A consistent estimator of the ACF is the sample autocorrelation function. It is defined as:

$$r_j = \frac{\sum_{t=j+1}^{T} (y_t - \overline{y})(y_{t-j} - \overline{y})}{\sum_{t=1}^{T} (y_t - \overline{y})^2} \qquad \forall j$$

In order to identify the underlying process, it is useful to check whether these coefficients are statistically nonzero or, more specifically, to check whether y_t

is a white noise. Under the assumption that $y_t \sim WN(0,\sigma^2)$, the distribution of these coefficients in large samples can be approximated by:

$$\sqrt{T} r_j \overset{a}{\sim} N(0,1) \tag{4.40}$$

Then a usual test of individual significance can be applied, *i.e.*, $H_0\colon \rho_j = 0$ against $H_a\colon \rho_j \neq 0$ for any $j = 1, 2, \ldots$. The null hypothesis H_0 would be rejected at the 5% level of significance if:

$$|r_j| > 1.96/\sqrt{T} \tag{4.41}$$

Usually, the correlogram plots the ACF jointly with these two-standard error bands around zero, approximated by $\pm 2/\sqrt{T}$, that allow us to carry out this significance test by means of an easy graphic method.

We are also interested in whether *a set* of M autocorrelations are jointly zero or not, that is, in testing $H_0\colon \rho_1 = \rho_2 = \cdots = \rho_M = 0$. The most usual test statistic is the **Ljung-Box statistic**:

$$Q_{LB} = T(T+2) \sum_{j=1}^{M} \frac{r_j^2}{T-j} \tag{4.42}$$

that follows asymptotically a $\chi^2_{(M)}$ distribution under H_0.

Partial Autocorrelation Function. The partial autocorrelation function is estimated by the OLS coefficient $\hat{\phi}_{ii}$ from the expression (4.11), that is known as sample PACF.

Under the assumption that $y_t \sim WN(0,\sigma^2)$, the distribution of the sample coefficients $\hat{\phi}_{ii}$ in large samples is identical to those of the sample ACF (4.40). In consequence, the rule for rejecting the null hypothesis of individual non-significance (4.41) is also applied to the PACF. The bar plot of the sample PACF is called the sample partial correlogram and usually includes the two standard error bands $\pm 2/\sqrt{T}$ to assess for individual significance.

4.5.2 Identification of ARIMA Models

The objective of the identification is to select a subclass of the family of $ARIMA$ models appropriated to represent a time series. We follow a two step procedure: first, we get a stationary time series, *i.e.*, we select the parameter λ of the Box-Cox transformation and the order of integration d, and secondly we identify a set of stationary $ARMA$ processes to represent the stationary process, *i.e.* we choose the orders (p, q).

Selection of Stationary Transformations. Our task is to identify if the time series could have been generated by a stationary process. First, we use the timeplot of the series to analyze if it is *variance stationary*. The series departs from this property when the dispersion of the data varies along time. In this case, the stationarity in variance is achieved by applying the appropriate Box-Cox transformation (4.17) and as a result, we get the series $y^{(\lambda)}$.

The second part is the analysis of the *stationarity in mean*. The instruments are the timeplot, the sample correlograms and the tests for unit roots and stationarity. The path of a nonstationary series usually shows an upward or downward slope or jumps in the level whereas a stationary series moves around a unique level along time. The sample autocorrelations of stationary processes are consistent estimates of the corresponding population coefficients, so the sample correlograms of stationary processes go to zero for moderate lags. This type of reasoning does not follow for nonstationary processes because their theoretical autocorrelations are not well defined. But we can argue that a 'non-decaying' behavior of the sample ACF should be due to a lack of stationarity. Moreover, typical profiles of sample correlograms of integrated series are shown in figure 4.14: the sample ACF tends to damp very slowly and the sample PACF decays very quickly, at lag $j = 2$, with the first value close to unity.

When the series shows nonstationary patterns, we should take first differences and analyze if $\Delta y_t^{(\lambda)}$ is stationary or not in a similar way. This process of taking successive differences will continue until a stationary time series is achieved. The graphics methods can be supported with the unit-root and stationarity tests developed in subsection 4.3.3. As a result, we have a stationary time series $z_t = \Delta^d y_t^{(\lambda)}$ and the order of integration d will be the number of times that we have differenced the series $y^{(\lambda)}$.

Selection of Stationary ARMA Models. The choice of the appropriate (p, q) values of the $ARMA$ model for the stationary series z_t is carried out on the grounds of its characteristics, that is, the mean, the ACF and the PACF.

The mean of the process is closely connected with the parameter δ: when the constant term is zero, the process has zero mean (see equation (4.22)). Then a

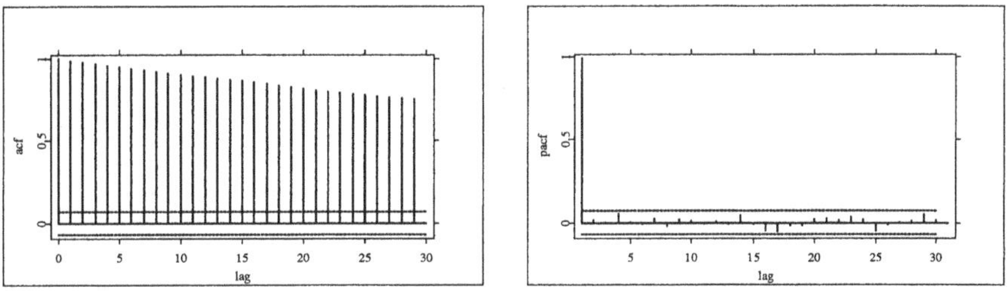

Figure 4.14. Sample correlograms of random walk

XEGutsm11.xpl

constant term will be added to the model if H_0: $\mathrm{E}(z) = 0$ is rejected.

The orders (p, q) are selected comparing the sample ACF and PACF of z_t with the theoretical patterns of $ARMA$ processes that are summarized in table 4.1.

Example: Minks time series. To illustrate the identification procedure, we analyze the annual number of mink furs traded by the Hudson's Bay Company in Canada from 1848 to 1909, denoted by $Minks$.

XEGutsm12.xpl

Figure 4.15 plots the time series $Minks$. It suggests that the variance could be changing. The plot of the $\ln(Minks)$ shows a more stable pattern in variance, so we select the transformation parameter $\lambda = 0$. This series $\ln(Minks)$ appears to be stationary since it evolves around a constant level and the correlograms

Process	ACF	PACF
$AR(p)$	Infinite: exponential and/or sine-cosine wave decay	Finite: cut off at lag p
$MA(q)$	Finite: cut off at lag p	Infinite: exponential and/or sine-cosine wave decay
$ARMA(p, q)$	Infinite: exponential and/or sine-cosine wave decay	Infinite: exponential and/or sine-cosine wave decay

Table 4.1. Autocorrelation patterns of ARMA processes

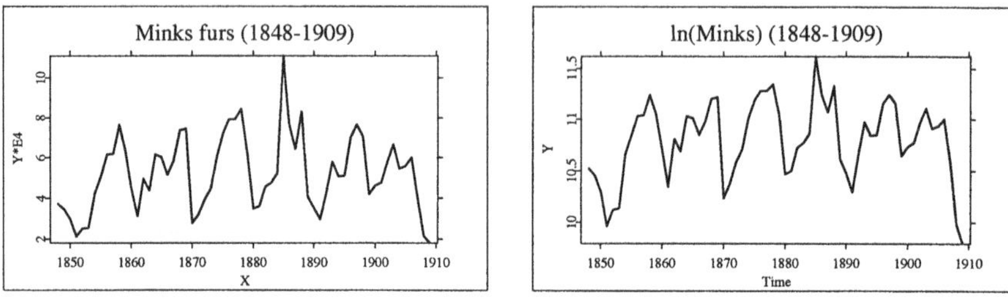

Figure 4.15. Minks series and stationary transformation

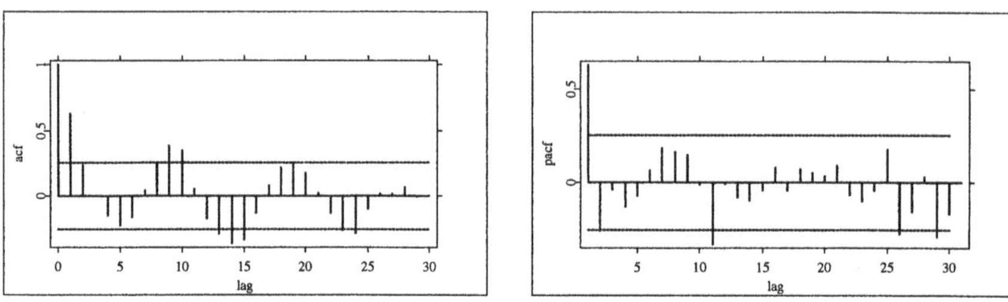

Figure 4.16. Minks series. Sample ACF and PACF of $\ln(Minks)$

lag	Two standard error	ACF	PACF
1	0.254	0.6274	0.6274
2	0.254	0.23622	-0.2596
3	0.254	0.00247	-0.03770
4	0.254	-0.15074	-0.13233
5	0.254	-0.22492	-0.07182

Table 4.2. Minks series. Sample ACF and PACF of $\ln(Minks)$

decay quickly (see figure 4.16). Furthermore the ADF test-value is -3.6, that clearly rejects the unit-root hypothesis. Therefore, the stationary time series we are going to analyze is $z_t = \ln(Minks)$.

As far as the selection of the orders (p, q) is concerned, we study the correlograms of figure 4.16 and the numerical values of the first five coefficients that are reported in table 4.2. The main feature of the ACF is its damping sine-cosine wave structure that reflects the behavior of an $AR(p)$ process with complex roots. The PACF, where the H_0: $\phi_{jj} = 0$ is rejected only for $j = 1, 2$, leads us to select the values $p = 2$ for the AR model.

The statistic for testing the null hypothesis H_0: $\mathrm{E}(z) = 0$ takes the value 221.02. Given a significance level of 5%, we reject the null hypothesis of zero mean and a constant should be included into the model. As a result, we propose an $ARIMA(2, 0, 0)$ model for $\ln(Minks)$:

$$z_t = \delta + \phi_1 z_{t-1} + \phi_2 z_{t-2} + \varepsilon_t \qquad \text{with} \quad z = \ln(Minks)$$

4.5.3 Parameter Estimation

The parameters of the selected $ARIMA(p, d, q)$ model can be estimated consistently by least-squares or by maximum likelihood. Both estimation procedures are based on the computation of the innovations ε_t from the values of the stationary variable. The least-squares methods minimize the sum of squares,

$$min \qquad \sum_t \varepsilon_t^2 \tag{4.43}$$

The log-likelihood can be derived from the joint probability density function of the innovations $\varepsilon_1, \dots, \varepsilon_T$, that takes the following form under the normality assumption, $\varepsilon_t \sim \mathrm{N.I.D.}(0, \sigma_\varepsilon^2)$:

$$f(\varepsilon_1, \dots, \varepsilon_T) \propto \sigma_\varepsilon^{-T} \exp\left\{ -\sum_{t=1}^{T} \frac{\varepsilon_t^2}{2\sigma_\varepsilon^2} \right\} \tag{4.44}$$

In order to solve the estimation problem, equations (4.43) and (4.44) should be written in terms of the observed data and the set of parameters (Θ, Φ, δ). An $ARMA(p, q)$ process for the stationary transformation z_t can be expressed as:

$$\varepsilon_t = z_t - \delta - \sum_{i=1}^{p} \phi_i z_{t-i} - \sum_{i=1}^{q} \theta_i \varepsilon_{t-i} \tag{4.45}$$

Then, to compute the innovations corresponding to a given set of observations $(z_1, \dots z_T)$ and parameters, it is necessary to count with the starting values $z_0, \dots, z_{p-1}$, $\varepsilon_0, \dots, \varepsilon_{q-1}$. More realistically, the innovations should be approximated by setting appropriate conditions about the initial values, giving to conditional least squares or conditional maximum likelihood estimators. One procedure consists of setting the initial values equal to their unconditional expectations, that is,

$$\varepsilon_0 = \cdots = \varepsilon_{q-1} = 0 \quad \text{and} \quad z_0 = \cdots = z_{p-1} = \delta(1 - \sum_{i=1}^{p} \phi_i)^{-1}$$

For example, for the $MA(1)$ process with zero mean, equation (4.45) is $\varepsilon_t = z_t - \theta\varepsilon_{t-1}$. Assuming $\varepsilon_0 = 0$, then we compute the innovations recursively as follows:

$$\begin{aligned}
\varepsilon_1 &= z_1 \\
\varepsilon_2 &= z_2 - \theta z_1 \\
\varepsilon_3 &= z_3 - \theta z_2 + \theta^2 z_1
\end{aligned}$$

and so on. That is,

$$\varepsilon_t = \sum_{i=0}^{t-1} (-1)^i \theta^i z_{t-i} \tag{4.46}$$

A second useful mechanism is to assume that the first p observations of y are the starting values and the previous innovations are again equal to zero. In this case we run the equation (4.45) from $t = p + 1$ onwards. For example, for an $AR(p)$ process, it is

$$\varepsilon_t = z_t - \delta - \phi_1 z_{t-1} - \cdots - \phi_p z_{t-p} \tag{4.47}$$

thus, for given values of δ, Φ and conditional on the initial values $z_1, \ldots, z_T$, we can get innovations from $t = p + 1$ until T. Both procedures are the same for pure $MA(q)$ models, but the first one could be less suitable for models with AR components. For example, let's consider an $AR(1)$ process with zero mean and AR parameter close to the nonstationary boundary. In this case, the initial value z_1 could deviate from its unconditional expectation and the condition $z_0 = 0$ could distort the estimation results.

Conditional Least Squares. Least squares estimation conditioned on the first p observations become straightforward in the case of pure AR models, leading to linear Least Squares. For example, for the $AR(1)$ process with zero mean, and conditioned on the first value y_1, equation (4.43) becomes the linear problem,

$$min \quad \sum_{t=2}^{T} (y_t - \phi y_{t-1})^2$$

leading to the usual estimator

$$\hat{\phi}_{LS} = \frac{\sum_t y_t y_{t-1}}{\sum_t y_{t-1}^2}$$

which is consistent and asymptotically normal.

In a general model with a MA component the optimization problem (4.43) is nonlinear. For example, to estimate the parameter θ of the $MA(1)$ process, we substitute equation (4.46) in (4.43),

$$min \sum_{t=2}^{T} \varepsilon_t^2 = min \sum_{t=2}^{T} \left(\sum_{i=0}^{t-1} (-1)^i \theta^i z_{t-i} \right)^2$$

which is a nonlinear function of θ. Then, common nonlinear optimization algorithms such as Gauss-Newton can be applied in order to get the estimates.

Maximum Likelihood. The ML estimator conditional to the first p values is equal to the conditional LS estimator. For example, returning to the $AR(1)$ specification, we substitute the innovations $\varepsilon_t = z_t - \phi z_{t-1}$ in the ML principle (4.44). Taking logarithms we get the corresponding log-likelihood conditional on the first value y_1:

$$\ell(\phi, \sigma_\varepsilon^2 | y_1) = -\frac{T-1}{2} \ln(\sigma_\varepsilon^2) - \frac{1}{2\sigma_\varepsilon^2} \sum_{t=2}^{T} (y_t - \phi y_{t-1})^2 \qquad (4.48)$$

The maximization of this function gives the LS estimator. Instead of setting the initial conditions, we can compute the unconditional likelihood. For an $AR(1)$ model, the joint density function can be decomposed as:

$$f(y_1, y_2, \ldots, y_T) = f(y_1) f(y_2, \ldots, y_T | y_1)$$

where the marginal distribution of y_1 is normal with zero mean, if $\delta = 0$, and variance $\sigma_\varepsilon^2 (1 - \phi^2)^{-1}$. Then, the exact log-likelihood under the normality assumption is:

$$\ell(\phi, \sigma_\varepsilon^2) = -\frac{1}{2} \ln(\sigma_\varepsilon^2) + \frac{1}{2} \ln(1 - \phi^2) - \frac{y_1^2 (1 - \phi^2)}{2\sigma_\varepsilon^2} + \ell(\phi, \sigma_\varepsilon^2 | y_1)$$

where the second term $\ell(\phi, \sigma_\varepsilon^2 | y_1)$ is equation (4.48). Then, the exact likelihood for a general $ARMA$ model is the combination of the conditional likelihood and the unconditional probability density function of the initial values. As can be shown for the $AR(1)$ model, the exact ML estimator is not linear and these estimates are the solution of a nonlinear optimization problem that becomes quite complex. This unconditional likelihood can be computed via the prediction error decomposition by applying the Kalman filter (Harvey, 1993), which is also a useful tool for bayesian estimation of $ARIMA$ models (Box, Jenkins and Reinsel, 1994; Bauwens, Lubrano and Richard, 1999). As the sample size increases the relative contribution of these initials values to the likelihood tends to be negligible, and so do the differences between conditional and unconditional estimation.

Example: Minks time series. As an example let us estimate the following models for the series $z = \ln(Minks)$:

$$AR(2) \quad z_t = \delta + \phi_1 z_{t-1} + \phi_2 z_{t-2} + \varepsilon_t \tag{4.49}$$

$$MA(1) \quad z_t = \delta + \theta \varepsilon_{t-1} + \varepsilon_t \tag{4.50}$$

$$ARMA(1,1) \quad z_t = \delta + \phi_1 z_{t-1} + \theta \varepsilon_{t-1} + \varepsilon_t \tag{4.51}$$

The `ariols` quantlet may be applied to compute the linear LS estimates of pure AR process such as the $AR(2)$ model (4.49). In this case we use the code `ar2=ariols(z,p, d, "constant")` with $p = 2, d = 0$ and the results are stored in the object `ar2`. The first three elements are the basic results: `ar2.b` is the vector of parameter estimates $(\hat{\delta}, \hat{\phi}_1, \hat{\phi}_2)$, `ar2.bst` is the vector of their corresponding asymptotic standard errors and `ar2.wnv` is the innovation variance estimate $\hat{\sigma}_\varepsilon^2$. The last three components `ar2.checkr`, `ar2.checkp` and `ar2.models` are lists that include the diagnostic checking statistics and model selection criteria when the optional strings `rcheck`, `pcheck` and `ic` are included and take zero value otherwise.

The $MA(1)$ model (4.50) is estimated by conditional nonlinear LS with the `arimacls` quantlet. The basic results of the code `ma1=arimacls(z,p,d,q, "constant")` with $p = d = 0, q = 1$ consist of: the vector `ma1.b` of the estimated parameters, the innovation variance estimate `ma1.wnv` and the vector `ma1.conv` with the number of iterations and a 0-1 scalar indicating convergence. The other output results, `ar2.checkr` and `ar2.ic`, are the same as the `ariols` components.

The exact maximum likelihood estimation of the $ARIMA(1,0,1)$ process (4.51) can be done by applying the quantlet `arima11`. The corresponding code is `arima11=arima11v(z,d, "constant")` with $d = 0$ and the output includes the vector of parameter estimates $(\hat{\delta}, \hat{\phi}, \hat{\theta})$, the asymptotic standard errors of ARMA components $(\hat{\phi}, \hat{\theta})$, the innovation variance estimate $\hat{\sigma}_\varepsilon^2$ and the optional results `arima11.checkr`, `arima11.checkp` and `arima11.ic`.

The parameter estimates are summarized in table 4.3.

Model	$AR(2)$	$MA(1)$	$ARMA(1,1)$
δ	4.4337	10.7970	4.6889
$\hat{\phi}_1$	0.8769		0.5657
$\hat{\phi}_2$	- 0.2875		
$\hat{\theta}$		0.6690	0.3477
$\hat{\sigma}_\varepsilon^2$	0.0800	0.0888	0.0763

Table 4.3. Minks series. Estimated models

XEGutsm13.xpl

4.5.4 Diagnostic Checking

Once we have identified and estimated the candidate $ARMA$ models, we want to assess the adequacy of the selected models to the data. This model diagnostic checking step involves both parameter and residual analysis.

Diagnostic Testing for Residuals.

If the fitted model is adequate, the residuals should be approximately white noise. So, we should check if the residuals have zero mean and if they are uncorrelated. The key instruments are the timeplot, the ACF and the PACF of the residuals. The theoretical ACF and PACF of white noise processes take value zero for lags $j \neq 0$, so if the model is appropriate most of the coefficients of the sample ACF and PACF should be close to zero. In practice, we require that about the 95% of these coefficients should fall within the non-significance bounds. Moreover, the Ljung-Box statistic (4.42) should take small values, as corresponds to uncorrelated variables. The degrees of freedom of this statistic take into account the number of estimated parameters so the statistic test under H_0 follows approximately a $\chi^2_{(M-k)}$ distribution with $k = p + q$. If the model is not appropriate, we expect the correlograms (simple and partial) of the residuals to depart from white noise suggesting the reformulation of the model.

Example: Minks time series. We will check the adequacy of the three fitted models to the $\ln(Minks)$ series. It can be done by using the optional string 'rcheck' of the estimation quantlets.

For example, for the $MA(1)$ model we can use the code `ma1= arimacls(z,0,0, 1, "constant","rcheck")`. This option plots the residuals with the usual standard error bounds $\pm 2\hat{\sigma}_\varepsilon$ and the simple and partial correlograms of $\hat{\varepsilon}_t$ (see figure 4.17). The output `ma1.checkr` also stores the residuals in the vector `a`, the statistic for testing H_0: $\mathrm{E}\varepsilon_t = 0$ in the scalar `stat` and the ACF, Ljung-Box statistic and the PACF in the matrix `acfQ`.

With regard to the zero mean condition, the timeplot shows that the residuals of the $MA(1)$ model evolve around zero and this behavior is supported by the corresponding hypothesis test $H_0: \mathrm{E}\varepsilon_t = 0$. The value of the statistic is 0.016 so the hypothesis of zero mean errors is not rejected. We can see in the correlogram of these residuals in figure 4.17 that several coefficients are significant and besides, the correlogram shows a decaying sine-cosine wave. The Ljung-Box statistics for some M take the following values: $Q_{LB}(10) = 26.65$ and $Q_{LB}(15) = 40.47$, rejecting the required hypothesis of uncorrelated errors. These results lead us to reformulate the model.

Next, we will check the adequacy of the AR(2) model (4.49) to $\ln(Minks)$ data by means of the code `ar2=ariols(z,2,0, "constant", "rcheck")`. The output `ar2.checkr` provides us with the same results as the `arimacls`, namely, `ar2.checkr.a`, `ar2.checkr.stat`, and `ar2.checkr.acfQ`. Most of the coefficients of the ACF lie under the non-significance bounds and the Ljung-Box statistic takes values $Q_{LB}(10) = 12.9$ and $Q_{LB}(15) = 20.1$. Then the hypothesis of uncorrelated errors is not rejected in any case.

`XEGutsm15.xpl`

Finally, the residual diagnostics for the $ARMA(1,1)$ model (4.51) are computed with the optional string "rcheck" of the code `arma11=arima11(z,0, "constant", "rcheck")`. These results show that, given a significance level of 5%, both hyphotesis of uncorrelated errors and zero mean errors are not rejected.

`XEGutsm16.xpl`

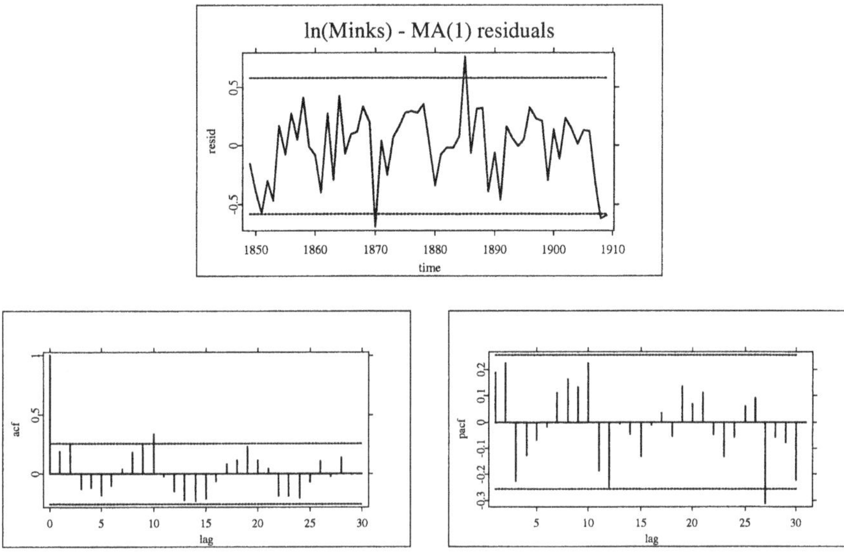

Figure 4.17. Minks series. Residual diagnostics of $MA(1)$ model

XEGutsm14.xpl

Diagnostic Testing for Parameters. The usual t-statistics to test the statistical significance of the AR and MA parameters should be carried out to check if the model is overspecified. But it is important, as well, to assess whether the stationarity and invertibility conditions are satisfied. If we factorize de AR and MA polynomials:

$$\begin{aligned} \Phi(L) &= (1 - R_1^{-1})(1 - R_2^{-1}) \dots (1 - R_p^{-1}) \\ \Theta(L) &= (1 - S_1^{-1})(1 - S_2^{-1}) \dots (1 - S_p^{-1}) \end{aligned}$$

and one of these roots is close to unity it may be an indication of lack of stationarity and/or invertibility.

An inspection of the covariance matrix of the estimated parameters allows us to detect the possible presence of high correlation between the estimates of some parameters which can be a manifestation of the presence of a 'common factor' in the model (Box and Jenkins, 1976).

Example: Minks time series. We will analyse the parameter diagnostics of the estimated $AR(2)$ and $ARMA(1,1)$ models (see equations (4.49) and (4.51)). The quantlets `ariols` for OLS estimation of pure $ARI(p,d)$ models and `arima11` for exact ML estimation of $ARIMA(1,d,1)$ models provide us with these diagnostics by means of the optional string "pcheck".

The `ariols` output stores the t-statistics in the vector `ar2.checkp.bt`, the estimate of the asymptotic covariance matrix in `ar2.checkp.bvar` and the result of checking the necessary condition for stationarity (4.16) in the string `ar2.checkp.est`. When the process is stationary, this string takes value 0 and in other case a warning message appears. The `arima11` output also checks the stationary and invertibility conditions of the estimated model and stores the t-statistics and the asymptotic covariance matrix of the $ARMA$ parameters ϕ, θ.

The following table shows the results for the $AR(2)$ model:

```
[1,] "           ln(Minks), AR(2) model                "
[2,] "   Parameter    Estimate       t-ratio           "
[3,] "_________________________________________________"
[4,] "    delta         4.434          3.598"
[5,] "    phi1          0.877          6.754"
[6,] "    phi2         -0.288         -2.125"
```

XEGutsm17.xpl

It can be observed that the parameters of the $AR(2)$ model are statistically significant and the roots of the polynomial $(1 - 0.877L + 0.288L^2) = 0$ are $1.53 \pm 1.07i$, indicating that the stationarity condition is clearly satisfied. Then, the $AR(2)$ seems to be an appropriate model for the $\ln(Minks)$ series. Similar results are obtained for the $ARMA(1,1)$ model.

4.5.5 Model Selection Criteria

Once a set of models have been identified and estimated, it is possible that more than one of them is not rejected in the diagnostic checking step. Although we may want to use all models to check which performs best in forecasting, usually we want to select between them. In general, the model which minimizes a certain criterion function is selected.

The standard goodness of fit criterion in Econometrics is the coefficient of determination:

$$R^2 = 1 - \frac{\hat{\sigma}_\varepsilon^2}{\hat{\sigma}_y^2}$$

where $\hat{\sigma}_\varepsilon^2 = \sum \hat{\varepsilon}_t^2/T$. Therefore, maximizing R^2 is equivalent to minimize the sum of squared residuals. This measure presents some problems to be useful for model selection. First, the R^2 cannot decrease when more variables are added to a model and typically it will fall continuously. Besides, economic time series usually present strong trends and/or seasonalities and any model that captures this facts to some extent will have a very large R^2. Harvey (1989) proposes modifications to this coefficient to solve this problem.

Due to the limitations of the R^2 coefficient, a number of criteria have been proposed in the literature to evaluate the fit of the model versus the number of parameters (see Postcher and Srinivasan (1994) for a survey). These criteria were developed for pure AR models but have been extended for $ARMA$ models. It is assumed that the degree of differencing has been decided and that the object of the criterion is to determine the most appropiate values of p and q. The more applied model selection criteria are the Akaike Information Criterion, AIC, (Akaike, 1974) and the Schwarz Information Criterion, SIC, (Schwarz, 1978) given by:

$$AIC = \ln(\hat{\sigma}_\varepsilon^2) + \frac{2k}{T} \tag{4.52}$$

$$SIC = \ln(\hat{\sigma}_\varepsilon^2) + \frac{k}{T}\ln(T) \tag{4.53}$$

where k is the number of the estimated $ARMA$ parameters $(p+q)$ and T is the number of observations used for estimation. Both criteria are based on the estimated variance $\hat{\sigma}_\varepsilon^2$ plus a penalty adjustment depending on the number of estimated parameters and it is in the extent of this penalty that these criteria differ. The penalty proposed by SIC is larger than AIC's since $\ln(T) > 2$ for $T \geq 8$. Therefore, the difference between both criteria can be very large if T is large; SIC tends to select simpler models than those chosen by AIC. In practical work, both criteria are usually examined. If they do not select the same model, many authors tend to recommend to use the more parsimonious model selected by SIC.

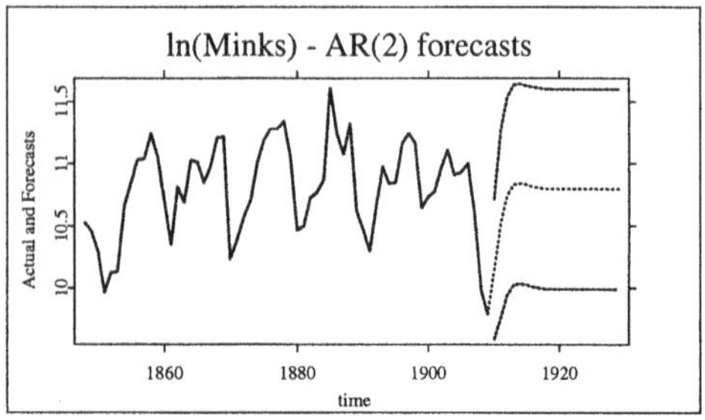

Figure 4.18. Mink series. Forecasts for $AR(2)$ model

XEGutsm19.xpl

Example: Minks time series. We will apply these information criteria to select between the $AR(2)$ and $ARMA(1,1)$ models that were not rejected at the diagnostic checking step. The optional string 'msc' of the estimation quantlets provide us with the values for both criteria, AIC and SIC. For example, the output of the code `ar2=ariols(z,0,2, "constant","nor", "nop", "msc")` includes the vector `ar2.ic` with these values. The following table summarizes the results for these fitted models:

	$AR(2)$	$ARMA(1,1)$
AIC	-2.510	-2.501
SIC	-2.440	-2.432

XEGutsm18.xpl

Both criteria select the $AR(2)$ model and we use this model to forecast.. This model generates a cyclical behavior of period equal to 10,27 years. The forecast function of this model for the $\ln(Minks)$ series can be seen in figure 4.18.

4.5.6 Example: European Union G.D.P.

To illustrate the time series modelling methodology we have presented so far, we analyze a quarterly, seasonally adjusted series of the European Union G.D.P. from the first quarter of 1962 until the first quarter of 2001 (157 observations).

This series is plotted in the first graphic of figure 4.19. It can be observed that the GDP series displays a nonstationary pattern with an upward trending behavior. Moreover, the shape of the correlograms (left column of figure 4.19) is typical of a nonstationary process with a slow decay in the ACF and a coefficient $\hat{\phi}_{11}$ close to unity in the PACF. The ADF test-values (see table 4.4) do not reject the unit-root null hypothesis both under the alternative of a stationary process in deviations to a constant or to a linear trend. Furthermore the KPSS statistics clearly reject the null hypothesis of stationarity around a constant or a linear trend. Thus, we should analyze the stationarity of the first differences of the series, $z = \Delta GDP$.

The right column of figure 4.19 displays the timeplot of the differenced series z_t and its estimated ACF and PACF. The graph of z_t shows a series that moves around a constant mean with approximately constant variance. The estimated ACF decreases quickly and the ADF test-value, $\tau_\mu = -9.61$, clearly rejects the unit-root hypothesis against the alternative of a stationarity process around a constant. Given these results we may conclude that z_t is a stationary series.

The first coefficients of the ACF of z_t are statistically significant and decay as AR or $ARMA$ models. With regard to the PACF, its first coefficient is clearly significant and large, indicating that an $AR(1)$ model could be appropriated for the z_t series. But given that the first coefficients show some decreasing structure and the $\hat{\phi}_{55}$ is statistically significant, perhaps an $ARMA(1,1)$ model should be tried as well. With regard to the mean, the value of the statistic for the hypothesis H_0: $Ez = 0$ is 14.81 and so we reject the zero mean hypothesis.

Therefore we will analyze the following two models:

$$
\begin{aligned}
(1-\phi L)\Delta GDP_t &= \delta + (1+\theta L)\varepsilon_t \\
(1-\phi L)\Delta GDP_t &= \delta + \varepsilon_t
\end{aligned}
$$

Estimation results of the $ARIMA(1,1,1)$ and $ARIMA(1,1,0)$ models are sum-

Statistic	**Testvalue**	**Critical value** ($\alpha = 5\%$)
τ_μ	0.716	-2.86
τ_τ	-1.301	-3.41
$KPSS_\mu$	7.779	0.46
$KPSS_\tau$	0.535	0.15

Table 4.4. GDP (E.U. series). Unit-root and stationarity tests

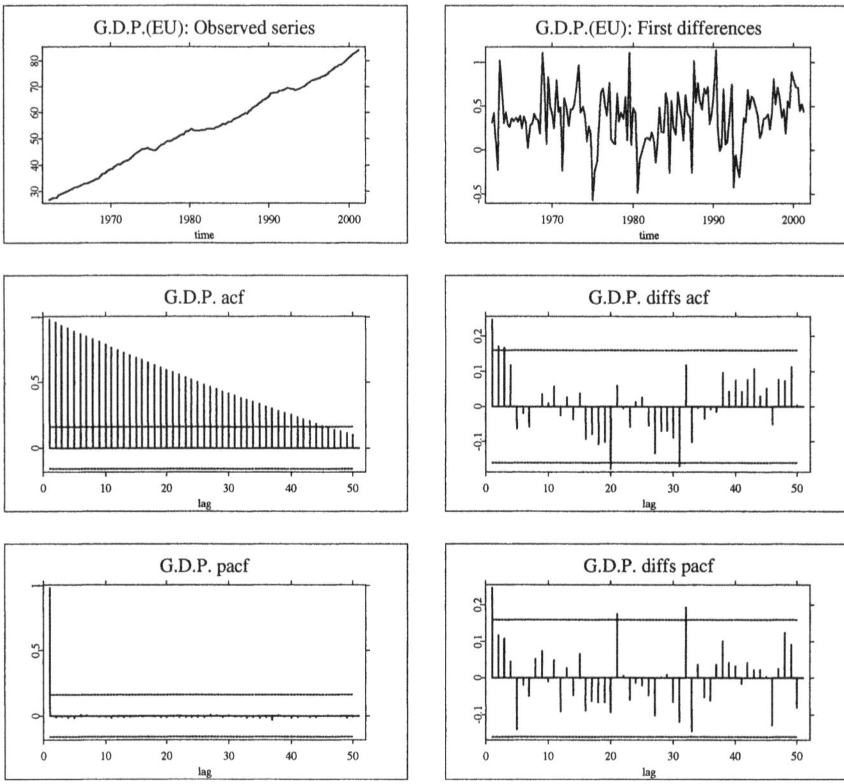

Figure 4.19. European Union G.D.P. (10^{11} US Dollars 1995)

XEGutsm20.xpl

marized in table 4.5 and figure 4.20. Table 4.5 reports parameter estimates, t-statistics, zero mean hypothesis test-value, Ljung-Box statistic values for $M = 5, 15$ and the usual selection model criteria, AIC and SIC, for the two models. Figure 4.20 shows the plot of the residuals and their correlograms.

Both models pass the residual diagnostics with very similar results: the zero mean hypothesis for the residuals is not rejected and the correlograms and the Ljung-Box statistics indicate that the residuals behave as white noise processes. However, the parameters of the $ARIMA(1, 1, 1)$ model are not statistically

	$ARIMA(1,1,1)$	$ARIMA(1,1,0)$
δ $(t - statistic)$	0.22	0.28 (7.37)
ϕ $(t - statistic)$	0.40 (0.93)	0.25 (3.15)
θ $(t - statistic)$	-0.24 (-0.54)	-
σ^2_ε	0.089	0.089
$H_0 : \mathrm{E}\varepsilon = 0$	0.020	-4.46e-15
$Q_{LB}(5)$	6.90	6.60
$Q_{LB}(15)$	9.96	10.58
AIC	-2.387	-2.397
SIC	-2.348	-2.377

Table 4.5. GDP (E.U. series). Estimation results

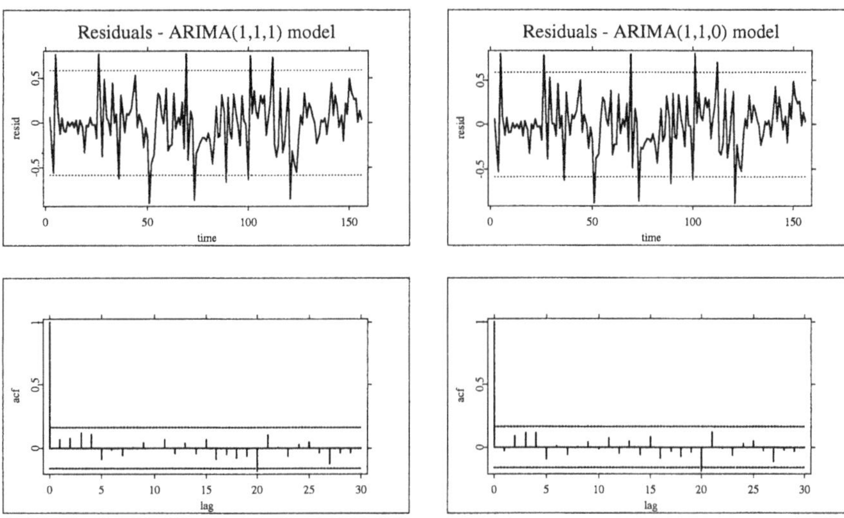

Figure 4.20. GDP (E.U. series). Residuals and ACF

significant. Given the fact that including an MA term does not seem to improve the results (see the AIC and SIC values), we select the more parsimonious $ARIMA(1,1,0)$ model.

Figure 4.21 plots the point and interval forecasts for the next 5 years generated by this model. As it was expected, since the model for the GDP series is

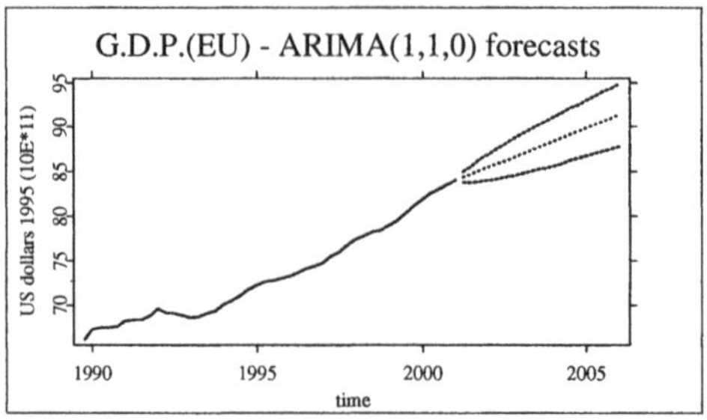

Figure 4.21. GDP (E.U. series). Actual and Forecasts

integrated of order one with nonzero constant, the eventual forecast function is a straight line with positive slope.

4.6 Regression Models for Time Series

In Econometrics the relationships between economic variables proposed by the Economic Theory are usually studied within the framework of linear regression models (see chapters 1 and 2). The data of many economic and business variables are collected in the form of time series. In this section we deal with the problems that may appear when estimating regression models with time series data.

It can be proved that many of the results on the properties of LS estimators and inference rely on the assumption of stationarity of the explanatory variables. Thus, the standard proof of consistency of the LS estimator depends on the assumption plim $(X'X/T) = Q$, where X is the data matrix and Q is a fixed matrix. This assumption implies that the sample moments converge to the population values as the sample size T increases. But the explanatory variables must be stationary in order to have fixed values in the matrix Q.

As it has been discussed in section 4.3.2, many of the macroeconomic, finance, monetary variables are nonstationary presenting trending behaviour in most cases. From an econometric point view, the presence of a deterministic trend (linear or not) in the explanatory variables does not raise any problem. But many economic and business time series are nonstationary even after eliminating deterministic trends due to the presence of unit roots, that is, they are generated by integrated processes. When nonstationary time series are used in a regression model one may obtain apparently significant relationships from unrelated variables. This phenomenom is called *spurious regression.* Granger and Newbold (1974) estimated regression models of the type:

$$y_t = \beta_0 + \beta_1 x_t + u_t \tag{4.54}$$

where y_t and x_t were unrelated random walks:

$$\begin{aligned} \Delta y_t &= \varepsilon_{1t} \qquad \varepsilon_{1t} \sim iid(0, \sigma_1^2) \\ \Delta x_t &= \varepsilon_{2t} \qquad \varepsilon_{2t} \sim iid(0, \sigma_2^2) \end{aligned}$$

Since x_t neither affects nor is affected by y_t, one expects the coefficient β to converge to zero and the coefficient of determination, R^2 to also tend to zero. However, they found that, frequently, the null hypothesis of no relationship is not rejected along with very high R^2 and very low Durbin-Watson statistics. It should be noted that the autocorrelation of the random walk x_t is projected into y_t which being a random walk as well is also highly correlated. Following these results they suggest that finding high R^2 and low D-W statistics can be a signal of a spurious regression.

These results found by Granger and Newbold (1974) were analytically explained by Phillips (1986). He shows that the t-ratios in model (4.54) do not follow a t-Student distribution and they go to infinity as T increases. This implies that for any critical value the ratios of rejection of the null hypothesis $\beta_1 = 0$ increase with T. Phillips (1986) showed as well that the D-W statistic converges to zero as T goes to infinity, while it converges to a value different from zero when the variables are related. Then, the value of the D-W statistic may help us to distinguish between genuine and spurious regressions. Summarizing, the spurious regression results are due to the nonstationarity of the variables and the problem is not solved by increasing the sample size T, it even gets worse.

Due to the problems raised by regressing nonstationary variables, econometricians have looked for solutions. One classical approach has been to detrend the series adjusting a determinist trend or including directly a deterministic function of time in the regression model (4.54) to take into account the nonstationary behaviour of the series. However, Phillips (1986) shows that this does not solve the problem if the series are integrated. The t-ratios in the regression model with a deterministic trend do not follow a t-Student distribution and therefore standard inference results could be misleading. Furthermore, it still appears spurious correlation between detrended random walks, that is, spurious regression. A second approach to work with nonstationary series is to look for relationships between stationary differenced series. However, it has to be taken into account that the information about the long-run relationship is lost, and the economic relationship may be different between levels and between increments.

4.6.1 Cointegration

When estimating regression models using time series data it is necessary to know whether the variables are stationary or not (either around a level or a deterministic linear trend) in order to avoid spurious regression problems. This analysis can be perform by using the unit root and stationarity tests presented in section 4.3.3.

It is well known that if two series are integrated to different orders, linear combinations of them will be integrated to the higher of the two orders. Thus, for instance, if two economic variables (y_t, x_t) are $I(1)$, the linear combination of them, z_t, will be generally $I(1)$. But it is possible that certain combinations of those nonstationary series are stationary. Then it is said that the pair (y_t, x_t) is cointegrated. The notion of cointegration is important to the analysis of long-run relationships between economic time series. Some examples are disposable income and consumption, goverment spending and tax revenues or interest rates on assets of differents maturities. Economic theory suggests that economic time series vectors should move *jointly*, that is, economic time series should be characterized by means of a long-run equilibrium relationship. Cointegration implies that these pairs of variables have similar stochastic trends. Besides, the dynamics of the economic variables suggests that they may deviate from this equilibrium in the short term, and when the variables are cointegrated the term z_t is stationary.

The definition of cointegration can be generalized to a set of N variables (Engle and Granger, 1987): The components of the vector y_t are said to be **co-integrated of order d,b** denoted $y_t \sim CI(d, b)$, if (i) all components of y_t are $I(d)$; (ii) there exists a vector $\alpha(\neq 0)$ so that $z_t = \alpha' y_t \sim I(d-b), b > 0$. The vector α is called the *co-integrating vector.*

The relationship $\alpha' y_t = 0$ captures the long-run equilibrium. The term $\alpha' y_t = z_t$ represents the deviation from the long-run equilibrium so it is called the equilibrium error. In general, more than one cointegrating relationship may exist between N variables, with a maximum of $N-1$. For the case of two $I(1)$ variables, the long-run equilibrium can be written as $y_t = \beta_0 + \beta_1 x_t$ and the cointegrating vector is $(1, -\beta_1)$. Clearly the cointegrating vector is not unique, since by multiplying both sides of $z_t = \alpha' y_t$ by a nonzero scalar the equality remains valid.

Testing for Cointegration Engle and Granger (1987) suggest to test whether the vector y_t is cointegrated by using standard unit-roots statistics such as the ADF to test the stationarity of the equilibrium error term. For example, in the simple case of two variables $x_t, y_t \sim I(1)$, to test the null hypothesis of cointegration is equivalent to test the stationarity of $u_t = y_t - \beta_0 - \beta_1 x_t$. Given that the error term u_t is not observable, it is approximated by the LS residuals:

$$\hat{u}_t = y_t - \hat{\beta}_0 - \hat{\beta}_1 x_t$$

and, in order to perform the Dickey-Fuller test, we could estimate the regressions:

$$\begin{aligned} \Delta \hat{u}_t &= \alpha + \rho\, \hat{u}_{t-1} + \varepsilon_t \\ \Delta \hat{u}_t &= \alpha + \beta t + \rho\, \hat{u}_{t-1} + \varepsilon_t \end{aligned}$$

and examine the corresponding τ_μ or τ_τ statistics. Since the ADF test is based on estimated values of u_t, the critical values must be corrected. Their asymptotical critical values were computed by Davidson and MacKinnon (1993) (see table 4.6) whereas the critical values for small sample sizes can be found in MacKinnon (1991).

Estimation. The cointegrating vector α can be estimated by least squares, that is, by minimizing the sum of the squared deviations from the equilibrium z_t. For example, for a set of two $I(1)$ variables this criteria is equal to:

$$min \sum_{t=1}^{T} (y_t - \beta_0 - \beta_1 x_t)^2$$

so, the estimate of the cointegrating vector is calculated by applying least squares on the linear regression:

$$y_t = \beta_0 + \beta_1 x_t + u_t \tag{4.55}$$

which captures the long-run pattern and it is called the *co-integrating regression.* Given that the variables are cointegrated, the LS estimators have good properties. Stock (1987) proves that this estimator is consistent with a finite sample bias of order T^{-1} and provides the expression for the asymptotic distribution.

No. variables	Test statistic	Significance level 0.01	0.05	0.10
N=2	τ_μ	-3.90	-3.34	-3.04
	τ_τ	-4.32	-3.78	-3.50
N=3	τ_μ	-4.29	-3.74	-3.45
	τ_τ	-4.66	-4.12	-3.84
N=4	τ_μ	-4.64	-4.10	-3.81
	τ_τ	-4.97	-4.43	-4.15
N=5	τ_μ	-4.96	-4.42	-4.13
	τ_τ	-5.25	-4.72	-4.43
N=6	τ_μ	-5.25	-4.71	-4.42
	τ_τ	-5.52	-4.98	-4.70

Source: Davidson and MacKinnon (1993)

Table 4.6. Asymptotic critical values for the cointegration test

Example: Consumption and GDP Let's analyze the relationship between consumption and GDP in the European Union with quarterly data from 1962 to 2001 (see figure 4.22). The unit root tests conclude that both series are $I(1)$. The value of the cointegration statistic is -3.79, so both variables are cointegrated. The estimated cointegration relationship is:

$$\hat{C}_t = -1.20 + 0.50\, GDP_t$$

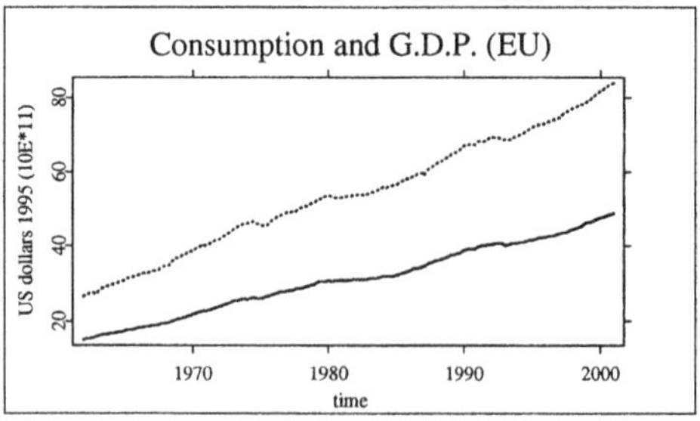

Figure 4.22. European Union GDP (dotted) and private consumption (solid)

XEGutsm21.xpl

4.6.2 Error Correction Models

At is has been mentioned above, a classical approach to build regression models for nonstationary variables is to difference the series in order to achieve stationarity and analyze the relationship between stationary variables. Then, the information about the long-run relationship is lost. But the presence of cointegration between regressors and dependent variable implies that the level of these variables are related in the log-run. So, although the variables are nonstationary, it seems more appropriate in this case to estimate the relationship between levels, without differencing the data, that is, to estimate the cointegrating relationship. On the other hand, it could be interesting as well to formulate a model that combines both long-run and short-run behaviour of the variables. This approach is based on the estimation of error correction models (ECM) that relate the change in one variable to the deviations from the long-run equilibrium in the previous period. For example, an ECM for two $I(1)$ variables can be written as:

$$\Delta y_t = \gamma_0 + \gamma_1(y_{t-1} - \beta_0 - \beta_1 x_{t-1}) + \gamma_2 \Delta x_t + v_t$$

The introduction of the equilibrium error of the previous period as explanatory variable in this representation allows us to move towards a new equilibrium, whereas the term v_t is a stationary disturbance that leads transitory deviations from the equilibrium path. The parameter γ_1 measures the speed of the movement towards the new equilibrium.

This model can be generalized as follows (Engle and Granger, 1987): a vector of time series y_t has an error correction representation if it can be expressed as:

$$A(L)(1-L)y_t = -\gamma z_{t-1} + v_t$$

where v_t is a stationary multivariate disturbance, with $A(0) = I, A(1)$ has all elements finite, $z_t = \alpha' y_t$ and $\gamma \neq 0$. The parameters of the correction error form are estimated by substituting the disequilibrium z_t by the estimate $\hat{z}_t = \hat{\alpha}' y_t$.

In the previous example it means that the following equation is estimated by least squares:

$$\Delta y_t \quad = \quad \gamma_0 + \gamma_1 \hat{u}_{t-1} + \gamma_2 \Delta x_t + v_t$$

where $\hat{u}_t$ are the least squares residuals from the cointegrating regression (4.55).

The resulting $\hat{\gamma}$ are consistent and asymptotically normal under standard assumptions.

Bibliography

Akaike, H. (1974). A new look at the statistical model identification, *IEEE Transactions on Automatic Control* **AC-19**: 716–723.

Bauwens, L. and Lubrano, M. and Richard, J.F. (1999). *Bayesian Inference in dynamic econometric models*, Oxford University Press, Oxford.

Box, G. E. P. and Cox, D. R. (1964). An analysis of transformations, *Journal of the Royal Statistical Society, Series B* **26**: 211–252.

Box, G. E. P. and Jenkins, G. M. (1976). *Time Series Analysis, Forecasting and Control*, Holden-Day, San Francisco.

Box, G. E. P. and Jenkins, G. M. and Reinsel, G. C. (1994). *Time Series Analysis, Forecasting and Control*, Prentice-Hall, Englewood Cliffs.

Cramer, H. (1961). On some classes of Non-Stationary Processes, *in Proceedings of the 4th Berkeley Symposium on Mathematical Statistics and Probability*, University of California Press, pp. 221–230.

Davidson, R. and MacKinnon, J. G. (1993). *Estimation and inference in Econometrics*, Oxford University Press, New York.

Dickey, D. A. (1976). *Estimation and hypothesis testing in Nonstationary Time Series*, PH. D. dissertation, Iowa State University, Ames.

Dickey, D. A. and Bell, W. R. and Miller, R. B. (1986). Unit roots in Time Series Models: Tests and Implications, *American Statistician* **40**: 12–26.

Dickey, D. A. and Fuller, W. A. (1979). Distribution of the Estimators for Autoregressive Time Series with a Unit Root, *Journal of the American Statistical Association* **74**: 427–431.

Dickey, D. A. and Pantula, S. G. (1987). Determining the Order of Differencing in Autoregressive Processes, *Journal of Business and Economics Statistics* **5**: 455–461.

Diebold, F. X. (1997). *Elements of Forecasting*, South-Western College Publishing, Cincinnati.

Engle, R. F. and Granger, C. W. J. (1987). Co-integration and error correction: representation, estimation, and testing, *Econometrica* **55**: 251–276.

Fuller, W. A. (1976). *Introduction to Statistical Time Series*, Wiley, New York.

Gardner, E.S. (1985). Exponential Smoothing: the state of the Art, *Journal of Forecasting* **79**: 616–23.

Granger, C. W. J. and Newbold, P. (1974). Spurious regressions in econometrics, *Journal of Econometrics* **2**: 111–120.

Granger, C. W. J. and Teräsvirta, T. (1993). *Modelling Nonlinear Economic Relationships*, Oxford University Press, Oxford.

Harvey, A. C. (1989). *Forecasting, structural time series models and the Kalman filter*, Cambridge University Press, Cambridge.

Harvey, A. C. (1993). *Time Series Models*, 2 edn, Harvester Wheatsheaf, Hemel Hempstead.

Kwiatkowski, D. and Phillips, P. C. B. and Schmidt, P. and Shin, Y. (1992). Distribution of the Estimators for Autoregressive Time Series with a Unit Root, *Journal of Econometrics* **54**: 159–178.

Lütkepohl, H. (1991). *Introduction to Multiple Time Series Analysis*, Springer Verlag, New York.

MacKinnon, J. G. (1991). Critical values for cointegration tests, Ch. 13 *in* R. F. Engle and C. W. J. Granger (eds.), *Long-run economic relationships: readings in cointegration*, Oxford University Press, Oxford.

Phillips, P.C.B. (1986). Understanding Spurious Regressions in Econometrics, *Journal of Econometrics* **33**: 311–40.

Postcher, B. and Srinivasan, S. (1994). A comparison of order determination procedures for ARMA models, *Statistica Sinica* **4**: 29–50.

Schwarz, G. (1978). Estimating the dimension of a model, *Annals of Statistics* **6**: 461–464.

Stock, J.H. (1987). Asymptotic properties of least squares estimators of cointegrating vectors, *Econometrica* **55**: 1035–1056.

Wold, H. (1938). *A Study in the Analysis of Stationary Time Series*, Almqvist and Wiksell, Stockholm.

5 Multiplicative SARIMA models

Rong Chen, Rainer Schulz and Sabine Stephan

5.1 Introduction

In the history of economics, the analysis of economic fluctuations can reclaim a prominent part. Undoubtedly, the analysis of business cycle movements plays the dominant role in this field, but there are also different perspectives to look at the ups and downs of economic time series. Economic fluctuations are usually characterized with regard to their periodic recurrence. Variations that last several years and occur in more or less regular time intervals are called business cycles, whereas seasonality (originally) indicates regularly recurring fluctuations within a year, that appear due to the season. Such seasonal patterns can be observed for many macroeconomic time series like gross domestic product, unemployment, industrial production or construction.

The term seasonality is also used in a broader sense to characterize time series that show specific patterns that regularly recur within fixed time intervals (e.g. a year, a month or a week). Take as an example the demand for Christmas trees: the monthly demand in November and especially in December will be generally very high compared to the demand during the other months of the year. This pattern will be the same for every year—irrespective of the total demand for Christmas trees. Moreover, one can also detect seasonal patterns in financial time series like in the variance of stock market returns. The highest volatility is often observed on Monday, mainly because investors used the weekend to think carefully about their investments, to obtain new information and to come to a decision.

As we saw so far, seasonality has many different manifestations. Consequently, there are different approaches to model seasonality. If we focus on macroeconomic time series the class of seasonal models is confined to processes with dynamic properties at periods of a quarter or a month. However, when financial time series are studied, then our interest shifts to seasonal patterns at the daily level together with seasonal properties in higher moments. Therefore, it is no surprise, that a rich toolkit of econometric techniques has been developed to model seasonality.

In the following we are going to deal with seasonality in the mean only (for seasonality in higher moments see Ghysels and Osborn (2001)), but there are still different ways to do so. The choice of the appropriate technique depends on whether seasonality is viewed as *deterministic* or *stochastic*. The well-known deterministic approach is based on the assumption, that seasonal fluctuations are fix and shift solely the level of the time series. Therefore, deterministic seasonality can be modeled by means of seasonally varying intercepts using seasonal dummies. Stochastic seasonality however is a topic in recent time series analysis and is modeled using appropriate ARIMA models (Diebold, 1998, Chapter 5). Since these *seasonal* ARIMA models are just an extension of the usual ARIMA methodology, one often finds the acronym SARIMA for this class of models (Chatfield, 2001).

The topic of this chapter is modeling seasonal time series using SARIMA models. The outline of this chapter is as follows: the next Section 5.2.1 illustrates, how to develop an ARIMA model for a seasonal time series. Since these models tend to be quite large, we introduce in Section 5.2.2 a parsimonious model specification, that was developed by Box and Jenkins (1976)—the *multiplicative SARIMA model.* Section 5.3 deals with the identification these models in detail, using the famous airline data set of Box and Jenkins for illustrative purposes. Those, who already studied the Section *ARIMA model building* in Chapter 4 on *Univariate Time Series Modeling*, will recognize that we use the same tools to identify the underlying data generation process. Finally, in Section 5.4 we focus on the estimation of multiplicative SARIMA models and on the evaluation of the fitted models.

All quantlets for modeling multiplicative SARIMA models are collected in XploRe's `times` library.

5.2 Modeling Seasonal Time Series

5.2.1 Seasonal ARIMA Models

Before one can specify a model for a given data set, one must have an initial guess about the data generation process. The first step is always to plot the time series. In most cases such a plot gives first answers to questions like: "Is the time series under consideration stationary?" or "Do the time series show a seasonal pattern?"

Figure 5.1 displays the quarterly unemployment rate u_t for Germany (West) from the first quarter of 1962 to the forth quarter of 1991. The data are published by the OECD (Franses, 1998, Table DA.10). The solid line represents

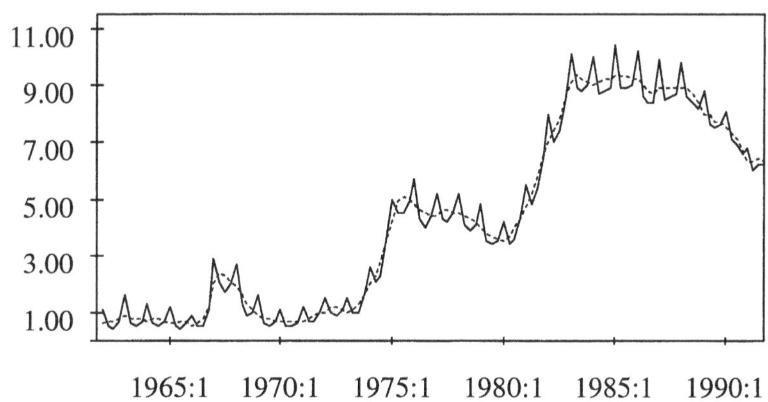

Figure 5.1. Quarterly unemployment rate for Germany (West) from 1962:1 to 1991:4. The original series (u_t) is given by the solid blue line and the seasonally adjusted series is given by the dashed red line.

XEGmsarima1.xpl

the original series u_t and the dashed line shows the seasonally adjusted series. It is easy to see, that this quarterly time series possesses a distinct seasonal pattern with spikes recurring always in the first quarter of the year.

After the inspection of the plot, one can use the sample autocorrelation function (ACF) and the sample partial autocorrelation function (PACF) to specify the order of the ARMA part (see `acf`, `pacf`, `acfplot` and `pacfplot`). Another convenient tool for first stage model specification is the extended autocorrelation function (EACF), because the EACF does not require that the time series under consideration is stationary and it allows a simultaneous specification of the autoregressive and moving average order. Unfortunately, the EACF can not be applied to series that show a seasonal pattern. However, we will present the EACF later in Section 5.4.5, where we use it for checking the residuals resulting from the fitted models.

Figures 5.2, 5.3 and 5.4 display the sample ACF of three different transformations of the unemployment rate (u_t) for Germany. Using the difference—or

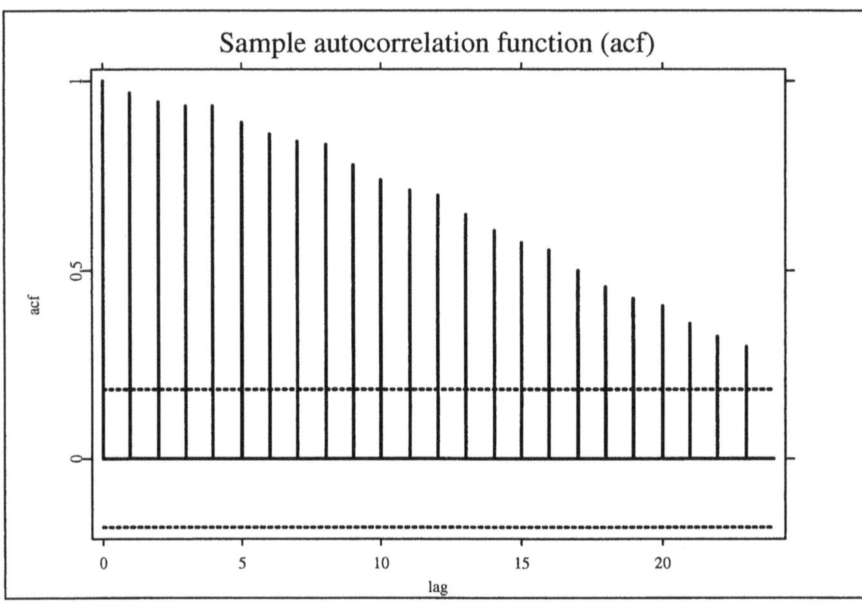

Figure 5.2. Sample ACF of the unemployment rate for Germany (West) (u_t) from 1962:1 to 1991:1.

`XEGmsarima2.xpl`

backshift—operator L, these kinds of transformations of the unemployment rate can be written compactly as

$$\Delta^d \Delta_s^D u_t = (1-L)^d (1-L^s)^D u_t ,$$

where L^s operates as $L^s u_t = u_{t-s}$ and s denotes the seasonal period. Δ^d and Δ_s^D stand for nonseasonal and seasonal differencing. The superscripts d and D indicate that, in general, the differencing may be applied d and D times.

Figure 5.2 shows the sample ACF of the original data of the unemployment rate (u_t). The fact, that the time series is neither subjected to nonseasonal nor to seasonal differencing, implies that $d = D = 0$. Furthermore, we set $s = 4$, since the unemployment rate is recorded quarterly. The sample ACF of the unemployment rate declines very slowly, i.e. that this time series is clearly nonstationary. But it is difficult to isolate any seasonal pattern as all autocorrelations are dominated by the effect of the nonseasonal unit root.

Figure 5.3 displays the sample ACF of the first differences of the unemployment rate (Δu_t) with

$$\Delta u_t = u_t - u_{t-1} .$$

Since this transformation is aimed at eliminating only the nonseasonal unit root, we set $d = 1$ and $D = 0$. Again, we set $s = 4$ because of the frequency of the time series under consideration. Taking the first differences produces a very clear pattern in the sample ACF. There are very large positive autocorrelations at the seasonal frequencies (lag 4, 8, 12, etc.), flanked by negative autocorrelations at the 'satellites', which are the autocorrelations right before and after the seasonal lags. The slow decline of the seasonal autocorrelations indicates seasonal instationarity. Analogous to the analysis of nonseasonal nonstationarity, this may be dealt by seasonal differencing; i.e. by applying the $\Delta_4 = (1 - L^4)$ operator in conjunction with the usual lag operator $\Delta = (1 - L)$ (Mills, 1990, Chapter 10).

Eventually, Figure 5.4 displays the sample ACF of the unemployment rate that was subjected to the final transformation

$$\begin{aligned} \Delta\Delta_4 u_t &= (1-L)(1-L^4)u_t \\ &= (u_t - u_{t-4}) - (u_{t-1} - u_{t-5}) . \end{aligned}$$

Since this transformation is used to remove both the nonseasonal and the seasonal unit root, we set $d = D = 1$. What the transformation $\Delta\Delta_4$ finally does is seasonally differencing the first differences of the unemployment rate.

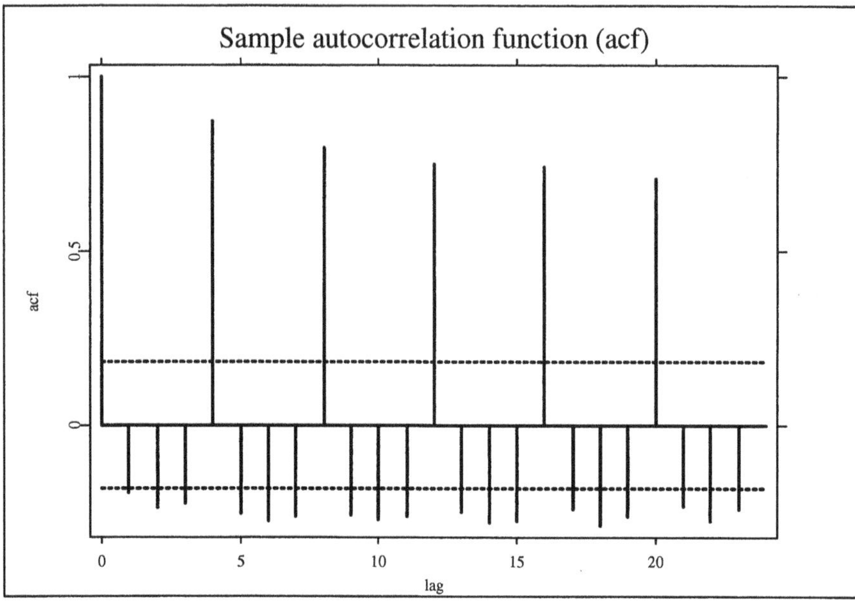

Figure 5.3. Sample ACF of the first differences of the unemployment rate (Δu_t) for Germany (West) from 1962:1 to 1991:1.

XEGmsarima3.xpl

By means of this transformation we obtain a stationary time series that can be modeled by fitting an appropriate ARMA model.

After this illustrative introduction, we can now switch to theoretical considerations. As we already saw in practice, a seasonal model for the time series $\{x_t\}_{t=1}^T$ may take the following form

$$\Delta^d \Delta_s^D x_t = \frac{\Theta(L)}{\Phi(L)} a_t , \tag{5.1}$$

where $\Delta^d = (1-L)^d$ and $\Delta_s^D = (1-L^s)^D$ indicate nonseasonal and seasonal differencing and s gives the season. a_t represents a white noise innovation. $\Phi(L)$ and $\Theta(L)$ are the usual AR and MA lag operator polynomials for ARMA models

$$\Phi(L) \equiv 1 - \phi_1 L - \phi_2 L^2 - \ldots - \phi_p L^p$$

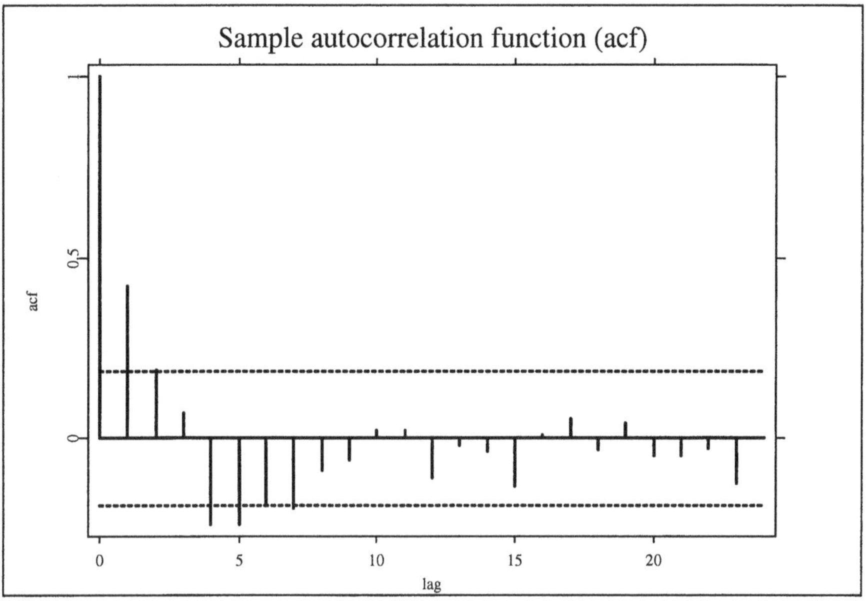

Figure 5.4. Sample ACF of the seasonally differenced first differences of the unemployment rate ($\Delta\Delta_4 u_t$) for Germany (West) from 1962:1 to 1991:1.

XEGmsarima4.xpl

and

$$\Theta(L) \equiv 1 + \theta_1 L + \theta_2 L^2 + \ldots + \theta_q L^q .$$

Since the $\Phi(L)$ and $\Theta(L)$ must account for seasonal autocorrelation, at least one of them must be of minimum order s. This means that the identification of models of the form (5.1) can lead to a large number of parameters that have to be estimated and to a model specification that is rather difficult to interpret.

5.2.2 Multiplicative SARIMA Models

Box and Jenkins (1976) developed an argument for using a restricted version of equation (5.1), that should be adequate to fit many seasonal time series.

Starting point for their approach was the fact, that in seasonal data there are two time intervals of importance. Suppose, that we still deal with a quarterly series, we expect the following to occur (Mills, 1990, Chapter 10):

- a seasonal relationship between observations for the same quarters in successive years, and
- a relationship between observations for successive quarters in a particular year.

Referring to Figure 5.1 that displays the quarterly unemployment rate for Germany, it is obvious that the seasonal effect implies that an observation in the first quarter of a given year is related to the observations of the first quarter for previous years. We can model this feature by means of a *seasonal model*

$$\Phi_s(L)\Delta_s^D x_t = \Theta_s(L)v_t \; . \tag{5.2}$$

$\Phi_s(L)$ and $\Theta_s(L)$ stand for a seasonal AR polynomial of order p and a seasonal MA polynomial of order q respectively:

$$\Phi_s(L) = 1 - \phi_{s,1}L^s - \phi_{s,2}L^{2s} - \ldots - \phi_{s,P}L^{Ps}$$

and

$$\Theta_s(L) = 1 + \theta_{s,1}L^s + \theta_{s,2}L^{2s} + \ldots + \theta_{s,Q}L^{Qs} \; ,$$

which satisfy the standard stationarity and invertibility conditions. v_t denotes the error series. The characteristics of this process are explained below.

It is obvious that the above given seasonal model (5.2) is simply a special case of the usual ARIMA model, since the autoregressive and moving average relationship is modeled for observations of the same seasonal time interval in different years. Using equation (5.2) relationships between observations for the same quarters in successive years can be modeled.

Furthermore, we assume a relationship between the observations for successive quarters of a year, i.e. that the corresponding error series (v_t, v_{t-1}, v_{t-2}, etc.) may be autocorrelated. These autocorrelations may be represented by a *nonseasonal model*

$$\Phi(L)\Delta^d v_t = \Theta(L)a_t \; . \tag{5.3}$$

v_t is ARIMA(p, d, q) with a_t representing a process of innovations (white noise process).

Substituting (5.3) into (5.2) yields the *general multiplicative seasonal model*

$$\Phi(L)\Phi_s(L)\Delta^d\Delta_s^D x_t = \delta + \Theta(L)\Theta_s(L)a_t \,. \tag{5.4}$$

In equation (5.4) we additionally include the constant term δ in order to allow for a deterministic trend in the model (Shumway and Stoffer, 2000). In the following we use the short-hand notation SARIMA $(p, d, q) \times (s, P, D, Q)$ to characterize a multiplicative seasonal ARIMA model like (5.4).

5.2.3 The Expanded Model

Before to start with the issues of identification and estimation of a multiplicative SARIMA model a short example may be helpful, that sheds some light on the connection between a multiplicative SARIMA $(p, d, q) \times (s, P, D, Q)$ and a simple ARMA (p, q) model and reveals that the SARIMA methodology leads to parsimonious models.

Polynomials in the lag operator are algebraically similar to simple polynomials $ax + bx^2$. So it is possible to calculate the product of two lag polynomials (Hamilton, 1994, Chapter 2).

Given that fact, every multiplicative SARIMA model can be telescoped out into an ordinary ARMA(p, q) model in the variable

$$y_t \stackrel{\text{def}}{=} \Delta_s^D \Delta^d x_t \,.$$

For example, let us assume that the series $\{x_t\}_{t=1}^T$ follows a SARIMA$(0, 1, 1) \times (12, 0, 1, 1)$ process. In that case, we have

$$(1 - L^{12})(1 - L)x_t = (1 + \theta_1 L)(1 + \theta_{s,1} L^{12})a_t \,. \tag{5.5}$$

After some calculations one obtains

$$y_t = (1 + \theta_1 L + \theta_{s,1} L^{12} + \theta_1 \theta_{s,1} L^{13})a_t \tag{5.6}$$

where $y_t = (1 - L^{12})(1 - L)x_t$. Thus, the multiplicative SARIMA model has an ARMA(0,13) representation where only the coefficients

$$\theta_1 \,, \quad \theta_{12} \stackrel{\text{def}}{=} \theta_{s,1} \quad \text{and} \quad \theta_{13} \stackrel{\text{def}}{=} \theta_1 \theta_{s,1}$$

are not zero. All other coefficients of the MA polynomial are zero.

Thus, we are back in the well-known ARIMA(p, d, q) world. However, if we know that the original model is a SARIMA(0,1,1)×(12,0,1,1), we have to estimate only the two coefficients θ_1 and $\theta_{s,1}$. For the ARMA(0,13) we would estimate instead the three coefficients θ_1, θ_{12}, and θ_{13}. Thus it is obvious that SARIMA models allow for a parsimonious model building.

In the following, a model specification like (5.6) is called an *expanded model*. In Section 5.4 it is shown, that this kind of specification is required for estimation purposes, since a multiplicative model like (5.5) cannot be estimated directly.

5.3 Identification of Multiplicative SARIMA Models

This section deals with the identification of a multiplicative SARIMA model. The required procedure is explained step by step, using the famous airline data of Box and Jenkins (1976, Series G) for illustrative purposes. The date give the number of airline passengers (in thousands) in international air travel from 1949:1 to 1960:12. In the following G_t denotes the original series.

The identification procedure comprises the following steps: plotting the data, possibly transforming the data, identifying the dependence order of the model, parameter estimation, and diagnostics. Generally, selecting the appropriate model for a given data set is quite difficult. But the task becomes less complicated, if the following approach is observed: one thinks first in terms of finding difference operators that produce a roughly stationary series and then in terms of finding a set of simple ARMA or multiplicative SARMA to fit the resulting residual series.

As with any data analysis, the time series has to be plotted first so that the graph can be inspected. Figure 5.5 shows the airline data of Box and Jenkins. The series G_t shows a strong seasonal pattern and a definite upward trend. Furthermore, the variability in the data grows with time. Therefore, it is necessary to transform the data in order to stabilize the variance. Here, the natural logarithm is used for transforming the data. The new time series is defined as follows

$$g_t \stackrel{\text{def}}{=} \ln G_t \,.$$

Figure 5.6 displays the logarithmically transformed data g_t. The strong seasonal pattern and the obvious upward trend remain unchanged, but the vari-

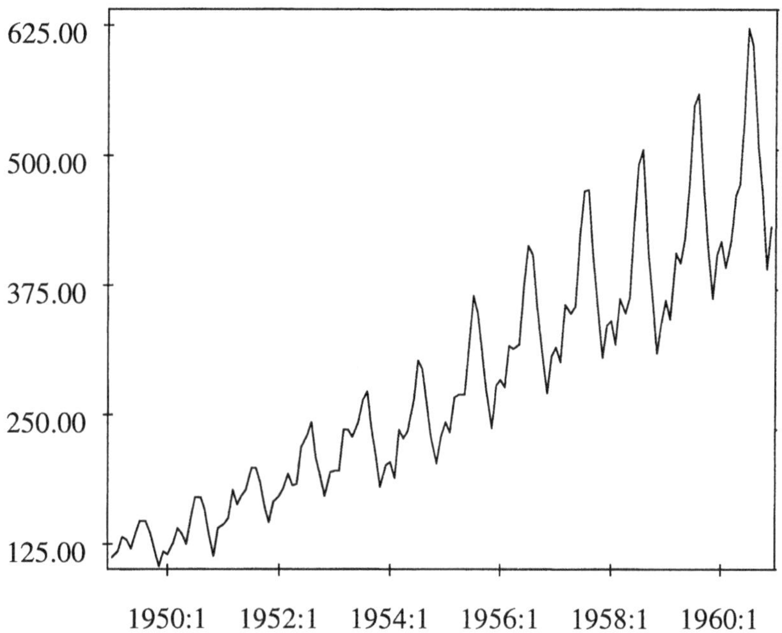

Figure 5.5. Number of airline passengers G_t (in thousands) in international air travel from 1949:1 to 1960:12.

XEGmsarima5.xpl

ability is now stabilized. Now, the first difference of time series g_t has to be taken in order to remove its nonseasonal unit root, i.e. we have $d = 1$. The new variable

$$\Delta g_t \equiv (1 - L) g_t \tag{5.7}$$

has a nice interpretation: it gives approximately the monthly growth rate of the number of airline passengers.

The next step is plotting the sample ACF of the monthly growth rate Δg_t. The sample ACF in Figure 5.7 displays a recurrent pattern: there are significant

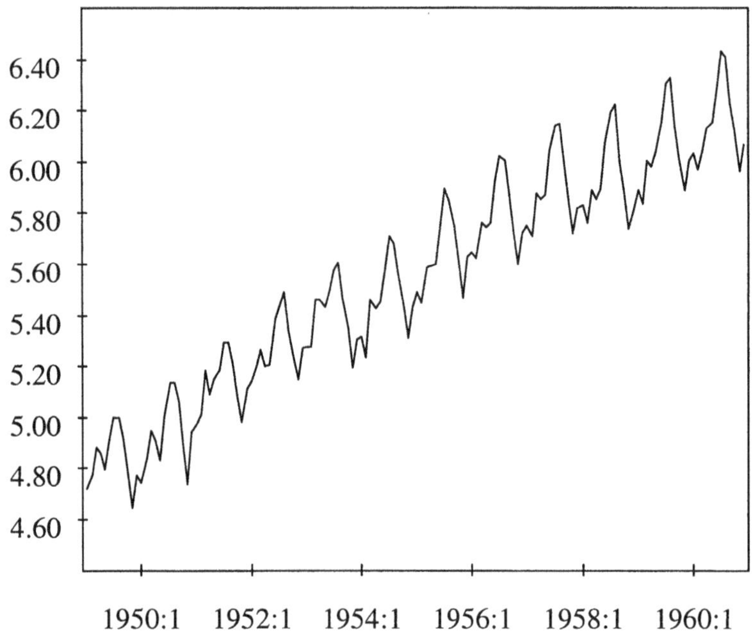

Figure 5.6. Log number of airline passengers g_t in international air travel from 1949:1 to 1960:12.

XEGmsarima6.xpl

peaks at the seasonal frequencies (lag 12, 24, 36, etc.) which decay slowly. The autocorrelation coefficients of the months in between are much smaller and follow a regular pattern. The characteristic pattern of the ACF indicates that the underlying time series possesses a seasonal unit root. Typically, $D = 1$ is sufficient to obtain seasonal stationarity. Therefore, we take the seasonal difference and obtain the following time series

$$\Delta_{12}\Delta g_t = (1 - L)(1 - L^{12})g_t$$

that neither incorporates an ordinary nor a seasonal unit root.

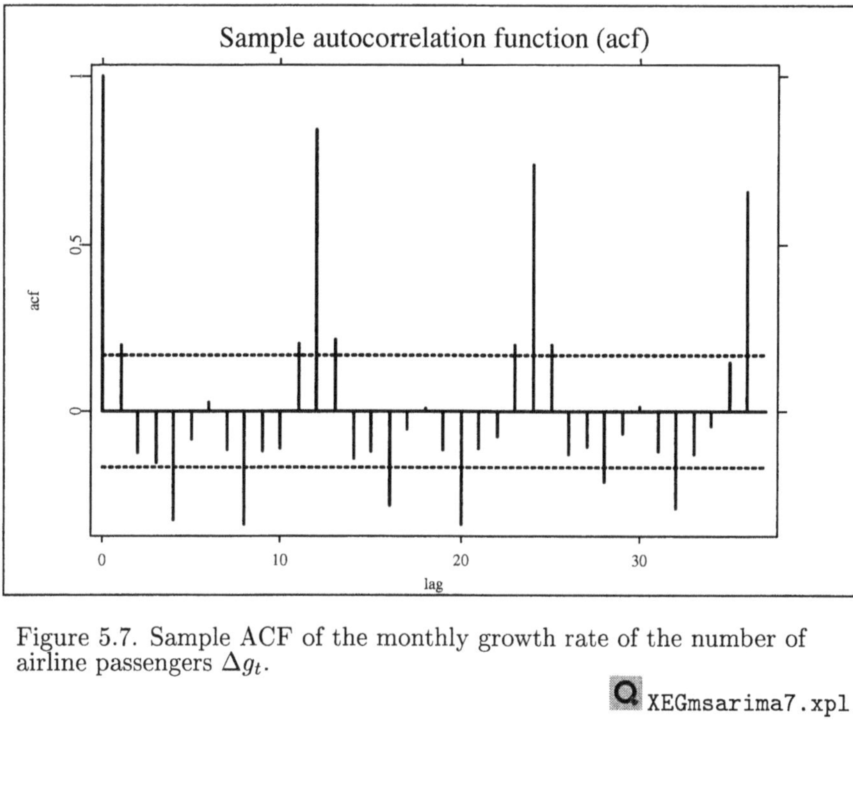

Figure 5.7. Sample ACF of the monthly growth rate of the number of airline passengers Δg_t.

XEGmsarima7.xpl

After that, the sample ACF and PACF of $\Delta_{12}\Delta g_t$ has to be inspected in order to explore the remaining dependencies in the stationary series. The autocorrelation functions are given in Figures 5.8 and 5.9. Compared with the characteristic pattern of the ACF of Δg_t (Figure 5.7) the pattern of the ACF and PACF of $\Delta_{12}\Delta g_t$ are far more difficult to interpret. Both ACF and PACF show significant peaks at lag 1 and 12. Furthermore, the PACF displays autocorrelation for many lags. Even these patterns are not that clear, we might feel that we face a seasonal moving average and an ordinary MA(1). Another possible specification could be an ordinary MA(12), where only the coefficients θ_1 and θ_{12} are different from zero.

Thus, the identification procedure leads to two different multiplicative SARIMA specifications. The first one is a SARIMA(0,1,1)$\times$(12,0,1,1). Using the lag-

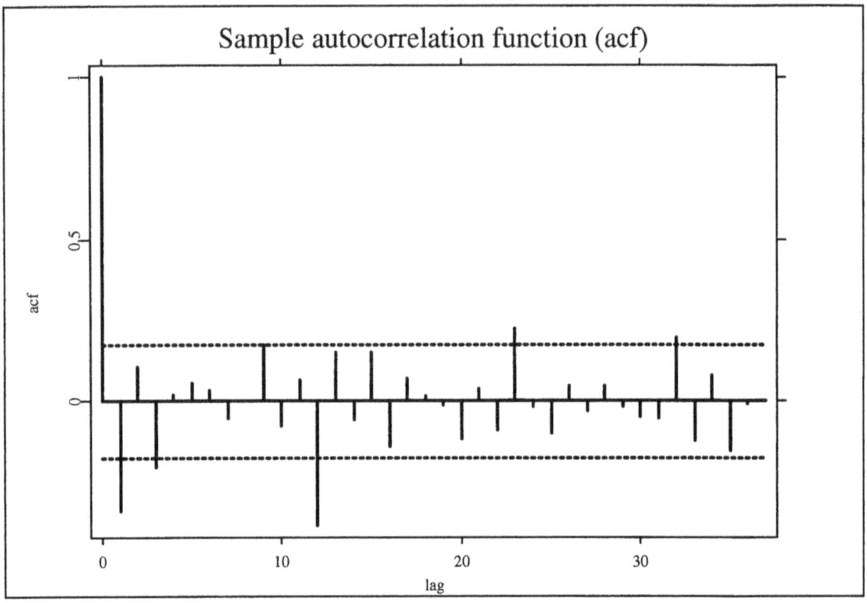

Figure 5.8. Sample ACF of the seasonally differenced growth rate of the airline data $\Delta_{12}\Delta g_t$.

XEGmsarima8.xpl

operator this model can be written as follows:

$$
\begin{aligned}
(1-L)(1-L^{12})G_t &= (1+\theta_1 L)(1+\theta_{s,1}L^{12})a_t \\
&= (1+\theta_1 L+\theta_{s,1}L^{12}+\theta_1\theta_{s,1}L^{13})a_t.
\end{aligned}
$$

The second specification is a SARIMA(0,1,12)×(12,0,1,0). This model has the following representation:

$$
(1-L)(1-L^{12})G_t = (1+\theta_1 L+\theta_{12}L^{12})a_t.
$$

Note, that in the last equation all MA coefficients other than θ_1 and θ_{12} are zero. With the specification of the SARIMA models the identification process is finished. We saw that modeling the seasonal ARMA after removing the nonseasonal and the seasonal unit root was quite difficult, because the sample

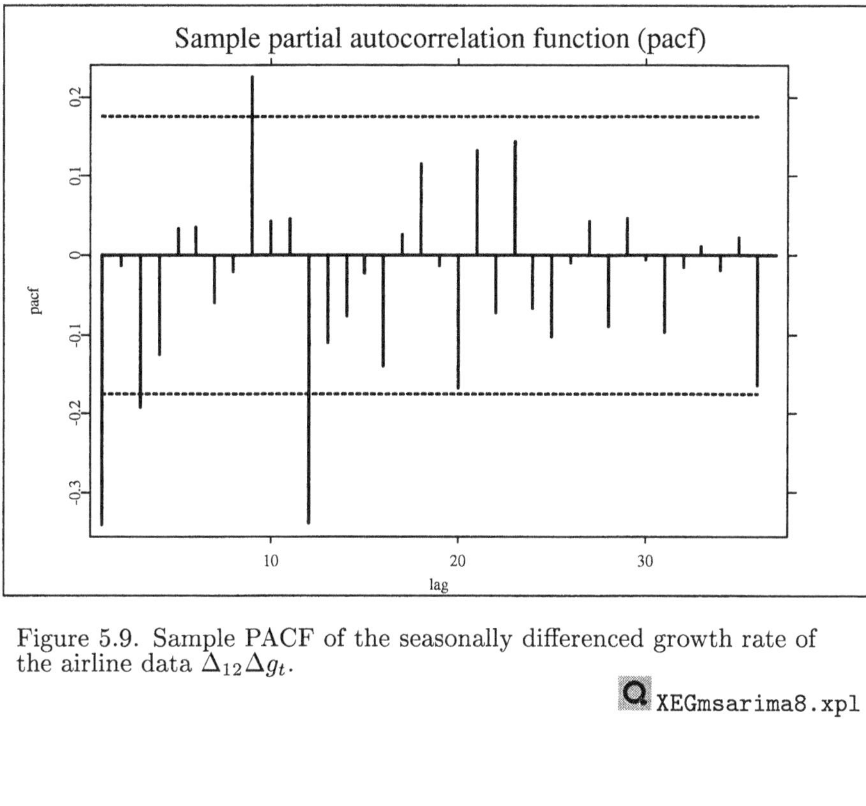

Figure 5.9. Sample PACF of the seasonally differenced growth rate of the airline data $\Delta_{12}\Delta g_t$.

XEGmsarima8.xpl

ACF and the PACF did not display any clear pattern. Therefore, two different SARIMA models were identified that have to be tested in the further analysis.

5.4 Estimation of Multiplicative SARIMA Models

This section deals with the estimation of identified SARIMA models, i.e. we want to estimate the unknown parameters ψ of the multiplicative SARIMA model. If the model contains only AR terms, the unknown coefficients can be estimated using ordinary least squares. However, if the model contains MA terms too, the task becomes more complicated, because the lagged values of the innovations are unobservable. Consequently, it is not possible to derive explicit expressions to estimate the unknown coefficients and therefore one has to use maximum likelihood for estimation purposes. In the next subsection 5.4.1 the theoretical background of maximizing a likelihood function is briefly outlined.

In order to convey an idea of what follows, we will shortly outline the procedure: first, one sets up the multiplicative SARIMA model—in the following also called *original model*— with some initial values for the unknown parameters ψ. In subsection 5.4.2 it is explained how to set the original SARIMA model using the quantlet `msarimamodel`. Restrictions can be imposed on the coefficients. The simplest restriction is that some of the coefficients are zero. Then the value of the likelihood function—given the initial parameters—is evaluated.

Unfortunately, in most cases the original SARIMA model cannot be estimated directly. If one looks at the SARIMA(3,1,1)×(12,1,0,0) model in section 5.4.3—equation (5.18)—one recognizes on the left hand side the product of two expressions. Both of them contain lag-operators. Such expressions have to be telescoped out first. XploRe provides a very convenient tool to do so: `msarimaconvert`. This quantlet is explained in detail in subsection 5.4.3. The result you get from `msarimaconvert` is an ordinary ARMA(p,q) model which can be estimated.

Under the assumption that an ARMA model is stationary and invertible and that the observations are normally distributed, it can be estimated using the maximum likelihood approach. By making suitable assumptions about initial conditions, the maximum likelihood estimators can be obtained by minimizing the conditional sum of squares. In subsection 5.4.4 the quantlet `msarimacond` is presented. It calculates the conditional sum of squares function and allows for zero restrictions on the coefficients. Given this function, numerical methods have to be applied to maximize the likelihood function with respect to ψ.

To evaluate the fit of the estimated model, the quantlet `msarimacond` also delivers several criteria for diagnostic checking. The residuals of the model should be white noise. The quantlet `eacf` provides an easy way to check the behavior of the residuals.

However, the conditional sum of squares is not always very satisfactory for seasonal series. In that case the calculation of the exact likelihood function becomes necessary (Box and Jenkins, 1976, p. 211). One approach is to set up the likelihood function via Kalman filter techniques. We briefly discuss how to set up the airline model in state space form and how to use the Kalman filter to evaluate the exact likelihood function. Once again, numerical methods are necessary to maximize the exact likelihood function.

5.4.1 Maximum Likelihood Estimation

The approach of maximum likelihood (ML) requires the specification of a particular distribution for a sample of T observations y_t. Let

$$f_{Y_T,Y_{T-1},\ldots,Y_1}(y_T, y_{T-1}, \ldots, y_1|\psi)$$

denote the probability density of the sample given the unknown $(n \times 1)$ parameters ψ. It can be interpreted as the probability of having observed the given sample (Hamilton, 1994, p. 117).

With the sample $y = \{y_T, \ldots, y_1\}$ at hand, the above given probability can be rewritten as a function of the unknown parameters given the sample y. Following the notation of Box and Jenkins (1976), we use the notation $L(\psi|y)$. In most cases it is easier to work with the log likelihood function $l(\psi|y) = \ln L(\psi|y)$.

The maximum likelihood estimate $\tilde{\psi}$ is the parameter vector that maximizes the probability for the observed sample y. Thus, the MLE satisfies the so-called likelihood equations, which are obtained by differentiating $l(\psi|y)$ with respect to each of the unknown parameters of the vector ψ and setting the derivatives to zero (Harvey, 1993). Using vector notation and suppressing y, we obtain

$$\frac{\partial l(\psi)}{\partial \psi} = 0. \tag{5.8}$$

As a rule, the likelihood equations are non-linear. Therefore, the ML estimates must be found in the course of an iterative procedure. This is true for the exact likelihood function of every Gaussian ARMA(p,q) process (see Hamilton, 1994, Chapter 5).

As already mentioned above, there are two different likelihood functions in use: the conditional and the exact likelihood function. Both alternatives can be estimated using XploRe.

In many applications of ARMA models the **conditional likelihood function** is an alternative to the exact likelihood function. In that case, one assumes that the first p observations of a Gaussian ARMA(p,q) process are deterministic and are equal to its observed values $\{y_p, \ldots, y_1\}$. The initial residuals a_t for $t \in \{p, \ldots, p-q+1\}$ are set to its expected values 0. The log likelihood function for this setting is of the following form with $\psi = (\psi', \sigma^2)$

$$l(\psi) = -\frac{1}{2}(T-p)\ln 2\pi - \frac{1}{2}(T-p)\ln\sigma^2 - \frac{S(\psi')}{2\sigma^2} \tag{5.9}$$

and $S(\psi')$ denoting the sum of squares function

$$S(\psi') = \sum_{t=p+1}^{T} \left(a_t(\psi')\right)^2 . \tag{5.10}$$

The notation $a_t(\psi')$ emphasizes that a_t is no longer a disturbance, but a residual which depends on the value taken by the variables in ψ'.

Note, that the parameter σ^2 is an additional one, that is not included in vector ψ'. It is easy to see that (5.9) is maximized with respect to ψ' if the sum of squares $S(\psi')$ is minimized. Using the condition (5.8), this leads to

$$\sum_{t=1}^{T} \frac{\partial a_t(\psi')}{\partial \psi'} a_t = 0. \tag{5.11}$$

Thus, the ML estimate for ψ' can be obtained by minimizing (5.10). Furthermore, we obtain from (5.9) and (5.8) that

$$\tilde{\sigma}^2 = \frac{S(\tilde{\psi}')}{T-p} . \tag{5.12}$$

Thus, given the parameter vector $\tilde{\psi}'$ that maximizes the sum of squares—and thus the conditional log likelihood function (5.9)—one divides the sum of squares by $T-p$ to obtain the ML estimate $\tilde{\sigma}^2$. Another estimator for the variance of the innovations corrects furthermore for the number of estimated coefficients k.

As already mentioned, one approach to calculate the **exact log likelihood** is to use the Kalman filter. We want to show this for the airline model. This model is rewritable in state space form (SSF) as

$$\alpha_t = \begin{bmatrix} 0 & I_{13} \\ 0 & 0 \end{bmatrix} \alpha_{t-1} + \begin{bmatrix} 1 & \theta_1 & 0 & \dots & \theta_{s,1} & \theta_1\theta_{s,1} \end{bmatrix}^\top a_t \tag{5.13a}$$

$$y_t = \begin{bmatrix} 1 & 0 & \dots & 0 \end{bmatrix} \alpha_t \tag{5.13b}$$

where I_{13} is a (13×13) identity matrix (Koopman, Shephard and Doornik, 1999). Here,

$$\begin{bmatrix} 0 & I_{13} \\ 0 & 0 \end{bmatrix} \tag{5.14}$$

is the so-called transition matrix.

Given Gaussian error terms a_t, the value of the log likelihood function $l(\psi)$ for the above given state space form is

$$-\frac{T}{2}\ln 2\pi - \frac{1}{2}\sum_{t=1}^{T} \ln |F_t| - \frac{1}{2}\sum_{t=1}^{T} v_t^\top F_t^{-1} v_t \, . \tag{5.15}$$

Here,

$$v_t \equiv y_t - Z_t \mathrm{E}[\alpha_t | \mathcal{F}_{t-1}]$$

are the *innovations* of the Kalman filtering procedure and $\mathcal{F}_{t-1}$ is the information set up to $t-1$. Z_t is the matrix from the above given state space form that contains the identity matrix. The matrix F_t is the covariance matrix of the innovations in period t and it is a by-product of the Kalman filter. The above log likelihood is known as the *prediction error decomposition form* (Harvey, 1989).

Given some initial values for ψ, the above exact log likelihood is evaluated with the Kalman filter. Using numerical methods, the function is maximized with respect to ψ.

Once the ML estimate $\tilde{\psi}$ is calculated, one wants to have standard errors for testing purposes. If T is sufficiently large, the ML estimate $\tilde{\psi}$ is approximately normally distributed with the inverse of the information matrix divided by T as covariance matrix. The inverse of the Hessian for $l(\tilde{\psi})$ is one way to estimate the covariance matrix (Hamilton, 1994, Section 5.8). One can calculate the Hessian applying numerical methods.

5.4.2 Setting the Multiplicative SARIMA Model

```
msarimamodelOut = msarimamodel(d,arma,season)
```
sets the coefficients of a multiplicative seasonal ARIMA model

The original model is specified by means of the quantlet `msarimamodel`. The three arguments are lists that give the difference orders (d, D), the ordinary

ARMA parts $\Phi(L)$ and $\Theta(L)$, and the seasonal AR and MA polynomials $\Phi_s(L)$ and $\Theta_s(L)$. If the model has no seasonal difference, one just omits D.

The `arma` list has at most four elements: the first element is a vector that specifies the lags of the AR polynomial $\Phi(L)$ that are not zero. The second element is a vector that specifies the lags of the MA polynomial $\Theta(L)$. If the model has only one polynomial, one sets the lags of the other one to 0.

The third element of the `arma` list is a vector with

- the AR coefficients
    - i) if the model has both an AR and a MA polynomial
    - ii) if the model has only an AR polynomial
- the MA coefficients if the model has only a MA polynomial .

If the model has both an AR and a MA polynomial then the fourth argument is necessary. It is a list that contains the coefficients of the MA polynomial. For example,

```
arma = list((1|3),0,(0.1|-0.25))
```

specifies an ARMA(3,0) part with $\phi_2 = 0$, $\phi_1 = 0.1$ and $\phi_3 = -0.25$.

The last argument `season` is a list that contains the information concerning the seasonal AR and MA polynomials. This list has at most five elements: the first element specifies the season s. If the data show no seasonal pattern, one sets $s = 0$ as the only argument of the list `season`. The second element is the lag structure of the seasonal AR polynomial. You have to fill in the lags that are different from zero. The third element is the lag structure of the seasonal MA polynomial. The last two elements are for the coefficient vectors of the polynomials. As explained for the `arma` list, one can omit the respective vector if the model has only one polynomial. For example,

```
season = list(12,0,(1|4),(-0.3|0.1))
```

gives a model with no seasonal AR polynomial and with the seasonal MA(4) polynomial

$$1 - 0.3L^{12} + 0.1L^{48} . \tag{5.16}$$

To understand what msarimamodel does, let us assume that the multiplicative SARIMA model is given as

$$(1 - 0.1L + 0.25L^3)\Delta x_t = (1 - 0.3L^{12} + 0.1L^{48})\varepsilon_t \,. \qquad (5.17)$$

Here $d = 1$ and $D = 0$, so that we can set d=1. The lists for the ordinary and seasonal polynomials are given above. To have a look at the output of msarimamodel, one just compiles the following piece of XploRe code

```
arma   = list((1|3),0,(0.1|-0.25))    ; ordinary ARMA part
season = list(12,0,(1|4),(-0.3|0.1)) ; seasonal ARMA part
msarimamodelOut = msarimamodel(1,arma,season)
msarimamodelOut ; shows the elements of msarimamodelOut
```

The output is

```
Contents of msarimamodelOut.d
[1,]         1
Contents of msarimamodelOut.arlag
[1,]         1
[2,]         3
Contents of msarimamodelOut.malag
[1,]         0
Contents of msarimamodelOut.s
[1,]        12
Contents of msarimamodelOut.sarlag
[1,]         0
Contents of msarimamodelOut.smalag
[1,]         1
[2,]         4
Contents of msarimamodelOut.phi
[1,]       0.1
[2,]     -0.25
Contents of msarimamodelOut.theta
[1,]         0
Contents of msarimamodelOut.Phi
[1,]         0
Contents of msarimamodelOut.Theta
[1,]      -0.3
[2,]       0.1
```

and it resembles our example in general notation (see equation (5.4)). The list `msarimamodelOut` is an easy way to check the correct specification of the model.

5.4.3 Setting the Expanded Model

```
{y,phiconv,thetaconv,k} = msarimaconvert(x,msarimamodelOut)
```

sets the coefficients of an expanded multiplicative seasonal ARIMA model

If you want to estimate the coefficients in (5.4), you have to telescope out the original model. Given the specification by the list `msarimaOut` (see Subsection 5.4.2) and the time series $\{x_t\}_{t=1}^T$, the quantlet `msarimaconvert` telescopes out the original model automatically.

Let us consider the following SARIMA(3,1,1)×(12,1,0,0) model with $\phi_2 = 0$:

$$(1 - \phi_{s,1}L^{12})(1 - \phi_1 L - \phi_3 L^3)\Delta x_t = (1 + \theta_1 L)a_t. \tag{5.18}$$

Telescoping out the polynomials on the left-hand side leads to an ordinary ARMA model:

$$(1 - \phi_1^e L - \phi_3^e L^3 - \phi_{12}^e L^{12} - \phi_{13}^e L^{13} - \phi_{15}^e L^{15})y_t = (1 + \theta_1^e L)a_t \tag{5.19}$$

with $y_t \stackrel{\text{def}}{=} \Delta x_t$, $\phi_1^e \stackrel{\text{def}}{=} \phi_1$, $\phi_3^e \stackrel{\text{def}}{=} \phi_3$, $\phi_{12}^e \stackrel{\text{def}}{=} \phi_{s,1}$, $\phi_{13}^e \stackrel{\text{def}}{=} -\phi_1\phi_{s,1}$, $\phi_{15}^e \stackrel{\text{def}}{=} -\phi_3\phi_{s,1}$, and $\theta_1^e \stackrel{\text{def}}{=} \theta_1$.

The superscript e denotes the coefficients of the expanded model. The output of the quantlet is thus self-explaining: the series y_t is just the differenced original series x_t and the other two outputs are the vector ϕ^e (with $\phi_0^e \stackrel{\text{def}}{=} 1$) and the vector θ^e (with $\theta_0^e \stackrel{\text{def}}{=} 1$). The first vector has the dimension $(sP + p + 1) \times 1$ and second one has the dimension $(sQ + q + 1) \times 1$. The scalar k gives the number of coefficients in the original model. For the above given example, we have $k = 4$, whereas the number of coefficients of the expanded model is 6. Later on, we need k for the calculation of some regression diagnostics.

5.4.4 The Conditional Sum of Squares

`{S,dia} = msarimacond(y,phiconv,thetaconv,mu{,k})`
calculates the conditional sum of squares for given vectors of coefficients

The sum of squares is a criterion that can be used to identify the coefficients of the best model. The output of the quantlet is the conditional sum of squares for a given model specification (Box and Jenkins, 1976, Chapter 7).

For an ARMA(p,q) model this sum is just

$$S(\psi') \stackrel{\text{def}}{=} \sum_{t=p+1}^{T} \left(a_t(\psi')\right)^2 = \sum_{t=p+1}^{T} \left(\phi^e(L)y_t - \mu - \theta^e_{-1}(L)a_t\right)^2 . \tag{5.20}$$

Here T denotes the number of observations y_t. Recall that the first entries of the lag-polynomials are for $L^0 = 1$. $\theta^e_{-1}(L)$ denotes the MA-polynomial without the first entry. The first q residuals are set to zero.

The arguments of the quantlet are given by the output of `msarimaconvert`. `mu` is the mean of the series $\{y_t\}_{t=1}^T$. k is the number of coefficients in the original model and will be used to calculate some regression diagnostics. This argument is optional. If you do not specify k, the number of coefficients in the expanded model is used instead.

Furthermore, the quantlet `msarimacond` gives the list `dia` that contains several diagnostics. After the maximization of the conditional sum of squares, one can use these diagnostics to compare different specifications. In the ongoing k denotes the number of ARMA parameters that are different from zero. In our example we have $k = 2$ for both specifications.

The first element of the list—that is `dia.s2`—is the estimated variance of the residuals

$$\hat{\sigma}_a^2 = \frac{S}{T-p-k} . \tag{5.21}$$

The second element `dia.R2` gives the coefficient of determination

$$R^2 = 1 - \frac{S}{(T-p-1)\hat{\sigma}_y^2} . \tag{5.22}$$

The variance of the dependent variables y_t is calculated for the observations starting with $t = p+1$. It is possible in our context that R^2 becomes negative.

The adjusted coefficient of determination $\bar{R}^2$ is calculated as

$$\bar{R}^2 = 1 - (1 - R^2)\frac{T - p - 1}{T - p - k}. \tag{5.23}$$

It is the third argument of the list and is labeled `dia.aR2`.

The fourth element `dia.logl` gives the values of the log likelihood function evaluated at $\tilde{\psi}$. Given the likelihood function (5.9), $\tilde{\sigma}^2$ is a function of $\tilde{\psi}'$. To take this into account, we plug (5.12) into (5.9) and obtain

$$l(\tilde{\psi}) = -\frac{T - p}{2}\left[1 + \ln 2\pi + \ln\left\{\frac{S(\tilde{\psi}')}{T - p}\right\}\right]. \tag{5.24}$$

This expression is the value of the log likelihood function.

The fifth element `dia.AIC` gives the Akaike Information Criteria (AIC)

$$\mathrm{AIC} = -\frac{2\{l(\tilde{\psi}) - k\}}{T - p}. \tag{5.25}$$

The sixth element `dia.SIC` gives the Schwarz Information Criteria (SIC)

$$\mathrm{SIC} = -\frac{2\{l(\tilde{\psi}) - k\ln(T - p)\}}{T - p}. \tag{5.26}$$

For both criteria see Shumway and Stoffer (2000). These criteria can be used for model selection (Durbin and Koopman (2001)). Eventually, the last element `dia.a` gives the $(T - p) \times 1$ vector of the residuals a_t.

Now we can come back to our example of the airline data: recall that we have identified two possible specifications for this data set. The first specification is a SARIMA(0,1,1)×(12,0,1,1) with $\psi_1 = (\theta_1, \theta_{s,1}, \sigma^2)$. The second is a SARIMA(0,1,12)×(12,0,1,0) with $\psi_2 = (\theta_1, \theta_{12}, \sigma^2)$.

We maximize the conditional sum of squares for both specifications using the BFGS algorithm. Given the estimates $\tilde{\psi}$, the standard errors are obtained by means of the Hessian matrix for the log likelihood. The Hessian is calculated for this function using numerical methods. The square roots of the diagonal elements of the inverse Hessian are the standard errors of the estimates $\tilde{\psi}'$.

The results of the first specification are obtained using the the quantlet

`XEGmsarima9.xpl`

and the results of the second specification can be also obtained with the quantlet

XEGmsarima10.xpl

It is obvious that both specifications deliver good results. However, the sum of squared resids is smaller for the specification with a seasonal MA term. Additionally, both information criteria indicate that this specification is slightly better.

5.4.5 The Extended ACF

`eacf(y,p,q)`
displays a table with the extended ACF for time series y_t

After estimating the unknown parameters $\tilde{\psi}$ for competing specifications, one should have a look at the residual series $\{\tilde{a}_t\}_{t=p+1}^{T}$. They should behave like a white noise process and should exhibit no autocorrelation. In order to check for autocorrelation, one could use the ACF and PACF. However, the extended autocorrelation function (EACF) is also a convenient tool for inspecting time series (Peña, Tiao and Tsay, 2001, Chapter 3) that show no seasonal pattern.

In general, the EACF allows for the identification of ARIMA models (differencing is not necessary). The quantlet `eacf` generates a table of the sample EACF for a time series. You have to specify the maximal number of AR lags (p) and MA lags (q). Every row of the output table gives the ACF up to q lags for the residuals of an AR regression with $k \leqslant p$ lags. Furthermore, the simplified EACF is tabulated. If an autocorrelation is significant according to Bartlett's formula the entry is 1. Otherwise the entry is 0. Bartlett's formula for an MA(q) is given as

$$\text{Var}[\hat{\rho}(q+1)] = \frac{1}{T}\left[1 + 2\sum_{j=1}^{q}\hat{\rho}(j)^2\right]$$

where T is the number of observations (Peña, Tiao and Tsay, 2001). For identification, look for the vertex of a triangle of zeros. You can immediately read off the order of the series from the table.

We use the EACF to explore the behavior of the residuals of both specifications. The next quantlet computes the EACF of the residuals that come from the SARIMA(0,1,1) ×(12,0,1,1) specification.

XEGmsarima11.xpl

It is obvious, that the vertex of zeros is at position $q = 0$ and $p = 0$. Thus we conclude that the residuals are white noise. Notice, that the first line in the above table at $p = 0$ just gives the ACF of the residual series. According to Bartlett's formula, all autocorrelation coefficients are not significantly different from zero.

The next quantlet computes the EACF of the residuals of the SARIMA(0,1,12)× (12,0,1,0) specification.

XEGmsarima12.xpl

We can conclude that the vertex of zeros is at position $q = 0$ and $p = 0$. Thus the residuals are white noise. According to Bartlett's formula, once again all autocorrelation coefficients are not significantly different from zero.

5.4.6 The Exact Likelihood

```
{gkalfilOut,loglike} = gkalfilter(Y,mu,Sig,ca,Ta,Ra,
                                  da,Za,Ha,l)
```
Kalman filters a SSF and gives the value of the log likelihood

As already mentioned in the introductory part of this section, the Kalman filter can be used to evaluate the exact log likelihood function. For the estimation of the unknown parameters the evaluated log likelihood function 5.15 is required. The second element of the quantlet provides the value of the exact log likelihood function.

We now shortly describe the procedure of the Kalman filter and the implementation with `gkalfilter`. Good references for the Kalman filter are—in addition to Harvey (1989)—Hamilton (1994), Gourieroux and Monfort (1997) and Shumway and Stoffer (2000). The first argument is an array with the observed time series. The vector `mu` specifies the initial conditions of the filtering procedure with corresponding covariance matrix `Sig`. Due to the fact that our SSF (5.13) contains no constants, we set `ca` and `da` to zero. Furthermore, we have no disturbance in the measurement equation—that is the equation for y_t in (5.13)—so we also set `Ha` to zero. The covariance matrix for the disturbance in the state equation is given as

$$R = \sigma^2 \begin{bmatrix} 1 & \theta_1 & 0 & \dots & 0 & \theta_{s,1} & \theta_1\theta_{s,1} \\ \theta_1 & \theta_1^2 & 0 & \dots & 0 & \theta_1\theta_{s,1} & \theta_1^2\theta_{s,1} \\ 0 & 0 & 0 & \dots & 0 & 0 & 0 \\ \vdots & \vdots & \vdots & \dots & \vdots & \vdots & \vdots \\ \theta_{s,1} & \theta_1\theta_{s,1} & 0 & \dots & 0 & \theta_{s,1}^2 & \theta_1\theta_{s,1}^2 \\ \theta_1\theta_{s,1} & \theta_1^2\theta_{s,1} & 0 & \dots & 0 & \theta_1\theta_{s,1}^2 & \theta_1^2\theta_{s,1}^2 \end{bmatrix}$$

Eventually, `Za` is an array for the matrix Z given in the measurement equation.

The state space form of the airline model is given in (5.13). It is a well known fact that the product of eigenvalues for a square matrix is equal to its determinant. The determinant of the transition matrix T for our model—given in equation (5.14)—is zero and so all eigenvalues are also zero. Thus our system is stable (Harvey, 1989, p. 114). In that case, we should set the initial values to the unconditional mean and variance of the state vector (Koopman, Shephard and Doornik, 1999). We easily obtain for our model (5.13) that

$$\mu \stackrel{\text{def}}{=} \mathrm{E}[\alpha_0] = 0 \tag{5.27}$$

and

$$\Sigma \stackrel{\text{def}}{=} \mathrm{Var}[\alpha_0] = T\Sigma T^\top + R\,.$$

A way to solve for the elements of Σ is

$$\mathrm{vec}(\Sigma) = (I - T \otimes T)^{-1}\mathrm{vec}(R)\,. \tag{5.28}$$

Here, vec denotes the vec-operator that places the columns of a matrix below each other and $\otimes$ denotes the Kronecker product.

For the estimation, we use the demeaned series of the growth rates g_t of the airline data. The standard errors of the estimates are given by the square roots of the diagonal elements of the inverse Hessian evaluated at $\tilde{\psi}'$. The following table shows the results:

```
"==================================================================="
```

```
" Estimation results for the SARIMA(0,1,12)x(12,0,1,0) specification"
" Exact Log Likelihood function is maximized                          "
"====================================================================="
" Convergence achieved after 12 iterations                            "
" 131 observations included                                           "
"                                                                     "
"     Variable       Coefficient        t-stat       p-value          "
"     -----------------------------------------------------           "
"     theta_1           -0.3998        -4.4726         0.00           "
"     theta_12          -0.5545        -7.5763         0.00           "
"     sigma2             0.0014         8.0632         0.00           "
"     -----------------------------------------------------           "
"     AIC               -3.6886         SIC          -3.5111          "
"====================================================================="
```

XEGmsarima13.xpl

The estimators are only slightly different from the estimators we have calculated with the conditional likelihood. The variance $\tilde{\sigma}^2$ is identical.

Bibliography

Box, G. E. P. and Jenkins, G. M. (1976). *Time Series Analysis, Forecasting and Control*, Revised Edition, Prentice Hall, Englewood Cliffs.

Chatfield, C. (2001). *Time-Series Forecasting*, Chapman & Hall/CRC, Boca Raton.

Diebold, F. X. (1998). *Elements of Forecasting*, South-Western College Publishing, Cincinnati.

Durbin, J. and Koopman, S J. (2001). *Time Series Analysis by State Space Methods*, Oxford Statistical Science Series 24, Oxford University Press, Oxford.

Franses, P. H. (1998). *Time Series Models for Business and Economic Forecasting*, Cambridge University Press, Cambridge.

Ghysels, E. and Osborn, D. R. (2000). *The Econometric Analysis of Seasonal Time Series*, Cambridge University Press, Cambridge.

Gourieroux, C. and Monfort, A. (1997). *Time Series and Dynamic Models*, Cambridge University Press, Cambridge.

Hamilton, J. D. (1994). *Time Series Analysis*, Princeton University Press, Princeton, New Jersey.

Harvey, A. C. (1989). *Forecasting, Structural Time Series Models and the Kalman Filter*, Cambridge University Press, Cambridge.

Harvey, A. C. (1993). *Time Series Models*, Harvester/Wheatsheaf, New York, London.

Koopman, S. J., Shepard, N. and Doornik, J. A. (1999). Statistical Algorithms for Models in State Space Using SsfPack 2.2, *Econometrics Journal* **2**: 107–160.

Mills, T. C. (1990). *Time series techniques for economists*, Cambridge University Press, Cambridge.

Peña, D., Tiao, G. C. and Tsay, R. S. (2001). *A Course in Time Series Analysis*, Wiley, New York.

Shumway, R. H. and Stoffer, D. S. (2000). *Time Series Analysis and Its Applications*, Springer, New York, Berlin.

6 AutoRegressive Conditional Heteroscedastic Models

Pilar Olave and José T. Alcalá

6.1 Introduction

The linear models presented so far in cross-section data and in time series assume a constant variance and covariance function, that is to say, the homoscedasticity is assumed.

The possibility of having dependence between higher conditional moments, most notably variances, implies to examine non-linear stochastic processes from a more realistic perspective in time series data. Moreover, as we have seen in previous chapter, some financial time series are approximated by random walk models, but the usual random walk assumptions are too restrictive because the asset price volatility changes over time and consequently, violating the conditional stationarity of the process.

From an empirical point of view, financial time series present various forms of non linear dynamics, the crucial one being the strong dependence of the variability of the series on its own past and furthermore, with the fitting of the standard linear models being poor in these series. Some non-linearities of these series are a non-constant conditional variance and, generally, they are characterised by the clustering of large shocks to the dependent variable.

That is to say, variance changes over time, and large (small) changes tend to be followed by large (small) changes of either sign and, furthermore, unconditional distributions have tails heavier than the normal distribution. The volume of data and the high-frequency sampling of data in financial and currency markets are increasing day to day, in such a way that we almost have a time-continuous information process and consequently, we need to adopt ad-hoc methods to allow shifts in the variance or may be a better alternative using a new class of models with non-constant variance conditional on the past. An additional advantage of these models is to take into account the conditional variance in the stochastic error to improve the estimation of forecasting intervals. A general study of the problem of heteroscedasticity and their consequences in regression and autocorrelation models can be seen in Mills (1993) and Johnston and DiNardo (1997).

Models which present some non-linearities can be modelled by conditional specifications, in both conditional mean and variance. The standard approach to heteroscedasticity is to introduce an exogenous variable x_t which takes into account the incertitude of the model. In figure 6.1 we can see a simulated time series $\{y_t\}$ and moreover, we can observe the existence of a non-constant variance in the right scatter plot of $\{y_t\}$ over the exogenous variable x_t. This behaviour is very often in time series data of high-frequency.

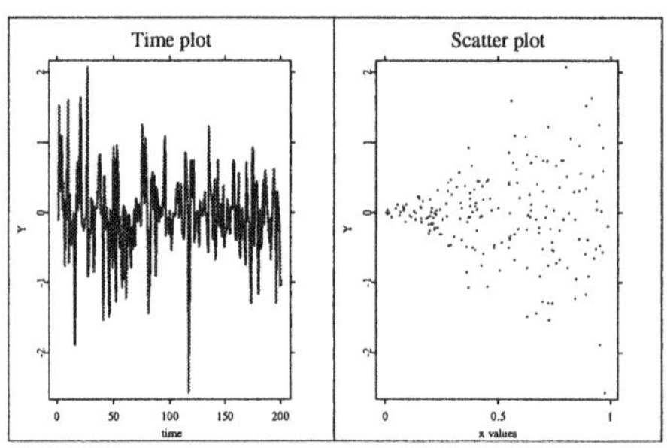

Figure 6.1. Time plot and scatter plot with the exogenous variable causing heteroscedasticity.

XEGarch01.xpl

One simple model which captures these features, might be

$$y_t = \varepsilon_t x_{t-1}$$

where, as usual $\mathrm{E}(\varepsilon) = 0$ and $V(\varepsilon) = \sigma^2$. The conditional variance of y_t is $\sigma^2 x_{t-1}^2$ and, therefore, the prediction interval depends on an exogenous variable changing over time.

However, the theory of finance does not usually provide adequate exogenous variables to explain changes in expected mean and variance of the rates of returns in asset prices. As consequence, a preferable model is

$$y_t = \varepsilon_t y_{t-1},$$

now the conditional variance is $\sigma^2 y_{t-1}^2$ but, unfortunately the unconditional variance is zero or infinity.

The basic models presented in this chapter are able to capture all observed phenomena and to give a satisfactory solution to most statistical requirements, such as asymptotic moments or stationarity, etc. The clustering volatility of these markets over time is a function of the most recent news, and in the next sections, we will describe the statistical properties of a basic autoregressive conditional heteroscedastic model and its generalisations.

In order to illustrate these ideas, we offer several examples. These are, respectively time series from the Spanish Stock Market, daily Spanish Peseta/US dollar exchange rate and several data sets simulated.

Ibex35 index Ibex35 index is a weighted mean of the 35 firms with the largest trading volumes. The series analysed corresponds to daily returns of the Ibex35 index, which is constructed as the logarithmic difference of the closing price, that is to say,

$$y_t = 100 * \log\left(\frac{S_t}{S_{t-1}}\right)$$

where S_t is the above mentioned closing price at time t, thus excluding dividend yields. We have a total of 499 data available to us. The time period analysed runs from 1st January 1999 to 29th December 2000. The return time series is plotted in 6.2

XEGarch02.xpl

Spanish peseta/US dollar data In this example, the data series is the daily spot exchange rate from January 1990 to December 1991. There are 500 observations. Let S_t denote the spot price of the one US dollar to Spanish pesetas. We then analyse the continuously compounded percentage rate of return,

$$y_t = 100 * \log\left(\frac{S_t}{S_{t-1}}\right).$$

These are the data plotted in figure 6.3

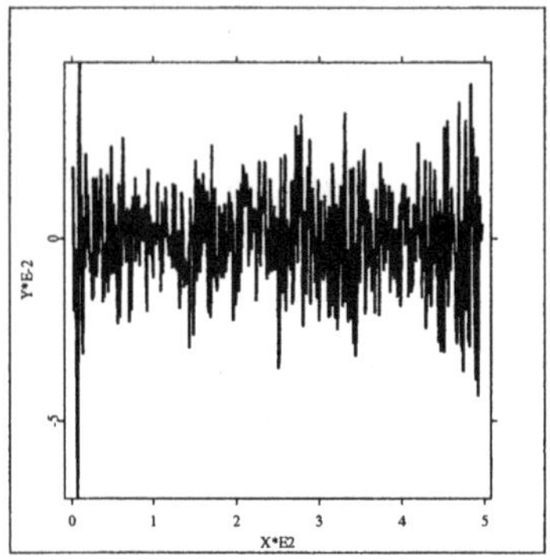

Figure 6.2. Daily returns of the Ibex35 Stock Market Index.

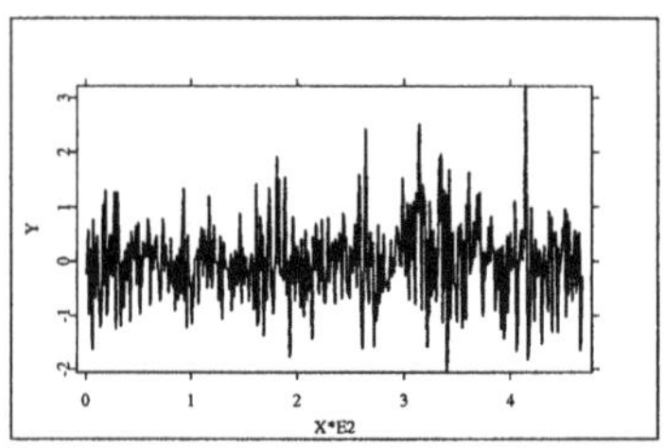

Figure 6.3. Daily rates of returns on Spanish peseta/US dollar exchange rate.

XEGarch03.xpl

Simulated Data The third example is a data set simulated in such a way that the mean is zero and the unconditional variance of the model is 1. The corresponding time plot is seen in figure 6.4,

The first aspect to note is that for all series the means appear to be constant, while the variances change over time.

Many researchers have introduced informal and ad-hoc procedures to take account of the changes in the variance. One of the first authors to incorporate variance changing over time was Mandelbrot (1963), who used recursive estimates of the variance for modelling volatility. More recently, Klein (1977) used rolling estimates of quadratic residuals.

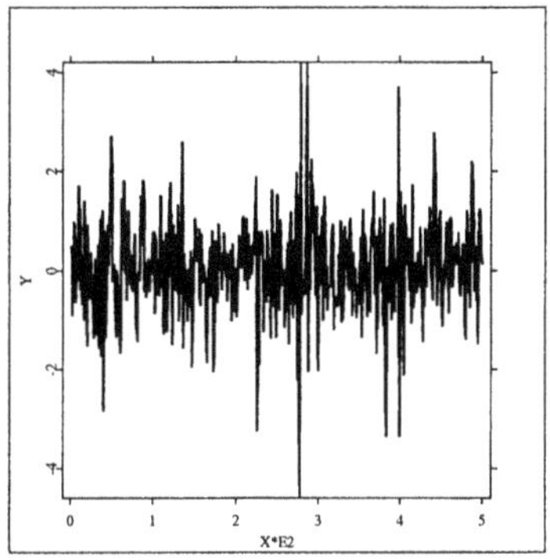

Figure 6.4. simulated ARCH(1) data. XEGarch04.xpl

Engle's ARCH model (see Engle, 1982) was the first formal model which seemed to capture the stylised facts mentioned above. The ARCH model (autoregressive conditional heteroscedastic models) has become one of the most important models in financial applications. These models are non-constant variances conditioned on the past, which are a linear function on recent past perturbations. This means that the more recent news will be the fundamental information that is relevant for modelling the present volatility.

Moreover, the accuracy of the forecast over time improves when some additional information from the past is considered. Specifically, the conditional variance of the innovations will be used to calculate the percentile of the forecasting intervals, instead of the homoscedastic formula used in standard time series models.

The simplest version of the ARCH disturbance model is the first-order, which can be generalised to a p-order model. The financial models do not use exogenous variables, but in another economic context a regression model with ARCH perturbations could be considered as in section 1.4. In what follows, we will describe the basic statistical properties of these proposed models, as well as the most appropriate estimation methods. Finally, we will present the usual hypothesis tests for detecting the structure and the order of the model. In addition, we present the extension of the ARCH model to a more general model in which the lagged conditional variance is included in the present conditional variance.

6.2 ARCH(1) Model

The basic model we consider is a parameterisation of the conditional variance of the time series based on the order one lag on squared past recent perturbations. For the sake of simplicity, we assume that the time series y_t has no structure in the mean, is conditionally gaussian and, furthermore, that the conditional variance is time dependent.

$$\begin{aligned} y_t &= u_t \\ u_t &= \epsilon_t \sigma_t, \epsilon_t \sim i.i.d.N(0,1) \\ \sigma_t^2 &= \alpha_0 + \alpha_1 u_{t-1}^2, \alpha_0 > 0, \alpha_1 \geq 0. \end{aligned} \tag{6.1}$$

A process that satisfies these three conditions is called autoregressive conditional heteroscedastic of order one.

This basic ARCH(1) process can be formulated as a linear model on squared perturbations. Let $\upsilon_t = u_t^2 - \sigma_t^2$, so that the square error can be written as

$$u_t^2 = \alpha_0 + \alpha_1 u_{t-1}^2 + \upsilon_t.$$

Because $\mathrm{E}(\upsilon_t | I_{t-1}) = 0$, where I_{t-1} is the information set up to time t; the law of iterated expectations reveals that υ_t has zero mean and is serially uncorrelated. Therefore, u_t^2 has an AR(1) representation, where υ_t is a non-gaussian white noise.

This ARCH process can be included as the innovation model of several other linear models (ARMA models, regression models, ...).

6.2.1 Conditional and Unconditional Moments of the ARCH(1)

The derivation of the unconditional moments of the ARCH(1) process is possible through extensive use of the law of iterated expectations on conditional distributions. Then, the following expressions are satisfied:

$$\begin{aligned} \mathrm{E}(u_t | I_{t-1}) &= 0 \\ V(u_t | I_{t-1}) &= \sigma_t^2 V(\epsilon_t | I_{t-1}) = \sigma_t^2 \end{aligned} \tag{6.2}$$

hence,

$$u_t | I_{t-1} \sim N(0, \sigma_t^2) \tag{6.3}$$

Therefore,

$$\begin{aligned} \mathrm{E}(u_t) &= E[\mathrm{E}(u_t|I_{t-1})] = 0 \\ \mathrm{E}(u_t^2) &= E[\mathrm{E}(u_t^2|I_{t-1})] = \mathrm{E}(\sigma_t^2) = \alpha_0 + \alpha_1 \mathrm{E}(u_{t-1}^2) \end{aligned}$$

which is a linear difference equation for the sequence of variances. Assuming the process began infinitely far in the past with a finite initial variance, the sequence of variances converge to the constant

$$\sigma^2 = \frac{\alpha_0}{1-\alpha_1}, \qquad \alpha_1 < 1.$$

When this unconditional variance exists, the prior information does not give any information to forecast the volatility at infinite horizon.

The difference between the conditional and the unconditional variance is a simple function of the deviation of squared innovations from their mean. Let $\sigma_t^2 - \sigma^2 = \alpha_1(u_{t-1}^2 - \sigma^2)$, in the ARCH(1) model with $\alpha_1 > 0$. Then the variance of the current error u_t, conditioned on the realised values of the lagged errors u_{t-1}, is an increasing function of the magnitude of the lagged errors, irrespective of their signs. Hence, large errors of either sign tend to be followed by a large error of either sign, similarly, small errors of either sign tend to be followed by a small error of either sign.

The nature of the unconditional density of an ARCH(1) process can be analysed by the higher order moments. Indeed,

$$\mathrm{E}(u_t^4|I_{t-1}) = \mathrm{E}(\epsilon_t^4 \sigma_t^4|I_{t-1}) = \mathrm{E}(\epsilon_t^4|I_{t-1}) E[(\sigma_t^2)^2|I_{t-1}] = 3(\alpha_0 + \alpha_1 u_{t-1}^2)^2$$

Applying once again the law of iterated expectations, we have

$$\mathrm{E}(u_t^4) = E[\mathrm{E}(u_t^4|I_{t-1})] = 3\mathrm{E}(\alpha_0 + \alpha_1 u_{t-1}^2)^2 =$$

$$3[\alpha_0^2 + 2\alpha_0\alpha_1 \mathrm{E}(u_{t-1}^2) + \alpha_1^2 \mathrm{E}(u_{t-1}^4)] = 3[\alpha_0^2 + 2\alpha_1 \frac{\alpha_0^2}{1-\alpha_1} + \alpha_1^2 \mathrm{E}(u_{t-1}^4)].$$

Assuming that the process is stationary both in variance and in the fourth moment, if $\mathrm{E}(u_t^4) = c$,

$$c = \frac{3\alpha_0^2[1-\alpha_1^2]}{(1-\alpha_1)^2(1-3\alpha_1^2)}.$$

Simple algebra then reveals that the kurtosis is

$$\kappa_u = \frac{\mathrm{E}(u_t^4)}{\sigma^4} = \frac{3(1-\alpha_1^2)}{1-3\alpha_1^2}$$

which is clearly greater than 3 (kurtosis value of the normal distribution). Moreover, it is required that $3\alpha_1^2 < 1$ for the fourth moment and, consequently, the unconditional kurtosis is finite.

Hence, the unconditional distribution of u_t is leptokurtic. That is to say, the ARCH(1) process has tails heavier than the normal distribution. This property makes the ARCH process attractive because the distributions of asset returns frequently display tails heavier than the normal distribution.

The quantlet XEGarch05 generates an ARCH(1) series with unconditional variance equal to 1 and obtain the basic descriptive statistics.

```
[ 1,] " " [ 2,]
"=============================================================" [ 3,]
" Variable 1" [ 4,]
"=============================================================" [ 5,]
" " [ 6,] " Mean           0.0675013" [ 7,] " Std.Error 0.987465
Variance           0.975087" [ 8,] " " [ 9,] " Minimum -4.59634
Maximum             4.19141" [10,] " Range 8.78775" [11,] " " [12,]
" Lowest cases                    Highest cases " [13,] "
278:      -4.59634                49: 2.69931" [14,] "         383:
-3.34884               442: 2.76556" [15,] "         400:
-3.33363               399: 3.69674" [16,] "         226:
-3.2339               279: 4.17015" [17,] "          40:
-2.82524               287: 4.19141" [18,] " " [19,] " Median
0.0871746"
[20,] " 25% Quartile    -0.506585      75% Quartile      0.675945"
[21,] " " [22,] " Skewness          -0.123027     Kurtosis 8.53126"
[23,] " " [24,] " Observations                         500" [25,] "
Distinct observations             500" [26,] " " [27,] " Total
number of {-Inf,Inf,NaN}    0" [28,] " " [29,]
"=============================================================" [30,]
" "
```

XEGarch05.xpl

We can see in the corresponding output that the unconditional standard error is not far from one. However, we can also observe a higher kurtosis and a wider range than we expect from a standardised white noise gaussian model.

6.2.2 Estimation for ARCH(1) Process

The process $\{u_t\}_{t=1}^T$ is generated by an ARCH(1) process described in equations (6.1), where T is the total sample size. Although the process define by (6.1) has all observations conditionally normally distributed, the vector of observations is not jointly normal. Therefore, conditioned on an initial observation, the joint density function can be written as

$$f(u) = \prod_{t=1}^{T} f(u_t|I_{t-1}). \tag{6.4}$$

Using this result, and ignoring a constant factor, the log-likelihood function $L(\alpha_0, \alpha_1)$ for a T sample size is

$$L(\alpha_0, \alpha_1) = \sum_{t=1}^{T} l_t$$

where the conditional log-likelihood of the tth observation for (α_0, α_1) is,

$$\begin{aligned} l_t &= -\frac{1}{2}\log(\sigma_t^2) - \frac{1}{2}\frac{u_t^2}{\sigma_t^2} \\ &= -\frac{1}{2}\log(\alpha_0 + \alpha_1 u_{t-1}^2) - \frac{1}{2}\frac{u_t^2}{\alpha_0 + \alpha_1 u_{t-1}^2} \end{aligned} \tag{6.5}$$

The first order conditions to obtain the maximum likelihood estimator are:

$$\begin{aligned} \frac{\partial l_t}{\partial \alpha_0} &= \frac{1}{2(\alpha_0 + \alpha_1 u_{t-1}^2)}\left(\frac{u_t^2}{\alpha_0 + \alpha_1 u_{t-1}^2} - 1\right) \\ \frac{\partial l_t}{\partial \alpha_1} &= \frac{1}{2(\alpha_0 + \alpha_1 u_{t-1}^2)} u_{t-1}^2 \left(\frac{u_t^2}{\alpha_0 + \alpha_1 u_{t-1}^2} - 1\right) \end{aligned} \tag{6.6}$$

More generally, the partial derivation of L is:

$$\frac{\partial L}{\partial \alpha} = \sum_t \frac{1}{2\sigma_t^2}\frac{\partial \sigma_t^2}{\partial \alpha}\left(\frac{u_t^2}{\sigma_t^2} - 1\right) = \sum_t \frac{1}{2\sigma_t^2} z_t \left(\frac{u_t^2}{\sigma_t^2} - 1\right) \tag{6.7}$$

where $z_t^\top = (1, u_{t-1}^2)$.

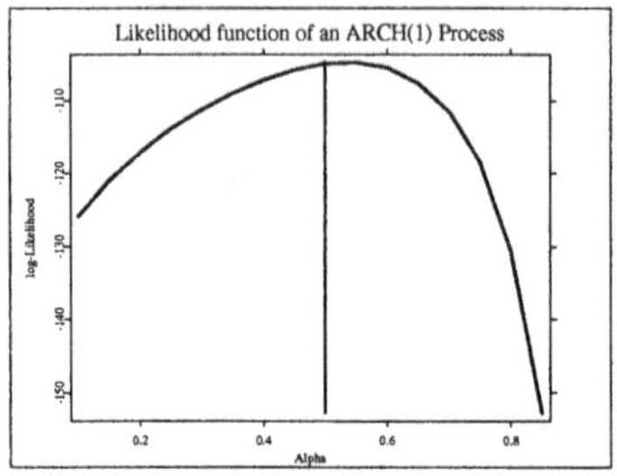

Figure 6.5. Log-likelihood function of ARCH(1) simulated data. Vertical line marks the true parameter value

`XEGarch06.xpl`

Example In the quantlet `XEGarch06`, we simulate an ARCH(1) process and plot the likelihood function of the α_1 parameter. Although the log-likelihood function depends on $\alpha = (\alpha_0, \alpha_1)$ we have simplified it by imposing the restriction $\hat{\alpha}_0 = \hat{\sigma}^2(1 - \hat{\alpha}_1)$ where $\hat{\sigma}^2$ is an unconditional variance estimate.

The ML estimators $\hat{\alpha} = (\hat{\alpha}_0, \hat{\alpha}_1)^\top$, under the usual assumptions, are asymptotically normal

$$\sqrt{T}(\hat{\alpha} - \alpha) \to N(0, I_{\alpha\alpha}^{-1})$$

where

$$I_{\alpha\alpha} = -E\left[\frac{\partial^2 l_t}{\partial\alpha\partial\alpha^\top}\right] = \begin{pmatrix} I_{\alpha_0\alpha_0} & I_{\alpha_0\alpha_1} \\ I_{\alpha_1\alpha_0} & I_{\alpha_1\alpha_1} \end{pmatrix}$$

where $I_{\alpha\alpha}$ must be approximated.

The elements of the Hessian matrix are:

$$\begin{aligned} \frac{\partial^2 l_t}{\partial\alpha_0^2} &= \frac{-1}{2\sigma_t^4}\left(\frac{2u_t^2}{\sigma_t^2} - 1\right) \\ \frac{\partial^2 l_t}{\partial\alpha_1^2} &= \frac{-1}{2\sigma_t^4}u_{t-1}^4\left(\frac{2u_t^2}{\sigma_t^2} - 1\right) \\ \frac{\partial^2 l_t}{\partial\alpha_0\alpha_1} &= \frac{-1}{2\sigma_t^4}u_{t-1}^2\left(\frac{2u_t^2}{\sigma_t^2} - 1\right) \end{aligned}$$

The information matrix is simply the negative expectation of the Hessian average over all observations, that is to say,

$$I_{\alpha\alpha} = -\frac{1}{T}\sum_{t=1}^{T} \mathrm{E}\left[\frac{\partial^2 l_t}{\partial\alpha\partial\alpha^\top}|I_{t-1}\right]. \tag{6.8}$$

Taking into account (6.3), the conditional expectations of the last terms is 1. Hence, to calculate the unconditional expectation of the Hessian matrix and, therefore, the information matrix, we approximate it by the average over all the conditional expectations. Then, $I_{\alpha\alpha}$ is consistently estimated by

$$\begin{aligned} \hat{I}_{\alpha_0\alpha_0} &= \frac{1}{2T}\sum_{t=1}^{T}\frac{1}{\hat{\sigma}_t^4} \\ \hat{I}_{\alpha_1\alpha_1} &= \frac{1}{2T}\sum_{t=1}^{T}\frac{u_{t-1}^4}{\hat{\sigma}_t^4} \\ \hat{I}_{\alpha_0\alpha_1} &= \frac{1}{2T}\sum_{t=1}^{T}\frac{u_{t-1}^2}{\hat{\sigma}_t^4} \end{aligned} \tag{6.9}$$

or, more generally,

$$\hat{I}_{\alpha\alpha} = \frac{1}{2T}\sum_{t=1}^{T}\frac{z_t z_t^\top}{\hat{\sigma}_t^4} \tag{6.10}$$

In practice, the maximum likelihood estimator is computed by numerical methods and, in particular gradient methods are preferred for their simplicity. They are iterative methods and at each step, we increase the likelihood by searching a step forward along the gradient direction. It is therefore desirable to construct the following iteration scheme, computing $\alpha^{(k+1)}$ from $\alpha^{(k)}$ by

$$\alpha^{(k+1)} = \alpha^{(k)} + \lambda^{(k)}\left(\hat{I}_{\alpha\alpha}^{(k)}\right)^{-1}\left(\frac{\partial L}{\partial\alpha}\right)^{(k)} \tag{6.11}$$

where the step length $\lambda^{(k)}$ is usually obtained by a one-dimensional search, (for details, see Bernt, Hall, Hall and Hausman, 1974)

Example In the following example we show the joint sample distribution of the parameter estimates. To that end, we plot the marginal kernel density estimates of both $\hat{\alpha}_0$ and $\hat{\alpha}_1$ and the corresponding scatter plot with the regression line drawn (kernel density estimation is a valuable tool in data analysis and to explore the unknown density function of a continuous variable, (see Silverman, 1989)) . Data are obtained by simulating and estimating 100 time series of size 400 of the same model ($\alpha_0 = 0.5, \alpha_1 = 0.5$).

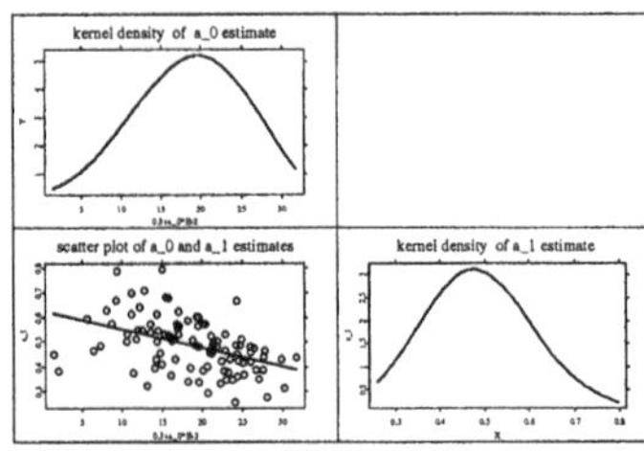

Figure 6.6. Kernel density of parameter estimators: In the top left hand panel for $\hat{\alpha}_0$, in the bottom right hand panel for $\hat{\alpha}_1$ and in the bottom left hand panel we have a scatter plot of parameter estimators

XEGarch07.xpl

In figure 6.6 we can see, as the asymptotic theory states, that both sampling distributions approach a bivariate normal density with a small correlation between them.

Example We will see the use of function `archest` in order to obtain the estimation of an ARCH(1) process. The data are simulated previously by function `genarch` (`yt=genarch(0.5|0.5,0,500)`). The function `archest` allows us estimate a general ARCH process (see section 6.6.1 for a complete description of this model). The result variable is a list with different information about the estimated model. For example, in the first element we have the parameter estimates and in the second element we have the standard error estimation for the estimates and , we easily obtain t-ratios values that show the statistical significance of the parameters.

Parameter	True Value	Estimates	t-ratio
α_0	0.5	0.4986	10.034
α_1	0.5	0.5491	6.9348

Table 6.1. Estimates and t-ratio values from an ARCH(1) model

In this example, we see that the estimated parameters agree with the theoretical values and they have a very high t-ratio. In the third component of the list we have the likelihood and in the fourth component we have the estimated volatility for the model. For example, we can plot the time series and add two lines representing twice the squared root of the estimated volatility around the mean value of the time series, as you can see in figure 6.7,

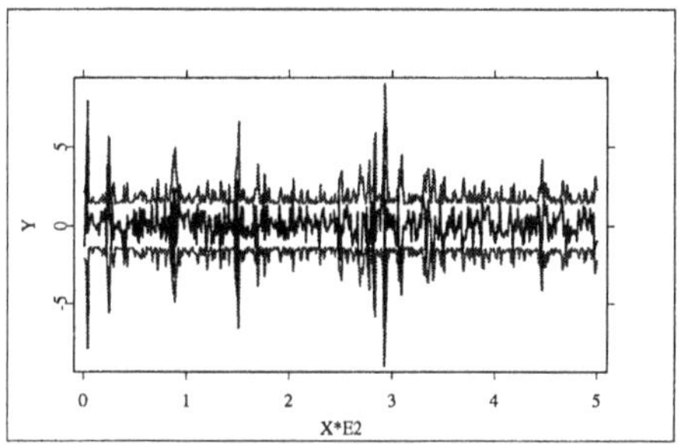

Figure 6.7. Simulated time series with the volatility bands estimated from the ARCH(1) model.

XEGarch08.xpl

6.3 ARCH(q) Model

Engle's (1982) original ARCH model assumes

$$
\begin{aligned}
y_t &= u_t \\
u_t &= \epsilon_t \sigma_t, \quad \epsilon_t \sim i.i.d.\ N(0,1) \\
\sigma_t^2 &= \alpha_0 + \sum_{i=1}^{q} \alpha_i u_{t-i}^2,
\end{aligned}
\tag{6.12}
$$

with $\alpha_0 > 0$, and $\alpha_i \geq 0$, $i = 1, ..., q$, to ensure that the conditional variance is positive.

The basic idea of these models is to increase the order of the autoregressive polynomial described in (1.1).

For this purpose, we define $v_t = u_t^2 - \sigma_t^2$, so that the square error is now

$$u_t^2 = \alpha_0 + \sum_{i=1}^{q} \alpha_i u_{t-i}^2 + v_t$$

where v_t is a non-gaussian white noise.

The derivation of the unconditional moments of the ARCH(q) process is analogous to ARCH(1). The necessary and sufficient condition for the existence of stationary variance is

$$\sum_{i=1}^{q} \alpha_i < 1$$

When this condition is satisfied, the variance of the process is

$$\sigma^2 = \frac{\alpha_0}{1 - \sum_{i=1}^{q} \alpha_i}$$

Although the variance of u_t conditioned on I_{t-1} changes with the elements of the information set (it depends on the past through the q most recent values of the squared innovation process) , the ARCH process is unconditionally homoscedastic.

Example We simulate an ARCH(2) process with parameters $\alpha_0 = 1/3$, and $\alpha_1 = \alpha_2 = 1/3$ and we compare the ACF function for the original and squared simulated values. The autocorrelation function of squared values reveals the first two significative lags.

After the model is estimated, we plot a similar picture as in figure 6.7 to show how the volatility does not vanish so quickly as in the ARCH(1) model.

The log-likelihood function of the standard ARCH(q) model in (6.27), conditoned on an initial observation, is given by

$$L(\alpha_0, \alpha_1, ..., \alpha_q) = \sum_{t=1}^{T} l_t$$

where

$$l_t = -\frac{1}{2}\log(\sigma_t^2) - \frac{1}{2}\frac{u_t^2}{\sigma_t^2} \tag{6.13}$$

apart from some constant in the likelihood.

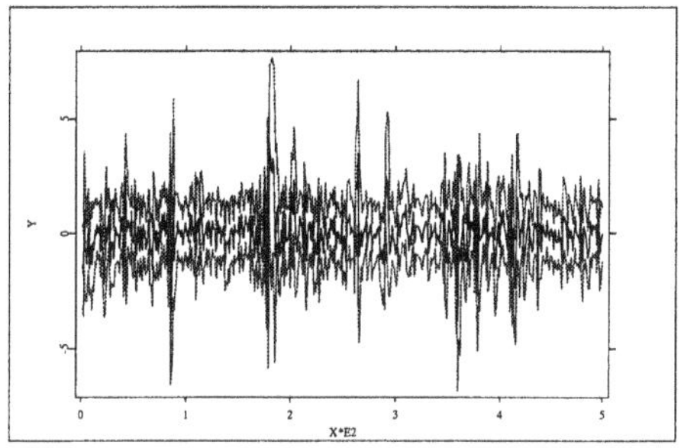

Figure 6.8. Simulated time series with the volatility bands estimated from the ARCH(2) model.

XEGarch09.xpl

Let $z_t^\top = (1, u_{t-1}^2, ..., u_{t-q}^2)$ and $\alpha^\top = (\alpha_0, \alpha_1, ..., \alpha_q)$ so that the conditional variance can be written as $\sigma_t^2 = z_t^\top \alpha$.

The first order conditions then become simply

$$\frac{\partial L}{\partial \alpha} = \frac{1}{2\sigma_t^2} z_t \left(\frac{u_t^2}{\sigma_t^2} - 1\right)$$

and the estimate of the information matrix is given in (6.10).

6.4 Testing Heteroscedasticity and ARCH(1) Disturbances

Most linear models and times series models estimated by OLS method assume homoscedastic disturbances. Heteroscedasticity is most expected in cross-sectional data, but also in financial time series. We present the Breusch-Pagan test valid for a general linear models and finally we show a specific LM test for testing the ARCH(1) model.

6.4.1 The Breusch-Pagan Test

If we assume an usual linear regression model,

$$y_t = x_t'\beta + u_t,$$

where $x_t'\beta$ is a linear combination of exogenous variables included in the information set I_{t-1} whit β a $k \times 1$ vector of unknown parameters. It is assumed that heteroscedasticity takes the form,

$$\sigma_t^2 = h(z_t'\alpha)$$

where $z_t' = [1, z_{1t}, \ldots, z_{pt}]$ is a vector of known variables and $\alpha' = [\alpha_0, \alpha_1, \ldots, \alpha_p]$ is a vector of unknown coefficients and $h(.)$ is an unspecified positive function. Let it the hypotheses be

$$H_0 : \alpha_1 = \cdots = \alpha_p = 0$$

that is, $\sigma^2 = h(\alpha_0)$ is constant. Under the null hypothesis, and taken in account that this test is a LM test, the model is estimated simply applying OLS method.

The test procedure is as follows:

- 1. We estimate the regression model by OLS, and let e_t be the residuals and then, we estimate the common variance $\hat{\sigma}^2 = \sum_t e_t^2/T$.
- 2. We estimate an auxiliary regression model by OLS method with endogenous variables and then, we compute the standardised residuals $e_t/\hat{\sigma}$ and exogenous variables of the z_t vector.
- 3. We compute the explained sum of squares (ESS) of the previous model and under the H_0 hypothesis ,

  $$\frac{1}{2}\text{ESS} \sim \chi^2_{p-1}, \text{ as } T \to \infty.$$

  Obviously, homoscedasticity is rejected if the statistic value exceeds the preselected critical value from the distribution.

It can be shown that this test procedure is equivalent to compute TR^2 where R^2 is the squared of the determination coefficient in a linear regression of e_t on z_t.

An inconvenient of this test, in practice, is the unacknowledge of the exogenous variables responsible of the heteroscedasticity. In that case, we present the following test.

6.4.2 ARCH(1) Disturbance Test

The Lagrange multiplier test procedure is also adequate to test particular form of an ARCH(1) model.

Let it the hypotheses be

$$\begin{array}{lcl} H_0 & \equiv & \alpha_1 = 0 \ (\sigma_t^2 = \sigma^2 = \alpha_0) \\ H_a & \equiv & \alpha_1 \neq 0 \ (\sigma_t^2 = \alpha_0 + \alpha_1 u_{t-1}^2) \end{array} \tag{6.14}$$

Under the null hypothesis, the test consists of deriving the score and the information matrix.

In this case, the score (1.6) can be written as

$$\begin{array}{lcl} \left.\frac{\partial l_t}{\partial \alpha_0}\right|_{H_0} & = & \frac{1}{2\alpha_0}\left(\frac{u_t^2}{\alpha_0} - 1\right) \\ \left.\frac{\partial l_t}{\partial \alpha_1}\right|_{H_0} & = & \frac{1}{2\alpha_0} u_{t-1}^2 \left(\frac{u_t^2}{\alpha_0} - 1\right) \end{array} \tag{6.15}$$

More generally, the partial derivation of the log-likelihood function for a T sample size is, under H_0,

$$\left.\frac{\partial L}{\partial \alpha}\right|_{H_0} = \frac{1}{2\alpha_0}\sum_{t=1}^{T} z_t \left(\frac{u_t^2}{\alpha_0} - 1\right) = \frac{1}{2\alpha_0} z^\top w_0$$

where

$$\begin{array}{lcl} z_t^\top & = & (1, u_{t-1}^2) \\ z^\top & = & (z_1^\top, \ldots, z_T^\top) \\ w_0^\top & = & \left(\frac{u_t^2}{\alpha_0} - 1\right) 1^\top \end{array} \tag{6.16}$$

The elements of the Hessian matrix can be calculated under the null hypothesis, and the information matrix is consistently estimated, taking into account expression (1.11), by

$$\left.\widehat{I}_{\alpha\alpha}\right|_{H_0} = \frac{1}{2\alpha_0^4} z^\top z$$

Applying previous Breusch-Pagan test and under the assumption that the u_t are normally distributed, is given by

$$\frac{1}{2} w_0^\top z (z^\top z)^{-1} z^\top w_0$$

and, under H_0, this statistic is asymptotically distributed as χ_1^2.

Again, a statistic that is asymptotically equivalent to this one, and which is also computationally convenient, can be obtained by considering the square of the multiple correlation coefficient (R^2) in the regression of w_0 on z. Given that adding a constant and multiplying by a scalar will not change the R^2 of a regression, this is also equivalent to the regression of u_t^2 on u_{t-1}^2 and a constant. The statistic will be asymptotically distributed as chi square of one degree of freedom.

To carry out this regression, we save the residuals of the OLS regression in the first stage. When we then regress the square residuals on a constant and u_{t-1}^2, and test TR^2 as χ_1^2.

In the ARCH(q) model the procedure is similar but taking in account that the z_t vector is q-dimensional containing the squared lagged perturbations and consequently the asymptotical reference distribution is a χ_q^2.

Ibex35 data (continued) A direct application of the LM test to the Ibex35 data with the function `archtest` reveals a presence of heteroscedastic effects of order one in the conditional variance. If we write

```
; LM test for ARCH effects to Ibex35 return data
arch= archtest(return,1,"LM")
```

we obtain,

```
Contents of archt

[1,] "Lag order  Statistic  95\% Critical Value  P-Value "
[2,] "_________________________________________________"
[3,] ""
[4,] "     1      4.58716           3.84146        0.03221"
```

XEGarch10.xpl

6.5 ARCH(1) Regression Model

The ARCH process defined in the previous sections is used as a tool to capture the behaviour of the volatility when it is time-varying in a high-frequency data. However, in a wide variety of contexts, the information set could also be determinant in specifying a time-varying mean. In this section, we will define the information set in terms of the distribution of the errors of a dynamic linear regression model.

The ARCH regression model is obtained by assuming that the mean of the endogenous variable y_t is given by $x_t^\top \beta$, a linear combination of lagged endogenous and exogenous variables included in the information set I_{t-1}, with β a $k \times 1$ vector of unknown parameters.

That is to say:

$$\begin{aligned} y_t|I_{t-1} &\sim N(x_t^\top \beta, \sigma_t^2) \\ \sigma_t^2 &= \alpha_0 + \alpha_1 u_{t-1}^2, \ \alpha_0 > 0, \ \alpha_1 \geq 0. \end{aligned} \tag{6.17}$$

where $u_t = y_t - x_t^\top \beta$.

Under these assumptions and considering that the regressors include no lagged endogenous variables, the unconditional mean and variance can be derived as:

$$\begin{aligned} E[u_t] &= 0, \ E[y_t] = x_t^\top \beta \\ V[y_t] &= V[u_t] = \frac{\alpha_0}{1-\alpha_1}, \ (\alpha_1 < 1) \end{aligned} \tag{6.18}$$

It can be shown that the u_t are uncorrelated, so that we have:

$$\begin{aligned} E[u] &= 0 \\ V[u] &= E[uu^\top] = \sigma^2 I \end{aligned} \tag{6.19}$$

where

$$\sigma^2 = \frac{\alpha_0}{1-\alpha_1}$$

Thus, the Gauss-Markov assumptions are satisfied and ordinary least squares is the best linear unbiased estimator for the model and the variance estimates are unbiased and consistent. However, OLS estimators do not achieve the Cramer-Rao bound.

By using maximum likelihood techniques, it is possible to find a nonlinear estimator that is asymptotically more efficient than OLS estimators.

The log-likelihood function for $\alpha = (\alpha_0, \alpha_1)^\top$ and β can be written, ignoring a constant factor as

$$L(\alpha, \beta) = \sum l_t$$

and

$$l_t = -\frac{1}{2}\log[\alpha_0 + \alpha_1(y_t - x_{t-1}^\top\beta)^2] - \frac{1}{2}\frac{(y_t - x_{t-1}^\top\beta)^2}{\alpha_0 + \alpha_1(y_t - x_{t-1}^\top\beta)^2}$$

The maximum likelihood estimator is found by solving the first order conditions. The derivative with respect to β is

$$\frac{\partial l_t}{\partial \beta} = \frac{x_t u_t}{\sigma_t^2} + \frac{1}{2\sigma_t^2}\frac{\partial \sigma_t^2}{\partial \beta}\left(\frac{u_t^2}{\sigma_t^2} - 1\right) \tag{6.20}$$

For the particular case $p = 1$, we obtain:

$$\frac{\partial l_t}{\partial \beta} = \frac{x_t u_t}{\sigma_t^2} - \frac{1}{\sigma_t^2}\left(\frac{u_t^2}{\sigma_t^2} - 1\right)\alpha_1 x_{t-1} u_{t-1} \tag{6.21}$$

The Hessian matrix for β is given by

$$\frac{\partial^2 l_t}{\partial \beta \partial \beta^\top} = -\frac{x_t x_t^\top}{\sigma_t^2} - \frac{1}{2\sigma_t^4}\frac{\partial \sigma_t^2}{\partial \beta}\frac{\partial \sigma_t^2}{\partial \beta^\top}\left(\frac{u_t^2}{\sigma_t^2}\right) -$$

$$\frac{2x_t u_t}{\sigma_t^4}\frac{\partial \sigma_t^2}{\partial \beta} + \left(\frac{u_t^2}{\sigma_t^2} - 1\right)\frac{\partial}{\partial \beta^\top}\left(\frac{1}{2\sigma_t^2}\frac{\partial \sigma_t^2}{\partial \beta}\right) \tag{6.22}$$

Taking into account (6.3) and as the conditional perturbations are uncorrelated, the information matrix is given by

$$I_{\beta\beta^\top} = \frac{1}{T}\sum_t E\left[\frac{x_t x_t^\top}{\sigma_t^2} + \frac{1}{2\sigma_t^4}\frac{\partial \sigma_t^2}{\partial \beta}\frac{\partial \sigma_t^2}{\partial \beta^\top}|I_{t-1}\right] \tag{6.23}$$

Simple calculus then reveals,

$$\frac{\partial \sigma_t^2}{\partial \beta} = \alpha_1 x_{t-1} u_{t-1} \tag{6.24}$$

and, finally the Hessian matrix is consistently estimated by,

$$\hat{I}_{\beta\beta^\top} = \frac{1}{T}\sum_t x_t x_t^\top \left[\frac{1}{\sigma_t^2} + 2\frac{\alpha_1^2}{\sigma_t^4}u_{t-1}^2\right] \tag{6.25}$$

The off-diagonal block of the information matrix is zero (see Engle (1982) for the conditions and the proof of this result). As a consequence, we can separately estimate vectors α and β.

The usual method used in the estimation is a two-stage procedure.

Initially, we find the OLS β estimate

$$\hat{\beta} = (X^\top X)^{-1} X_t^\top y \tag{6.26}$$

where X is the usual design matrix $T \times k$ and y is the $(T \times 1)$ vector of the endogenous variable. We calculate the residuals $\hat{u}_t = y_t - x_t^\top \hat{\beta}$.

Secondly, given these residuals, we find an initial estimate of $\alpha = (\alpha_0, \alpha_1)$, replacing $y_t = u_t$ by $\hat{u}_t$ in the maximum likelihood variance equations (6.6). In this way, we have an approximation of the parameters α and β.

The previous two steps are repeated until the convergence on $\hat{\alpha}$ and $\hat{\beta}$ is obtained.

Additionally, the Hessian matrix must be calculated and conditional expectations taken on it.

If an ARCH regression model is symmetric and regular, the off-diagonal blocks of the information matrix are zero [(see theorem 4, in Engle, 1982)].

Because of the block diagonality of the information matrix, the estimation of (α_0, α_1) and β can be considered separately without loss of asymptotic efficiency.

Alternatively, we can use an asymptotic estimator that is based on the scoring algorithm and which can be found using most least squares computer programs.

A homoscedastic test for this model is follows by a general LM test, where under the restricted model the conditional variance does not depend on the α_1. For a more detailed derivation of this test (see section 4.4, in Gouriéroux , 1997).

6.6 GARCH(p,q) Model

The ARCH model is based on an autoregressive representation of the conditional variance. One may also add a moving average part. The GARCH(p,q) process (Generalised AutoRegressive Conditionally Heteroscedastic) is thus obtained. The model is defined by

$$\begin{aligned} y_t &= u_t \\ u_t &= \epsilon_t \sigma_t, \quad \epsilon_t \sim i.i.d.\ N(0,1) \\ \sigma_t^2 &= \alpha_0 + \sum_{i=1}^{q} \alpha_i u_{t-i}^2 + \sum_{j=1}^{p} \beta_j \sigma_{t-j}^2, \end{aligned} \tag{6.27}$$

where $\alpha_i \geq 0, \beta_i \geq 0, \alpha_0 > 0$ are imposed to ensure that the conditional variance is strictly positive.

The conditional variance can be expressed as

$$\sigma_t^2 = \alpha_0 + \alpha(B)u_t^2 + \beta(B)\sigma_t^2$$

where $\alpha(B) = \alpha_1 B + ... + \alpha_q B^q$ and $\beta(B) = \beta_1 B + ... + \beta_p B^p$ are polynomials in the backshift operator B. If the roots of $1 - \beta(Z)$ lie outside the unit circle, we can rewrite the conditional variance as

$$\sigma_t^2 = \frac{\alpha_0}{1-\beta(1)} + \frac{\alpha(B)}{1-\beta(B)} u_t^2.$$

Hence, this expression reveals that a GARCH(p,q) process can be viewed as an ARCH(∞) with a rational lag structure imposed on the coefficients.

The GARCH(p,q) model may be rewritten in an alternative form, as an ARMA model on squared perturbations.

For this purpose, let us introduce $v_t = u_t^2 - \sigma_t^2$. Replacing σ_t^2 by $u_t^2 - v_t$ in the GARCH representation yields

$$u_t^2 - v_t = \alpha_0 + \sum_{i=1}^{q} \alpha_i u_{t-i}^2 + \sum_{j=1}^{p} \beta_j (u_{t-j}^2 - v_{t-j})$$

that is to say

$$u_t^2 = \alpha_0 + \sum_{i=1}^{\max(p,q)} (\alpha_i + \beta_i) u_{t-i}^2 + v_t - \sum_{j=1}^{p} \beta_j v_{t-j}$$

with $\alpha_i = 0$ for $i > q$ and $\beta_i = 0$ for $i > p$.

It is an ARMA (max(p, q),p) representation for the process u_t^2 but with an error term, which is a white noise process that does not necessarily have a constant variance.

6.6.1 GARCH(1,1) Model

The most used heteroscedastic model in financial time series is a GARCH(1,1), (see Bera and Higgins (1993) for a very complete revision).

This particular model parameterises the conditional variance as

$$\sigma_t^2 = \alpha_0 + \alpha_1 u_{t-1}^2 + \beta_1 \sigma_{t-1}^2 \tag{6.28}$$

Using the law of iterated expectations

$$\begin{aligned} \mathrm{E}(u_t^2) = \mathrm{E}(\mathrm{E}(u_t^2|I_{t-1})) &= \mathrm{E}(\sigma_t^2) = \alpha_0 + \alpha_1 \mathrm{E}(u_{t-1}^2) + \beta_1 \mathrm{E}(\sigma_{t-1}^2) \\ &= \alpha_0 + (\alpha_1 + \beta_1)\mathrm{E}(u_{t-1}^2) \end{aligned} \tag{6.29}$$

Assuming the process began infinitely far in the past with a finite initial variance, the sequence of the variances converge to a constant

$$\sigma^2 = \frac{\alpha_0}{1 - \alpha_1 - \beta_1}, \quad \text{if } \alpha_1 + \beta_1 < 1$$

therefore, the GARCH process is unconditionally homoscedastic. The α_1 parameter indicates the contributions to conditional variance of the most recent news, and the β_1 parameter corresponds to the moving average part in the conditional variance, that is to say, the recent level of volatility. In this model, it could be convenient to define a measure, in the forecasting context, about the impact of present news in the future volatility. To carry out a study of this impact, we calculate the expected volatility k-steps ahead, that is

$$\mathrm{E}(\sigma_{t+k}^2|\sigma_t^2) = (\alpha_1 + \beta_1)^k \sigma_t^2 + \alpha_0 (\sum_{i=0}^{k-1} (\alpha_1 + \beta_1)^i).$$

Therefore, the persistence depends on the $\alpha_1 + \beta_1$ sum. If $\alpha_1 + \beta_1 < 1$, the shocks have a decaying impact on future volatility.

	α_0	α_1	β_1
Model A	0.05	0.85	0.10
estimates	0.0411	0.8572	0.0930
t-ratio	(1.708)	(18.341)	(10.534)
Model B	0.05	0.10	0.85
estimates	0.0653	0.1005	0.8480
t-ratio	1.8913	3.5159	18.439

Table 6.2. Estimates and t-ratios of both models with the same $\alpha_1 + \beta_1$ value

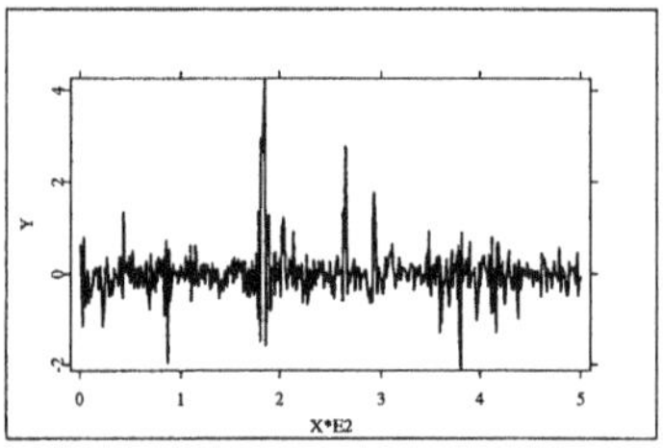

Figure 6.9. Simulated GARCH(1,1) data with $\alpha_1 = 0.85$ and $\beta_1 = 0.10$.

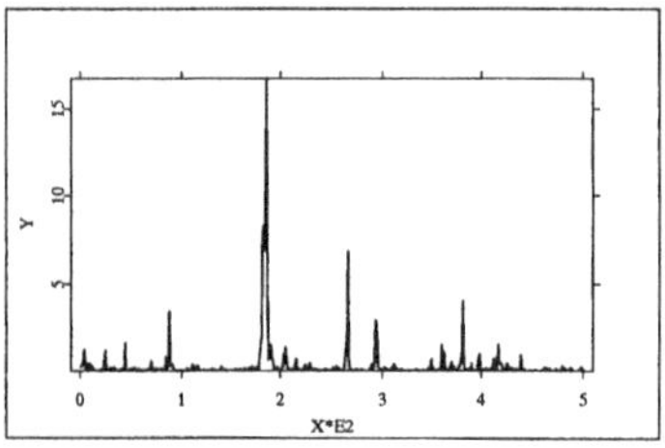

Figure 6.10. Estimated volatility of the simulated GARCH(1,1) data with $\alpha_1 = 0.85$ and $\beta_1 = 0.10$.

Example In this example we generate several time series following a GARCH(1,1) model, with the same value of $\alpha_1 + \beta_1$, but different values of each parameter to reflect the impact of β_1 in the model.

All estimates are significant in both models. The estimated parameters $\hat{\alpha}_1$ and $\hat{\beta}_1$ indicate that the conditional variance is time-varying and strongly persistent

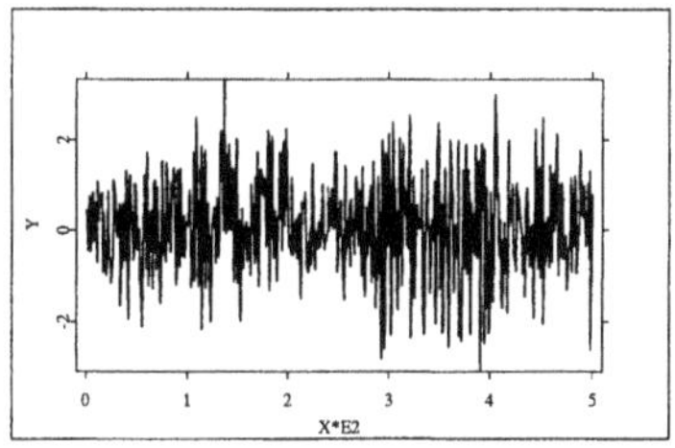

Figure 6.11. Simulated GARCH(1,1) data with $\alpha_1 = 0.10$ and $\beta_1 = 0.85$.

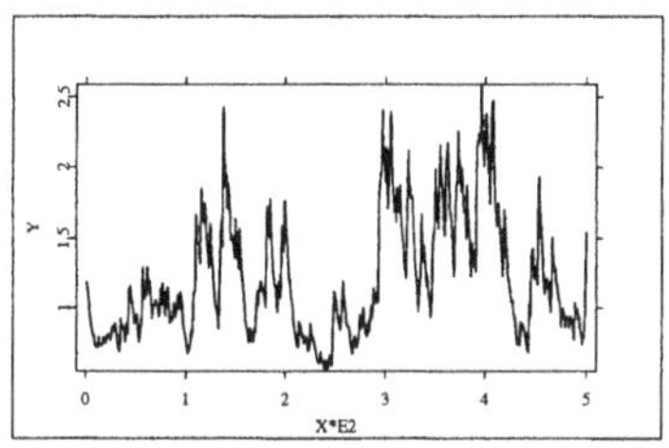

Figure 6.12. Estimated volatility of the simulated GARCH(1,1) data $\alpha_1 = 0.10$ and $\beta_1 = 0.85$.

XEGarch11.xpl

$(\hat{\alpha}_1 + \hat{\beta}_1 \approx 0.95)$. But the conditional variance is very different in both models as we can see in figures 6.10 and 6.12.

6.7 Extensions of ARCH Models

The ARCH model has been extended to allow the conditional variance to be a determinant of the mean, and under the name ARCH-M was introduced by Engle, Lilien and Robins (1987). This is an attractive form in financial applications, since it is natural to suppose that the expected return on an asset is proportional to the expected risk of the asset. The general model used in financial series is an ARMA process in the mean and innovations with time dependent conditional heteroskedasticity are represented by an ARCH process.

Its expression is given by

$$\begin{aligned} y_t &= \mu + \delta\sigma_t^2 + \sum_{i=1}^{p} \phi_i y_{t-i} + \sum_{i=1}^{q} \theta_i u_{t-i} + u_t \\ u_t &= \epsilon_t \sigma_t, \quad \epsilon_t \sim i.i.d.\ N(0,1) \\ \sigma_t^2 &= \alpha_0 + \alpha_1 u_{t-1}^2 + \beta_1 \sigma_{t-1}^2. \end{aligned} \tag{6.30}$$

Note that the greatest complexity introduced in this model comes from evaluating the derivatives of innovations and the conditional variance with respect to the parameters in a non obvious way and consequently, the explicit expression in the first order likelihood conditions are not available in a such simple form. Moreover, the information matrix is not block diagonal between the parameters of the mean and variance, so the estimation procedure must be carried out simultaneously (for more details, see McCurdy and Morgan (1988)).

The conditions in a GARCH process to have a finite unconditional variance are often unsatisfied in a high frequently sampled financial series. Engel and Bollerslev (1986) introduced a new variety of ARCH models, in which $\alpha_1 + \beta_1 = 1$, in the formulation of GARCH(1,1) given in (6.28), named Integrated GARCH model (IGARCH). It is easy to see in this model, that

$$E[\sigma_{t+k}^2 | \sigma_t^2] = \sigma_t^2 + \alpha_0 k$$

very similar to the conditional mean specification of a random walk, however this model is strictly stationary unlike a random walk. Consequently, the IGARCH model has some characteristics of integrated processes. At this stage, could be interesting to go further in understanding the persistence effect. In a few words, if the shocks (imputs) in the conditional variance persist indefinitely, the process is said to be persistent in variance. It is clear from (6.6.1), that the effect of a shock persists faraway but not very much only when $\alpha_1 + \beta_1 < 1$. That is to say, the persistence disappears in terms of the past of the process , i.e. in an unconditional sense(for more details, see section 5.5 in Gouriéroux , 1997). Many empirical researchers in financial markets have found evidence that bad news and good news have different behaviour in the models, revealing an asymmetric behaviour in stock prices, negative surprises give to increase the volatility more than positive surprise, this effect is described as the leverage effect. For this reason,Nelson (1991) proposes a new model, in which the conditional variance is

$$\log \sigma_t^2 = \alpha_0 + \sum_{j=1}^{q} \alpha_j \log \sigma_{t-j}^2 \sum_{j=1}^{p} \beta_j \{\theta \varepsilon_{t-j} + (\gamma |\varepsilon_{t-j}| - (2/\pi)^{1/2})\}$$

where the γ parameter allows this asymmetric effect.

6.8 Two Examples of Spanish Financial Markets

6.8.1 Ibex35 Data

The use of ARCH models, which have enjoyed increasing popularity during the last decade, solves important statistical problems in the estimation of the volatility, as well as in the goodness of these models in forecast intervals. Apart from their simplicity, the main reason for the success of ARCH models is that they take into account non-linearities and changes in the forecasting of future values (a comparative forecasting approach between traditional and bootstrap methodology can be seen in Olave and Miguel (2001)). Moreover, the joint estimation of the mean and the variance can be easily made.

In the following example of financial markets, we will apply different statistical tools in order to fit the best model to the data.

First, we analyse whether there is any type of dependence in the mean of this series. To that end, we analyse graphically the existence of ARMA structure in the mean. The autocorrelation plots obtained by functions `acfplot` and `pacfplot` of y_t reveal no presence of statistically significant autocorrelations or partial autocorrelations, at least in the first lags. In the light of these results (see figures 6.13 and 6.14), we will not fit a usual MA(1), which is very often the model in this financial series, where the "leverage" effect in the mean appears as a moving average effect in the residuals.

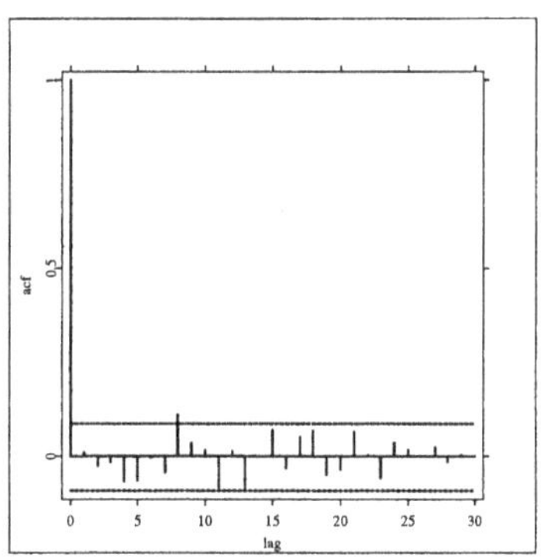

Figure 6.13. ACF for daily returns of Ibex35 data

In a second stage, we would determine the type of heteroscedasticity by means

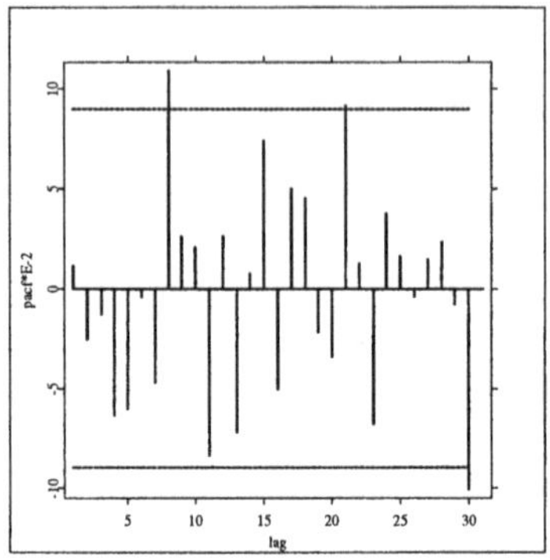

Figure 6.14. PACF for daily returns of Ibex35 data

XEGarch12.xpl

of the squared residuals (in our particular example the squared data). Note that the ARCH model can be seen as an ARMA on squared residuals. Figures 6.15 and 6.16 show a slow decreasing of significative lags up to a high order, indicating the convenience of selecting a GARCH(1,1) model. In this case we can say that the "leverage" effect is present in the conditional variance.

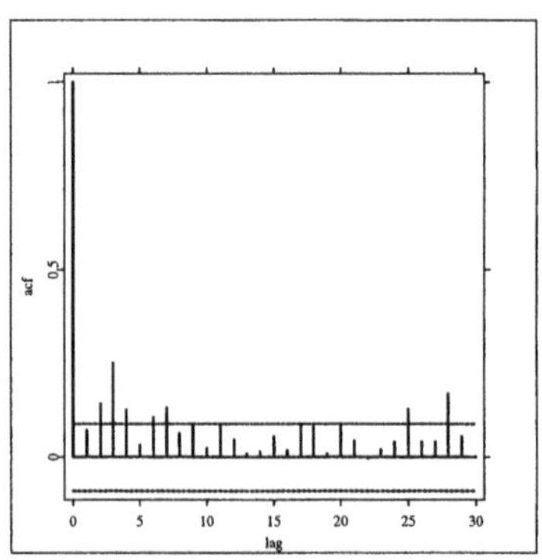

Figure 6.15. ACF for squared daily returns of Ibex35 data

The usual ARCH test confirms us the presence of ARCH effects. So, finally we use the function `garchest` to obtain the estimations of the model. The order

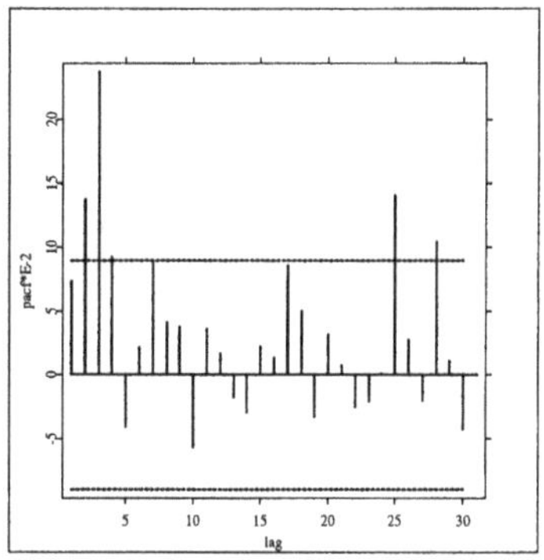

Figure 6.16. PACF for squared daily returns of Ibex35 data

XEGarch13.xpl

of the model fitted to the data depends on the autocorrelation and partial autocorrelation structure.

The results of the GARCH(1,1) model fitted to the data can be seen in table 6.3.

Parameter	estimates	t-ratio
α_0	0.08933	1.657
α_1	0.095954	2.915
β_1	0.85825	17.441

Table 6.3. Estimated parameters and t-ratio values for the Ibex35 data model

XEGarch14.xpl

We can see that the sum of $\hat{\alpha}_1 + \hat{\beta}_1 = 0.954$ and both parameters are significant, indicating a high persistence of volatility for this data in this period of time.

6.8.2 Exchange Rate US Dollar/Spanish Peseta Data (Continued)

This time series only shows a moderate significant autocorrelation coefficient in lag 5, but we do not take it into account by filtering the data. The squared data show a clearly significant pattern in the ACF and PACF functions, meaning again a strong ARCH effect in this time series. In figures 6.17 and 6.18 we see the corresponding autocorrelations of the squared centred time series.

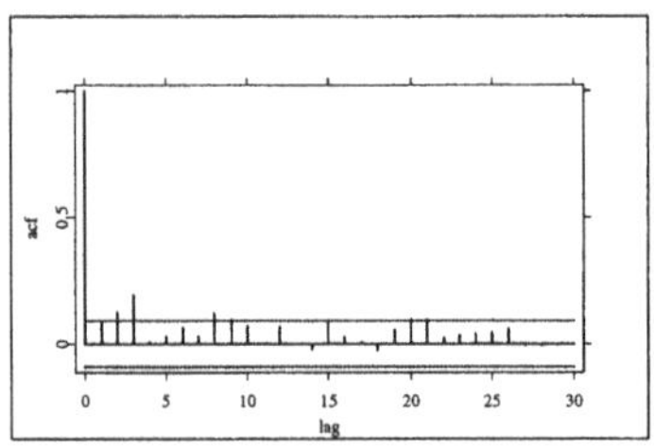

Figure 6.17. ACF for the US Dollar/Spanish peseta squared data

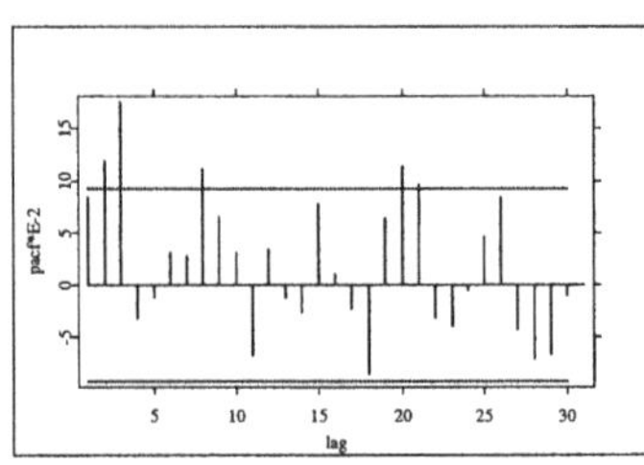

Figure 6.18. PACF for the US Dollar/Spanish peseta squared data

XEGarch15.xpl

The main information given by the autocorrelation plots is confirmed by the LM test of the ARCH effect, and similarly by the "TR2" test, as you can see if you execute XEGarch16.

At the sighting of the results, we opt for fitting a GARCH(1,1) model to the data in XEGarch17.

Figure 6.19 represents the original time series plus the two volatility bands around it. We see that the strong moving average does not allow very high variations in the estimated conditional variance

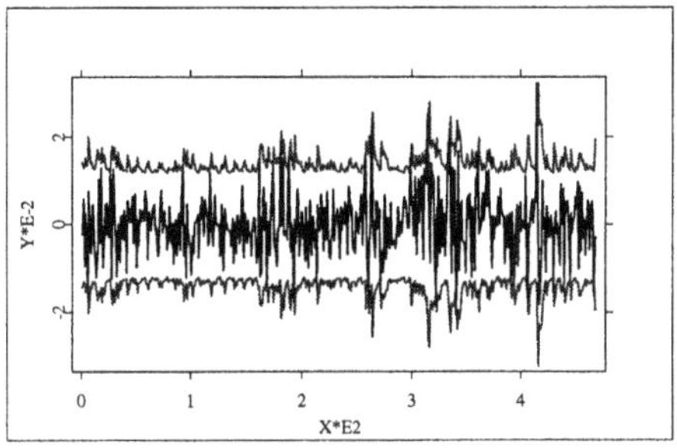

Figure 6.19. Daily rate of return of Spanish peseta/US dollar series and volatility estimated by the GARCH(1,1) model

XEGarch18.xpl

Bibliography

Bera, A.K. and Higgins, M.(1993). ARCH models: properties, estimation and testing. *Journal of Economic Surveys,* **7**: 305-366.

Bernt, E.K., Hall, B.H., Hall, R.E., and Hausman, J.A. (1974). Estimation and inference in nonlinear structural models. *Annals of Economic and Social Measurement,* **3-4**: 653–665.

Breusch, T.S. and Pagan, A.R.(1978). A simple test for heteroskedasticity and random coefficient variation. *Econometrica,* **46**: 1287-1294.

Engle, R.F.(1982). Autoregresive conditional heteroscedasticity with estimates of the variance of U.K. inflation *Econometrica,* **50**: 987–1008.

Engle, R.F., and Bollerslev T. (1986). Modelling the persistence of conditional variance. *Econometric Reviews,* **5**: 1-50.

Engle, R.F., Lilien D.M. and Robins R.P. (1987). Estimating time varying risk premia in the term structure: the ARCH-M model. *Econometrica,* **55**: 391-408.

Gouriéroux,Ch. (1997). *ARCH models and Financial Applications*, Springer.

Härdle, W., Klinke, S., and Müller, M. (2000). *XploRe Learning Guide*, Springer.

Johnston, J. and DiNardo J.(1997). *Econometric Methods*, McGraw-Hill, New York.

Klein, B. (1977). The demand for quality-adjusted cash balances: Price incertity in the US demand for money functions, *Journal of Political Economy,* **85**: 692–715.

Mandelbrot, B. (1963). The variation of certain speculative prices, *Journal of Business,* **36**: 394–419.

McCurdy, T.H. and Morgan, I. (1988). Testing the martingale hypothesis in Deutsche mark futures with models specifying the form of heteroscedasticity. *Journal of Applied Econometrics,* **3**: 187–202.

Mills, T.C. (1993). *The econometric modelling of financial time series*, Cambridge University Press, U.K.

Nelson, D.B. (1991). Conditional heteroskedasticity in asset returns: a new approach. The econometric modelling of finacial time series, , *Econometrica,* **59**: 318-34.

Olave, P. and Miguel, J.(2001). The risk premium and volatility in the Spanish Stock Market. A forecasting approach, *Économie Appliquée,* LIV**4**:63-77.

Silverman, B.(1989). Kernel density estimation, Springer-Verlag.

7 Numerical Optimization Methods in Econometrics

Lenka Čížková

7.1 Introduction

Techniques of numerical mathematics are often used in statistics, e.g., r oot finding and optimization (minimization or maximization) in maximum likelihood, where analytical methods usually cannot be used because closed form solutions do not exist. This chapter explains the principles of some important numerical methods and their usapes.eunet.cy

Sections 7.2 and 7.3 describe methods for solving nonlinear equations and their systems. One can also learn the basic facts about iterative methods and their termination here. Sections 7.4 and 7.5 are dedicated to methods of local unconstrained optimization for uni- and multivariate functions, respectively. Section 7.6 deals with numerical evaluation of function derivatives which is very often used in optimization methods.

7.2 Solving a Nonlinear Equation

This section describes some numerical methods for finding real roots of the one-dimensional nonlinear function $f(x)$, i.e., solving the nonlinear equation $f(x) = 0$. The multidimensional case is treated in Section 7.3.

Our aim is to construct a sequence $\{x_i\}$ of real numbers or real vectors that converges to the root we search for. n-point iterative methods are used, i.e., x_{i+1} is computed as an n-point iteration function depending upon the n previous values:

$$x_{i+1} = f_i(x_i, x_{i-1}, \ldots, x_{i-n+1}) \quad \text{for } i = n-1, n, \ldots.$$

One-point iterative methods with the same function $f_i = f$ for all i are used most often. In commonly used methods, the sequence is known to converge if the initial approximation is close enough to the root.

7.2.1 Termination of Iterative Methods

For any iterative method, one has to specify termination criteria. Natural ones are:

- Function value is close enough to zero, i.e., the procedure stops in i-th step if $|f(x_i)| < \epsilon_f$ for given ϵ_f.
- Successive values of x_i are close to each other (hence, we are approaching the root probably), i.e., stop the procedure if $|x_{i+1} - x_i| < \epsilon_x$ for given ϵ_x.
- The procedure should be stopped if the number of iterations reaches a given maximal number of iterations; in this case, one should inspect the sequences x_i and $f(x_i)$ for eventual loops and possibly start with a different initial approximation.

7.2.2 Newton-Raphson Method for One-dimensional Problems

The Newton-Raphson method (or just Newton method) is one of the most popular methods for root finding. Let x_i be i-th approximation of the root. The function f in the vicinity of the root is approximated by the tangent to the curve $y = f(x)$ at $(x_i, f(x_i))$; the intersection of the tangent with the x-axis defines the next approximation, x_{i+1} (see Fig. 7.1).

The formula describing this procedure is

$$x_{i+1} = x_i - \frac{f(x_i)}{f'(x_i)}. \tag{7.1}$$

This formula can be also derived as follows: start with the Taylor series of f centered in x_i:

$$f(x_i + h) = f(x_i) + hf'(x_i) + O(h^2)$$

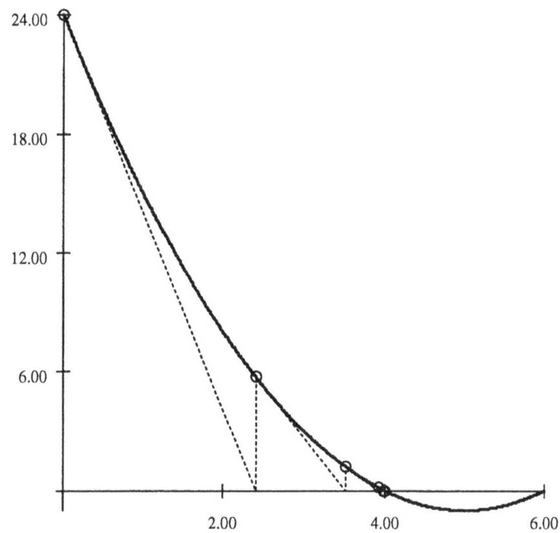

Figure 7.1. Principle of Newton-Raphson Method, `XEGnum01.xpl`

and take $h = x_{i+1} - x_i$; then

$$f(x_{i+1}) = f(x) + hf'(x_i) + O(h^2).$$

Now we neglect the term $O(h^2)$ and setting $f(x_{i+1}) = 0$ implies the formula (7.1).

REMARK 7.1 *The Newton-Raphson method converges quadratically in case of distinct roots. Hence, it is very efficient for functions that have continuous and nonzero derivative in some neighbourhood of a root, having a good initial guess.*

REMARK 7.2 *If $f'(x)$ is not known (or its computation is time-consuming too much), it can be approximated by differences as shown, e.g., in (Rektorys,*

1995); see Section 7.6.1 for details. However, the convergence rate is lower in this case.

7.3 Solving a System of Nonlinear Equations

Here we deal with numerical methods for approximation of real solutions of a system of nonlinear equations $f_j(x) = 0$, $j = 1, \dots, n$, i.e., finding the roots of a vector function $F = (f_1, \dots, f_n)$. Compared with the one-dimensional case, root-finding in the multidimensional case is much more complicated. For example, in one-dimensional case one can relatively easily bracket the roots of a given function (i.e., determine the intervals, in which at least one root of the function lies) but there are no methods for bracketing of roots of general functions in the multidimensional case! Usually we even do not know whether a root (solution of the system) exists and whether it is unique.

7.3.1 Newton-Raphson Method for Nonlinear Systems of Equations

The Newton-Raphson method is very popular also in the multidimensional case (here we have far less methods to choose from). As well as in the one-dimensional case, it is very efficient if one has a good initial approximation.

The formula for the multidimensional Newton-Raphson method can be derived similarly as in Section 7.2.2. Start again with the Taylor series of f_j centered in (vector!) x_i

$$f_j(x_i + h) = f_j(x_i) + \sum_{k=1}^{n} \frac{\partial f_j(x_i)}{\partial x_k} h_k + O(h^2) \text{ for } j = 1, \dots, n.$$

The same can be written in matrix notation as

$$F(x_i + h) = F(x_i) + JF(x_i)h + O(h^2)$$

where $JF(x_i) = (\partial_k f_j)_{j,k=1,\dots,n}$ is the Jacobian of the vector function $F = (f_1, \dots, f_n)$. Neglecting the term $O(h^2)$ and setting $f(x_i + h) = 0$ implies

$$JF(x_i)h = -F(x_i).$$

This system of linear equations can be solved for the vector h. The new iteration is computed as $x_{i+1} = x_i + h$.

REMARK 7.3
Vector *h points in the descent direction of the function* $|F|^2$ *from* x_i *as shown in (Press, Teukolsky, Vetterling, and Flannery, 1992).*

Computing the derivative $f'(x)$**:** *As well as* $f'(x)$ *in one-dimensional case,* $JF(x_i)$ *can be also approximated by differences (see 7.6.3).*

Termination: *For usual termination criteria, see Section 7.2.1.*

7.3.2 Example

We can solve a nonlinear system of equations by Newton-Raphson method using the following quantlet:

```
z = nmnewton(fname, fder, x0{, epsf, epsx,
                              maxiter, checkcond})
```

Its simplest usage is in form

```
z = nmnewton(fname,"",x0),
```

as shown in example `XEGnum02.xpl`, searching for a solution of the following system of two nonlinear equations:

$$\begin{aligned} x^2 - 2y - 2 &= 0 \\ x - y^2 - 1 &= 0 \end{aligned}$$

Starting from initial estimate $x = 0$, $y = 0$, we get an approximation of the solution $x = 0$, $y = -1$:

```
Contents of sol.x
[1,] -1.7807e-15
[2,]          -1

Contents of sol.fval
[1,]  1.5987e-14
[2,]  2.2204e-14

Contents of sol.fderval
```

```
[1,]          0         -2
[2,]          1         -3
```

XEGnum02.xpl

If functions computing the derivatives of `fname` are not available and the precision of the numerical approximation of the derivatives should be influenced, one can input a step `h` for `nmjacobian` (see Section 7.6.3):

```
z = nmnewton(fname,h,x0).
```

Having the functions for computation of the derivatives of `fname` available, one may input their name(s) as a parameter `fder`:

```
z = nmnewton(fname,fder,x0);
```

`fder` should be either a string with a name of the function computing the Jacobian of `fname` or a vector of strings with names of functions that compute gradients of the first, second, ..., n-th component of the vector function `fname`.

This possibility is shown in example XEGnum03.xpl that solves the following system:

$$\begin{aligned}\sin(x+y) &= 0\\ \cos(x-y) &= 0\end{aligned}$$

The Jacobian is computed using the formula

$$J = \begin{pmatrix} \cos(x+y) & \cos(x+y) \\ -\sin(x-y) & \sin(x-y) \end{pmatrix}$$

Setting an initial estimate to $x = 1$, $y = -1$, we get a solution $x = 0.7854$, $y = -0.7854$. This is an approximation of $(\pi/4, -\pi/4)$:

```
Contents of _tmp.x
[1,]    0.7854
[2,]   -0.7854

Contents of _tmp.fval
[1,]          0
```

```
[2,]  6.1257e-17

Contents of _tmp.fderval
[1,]          1         1
[2,]         -1         1
```

XEGnum03.xpl

The parameters `epsf, epsx and maxiter` influence the termination of an iterative process of finding the solution (see Section 7.2.1): the procedure ends if sum of absolute values of `fname` or corrections to `z` are less or equal to `epsf` or `epsx`, respectively; the process is also terminated if the number of iterations exceeds `maxiter`.

In each iteration we multiply by $JF(x_i)^{-1}$, the inverse matrix to the Jacobian of `fname`; the high condition number of the Jacobian can cause a numerical instability of the iterative process. Set the last parameter `checkcond` for checking the stability; A warning message will be produced if the condition number exceeds `checkcond`.

Unfortunately, the Newton-Raphson method can fail if the initial approximation is not close enough to the root. Failing of the method (i.e., convergence is not achieved after any reasonable number of iterations) means either that F has no roots or that the Newton-Raphson steps h were too long in some iterations (as mentioned above, each step of the Newton-Raphson method goes in the descent direction of the function $|F|^2$, having its minimum $|F|^2 = 0$, if a root exists). The latter possible difficulty can be solved using a modification of the Newton-Raphson method described in the Section 7.3.3

REMARK 7.4 *The sensitivity of the Newton-Raphson method applied to problems with oscillating functions is increased by using numerically computed derivatives.*

7.3.3 Modified Newton-Raphson Method for Systems

The Newton-Raphson method can be modified following way to achieve higher numerical stability: In each iteration, compute the Newton-Raphson step h and check whether $|F(x_i + h)| < |F(x_i)|$. If this condition is not valid, we have to reduce step size until having an acceptable h. More or less ingenious ways of reducing step size were introduced (see, e.g., (Press, Teukolsky, Vetterling, and Flannery, 1992)); however, reducing it too much can substantially decrease the convergence rate.

7.3.4 Example

The following quantlet solves a nonlinear system of equations using the modified Newton-Raphson method:

```
z = nmnewtonmod(fname, fder, x0{, epsf, epsx,
                                  maxiter, checkcond})
```

Its usage is the same as for the quantlet `nmnewton`, see Section 7.3.2.

An example `XEGnum04.xpl` shows a problem where using the modified Newton-Raphson method instead of the original one is desirable. The following equation is to be solved:

$$x \cdot \sin\left(\frac{1}{x^2}\right) = 0.$$

Its left-side function $f(x) = x \sin(1/x^2)$ is highly oscillating (see Fig. 7.2).

Setting an initial estimate to $x = 0.01$, the modified Newton-Raphson method gives a solution $x = 0.010002$ in 5 iterations (shown as a filled circle at Fig. 7.2). On the other hand, the original Newton-Raphson method needs 88 iterations to find a much more distant root $x = 0.010702$.

```
Contents of _tmp
[1,] "Newton-Raphson method:"

Contents of x
[1,]  0.010702

Contents of fval
[1,]  4.7088e-05

Contents of _tmp
[1,] "Modified Newton-Raphson method:"
```

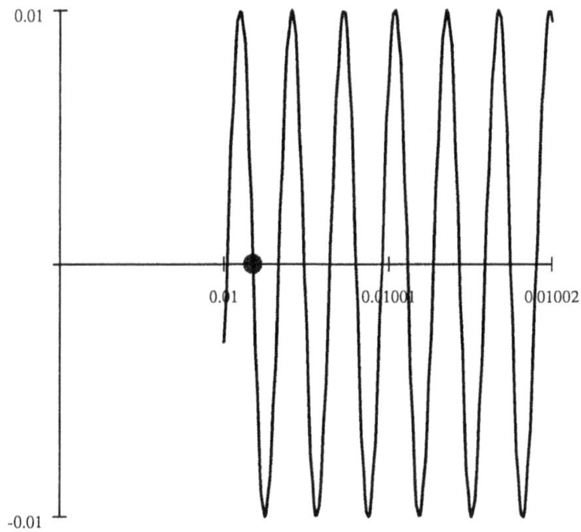

Figure 7.2. Graph of $f(x) = x \sin(1/x^2)$ for $x \in [0.01, 0.01002]$. The filled circle shows the solution found by the modified Newton-Raphson method, XEGnum04.xpl

```
Contents of x
[1,]  0.010002

Contents of fval
[1,] -1.9808e-05
```

XEGnum04.xpl

7.4 Minimization of a Function: One-dimensional Case

Some numerical methods for finding a local minimum of a given one-dimensional function $f(x)$ will be described in this section.

The same methods can be used for finding a maximum as well because the function $f(x)$ has its (local, global) maximum at x_0 if and only if $-f(x)$ has its (local, global) minimum at x_0.

7.4.1 Minimum Bracketing

Before starting any optimum-searching procedure, it is advisable to bracket the minimum (or maximum); otherwise one cannot be sure that there *exists* any solution to the given optimization problem.

A minimum (or maximum) is bracketed by three points (a, b, c), if $a < b < c$ and $f(b)$ is less (or greater in case of maximum) than both $f(a)$ and $f(c)$. If this condition holds and the function $f(x)$ is continuous in the interval (a, c), then $f(x)$ has a minimum for some x, $a < x < c$. A very simple iterative minimum bracketing procedure follows:

Start from any initial point. Moving a step in the downhill direction, one gets a new point in each iteration. From the third iteration on, store the last three points. New one in each iteration substitutes the oldest one in the triplet. Take larger and larger steps (the new step being computed by simple multiplying the previous one by a constant factor or obtained as a result of a parabolic interpolation applied on a previous triplet of points, see Section 7.4.3) until the downhill trend stops and one gets the last point, where the function value is *greater* than in the previous one.

An analogous procedure can be used for maximum bracketing; alternatively, one can use the minimum bracketing procedure for $-f(x)$.

7.4.2 Example

The following quantlet can be used for bracketing of a minimum of a scalar function:

```
{a,b,c,fa,fb,fc} = nmbracket(fname {,a0,b0})
```

`fname` has to be a string with a name of the function whose minimum should be bracketed. If one has some idea about the location of the minimum, the input parameters `a0` and `b0` can be set to start the bracketing from `a0` in the direction to `b0` or vice versa, depending on the downhill direction. Otherwise one can use the simplest form

```
{a,b,c,fa,fb,fc} = nmbracket(fname)
```

starting the bracketing with the defaults values `a0` $= 0$ and `b0` $= 1$.

An example XEGnum05.xpl gives the following brackets for function $f(x) = x^2 \cdot \cos\left(\frac{x+3\pi}{4}\right)$:

```
Contents of bracket.a
[1,]    2.618
Contents of bracket.b
[1,]   5.2361
Contents of bracket.c
[1,]   9.4721

Contents of bracket.fa
[1,]  -6.7955
Contents of bracket.fb
[1,]  -23.743
Contents of bracket.fc
[1,]   1.0622
```

XEGnum05.xpl

Fig. 7.3 shows a graph of $f(x)$ and the bracketing points shown as stars.

7.4.3 Parabolic Interpolation

The bracketing procedure described in Section 7.4.1 involves a parabolic interpolation. Given a triplet of points and the respective functional values,

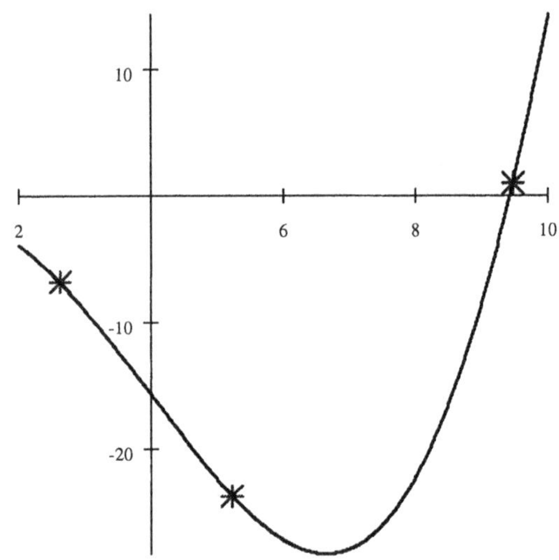

Figure 7.3. Graph of $f(x) = x^2 \cdot \cos\left(\frac{x+3\pi}{4}\right)$ with stars representing the bracketing points, XEGnum05.xpl

parabolic interpolation fits a parabola through these points and finds its extremum (i.e., its minimum or maximum). Using parabolic interpolation can speed up the optimizing procedure if the function is approximately parabolic near the minimum or maximum.

Let us denote the three points a, b, c and the respective function values $f(a), f(b), f(c)$. We are looking for point x minimizing (or maximizing) $f(x)$. Providing the parabola can be described as

$$f(x) = \alpha_2 x^2 + \alpha_1 x + \alpha_0,$$

we can find the values of α_i, $i = 0, 1, 2$ by solving the following system:

$$
\begin{aligned}
f(a) &= \alpha_2 a^2 + \alpha_1 a + \alpha_0, \\
f(b) &= \alpha_2 b^2 + \alpha_1 b + \alpha_0, \\
f(c) &= \alpha_2 c^2 + \alpha_1 c + \alpha_0.
\end{aligned}
$$

Now we want to find the point x, at which the parabola has its extremum. Hence, the condition $f'(x) = 0$ should be valid, i.e., $2\alpha_2 x + \alpha_1 = 0$. From here we have

$$x = \frac{-\alpha_1}{2\alpha_2}$$

and after substituting for alphas

$$x = \frac{1}{2}\frac{(b^2 - a^2)\{f(b) - f(c)\} - (b^2 - c^2)\{f(b) - f(a)\}}{(b - a)\{f(b) - f(c)\} - (b - c)\{f(b) - f(a)\}}$$

or, alternatively

$$x = b - \frac{1}{2}\frac{(b - a)^2\{f(b) - f(c)\} - (b - c)^2\{f(b) - f(a)\}}{(b - a)\{f(b) - f(c)\} - (b - c)\{f(b) - f(a)\}}.$$

REMARK 7.5

Minimum or maximum? *As shown by the formulas above, the parabolic interpolation finds the only extremum of the parabola, not distinguishing between a minimum and a maximum. If one needs to know whether a minimum or a maximum was found, the signum of α_2 can be used to determine: if it is positive, the extremum is a minimum; if it is negative, one has a maximum.*

Can parabolic interpolation fail? *The parabolic interpolation fails if the denumerator of the formula for x is equal to zero. This happens if and only if the three given points $[a, f(a)], [b, f(b)], [c, f(c)]$ are linear dependent, i.e., they are on the same line. In this case, the information for parabolic interpolation is insufficient.*

7.4.4 Example

One can use the following quantlet to find the extremum of a parabola determined by three points.

```
x = nmparabint(a,b,c,fa,fb,fc)
```

The input parameters include the abscissas `a,b and c` as well as the respective function values `fa, fb and fc`. Using `nmparabint`, one can execute the inverse parabolic interpolation for more parabolas at the same time. In this case all the input parameters will be vectors whose i-th components refer to the i-th parabola. `nmparabint` returns INF if the three points are linear dependent (i.e., on the same line).

An example `XEGnum06.xpl` uses the parabolic interpolation through the points $(-1, 4)$, $(0, 2)$ and $(3, 8)$ to find the parabola extremum at $x = 0.5$:

```
Contents of res
[1,]       0.5
```

`XEGnum06.xpl`

Fig. 7.4 shows the parabola $f(x) = x^2 - x + 2$ from which the input points (represented by stars) were taken. The minimum found by `nmparabint.xpl` is represented by a triangle.

7.4.5 Golden Section Search

The principle of the golden section search method is very simple and can be used even for functions without continuous second (or even first) derivative–in such case the parabolic interpolation used in Brent's method (see Sections 7.4.7 and 7.4.9) cannot provide any additional information.

For golden section search, one has to bracket the minimum by some triplet $a < b < c$ first (see Section 7.4.1 for details on minimum bracketing). Now, let us choose a new point x in the bracketing interval, for example between a and b ($a < x < b < c$), and evaluate $f(x)$. The new point x substitutes one of the original points in bracketing triplet: if $f(x) > f(b)$, then (x, b, c) is the new triplet (with $f(b)$ less then both $f(x)$ and $f(c)$); if $f(x) < f(b)$, then (a, x, b) is the new triplet (with $f(x) < f(b) < f(a)$). The minimum function value we have found until now is at the middle point of the new triplet in both cases. Continue this procedure until the size of the bracketing interval (i.e., the distance of its outer points) is small enough.

It can be shown divides the interval (a, c) in the ratio $g : (1 - g)$ or, vice versa, $(1 - g) : g$, with $g = \frac{3-\sqrt{5}}{2} \approx 0.38$. This g is the so called *golden section.*

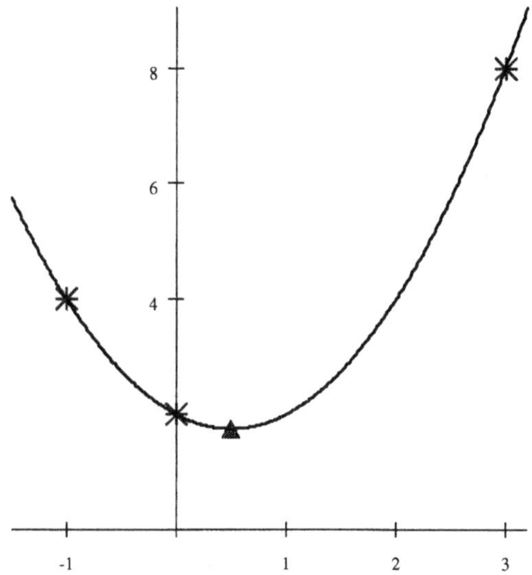

Figure 7.4. Graph of $f(x) = x^2 - x + 2$ with an interpolated minimum shown as a triangle, XEGnum06.xpl

7.4.6 Example

The following quantlet implements the golden section search method described above:

```
min = nmgolden(fname{,a,b,c,xtol})
```

If used in the very basic form

```
min = nmgolden(fname),
```

`fname` being a string with a name of function to be minimized, `nmgolden` calls the quantlet `nmbracket` to bracket a minimum of `fname`. Use

```
min = nmgolden(fname,a,b,c)
```

if a bracketing triplet a, b, c is known, i.e., the values $a < b < c$ whose function values satisfy the conditions $f(b) < f(a)$ and $f(b) < f(c)$. The optional parameter `xtol` sets the fractional presicion of the minimum; the iterative process stops after achieving this value.

An example `XEGnum07.xpl` uses a golden section search with a function $\sin(x)$ given a bracketing triplet $\{\pi, 1.3\pi, 2\pi\}$ and finds its minimum $\sin(3/2\ \pi) = -1$:

```
Contents of res.xmin
[1,]   4.7124

Contents of res.fmin
[1,]        -1
```

`XEGnum07.xpl`

Fig. 7.5 depicts a graph of $\sin(x)$ with bracketing triplet represented by stars and the minimum shown as a triangle.

7.4.7 Brent's Method

The golden section search method described in Section 7.4.5 can be easily used with any continuous function; however, its convergence is only linear. If the function has at least a continuous second derivative, Brent's method finds the minimum quicker (its convergence is superlinear).

Before starting the procedure, one should bracket the minimum (see section 7.4.1 for more details). In each iteration, Brent's method reduces the bracketing interval and updates six stored points: outer points of bracketing interval a, b, three points (x_{min_i}, $i = 1, 2, 3$) with the three least values found so far and the most recently evaluated point x_{new}. The method combines parabolic interpolation through x_{min_i} (as long as the process is convergent and does not leave the bracketing interval) with golden section search.

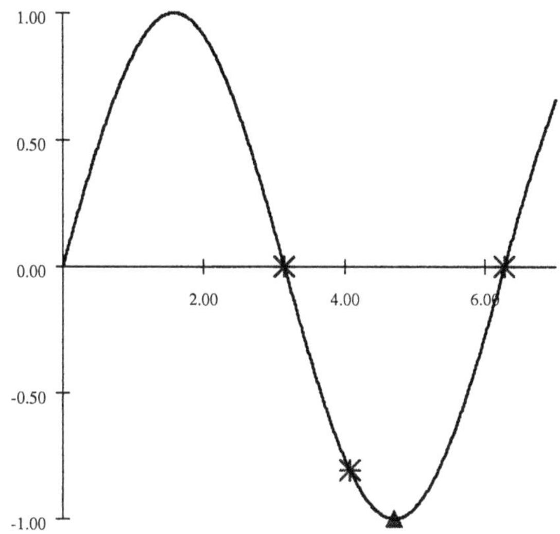

Figure 7.5. Graph of $f(x) = \sin(x)$ with a minimum shown as a triangle, XEGnum07.xpl

7.4.8 Example

The following quantlet implements Brent's method for minimization of a scalar function:

```
min = nmbrent(fname{,a,b,c,xtol})
```

It is used the same way as `nmgolden` described in Section 7.4.6.

An example XEGnum07b.xpl uses the Brent's method for a function $\sin(x)$ given a bracketing triplet $\{0, 1.1\pi, 2\pi\}$ and finds its minimum $\sin(3/2\,\pi) = -1$:

```
Contents of res.xmin
```

```
[1,]    4.7124

Contents of res.fmin
[1,]         -1
```

XEGnum07b.xpl

Fig. 7.6 depicts a graph of sin(x) with bracketing triplet represented by stars and the minimum shown as a triangle.

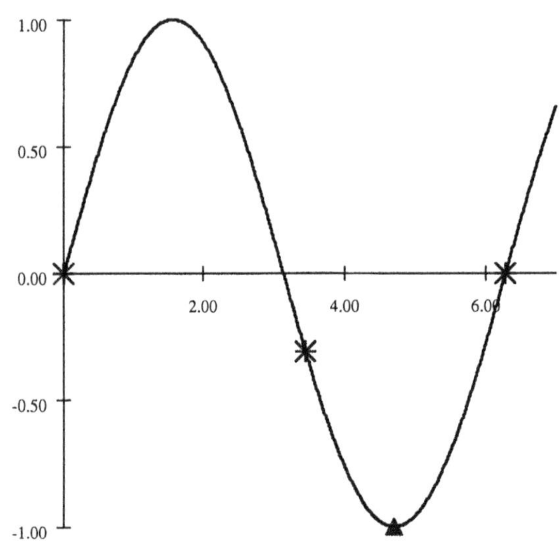

Figure 7.6. Graph of $f(x) = \sin(x)$ with a minimum shown as a triangle, XEGnum07b.xpl

7.4.9 Brent's Method Using First Derivative of a Function

This method is based on Brent's method from the Section 7.4.7. If it is possible to calculate the first derivative of the function f to be minimized, one can utilize this additional information for minimization. However, it is not very practical to simply search for roots of $f'(x)$: first, one cannot easily distinguish maxima and minima; second, the downhill search in the root-finding method can lead out of the bracketing interval! Hence, the derivative only helps us to choose a new point within the bracket in each iteration: the sign of the derivative in the middle point b of the bracketing triplet indicates whether the new trial point x_{new} should be taken from the interval (a, b) or (b, c). The point x_{new} is computed by extrapolating $f'(b)$ and $f'(x_{min_2})$ to zero (using secant method, i.e., linear interpolation) or by bisection, if extrapolation takes us out of the bracketing interval.

7.4.10 Example

The quantlet

```
min = nmbrentder(fname{,fder,a,b,c,xtol})
```

finds a minimum of a given scalar function using Brent's method with first derivative. Its usage is very similar to `nmgolden`; see Section 7.4.6 for description of the input parameters `a,b,c and xtol`. In the simplest form

```
min = nmbrentder(fname)
```

without the derivative of `fname` the quantlet calls `nmgraddiff` to compute the derivative numerically. One can influence the precision of the numerical approximation of the derivative by setting the step h for quantlet `nmgraddiff`, see Section 7.6.1:

```
min = nmbrentder(fname,h)
```

If a function computing the first derivative of `fname` is available, one can input its name as a string `fder`:

```
min = nmbrentder(fname,fder),
```

as in example XEGnum07c.xpl searching for a local minimum of $f(x) = \sin(x)$. As a result, one gets Fig. 7.7 and the following approximation of the minimum at $x = -\pi/2$:

```
Contents of res.xmin
[1,]  -1.5708

Contents of res.fmin
[1,]       -1
```

XEGnum07c.xpl

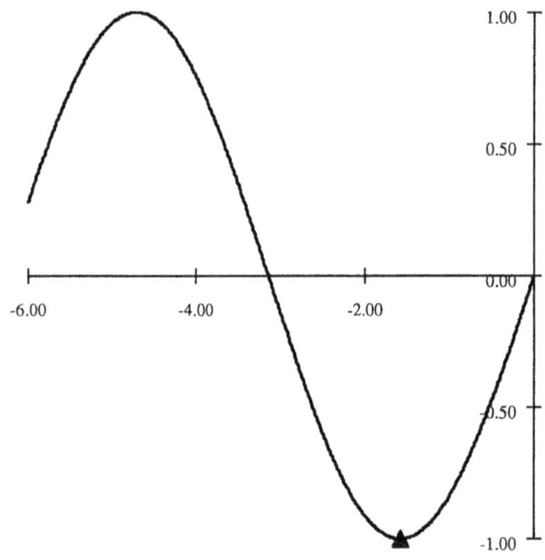

Figure 7.7. Graph of $f(x) = \sin(x)$ with a minimum shown as a triangle, XEGnum07c.xpl

7.5 Minimization of a Function: Multidimensional Case

Several numerical methods for the multidimensional minimization will be described in this section. Many of such algorithms except the Nelder & Mead's method (see Section 7.5.1) use a one-dimensional minimization method in their individual iterations.

REMARK 7.6 *Analogously to root-finding, we are generally not able to bracket a minimum in the multidimensional case.*

7.5.1 Nelder and Mead's Downhill Simplex Method (Amoeba)

The downhill simplex method is a very simple iterative multidimensional ($n \approx 20$) minimization method, not requiring evaluation nor existence of derivatives. On the other hand, it requires many function evaluations. However, it can be useful when f is nonsmooth or when its derivatives are impossible to find.

The simplex method attempts to enclose the minimum inside a simplex (i.e., an n-dimensional convex volume defined by $n+1$ linearly independent points—vertices). Starting from an initial simplex, the algorithm inspects the function values in vertices and constructs a new simplex using operations of reflection, expansion or contraction, so that the final simplex is small enough to contain the minimum with the desired accuracy.

7.5.2 Example

The quantlet

```
x = nelmin(x0,f,maxiter{,eps,step})
```

finds a minimum of a given function using Nelder and Mead's simplex method. The method can be started from more initial points at the same time; input all the initial points as columns of input matrix `x0`. The string parameter `f` contains a name of the minimized function. It is necessary to specify a maximal number of iterations `maxiter`. The optional parameter `eps` sets the termination criterium of the iterative process (it is compared with the variance of function values at vortices, hence a smaller value should be set to get the same precision as by e.g., conjugate gradients described in Section 7.5.3). The parameter `step` sets the length of an initial simplex. The output parameter `x` has three components: columns of `x.minimum` contain the minima of `f` found in the search started from the respective initial points, `x.iter` is the number of executed iterations and `x.converged` is equal to 1 if the process converged for all initial points, otherwise it is 0.

Example `XEGnum22.xpl` implements minimization of $f(x) = \sum_{i=1}^{n} x_i^2$ using the downhill simplex method. Starting from an initial estimate $(28, -35, 13, -17)^T$, amoeba needs 410 iterations to find the following approximation of the minimum in $(0, 0, 0, 0)^T$:

```
Contents of minim.minimum
[1,]  8.6837e-19
[2,]  8.9511e-19
[3,]  1.6666e-18
[4,]  2.0878e-18

Contents of minim.iter
[1,]      410

Contents of minim.converged
[1,]        1
```

`XEGnum22.xpl`

7.5.3 Conjugate Gradient Methods

A whole family of conjugate gradient methods exists. Their common principle as well as some details of Fletcher-Reeves algorithm and its modification by Polak and Ribiere are described in this section. As the name of methods suggests, it is necessary to compute the gradient of function f whose minimum is to be found. Gradient information can be incorporated into the minimization procedure in various ways. The common principle of all conjugate gradient method is following:

Start at an initial point x_0. In each iteration, compute x_{i+1} as a point minimizing the function f along a new direction, derived in some way from the local gradient. The way of choosing a new direction distinguishes the various conjugate gradients methods. For example, very simple *method of steepest descent* searches along the line from x_i in the direction of the local (downhill) gradient $-\operatorname{grad} f(x_i)$, i.e., computes the new iteration as $x_{i+1} = x_i - \lambda \operatorname{grad} f(x_i)$, where λ minimizes the restricted function $f(x_i + \lambda \operatorname{grad} f(x_i))$. However, this method is not very efficient (each step has to go in perpendicular direction to the previous one, which is usually not a direction leading to the minimum). Hence, we would like to choose a new direction based on the negative local gradient direction but at the same time *conjugated*, i.e., Q-orthogonal to the previous direction(s).

In the original Fletcher-Reeves version of conjugate gradient algorithm, the new direction in all steps is taken as a linear combination of the current gradient and the previous direction, $h_{i+1} = -\operatorname{grad} f(x_{i+1}) + w_i h_i$, with the factor w_i calculated from the ratio of the magnitudes of the current and previous gradients:

$$w_i = \frac{\operatorname{grad} f(x_{i+1})^T \operatorname{grad} f(x_{i+1}))}{\operatorname{grad} f(x_i)^T \operatorname{grad} f(x_i)}.$$

Polak and Ribiere proposed to use the factor w_i in the form

$$w_i = \frac{(\operatorname{grad} f(x_{i+1}) - \operatorname{grad} f(x_i))^T \operatorname{grad} f(x_{i+1})}{\operatorname{grad} f(x_i)^T \operatorname{grad} f(x_i)}.$$

There is no difference between these two versions on an exactly quadratic hypersurface; otherwise, the latter version converges faster than the former one.

7.5.4 Examples

Fig. 7.8 shows a principle of conjugate gradient method. It was produced by example `XEGnum08.xpl` that minimizes the function $f(x) = x^2 + 3(y-1)^4$ starting from point $(1,2)^T$. The exact solution $(0,1)^T$ is approximated in 10 iterations as follows:

```
Contents of minim.xmin
[1,]  7.0446e-12
[2,]           1
```

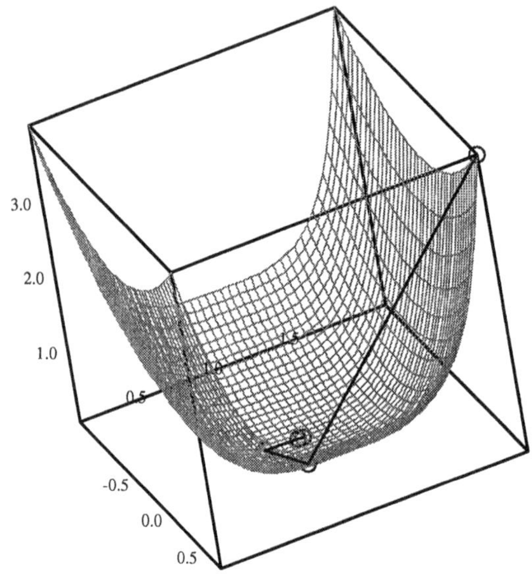

Figure 7.8. Graph of $f(x) = x^2 + 3(y-1)^4$; red line shows the progress of conjugate gradient method, XEGnum08.xpl

```
Contents of minim.fmin
[1,]  4.9822e-23

Contents of minim.iter
[1,]        10
```

XEGnum08.xpl

The example XEGnum08.xpl uses the quantlet

```
min = nmcongrad(fname,x0{,fder,linmin,ftol,maxiter})
```

implementing the Polak and Ribiere version of conjugate gradient method. One can call this function with only two parameters—string `fname` containing the name of a function to be minimized and a vector `x0` with the initial estimate of the minimum location:

```
min = nmcongrad(fname,x0)
```

In this case, the gradient of `fname` will be computed numerically using the quantlet `nmgraddiff`. The precision of the gradient computation can be influenced by setting the step `h` of `nmgraddiff`—call `nmcongrad` in the form

```
min = nmcongrad(fname,x0,h).
```

If a function computing the derivatives (gradient) of `fname` is available, one can input its name as a string `fder` and call the quantlet `nmcongrad` in the form

```
min = nmcongrad(fname,x0,fder).
```

Another example illustrating the usage of `nmcongrad` is implemented in `XEGnum09.xpl`. The function to be minimized is defined as $f(x) = \sum_{i=1}^{n} x_i^2$. Starting from an initial estimate $(28, -35, 13, -17)^T$, `nmcongrad` needs four iterations to find a following approximation of the minimum in $(0, 0, 0, 0)^T$:

```
Contents of minim.xmin
[1,] -3.1788e-18
[2,] -4.426e-18
[3,] -4.1159e-18
[4,]  7.2989e-19

Contents of minim.fmin
[1,]  4.7167e-35

Contents of minim.iter
[1,]        4
```

`XEGnum09.xpl`

The conjugate gradient method involves a line minimization (see Section 7.5.7 for more details); the quantlet `nmlinminder` is used by default. One can specify the name of another line minimization function in the parameter `linmin`. Line minimum should be computed as precisely as possible, otherwise the convergence of the conjugate gradient method is slower; hence, the quantlet `nmlinminappr` is not suitable for line minimization in context of `nmcongrad`.

The termination of the iterative process can be influenced by the parameters `ftol` and `maxiter`, setting the tolerance limit for the function values and maximal number of iterations, respectively.

7.5.5 Quasi-Newton Methods

Recall the steepest descent method mentioned in Section 7.5.3. Its straightforward idea is to choose the search direction always in the direction of the negative gradient $-\operatorname{grad} f(x_i)$ (steepest descent direction). Another simple idea is based on Newton-Raphson method for solving systems of equations used to find a stationary point of the function f (i.e., a root of f's gradient); this yields

$$x_{i+1} = x_i - H^{-1} \operatorname{grad} f(x_i),$$

where $H = Hf(x_i)$ denotes the Hessian matrix of f at x_i. The Newton-Raphson algorithm converges quadratically but, unfortunately, it is not globally convergent. In addition, for x_i not close enough to a minimum, H does not need to be positive definite. In such cases, the Newton-Raphson method is not guaranteed to work. An evaluation of H can be difficult or time-demanding as well. Consequently, the so-called quasi-Newton methods producing a sequence of matrices H_i approximating the Hessian matrix were developed. To prevent a possible overshooting of the minimum, the same backtracking strategy as in the modified Newton-Raphson method (see Section 7.3.3) is used.

Together with conjugate gradient methods, the family of quasi-Newton methods (called also variable metric methods) belongs to the class of conjugate directions methods. The search direction in i-th step is computed according to the rule

$$d_i = -A_i \operatorname{grad} f(x_i),$$

where A_i is a symmetric positive definite matrix (usually $A_1 = I$, the unit matrix) approximating H^{-1}. One question remains open: given A_i, what A_{i+1} should we use in the next iteration? Let us return to Newton's method that gave us $x - x_i = -H^{-1} \operatorname{grad} f(x_i)$; taking the left-hand side step with a quadratic function f would take us to the exact minimum. The same equation for x_{i+1} reads $x - x_{i+1} = -H^{-1} \operatorname{grad} f(x_{i+1})$. Subtracting these two equations gives

$$x_{i+1} - x_i = H^{-1}(\operatorname{grad} f_{i+1} - \operatorname{grad} f_i),$$

where $\operatorname{grad} f_i$, $\operatorname{grad} f_{i+1}$ stand for $\operatorname{grad} f(x_i)$ and $\operatorname{grad} f(x_{i+1})$, respectively. Hence, a reasonable idea is to take a new approximation A_i satisfying

$$x_{i+1} - x_i = A_{i+1}(\operatorname{grad} f_{i+1} - \operatorname{grad} f_i)$$

(the quasi-Newton condition). Updating formulas for A_i, usually of the form $A_{i+1} = A_i + \text{correction}$, differentiate various quasi-Newton methods. The most commonly used is the Broyden-Fletcher-Goldfarb-Shanno method (BFGS) that uses the following update:

$$A_{i+1} = A_i + \frac{s_i s_i^T}{s_i^T v_i} - \frac{A_i v_i v_i^T A_i}{v_i^T A_i v_i} + (v_i^T A_i v_i) \cdot u_i u_i^T$$

with

$$u_i = \frac{s_i}{s_i^T v_i} - \frac{A_i v_i}{v_i^T A_i v_i},$$

where $s_i = x_{i+1} - x_i$ and $v_i = \operatorname{grad} f_{i+1} - \operatorname{grad} f_i$. It can be easily shown that if A_i is a symmetric positive definite matrix, the new matrix A_{i+1} is also symmetric positive definite and satisfies the quasi-Newton condition.

7.5.6 Examples

Fig. 7.9 shows a principle of BFGS method. It was produced by example XEGnum10.xpl that minimizes function $f(x) = x^2 + 3(y-1)^4$ starting from point $(1, 2)$. The exact solution $(0, 1)$ is approximated in 25 iterations as follows:

```
Contents of minim.xmin
[1,]  2.1573e-21
[2,]  0.99967

Contents of minim.fmin
[1,]  3.6672e-14

Contents of minim.iter
[1,]        25
```

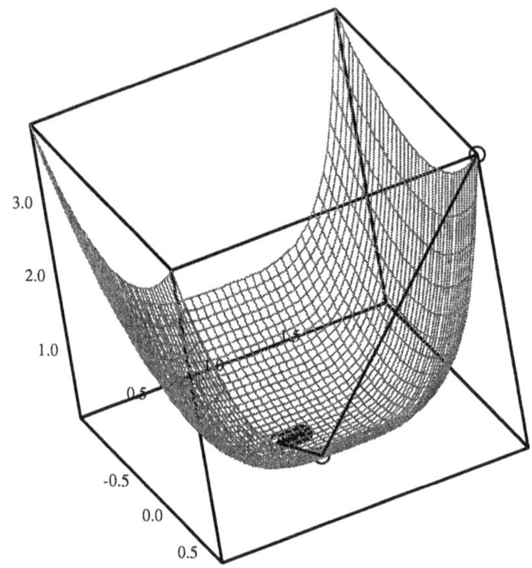

Figure 7.9. Graph of $f(x) = x^2 + 3(y-1)^4$; red line shows the progress of BFGS method, `XEGnum10.xpl`

`XEGnum10.xpl`

The following quantlet

```
min = nmBFGS(fname,x0{,fder,linmin,ftol,gtol,maxiter})
```

is used to find a minimum of a given function using Broyden-Fletcher-Goldfarb-Shanno method. Similarly to `nmcongrad`, this quantlet can be called with only two parameters—string `fname` containing the name of a function to be minimized and a vector `x0` with the initial estimate of the minimum location:

```
min = nmBFGS(fname,x0)
```

The gradient of `fname` will be computed numerically using the quantlet `nmgraddiff` (see Section 7.6.1) in this case. The precision of this computation can be influenced by setting the step `h` of `nmgraddiff`—call `nmBFGS` in the form

```
min = nmBFGS(fname,x0,h).
```

If a function computing the derivatives (gradient) of `fname` is available, one can call the quantlet `nmBFGS` with its name as an input string `fder`:

```
min = nmcongrad(fname,x0,fder).
```

An example `XEGnum11.xpl` calls the quantlet `nmBFGS` to minimize $f(x) = \sum_{i=1}^{n} x_i^2$ (see Section 7.5.3 for minimization of the same function by conjugate gradient method). Starting from an initial estimate $(28, -35, 13, -17)^T$, `nmBFGS` finds the following approximation of the minimum $(0, 0, 0, 0)^T$ in two iterations:

```
Contents of minim.xmin
[1,]  1.0756e-08
[2,]  1.4977e-08
[3,]  1.3926e-08
[4,] -2.47e-09

Contents of minim.fmin
[1,]  5.4004e-16

Contents of minim.iter
[1,]        2
```

`XEGnum11.xpl`

The BFGS method also involves a line minimization; the quantlet `nmlinminappr` is used by default, because it gives a result quicker then `nmlinmin` or `nmlinminder` and its precision is sufficient in context of `nmBFGS`. The name of another line minimization function can be specified in the parameter `linmin`.

The termination of the iterative process can be influenced by the parameters `ftol`, `gtol` and `maxiter`, setting the tolerance limit for the convergence of function values, function gradients and maximal number of iterations, respectively.

7.5.7 Line Minimization

As mentioned already at the beginning of the Section 7.5, multidimensional optimization routines call often some of the one-dimensional methods for finding a minimum on a line going through the last trial point in a given direction. The easy way how to include these one-dimensional optimizers into a multi-dimensional procedure is to minimize the function f restricted to the given line.

In other words, minimizing f on the line $x_i + \lambda g_i$ is equivalent to the one-dimensional minimization of a newly defined (one-dimensional, of course) function $f_{1D}(t) = f(x_i + t \cdot g_i)$ using any one-dimensional minimization method.

REMARK 7.7 *If a chosen one-dimensional method needs also the derivative of a function, this has to be a derivative in the direction of the line of minimization. It can be computed using the formula* $f'_g(x) = g^T \operatorname{grad} f(x)$*; of course, one can also compute the (numerical, if necessary) derivative of the restricted function* f_{1D}.

REMARK 7.8 *Note that there is a substantial difference between the gradient and a derivative in the direction of a given line. For example, gradient and a derivative in the direction* $d = (1, -1)$ *of a function* $f(x, y) = x^2 + y^3$ *at* $(1, 1)$ *can be computed using* `XEGnum17.xpl`*, with the following output:*

```
Contents of grad
[1,]        2
[2,]        3

Contents of fdert
[1,]       -1
```

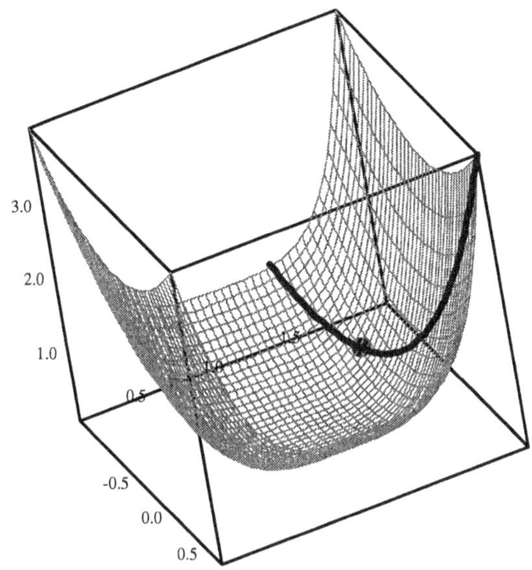

Figure 7.10. Graph of $f(x) = x^2 + 3(y-1)^4$; a line $(1,2) + t \cdot (3,1)$ is shown in red with a big point representing the line minimum, XEGnum12.xpl

7.5.8 Examples

The quantlet

```
lmin = nmlinmin(fname,fder,x0,direc)
```

serves to find a minimum of a given function along the direction `direc` from the point `x0` not using derivatives of `fname`. The input string `fname` contains a name of a function to be minimized; both `x0` and `direc` are vectors. The second parameter `fder` is a dummy necessary for the compatibility with `nmlinminder`; it can be set to any value.

Example XEGnum12.xpl illustrates a line minimization using the quantlet `nmlinmin`. A function $f(x) = x^2+3(y-1)^4$ is minimized on a line $(1,2)+t\cdot(3,1)$ and a graph of the function is produced (see Fig. 7.10).

```
Contents of minim.xlmin
[1,] -0.33928
[2,]    1.5536

Contents of minim.flmin
[1,]  0.39683

Contents of minim.moved
[1,]  -1.3393
[2,] -0.44643
```

XEGnum12.xpl

The output parameter `lmin` consists of the abscissa `lmin.xlmin` of the minimum of `fname` on a line $x0 + span\{direc\}$, `lmin.flmin` is a minimum function value $flmin = f(xlmin)$ and `lmin.moved` gives the vector displacement during the minimization: $moved = xlmin - x0$.

The following quantlet is similar to `nmlinmin` but the implemented method involves the evaluation of the derivatives of `fname`:

```
lmin = nmlinminder(fname,fder,x0,direc)
```

Hence, the string `fder` should contain a name of function computing the derivatives (gradient) of `fname`; if left empty, the quantlet `nmgraddiff` will be used for computing the gradient.

Example XEGnum13.xpl is equivalent to the example XEGnum12.xpl above except of using the quantlet `nmlinminder` for line minimization. It produces the same output and Fig. 7.10.

The quantlet `nmlinminappr` finds an approximated minimum of a function on a given line:

```
lmin = nmlinminappr(fname,fder,x0,direc,stepmax)
```

In contrast to the quantlets `nmlinmin` and `nmlinminder` described above, it finds a minimum with lower precision; on the other hand, the computation is quicker. Hence, it is used as a default line minimization routine for `nmBFGS` but it is not convenient for `nmcongrad`.

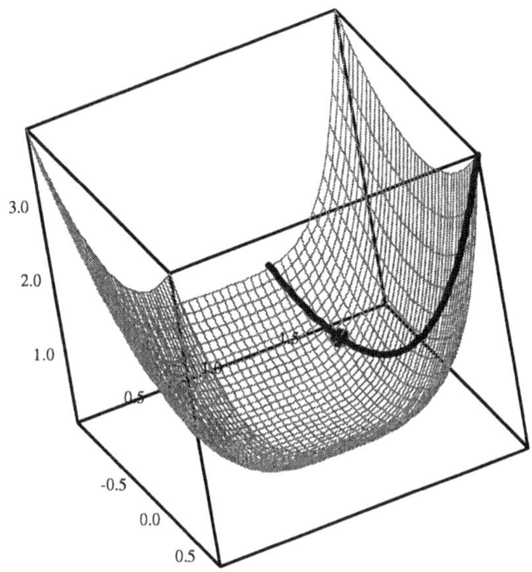

Figure 7.11. Graph of $f(x) = x^2 + 3(y-1)^4$; a line $(1,2) + t \cdot (3,1)$ is shown in red with a big point representing an approximation of the line minimum, `XEGnum14.xpl`

Example `XEGnum14.xpl` is another modification of the example `XEGnum12.xpl`, using the line-minimizing quantlet `nmlinminappr`. Fig. 7.11 and the following output show that the approximation of the line minimum found by `nmlinminappr` is less precise then the approximation found by `nmlinmin` or `nmlinminder`:

```
Contents of minim.xlmin
[1,]     -0.5
[2,]      1.5
```

```
Contents of minim.flmin
[1,]   0.4375

Contents of minim.moved
[1,]     -1.5
[2,]     -0.5

Contents of minim.check
[1,]        0
```

XEGnum14.xpl

Please note that `nmlinminappr` searches for a line minimum only in the positive direction of a given direction vector `direc`. An additional input parameter `stepmax` can be used to prevent evaluation of the function `fname` outside its domain. Except of output parameters `lmin.xlmin`, `lmin.flmin` and `lmin.moved` described above, `nmlinminappr` returns also `lmin.check`. `lmin.check` is equal to zero in case of numerical convergence of line minimization and equals one for `lmin.xlmin` too close to `x0`; `lmin.check` = 1 means usually convergence when used in a minimization algorithm, but a calling method should check the convergence in case of a root-finding problem.

7.6 Auxiliary Routines for Numerical Optimization

7.6.1 Gradient

The first derivative of a one-dimensional function f at x can be approximated by the difference $f'(x) = \frac{1}{2h}\{f(x+h) - f(x-h)\}$ with a precision of $O(h^2)$. Similarly, the partial derivative of function f of n variables x_i, $i = 1, \ldots, n$, with respect to the i-th variable at point $x = (x_1, \ldots, x_n)$ can be approximated by $\partial_{x_i} f = \frac{1}{2h}\{f(x_1, \ldots, x_i + h, \ldots, x_n) - f(x_1, \ldots, x_i - h, \ldots, x_n)\}$ with a precision of $O(h^2)$.

7.6.2 Examples

Example XEGnum23.xpl approximates the first derivative of $f(x) = x^3$ at $x = 0.1$ by the difference with a step $h = 0.05$. It shows Figure 7.12 and the following output:

```
Contents of string
[1,] "Gradient - analytic computation: 0.030000"

Contents of string
[1,] "Gradient - numeric computation : 0.032500"
```

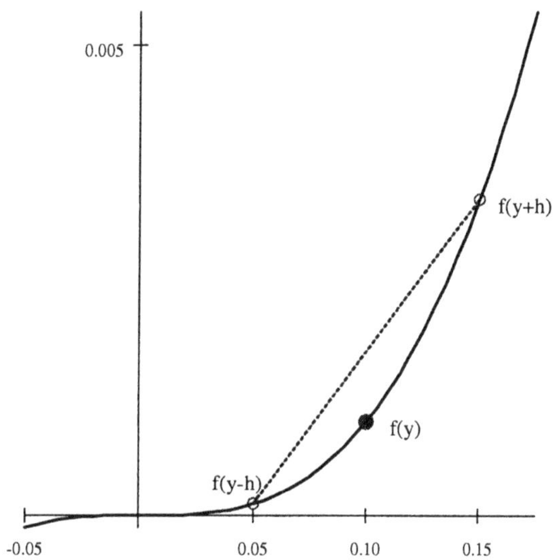

Figure 7.12. Approximation of the gradient of $f(y) = y^3$ at $y = 0.1$ by symmetric difference with $h = 0.05$, XEGnum23.xpl

This example uses a quantlet

```
grad = nmgraddiff(fname,x0{,h})
```

implementing the symmetric difference approximation of gradient of **fname** at a given point x0. The input parameter **fname** should be a string containing a name of a function whose gradient is to be computed; x0 is a vector. One can influence the precision of the approximation by setting the optional parameter h—step of the symmetric difference; the step h can be set separately for each component—input a vector of steps in this case—or it can be the same for every component—inputing a single scalar is then enough. The output parameter grad contains the computed gradient.

Example XEGnum15.xpl computes the gradient of $f(x) = 1 - x + y^2$ at point $x_0 = (1, 2)^T$. As one can easily see, $\operatorname{grad} f(x) = (-1, 2y)^T$ and $\operatorname{grad} f((1, 2)) = (-1, 4)^T$:

```
Contents of grad
[1,]        -1
[2,]         4
```

XEGnum15.xpl

If you need to compute the gradient of a given function more precisely, use the following quantlet:

```
z = nmgraditer(fname,x0{,h})
```

It calls iteratively the quantlet **nmgraddiff** with various values of parameter h and extrapolates the results to obtain the limit value for $h = 0$. Ridder's polynomial extrapolation is used. The quantlet **nmgraditer** is used the same way as **nmgraddiff**. The output parameter z consists of the computed gradient z.grad, a vector of estimated errors of partial derivatives z.err and a vector z.hfin of stepsizes h is the last iteration.

REMARK 7.9 *For differentiable functions,* nmgraditer *gives very precise results but the iterative process is more time-consuming, of course. Hence, use* nmgraddiff *for less accurate but quick results (e.g., in another iterative method) and* nmgraditer *for precise but slower computation.*

REMARK 7.10 *An advantage of* `nmgraditer` *is a fact that it computes also an estimated error of the computed gradient. In case of oscillating functions, it is advisable to compare the error with a computed value of the gradient: if the error estimate is relatively high, the initial stepsize should be decreased.*

Table 7.1 generated by example `XEGnum16.xpl` compares the results of several gradient evaluations for $f(x) = x \sin(1/x^2)$ at $x_0 = 0.01$ (see Fig. 7.2). The gradient was computed analytically using the formula

$$\operatorname{grad} f(x) = \sin\left(\frac{1}{x^2}\right) - \frac{2}{x^2} \cdot \cos\left(\frac{1}{x^2}\right)$$

and numerically using the quantlets `nmgraddiff` and `nmgraditer`. The table summarizes step h for `nmgraddiff`, initial and final step used in `nmgraditer`, the computed gradient and an error estimated by `nmgraditer`.

7.6.3 Jacobian

The Jacobian of a vector function f (see Section 7.3.1) consists of the gradients of components f_i, $i = 1, \ldots, n$. Hence, we can use the analogous approximation as for the gradients, described in Section 7.6.1.

7.6.4 Examples

The quantlet

```
jacobi = nmjacobian(fname,x0{,h,iter})
```

computes not only the Jacobian of a vector function; it can compute the gradients of components of a vector function `fname` even when $\dim f \neq \dim x_0$. Input the name of the function(s) whose gradients should be computed as a string or a vector of strings `fname`. The gradients will be computed at a point `x0`, using the quantlet `graddiff` when the parameter `iter` is equal to zero or not given, or using `graditer` otherwise—see Remark 7.9. In both cases, `h` is an input parameter for gradient-computing quantlet. The rows of output matrix `jacobi` contain the gradients of respective components of `fname`.

Example `XEGnum18.xpl` computes the Jacobian of a function f defined as $f(x) = (\sin(x_1) + x_2^2, x_1 - x_2)$ at a point $(\pi, 2)^T$.

```
Contents of out

[ 1,] ==============================================================
[ 2,]
[ 3,]            Comparison of gradient computations
[ 4,]
[ 5,] ==============================================================
[ 6,] Method     Initial h   Final h      Result      Est. error
[ 7,] ==============================================================
[ 8,] analytic                          19042.8018
[ 9,] --------------------------------------------------------------
[10,] graddiff   1.0e-05                  860.3846
[11,] graddiff   1.0e-06                 8657.2173
[12,] graddiff   1.0e-07                18916.0892
[13,] graddiff   1.0e-08                19041.5321
[14,] graddiff   1.0e-09                19042.7890
[15,] --------------------------------------------------------------
[16,] graditer   1.0e-03  7.1429e-04      11.3483        3.3653
[17,] graditer   1.0e-04  7.1429e-05     -11.3496        95.527
[18,] graditer   1.0e-05  7.1429e-06    1781.9238        921.54
[19,] graditer   1.0e-06  1.3281e-07   19042.8018    1.1133e-07
[20,] ==============================================================
```

Table 7.1. Comparison of gradient evaluations, XEGnum16.xpl

```
Contents of jacobi
[1,]        -1         4
[2,]         1        -1
```

XEGnum18.xpl

7.6.5 Hessian

The partial derivative of the second order of a function f at a point $x = (x_1, \ldots, x_n)$ with respect to the i-th variable (i.e., the diagonal of the Hessian) can be approximated by the symmetric difference

$$\partial_i^2 f(x) \approx \frac{1}{h^2}\{f(x_1,\ldots,x_i+h,\ldots,x_n) - 2f(x_1,\ldots,x_n) + \\ + f(x_1,\ldots,x_i-h,\ldots,x_n)\}$$

with a precision of order $O(h^2)$.

Let us suppose that the partial derivatives of the second order of f are continuous; then $\partial_{ij}^2 f = \partial_{ji}^2 f$ for all $i,j = 1,\ldots,n$. The non-diagonal elements of the Hessian contain the mixed partial derivatives of the second order that can be approximated by the difference

$$\partial_{ij}^2 f(x) = \partial_{ji}^2 f(x) \approx \frac{1}{4h^2}\{f(x_1,\ldots,x_i+h,\ldots,x_j+h,\ldots,x_n) - \\ - f(x_1,\ldots,x_i+h,\ldots,x_j-h,\ldots,x_n) - \\ - f(x_1,\ldots,x_i-h,\ldots,x_j+h,\ldots,x_n) + \\ + f(x_1,\ldots,x_i-h,\ldots,x_j-h,\ldots,x_n)\}$$

providing $i < j$. The error of the approximation is $O(h^2)$.

7.6.6 Example

The following quantlet can be used for numerical approximation of the Hessian:

```
hess = nmhessian(fname,x0{,h})
```

The input parameter `fname` is a string with a name of the function, `x0` is a point (vector) at which the Hessian is to be computed. The optional parameter `h` is a stepsize h used in the approximation; it can influence the precision of the approximation. `h` can be either a vector or a scalar; in the first case, i-th component of `h` is a step size for the difference in the i-th variable, in the latter case, the same value `h` is used for all variables.

Example XEGnum19.xpl computes the Hessian of $f(x) = (\cos(x_1)\cdot\sin(x_2))$ at a point $(\pi/4, -\pi/4)^T$:

```
Contents of hess
[1,]       0.5      -0.5
[2,]      -0.5       0.5
```

XEGnum19.xpl

7.6.7 Restriction of a Function to a Line

It is often useful to restrict a multidimensional function to a line (for example, in multidimensional optimization methods based on a series of one-dimensional optimizations) and deal with it as with a function of only one parameter. The function restricted to a line given by a point x_0 and a direction *direc* is defined as $f_{1D}(t) = f(x_0 + t \cdot direc)$. Refer to the Section 7.6.9 for information on a derivative of a restricted function.

7.6.8 Example

The quantlet

```
ft = nmfunc1d(t)
```

restricts the function `fname` to a line: $f(t) = fname(x0 + t \cdot direc)$. In the context of optimization, the main goal of a restriction of a function to a line is to get a function of only one variable. Therefore, given a function $fname$, we construct a new one-dimensional function f defined as $f(t) = fname(x0 + t \cdot direc)$. A variable `t` is the only parameter of f. However, to be able to compute the values of $f(t)$, the values of `x0` and `direc` have to be given. They should be stored in the global variables `nmfunc1dx` and `nmfunc1dd` before calling `nmfunc1d`. The global variable `nmfunc1dfunc` should be a string with the name of a function computing $fname$. The resulting value $f(t)$ is returned in an output parameter `ft`.

Example `XEGnum20.xpl` evaluates $f(x) = x_1^2 + 3(x_2 - 1)^4$ restricted to a line $(2, -1) + t \cdot (0, 1)$ at $t = 3$ and produces the following result:

```
Contents of ft
[1,]        7
```

`XEGnum20.xpl`

7.6.9 Derivative of a Restricted Function

Some line-minimizing methods use also the derivative of a restricted function (see Section 7.6.7), i.e., the derivative of a multidimensional function in a direction of a given line. Providing one has restricted the multidimensional function $fname$ to $f(t) = fname(x0 + t \cdot direc)$, its derivative can be computed either as a derivative of a one-dimensional function $f'(t) = \frac{df(t)}{dt}$ or by multiplication of a local gradient of the original function $fname$ by the direction vector of the line: $f'(t) = direc^T \cdot \operatorname{grad} fname(x0 + t \cdot direc)$.

7.6.10 Example

The quantlet

```
fdert = nmfder1d(t)
```

computes the derivative of a function `fname` restricted to a line using the formula

$$\frac{d(fname(x0 + t \cdot direc))}{dt} = direc^T \cdot \operatorname{grad} fname(x0 + t \cdot direc).$$

Similarly as `nmfunc1d`, it has only one input parameter `t`. The values `x0` and `direc` are taken from the global variables `nmfder1dx` and `nmfder1dd` which are set before calling `nmfder1d`. The global variable `nmfder1dfunc` should be a string with a name of a function to be restricted. If a function computing the gradient of $fname$ is available, the global variable `nmfder1dfder` should be set to its name. Otherwise, the gradient is computed numerically using the quantlet `nmgraddiff`: if `nmfder1dfder` is left empty, the default value of a step h is used in `nmgraddiff` or one can set `nmfder1dfder` to a value of h for the numerical approximation by `nmgraddiff`.

Example `XEGnum21.xpl` computes the derivative of $f(x) = x_1^2 + 3(x_2 - 1)^4$ restricted to a line $(2, -1) + t \cdot (0, 1)$ at $t = 3$:

```
Contents of fdert
[1,]       12
```

`XEGnum20.xpl`

Bibliography

Press, W. H., Teukolsky, S. A., Vetterling, W. T. and Flannery, B. P. (1992). *Numerical Recipes in C – Second Edition*, Cambridge University Press, Cambridge. Texts of the book (by sections) are available at http://lib-www.lanl.gov/numerical/index.html

Rektorys, K. et al. (1995). *Přehled užité matematiky* (in Czech), Prometheus, Praha.

Rustagi, J. S. (1994). *Optimization Techniques in Statistics*, Academic Press, San Diego.

Stoer, J. (1989). *Numerische Mathematik 1 – 5. Auflage* (in German), Springer-Verlag, Berlin.

Woodford, C. and Phillips, C. (1997). *Numerical Methods with Worked Examples*, Chapman & Hall, London.

Index

www.ingramcontent.com/pod-product-compliance
Lightning Source LLC
Chambersburg PA
CBHW071239230926
51849CB00001B/156
9783540441144